Food for Life

A Guidebook to
Better Eating, Better Living

NATIONAL Health &Wellness CLUB®

Health & Wellness Reference Library™

About the Author

Julie Metcalf Cull, R.D., has been working in the nutrition field for more than 20 years. *Food for Life* is Julie's third book. Author of two cookbooks, *The Quality Time Family Cookbook* and *Magic Herbs*, Julie also contributes to *Today's Health & Wellness* magazine. As proprietor of The Parson's Inn Bed & Breakfast near the Mississippi River in beautiful southwestern Wisconsin, Julie treats her guests to delicious and nutritious breakfast entrees, some of which you will find included in *Food for Life*.

Food for Life: A Guidebook to Better Eating, Better Living

Printed in 2007.

The nutritional and health information presented in this book is based on an in-depth review of the current scientific literature. It is intended only as an informative resource guide to help you make informed decisions; it is not meant to replace the advice of a physician or to serve as a guide to self-treatment. Always seek competent medical help for any health condition or if there is any question about the appropriateness of a procedure or health recommendation.

Portions of the text in chapter 2 were previously printed in the National Health & Wellness Club's *Smart Nutrition* by Felicia Busch.

National Health & Wellness Club
12301 Whitewater Drive
Minnetonka, MN 55343
www.healthandwellnessclub.com

1 2 3 4 5 6 / 12 11 10 09 08 07
ISBN: 978-1-58159-362-4
© 2003 National Health & Wellness Club

Tom Carpenter
Creative Director

Heather Koshiol
Managing Editor

Sandy Zilka
Heather Koshiol
Copyeditors

Pam Myhre, R.N., B.S.N., C.D.E.
Technical Editor

M. J. Smith, R.D./L.D., F.A.D.A.
Recipe Contributor

Laura Holle
Book Development Assistant

Teresa Marrone
Book Production

Special thanks from the author to: Diane Barton, Felicia Busch, Jacqueline Cale, Angela Conklin, Anne Cull, James and John Cull, Diane Foreyt, Mary Metcalf Huser, Dennis Marshall, Pam Myhre, Kris Sitz, Deborah Prelesnik, M.J. Smith, Pat Udelhofen.

Photo Credits
Front Cover: NHWC photo Archive; Zane Williams/Getty Images; James Noble/Corbis; Lori Adamski Peek/Getty Images; NHWC photo Archive (2).

Back Cover: NHWC photo Archive (3); Rob Lewine/Corbis.

Contents

Introduction

Are you overwhelmed and perhaps even a little confused by the volume and inconsistency of nutrition advice nowadays?

I share your concern. My name is Julie Metcalf Cull, and I'm a registered dietitian. I've studied and practiced nutrition for more than 20 years now, and let me tell you, it's constantly changing. No wonder there are inconsistencies. But as a practitioner of nutrition and dietetics, I can help you sort out:

- the good from the bad
- the science from the junk
- the "need to know" from the "nice to know"
- the "pertinent" from the "interesting"

In my years of working with people every day to shape their nutrition plans, I've found that you need to take some nutrition advice, meditate a little, listen to your gut and then experiment a little to find the plan that works right for you.

You may be wondering why in the world I care. Or what I can provide that's different from all the other food, diet and recipe books that are out there.

In a nutshell, I have a passion for nutrition. Once upon a time, I wasn't interested in nutrition as a career. I was enrolled in college as a physical education major. In fact, I was getting A's in the theory, but guess what? When it came to track and field that first semester, I couldn't even cross a single hurdle. Not even the lowest one!

What I didn't know then was that just the year before, events had conspired to change the path of my life forever. On a May evening in 1969, at the young age of 37, my father, Jack, lay down and died. He suffered a massive heart attack with absolutely no warnings. I still remember ironing his white shirt—two days before I turned 17. I remember how his shirt smelled. And how Grandpa woke me that night, as they carried his body down the stairs. My dad would wear his white shirt forever.

Our loving grandparents gave Dad everything—the newest cars; an Army jeep; rich, tweedy clothes; even an airplane. They also gave him the penchant for his early MI (heart attack). Passing

along the favor, Dad's genes diced my siblings' luck—at least three of the six of us are prone to heart disease.

How do we know we're at risk? Statistics tell us that at least 50 percent of children of parents who suffer early cardiac death and have an inherited hyperlipoproteinemia (a genetic tendency to have elevated fats in the blood), are at risk for similar cardiac fate. And the story doesn't end there.

As the statistics might predict, Dad's younger brother, Jim, suffered the same fate at age 42. As you now know, my path in life has certainly changed. I never taught physical education. I don't try to go over hurdles any more, although I do enjoy watching the track stars make it look so easy. My path, filled with different hurdles and tremendous joy, has led me to dietetics. For me, this passion for nutrition is personal, and I hope I can help you make the right choices on your own journey to good nutrition.

You may be able to tell a story similar to mine. My pledge to you, in *Food for Life*, is that together, we will sort through all your personal nutrition, health risk and lifestyle questions.

I'll take the volume of nutrition information, facts, theories (and even quackery) and help you sift out what works for you.

Always remember, there's another crucial member of this team, and that's your healthcare provider. As important as nutrition is, it is still just one piece of the puzzle. You need to be comfortable sharing your nutrition goals and practices with your healthcare provider and/or your alternative therapy practitioner to optimize your total healthcare management.

What Will You Get in *Food for Life*?

Reading and applying the information in *Food for Life* will clarify nutrition facts for you and help you feel less overwhelmed with the volume and inconsistency of nutrition advice. You can be sure that nutrition information in *Food for Life* will:

- Emphasize total diet over your lifetime. "You are what you eat," and this occurs cumulatively. There are very few quick fixes in regard to nutritional health (chapter 1).
- Acquaint you with the nutrients that help you live longer and stay healthier—vitamins, minerals and antioxidants (chapter 2).

■ Help you avoid common diseases and conditions, or help you work with your healthcare provider to include nutrition to better self-manage them. (Note that nutritional recommendations will follow the first code of medicine: Do no harm.) Provide a bulleted, easy-to-use list of both Eastern and Western nutrition practices for more than 50 chronic diseases that you may develop in midlife (chapter 3).

■ Save you cooking time and help you eat right with more than 100 quick and easy-to-fix recipes and menus (chapter 5).

Eastern & Western Medicine and *Food for Life*

Food for Life is written on the premise that many of us already self-manage our health with a blend of Eastern and Western nutrition practices. Seeing a traditional healthcare provider today may allow just 8 to 10 minutes of face-to-face time. *Food for Life* will help you maximize those precious minutes. And this book may help you become more comfortable discussing alternative therapies with your healthcare provider. One recent study found that only one-third of patients who use alternative therapies talk to their conventional healthcare providers about them. This fosters the element of surprise for the Western medicine practitioner, and eliminates the patient's opportunity to seek helpful advice on integrating alternative remedies with conventional treatments.

The best nutritional advice today is probably this blend of Eastern and Western medicine found within an evolving practice called *integrative therapies* (also called *alternative* or *complementary therapy* or *medicine*). The demand for complementary and alternative medicine (CAM) continues to grow in popularity. The number of visits to CAM providers increased by 47 percent in the last decade. Total visits to CAM providers exceeded total visits to all primary care physicians. In one year, out-of-pocket expenditures for herbal products and high-dose vitamins were estimated at $8 billion and out-of-pocket expenditures for CAM professional services during the same time were estimated at $12.2 billion. These numbers exceeded the out-of-pocket expenditures for all U.S. physician services during the same period.

Nutritional practices from both

camps have value. Eastern medicine includes nutrition dogma practiced for thousands of years. These tenets are applied in cultures and lifestyles that are very different from those of the West, but many are applicable to our lives in the United States. Western medicine, with its scientific studies and experiments that validate or refute nutritional practices, accumulated most of its body of evidence during the 20th century. Today's dietitians and healthcare providers recognize that value-added service may come from designing medical nutritional therapy (MNT) protocols that include both.

It is easy to mix and match foods, recipes and snack choices with lifestyle practices that promote longevity. The wrong mix precipitates disease. The right combinations help you live better when you already have a particular disease, or are worried about getting one. All foods can fit in your diet, and it can be fun to find the right mix.

Eating Joyfully

No matter who you are, food choices make a difference in your health and in the health of the people you love. Once you learn to recognize basic nutrition principles, you can apply them and practice joyous and healthful dining. After all, the simplest, most important nutrition action is just eating well most of the time.

Andrew Weil, M.D., coined a definition of nutrition in *Eating Well for Optimum Health*. He said, "Eating well simply means using a basic understanding of human nutrition to maximize as much as you can both the nourishing and pleasure-giving qualities of food."

I think that I can do that; how about you? That is the premise of *Food for Life*, as well. This is not just another "Food Bible." But you may decide to keep it among your most treasured volumes, and share it with your best friends.

Enjoy!

Then an old man, a keeper of an inn, said,
"Speak to us of eating and drinking."
And he said:
Would that you could live on the fragrance of the earth,
and like an air plant be sustained by the light.
But since you must kill to eat, and rob the newly born of
its mother's milk to quench your thirst, let it then be an
act of worship.

—Kahlil Gibran
The Prophet

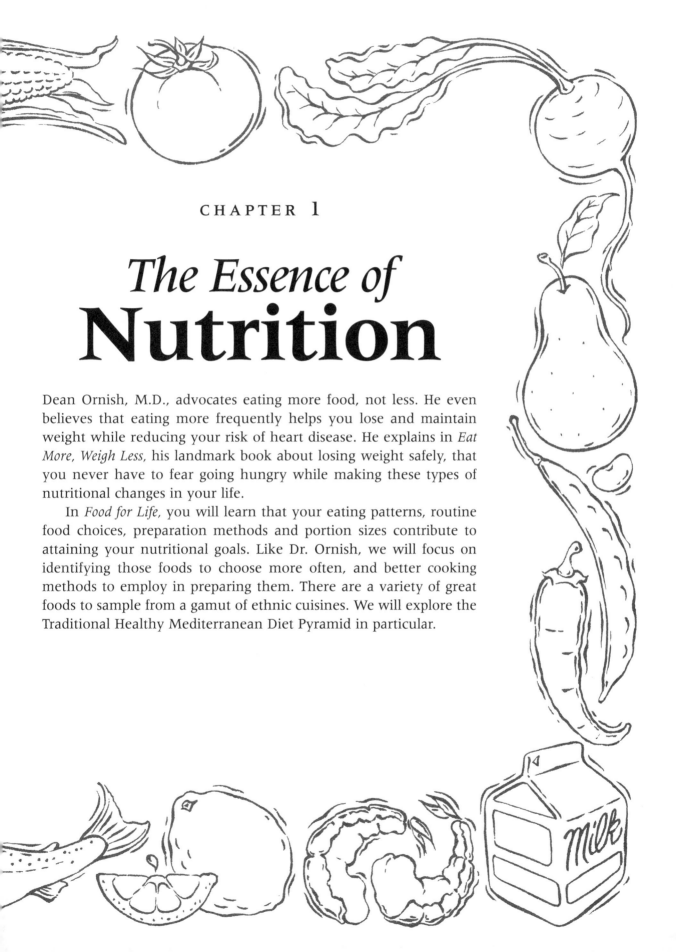

CHAPTER 1

The Essence of Nutrition

Dean Ornish, M.D., advocates eating more food, not less. He even believes that eating more frequently helps you lose and maintain weight while reducing your risk of heart disease. He explains in *Eat More, Weigh Less,* his landmark book about losing weight safely, that you never have to fear going hungry while making these types of nutritional changes in your life.

In *Food for Life,* you will learn that your eating patterns, routine food choices, preparation methods and portion sizes contribute to attaining your nutritional goals. Like Dr. Ornish, we will focus on identifying those foods to choose more often, and better cooking methods to employ in preparing them. There are a variety of great foods to sample from a gamut of ethnic cuisines. We will explore the Traditional Healthy Mediterranean Diet Pyramid in particular.

How Does Eating Relate to Illness?

Eating is the most natural way to combine all of the 40-plus known nutrients the body demands for good nutrition. Later in this chapter, you will learn more about carbohydrates, fats, proteins and alcohol. In chapter 2, we'll review the importance of the four classes of micronutrients (nutrients needed in small amounts):

■ vitamins
■ minerals
■ fiber
■ protective phytochemicals (such as antioxidants and flavonoids)

If you learn how to eat with optimum nutrition in mind, you will be healthier and less likely to develop certain diseases. Maybe you have already developed a disease, or are at risk of developing one because of genetics, environment or fate. After reading this chapter, consider checking out the recommendations in chapter 3 to better help you manage your particular condition or disease.

A Look Back in Time

How do we begin rethinking our food choices if they have gone awry? Taking a look backward in time may help us understand the habits thrust upon us over the eons our bodies have evolved. What did our ancestors eat, and why? Loren Cordain,

Ph.D., who has been working on that question for more than 20 years, states in *The Paleo Diet*, "We are designed to run best on the wild plant and animal foods that all humans gathered and hunted just 500 generations ago."

Surprisingly, the human body resembles and works much as it did when *Homo sapiens sapiens* first evolved 12,000 to 40,000 years ago.

We're talking about very few changes within the human digestive system and other things biological. Cordain goes on to say " ... we are Stone Agers living in the Space Age; our dietary needs are the same as theirs. Our genes are well adapted to a world in which all the food eaten daily had to be hunted, fished, or gathered from the natural environment—a world that no longer exists."

For the most part, ancestors of *Homo sapiens sapiens* had a diet focused on the capture, preparation and consumption of meat. By 430,000 B.C.E., *Archaic Homo sapiens* and other species of hominids had a dietary intake of meat that greatly surpassed levels seen in more distant ancestors. Cordain further explains that "wild, lean animal foods dominated Paleolithic diets, so their protein intake was quite high by modern standards, while their carbohydrate consumption was much lower, and virtually all of the carbohydrates Paleolithic people ate came from

Origins

Homo sapiens sapiens is the scientific name for "modern" humans, and should not be confused with our early ancestor *Homo sapiens*. All races living today are members of the subspecies *Homo sapiens sapiens*.

nonstarchy, wild fruits and vegetables … their carbohydrate intake was much lower and their fiber intake much higher than those obtained by eating the typical modern diet." In addition, this "free-range" meat was quite different from what we buy at today's supermarkets. The meat we get today is higher in total fat, saturated fats and calories, and much lower in polyunsaturated fats and omega-3 fatty acids. The contrast of available foods for current diets to those fulfilling the needs of Paleolithic man continue to influence our needs and choices today, for illness or for health.

We'll explore the growing practice of vegetarianism. It may surprise you to learn that more than 12.4 million Americans call themselves vegetarians. This appears to be a wholesome and viable alternative to including meat in your diet and is endorsed by the American Dietetic Association and the National Institute for Cancer Research. It is growing in popularity for several reasons:

- religious
- medical
- environmental
- animal rights

Playing the Nutrition Game to Win

Although our bodies still resemble those of our distant ancestors, and even though some of us no longer eat animal products, our broadened knowledge of nutrition has indeed "evolved." Science is at the heart of the practice of modern Western nutrition. And with rigorous training and dedication to improving health and health awareness, nutritional science meets an all-important need. But a lot of new facts and information come along with it.

On an old TV game show called "Video Village," the contestants traveled along an enlarged game board in a make-believe village and had so much fun. Discovering the essence of nutrition (found in this chapter) can be just as much fun. This chapter will help lay the groundwork to "win" the nutrition "game."

Let's walk through some of these facts together, as if we were part of that old TV game show. Each time we pause to mull over a nutrition truth that might personally benefit us, we have a chance to accumulate coins, similar to the game show contestants who dug for pennies along the village street. Nutrition truths are like "nutrition coins"—because they hold value for us.

Accumulating Your Personalized Nutrition "Stash"

And just like those pennies, these "nutrition coins" accumulate and help us to win the nutrition game. We will collect those coins in our "nutrition bucket." Our buckets are uniquely designed to hold the special nutritional needs of each individual participant playing to win the nutrition game. And, in our game, really everyone can win, as long as they are willing to make the necessary changes and adjustments to dining and health. (Notice I didn't say "make necessary sacrifices … "!)

Later, in chapter 4, we will sort through the "nutrition stash" we have collected. This information will help us fashion nutrition goals and design personalized menus that fit our individual needs.

Junk Science vs. Nutrition Facts

The most useful nutrition skill you can learn is how to sort out the junk science from the nutrition fact. This will help you decode the confusing nutrition messages you are bombarded with every day. Spotting the fiction interspersed with the fact could very well save your life. The 10 "Red Flags of Junk Science" will give you guidelines for analyzing information you hear or read.

Conventional Medicine vs. Integrative Therapies

You may opt to blend the best of conventional therapies (Western medicine) with alternative or integrative recommendations (usually Eastern medicine). Some integrative therapies are new and some are thousands of years old, but their use is becoming increasingly popular. This renewed interest in integrative therapies comes from a desire to find something more than just the medications and surgery that form the backbone of Western medicine.

Food for Life will provide nutrition recommendations and introduce you to some of the integrative therapies that certain practitioners may recommend. Not all therapies fit all diseases, but we want you to be aware of the vast number of options available.

You are probably wondering: What is integrative therapy? This term refers to a collection of therapies like acupuncture,

10 Red Flags of Junk Science

Be wary of information that:
- Promises a quick fix
- Presents dire warning or danger
- Appears too good to be true
- Draws simplistic conclusions
- Gives one person's opinion or comes from a single study
- Involves statements that can be refuted by other respected scientists
- Lists good/bad foods
- Pushes a product or name brand
- Has no peer review; other scientists haven't found similar results
- Ignores individual differences

Source: American Dietetic Association

massage, guided imagery, biofeedback and more. These therapies are practiced all over the world and are gaining acceptance in the United States. This collection of therapies was once called "alternative medicine," and may still be called that by some. But now, many medical experts say that these therapies shouldn't be *alternatives to* Western medicine. Instead, these therapies should be used to *complement* Western medicine. So they are called "complementary medicine" or "complementary therapy."

Now, healthcare practitioners are beginning to look at these therapies in conjunction with, or as an integral part of, treatment with conventional medicine—thus, "integrative therapies." These therapies are briefly described below. It's important to remember that most of these therapies are used in conjunction with other healthcare therapies. In addition, almost all are supplemented with exercise prescriptions and specific nutritional remedies or diets.

It's important for you to remember that definitive research does not exist, and may never exist, for most integrative therapies. Because of this, these therapies are just now making their way into the scope of dietetic practice. The practice of dietetics is primarily within the realm of Western medicine. Therefore, the integrative therapies included in chapter 3 are based on researched recommendations outside of the scope of dietetics. Although a variety of integrative therapies are included, none are specifically recommended for you. Rather, they represent the options that some alternative therapy practitioners suggest. However, when an integrative therapy is documented as detrimental to your health, it will be pointed out. Remember, every change in your healthcare regimen should be integrated with your healthcare provider's recommendations and action plan, and all recommendations should fit within the "do no harm" tenet of medicine.

Acupuncture. Did you know that more than 1,000 needle locations are used in the practice of acupuncture? The trained acupuncturist inserts tiny needles into the body's meridians (fine duct-like tubes through which fluids travel) in an attempt to balance the flow of vital life energy. The acupuncturist completes a thorough and lengthy medical history and interview; observes the patient's color, body language and voice; then assesses the wrist for 12 radial pulses, all before treatment is started. A treatment can last from just a few seconds to 45 minutes or more.

Applied Kinesiology. The practitioner of kinesiology studies the muscles in the body and correlates health imbalances with weaknesses in muscles. Muscles are evaluated to determine if they are stuck "on" or "off," resulting in flaccid muscles or chronically tight or spasming muscles. Then the muscles are stimulated or relaxed to restore health. The body can further be corrected with joint manipulation, muscle sheath therapies, cranial (head) adjustments, meridian therapy and reflex procedures.

Aromatherapy. How's your sniffer? Most people think aromatherapy is just the smelling of different scents to result in stimulation or calmness. Aromatherapy practitioners use medicinal essential oils (from plants and herbs) in a number of ways to treat infections, stress and even immune deficiencies. These oils are utilized in the following ways:
- through a diffuser (into the air)
- as external applications
- in floral waters (sprayed in the air or on the skin)
- as internal treatments (ingesting)

Ayurvedic Medicine. In Ayurvedic medicine, which is more than 5,000 years old, the body, mind and spirit are all evaluated in order to restore harmony to the individual. The practitioner looks at three metabolic body types (doshas), and helps the patient make changes in their diet, lifestyle and environment to best suit their dosha.

Biofeedback Training. I was amazed when I first heard about diabetes patients who raised the temperature in their feet through biofeedback. If they could raise the temperature, they were certainly increasing circulation, weren't they? And they were using a drug-free, low-cost and highly effective method, all the while lowering their risk of foot ulcers. In biofeedback training, you learn to control your heart rate, breathing and blood pressure. This is done by paying attention to, and visualizing with a simple biofeedback device that blinks or beeps in response to, your heartbeat and body temperature.

Biological Dentistry. How many of us have a mouthful of silver from years of sitting in that dentist's chair? And what is being released into our bodies from those fillings? Mercury, tin, copper, silver and sometimes zinc. This observation is one concern of biological dentistry; its goal is to replace older, possibly toxic, materials in fillings. Biological dentistry also looks for hidden infections under the teeth and in the gums, and correlates illness to many disturbances in the mouth.

Bodywork. Have you ever enjoyed a relaxing massage? Have you heard of rolfing, aston-patterning, hellerwork, the trager approach, Bonnie Prudden myotherapy, reflexology, acupressure, polarity therapy and therapeutic touch? All of these are schools of therapies called bodywork. Bodywork therapies are used to treat pain and sore muscles, enhance circulation (of blood and the lymph system) and provide deep relaxation by manipulating or literally restructuring the muscles of the body.

Chelation Therapy. Instead of heart bypass surgery, Joe decided to have his system "cleansed" with intravenous (IV) chelating agents. Sounds like something out of a sci-fi movie, doesn't it? But it's not. It's chelation therapy, where an IV solution containing medication, vitamins and minerals is infused through the body in about 3½ hours. The goal is to improve circulation to all the tissues of the body by eliminating toxins and plaque, and reducing the effects of atherosclerosis. Oral chelation therapy is also available.

Chiropractic. Many people will argue whether chiropractic should even be listed under integrative or alternative medicine. Insurance companies, medical experts and healthcare providers now recognize this therapy as beneficial and medically appropriate for many ailments.

Chiropractic care focuses on how the nervous system is affected by the spinal column and musculoskeletal system. The most common treatment is adjustment of a subluxation (misalignment of the spine), which may be causing nerve interference. When you consider that all the body's functions are based on nerves coming from the spinal column, subluxations can cause obvious problems (pain, tightness, stiffening) and less obvious problems (infections, shortness of breath, fatigue). But what is that popping noise? Chiropractors explain that this is a harmless release of gases from the joint fluid when a joint is precisely stretched to just beyond its normal range of motion. Many chiropractors are now working in conjunction with other healthcare therapies, other medical physicians in hospitals, massage specialists and therapists using heat and ultrasound.

Colon Therapy. It's more than just an enema—it's colon therapy. In colon therapy, flushes of 2 to 6 liters of water (sometimes with herbs and oxygen) are used to clean and detoxify the entire 5 feet of the lower intestine called the colon. Treatments last from 30 to 45 minutes.

Craniosacral Therapy. Cranio is Latin for cranium, or head. Sacral is the area at the base of the spine and tailbone. And between these two areas lie the brain, spinal cord, cerebrospinal fluid and the membranes around the brain and spinal cord. The fluid in and around the brain and spinal column (cerebrospinal fluid) moves and shifts in waves that can be felt as a rhythm. Craniosacral therapists feel them, then treat the patient based on these rhythms of approximately 6 to 10 cycles per minute.

Detoxification Therapy. Getting rid of body toxins, and thereby restoring health, is the key to this therapy. Chelation and colon therapy are examples of detoxification therapy, as are:
- fasting (juice fasting, weekend water fast)
- diets (weekend monodiet, alkaline-

detoxification diet)
- vitamin C therapy
- heat stress detoxification

Energy Therapy. A practitioner waves a device over your body, checks your hands and feet, reviews meter readings and makes a diagnosis about any imbalance in your body. Treatments include energy devices that:
- Read and correct energy waves emitting from your body, using no outside electricity or energy.
- Provide nerve stimulation with tiny amounts of electrical current.
- Radiate a light beam to allow the body to heal itself.
- Provide sound tones (alternating frequencies to destroy things like bacteria, viruses and fungi that don't resonate with the body energy).
- Produce radio waves for electromagnetic pulses for deep heat tissue treatments.
- Use electroacoustical technology (to simulate infrasonic sound waves) for ailing body parts.
- Alter electromagnetic frequencies in the body. Included here is magnetic field therapy, where magnets are placed on and around the body to change magnetic fields.

Enzyme Therapy. You can eat a diet rich in raw foods and organic produce, and add vitamin and mineral supplements. But without enzymes, all this would be useless. Along with healthier eating, enzyme therapy (taking plant and pancreatic enzymes by mouth) treats digestive disorders, and thus helps restore health and well-being.

Guided Imagery. "Imagine you are your favorite Popsicle on a warm summer day. Picture the sun beating down on you. Now focus on the melting process as you turn to liquid and slowly melt off the stick." If you've never heard of guided imagery, you've just done it—well, at least a baby version of it!

Using imagination and the power of the mind, this therapy will help you deal with stress and pain, and can even boost your immune system. It's based on the premise that the body cannot distinguish between an actual experience and an "imagined" experience, especially when it is vivid in the mind.

Let's say heights make you nervous. Now imagine yourself at the top of the Empire State Building, looking over the edge with no protective fencing. Guess what? Your body will respond with stress symptoms (increase in heart rate and blood pressure, sweatiness, clamminess), even though you're not in any actual physical danger. The reverse is true as you picture a healing, calming place during times of stress.

Herbal Medicine. For thousands of years, humans have used external and internal remedies and treatments derived from plants. As modern medicine evolved, we relied less on plants. However, we still get 25 percent of all prescription drugs from trees, shrubs or herbs. Naturopathic physicians are professionally trained herbalists who know both the historical and medicinal use of plants.

Herbal medicines are gaining acceptance in the United States, but because there is no U.S. licensing body for herbs, getting the correct herb in the correct amount is often a challenge. Some bottles of herbs have been shown to be totally devoid of the listed herb or active ingredient. That's cause for concern. And caution must be used because many herbs can be toxic when taken in higher than recommended doses or in combination with other therapies.

Homeopathy. Take a remedy (tablets) of onion to treat the runny eyes of a cold. This is one of the principles of homeopathic medicine: like cures like (Law of Similars). Two other foundations include: the more a remedy is diluted, the greater its potency (Law of Infinitesimal Dose); and an illness is specific to the individual. George Vithoulkas, Director, Athenian School of Homeopathic Medicine, states in *Alternative Medicine* that "the long-term benefit of homeopathy to the patient is that it not only alleviates the presenting symptoms but it reestablishes internal order at the deepest levels and thereby provides a lasting cure."

Hydrotherapy. In hydrotherapy, water is used in many different forms and therapies to treat illness and injury. Simple hydrotherapy includes showers and baths, ice and hot packs, as well as sitz baths and foot or hand baths. Other options are cold and heat compresses, cold friction rubs, constitutional hydrotherapy, immersion baths, enema/colon irrigation and wet sheet packs.

Hypnotherapy. Imagine having open-heart surgery with no anesthesia. It's possible with hypnosis! The basis of hypnosis is to access the unconscious mind and to quiet the conscious mind.

Successful hypnosis comes about when you trust your hypnotist and understand that you're not giving up control, you're just moving into an advanced form of relaxation. Hypnosis is not a one-time treatment. Average treatment is 6 to 12 sessions that last from 60 to 90 minutes.

Macrobiotic Diet. Popular in the 1960s and '70s, the macrobiotic diet emphasizes liberal and varied amounts of whole grains, fish, nuts, seeds, tofu and vegetables. The good news is that it is consistent with dietary recommendations for preventing cancer. The bad news is that people who already have cancer should avoid macrobiotic diets of any kind because they may not provide enough calories and protein to protect against the wasting associated with the disease.

Magnetic Field Therapy. See Energy Therapy.

Meditation. Meditation is simple, but highly effective, especially if you use it for stress and pain relief. A basic definition: "Any activity that keeps the attention pleasantly anchored in the present moment." Two basic meditative types are concentrative (focused on breathing, images or sound) and mindfulness (paying attention to all aspects and sensations of an event or object).

Music Therapy. You don't have to sing. You don't even have to carry a tune. Music therapists design music sessions for individuals and groups as an adjunct to treating everything from mental health to Alzheimer's disease to substance abuse. Music therapy has been particularly effective in helping people

deal with acute and chronic pain. The music therapist assesses the client's emotional well-being, physical health, social functioning, communication abilities and cognitive skills through musical responses.

Neural Therapy. Do you have a blocked flow of energy? This is what neural therapy aims to treat. Injections or shots of anesthetics (numbing agents) are used in special nerve sites, acupuncture points, glands and scars. The goal is to free up energy pathways, like repairing a short circuit in an electrical pathway.

Neuro-Linguistic Programming. What you think about, how healthy you think you are and what you believe about your future all affect your degree of health and wellness. In neuro-linguistic programming, you're trained to recognize verbal and nonverbal responses (thoughts, behaviors and actions) to health issues. Then you learn to reprogram negative responses with positive ones.

Oxygen Therapy. Every cell in our bodies needs oxygen to live. Usually we get that oxygen from red blood cells carried through our arteries. But oxygen can be delivered to the body in different, more powerful, ways: by mouth, through the rectum or vagina, into a vein or artery or into the skin (by absorption or injection). Hydrogen peroxide therapy and ozone therapy are parts of this type of therapy.

Qigong. Imagine checking into a hospital where your disease will be treated with IVs and medications, as well as a combination of moving, meditating and special breathing exercises. Talk about the meeting of Eastern and Western Medicine! The focus of qigong is the flow of *qi*, which is vital life energy. Exercise and massage are also adjuncts to qigong.

Traditional Chinese Medicine. More than 3,000 years old, traditional Chinese medicine combines many of the therapies already covered: herbs, acupuncture, food therapy (diets), massage and therapeutic exercise.

Writing Therapy. There are a number of different types of writing therapy: journal therapy, letter therapy and poetry therapy. Writing helps people put difficult emotions and memories into words. Some scientists believe that the therapeutic release offered by writing affects the body's physical capacity to withstand stress and to fight off stress-related infection and disease. Studies have also shown that when people write about emotionally difficult events for just 20 minutes a day for 3 or 4 days, the function of their immune system improves.

Yoga. You may think yoga is just a funky, twisted-body exercise, but it's definitely more than that. Yoga is a combination of physical, mental and spiritual energies that enhance health and well-being. The meaning of the word *yoga* is "union," and it ranks among the oldest known systems of health practiced in the world today. Research shows its strong impact on the fields of mind/body medicine, stress reduction and energy medicine. Yoga combines specific body positioning with specific breathing exercises and meditations. Its use has been

proven to reduce stress, lower blood pressure, regulate heart rate and even retard the aging process.

As you can see, there are a wide variety of integrative therapies that may be recommended or tried for preventing or treating diseases and illnesses. Let's step back in time to begin the exploration of some nutrition truths together.

Eating to Maintain Life

The migration of early man, about one million years ago, took our earliest relatives from Africa northward to the colder regions of Europe. Plant foods generally were not shared with others but instead were used by members of the immediate family circle—a group of between 10 and 14 people. When our ancestors adopted the concept of "hunting and gathering," a major change came about: that of learning to share.

Up to this point, man could not yet be considered much of a true social being. But the hunter/meat-eater changed that. Meat from a hunt was shared, and thus the mixed economy emerged. This mixture of hunting and gathering created a new and powerful social pattern, as foodstuffs were shared with members of other groups. The widening of social circles was underway.

And in the process, meat gained dominance over plants. Its importance wasn't so much because it tasted good or provided nutrition, but because it cast the skillful hunter, the provider of meat, into an admiring light. Sharing meat with others beyond his own clan enhanced his social status, placing him front and center. This sharing and eating of meat helped form relationships with other groups. In his book *Origins*, Richard E. Leakey says that meat was used as a prime currency in the development of politics in human society.

Evolution & Diet

The word "diet" derives from the Greek *diata,* meaning "way of life." The most ancient documents known to us are actually lists that itemize quantities of cattle, grain and wine. Today, we essentially have the same body and brain our ancestors had more than 12,000 years ago. Few significant biological changes in how our bodies handle food, bacteria, toxins and air pollutants have occurred. Elizabeth Somer, M.A., R.D., in *The Origin Diet: How Eating Like Our Stone Age Ancestors Will Maximize Your Health*, tells us: "Starchy vegetables, such as roots and tubers, fruits and legumes, provided the main source of calories—carbohydrates—in our evolutionary diets. Carbohydrates in primitive tribal diets even today average about 50 percent of total calories, which is similar to current Western recommendations. However, all the carbohydrates on which our bodies evolved came from unprocessed, high-fiber, nutrient-packed wild plants."

Carbohydrate Consumption throughout Evolution

Carbohydrates provide 45 to 80 percent of the calories in various cultures. And the history of carbohydrates in our ancestral diet goes back to times long before wild wheat grass and wild barley grew in the area called Mesopotamia, now confirmed as the cradle of civilization in research done by the likes of Bryan Sykes, Professor of Human Genetics at the University of Oxford. Mr. Sykes and his research team work with ancient DNA, when available, and test today's populations. They are able to identify where our Paleolithic ancestors lived, how long ago and even who our most distant ancestors were.

This type of research has an obvious extension to "ancestral diets" and helps us learn what foods were abundant then, and how some genetic needs may still guide us in healthy choices today. Remember, our bodies have barely changed for about 12,000 to 40,000 years—and this estimate is probably closer to 40,000 than 12,000. Elizabeth Somer, M.A., R.D., explains in *The Origin Diet*, "Up to 65 percent of our original diets were fresh fruits and vegetables, nuts, seeds and other plants. Our ancient ancestors ate pounds of produce every day. The other 35 percent came from wild game, low in saturated fats and rich in polyunsaturated fats called the omega-3 fatty acids."

Caloric Needs, Then & Now

It has been said that earliest man (as we know *Homo sapiens* today) was a hunter/gatherer. An adult at that time may have needed as many as 10,000 to 14,000 calories per day to maintain weight and carry on the extensive physical exercise which included the daily walk of many miles to forage for food. Now, dietitians who specialize in sports nutrition and work, for example, with professional football teams or with people who climb Mount Everest, still design diets with high-range caloric needs. My neighbors and I had the opportunity to see the Chicago Bears football team practice while they summered in a small town nearby. In fact, I knew the dietitian who designed those training camp meals: Susan Davis, M.S., R.D. She would tell us tongue-in-cheek stories of how she had to advise William Perry, nicknamed "The Fridge," to eat less meat and more spaghetti. And I'm sure it was a funny sight—this petite dietitian going nose-to-nose with this 400-pound hulk. But knowing Susan, I'll bet she won.

It's helpful to keep those dramatic caloric needs in mind when you consider the maximum amounts most of us will need with our more sedentary lifestyles. If we are quite active each day—engaging in daily walks or tennis twice a week, for example—we may need between 2,000 and 2,400 calories per day. Many of us will need a lot less, and few of us will need the number of calories needed by our evolutionary ancestors or the infamous "Fridge" of the Chicago Bears.

While the amount of calories has changed, our need for whole grains has not. They remain the most readily available type of carbohydrate that mimic the wild grasses growing in Mesopotamia long ago.

More Ancient Foods

Our bodies adapted early on to meet the needs of people who ate this grain-rich diet and lived millions of years before the industrial era. One *National Geographic* article even pegs what the biblical figure Abram might have eaten. Abram grew up near the Tigris and Euphrates rivers between 2000 and 1800 B.C.E. His diet would have included dates, barley, lentils, onions, garlic and lamb.

Picture our bodies marching in place in Abram's costume—as our hands reach for a handful of greasy french fries. Our age-old bodies might be cringing in reaction to modern diets. And the scope of this book does not even include the other changes that affect our bodies—new and different levels of stress, jobs that require stationary work, "couch-potato" down-time and constantly being "on" (tied to our phones, beepers and e-mail).

But there's more to eating than the intake of food. It is said that civilization occurs when something we never missed becomes a necessity. Particular foods and food practices have begun to fashion a social identity for most of us. This connection with what foods are served and how they are prepared forms a connection with the section or region of the country in which we live.

Dietetics as a Science

Dietetics is the study of the science of food and how it relates to health and disease through the practice of nutrition. Registered dietitians like myself strive to communicate "eating" messages to the public, patients and clients that focus on the total diet rather than any one food or nutrient. When patients' needs dictate, we fashion specific diets that may eliminate or substitute one food for another.

The science of dietetics has existed since Hippocrates, but 2,400 years ago, it was basically a form of preventive medicine. In the United States today, manipulating diets is part of the treatment of disease. For example, when someone newly diagnosed with type 2 diabetes begins treatment, losing weight and moderating their intake of carbohydrate and fat are the first recommended steps. Following these straightforward measures, along with increased activity (as tolerated), can positively work to control the blood sugar level, and thus control the disease.

A person who gets type 2 diabetes, like my sister Carol, who developed it in her early 40s, might not have to use medications as treatment—if nutrition recommendations are followed and her body responds favorably to them. Adopting such recommendations will certainly reduce the heightened level of cardiac risk associated with diabetes, and in doing so, it can literally prolong and improve the quality of your life, just like it has my sister's.

There is no one way to eat properly; nutritional needs change over time. Nutrition in America is not regarded as a religion (unlike its exalted status in Europe). Here, it is based firmly on research and science. Medical nutritional therapy (MNT) is the name healthcare has given to the treatment of nutrition by registered dietitians and other qualified individuals. The American Dietetic Association (ADA) holds the position that all foods "belong" within a healthful eating style. And that is the philosophy I bring to *Food for Life* as well.

Setting Goals & Taking Action

A good many health and wellness publication readers report they know what healthful eating behaviors are but don't follow them. More than 40 percent of us like to hear about new studies, but feel that those studies just tell us what not to eat. The approach found in *Food for Life* for improving diet choices and identifying food behaviors that need modification should feel refreshing.

You can learn to combine better eating behaviors with meals and snacks you like, and believe me, variety holds the key. Later, in chapters 2 and 4, you will learn more about food pyramids, national guidelines and recommendations that are available to guide you. Armed with all of that information, you will be ready to further sort the junk science from the wholesome. As you enlist national recommendations to help you bring choices and variety to your diet, you will also learn more about appropriate portion sizes and eating in moderation. And, of course, the final key is physical activity. Although the confines of this book do not allow a lengthy review, physical activity provides the balance for the types of foods and beverages that provide calories.

Bridging the Gaps

Lots of reasons can explain why you might consider adopting the diet and nutrition recommendations in *Food for Life*. You may be driven by the fact that 70 percent of cancers and at least 50 percent of heart diseases are related to diet and lifestyle. Or you might wish to lose weight, better manage a nutrition-related disease or desire increased energy and vitality. Your list may go on and on.

These things are all important and most definitely attainable when the information provided in this book is put to use. However, the real benefit of implementing nutritional lifestyle changes is simple: a better living experience. This is not something that happens in the future, but something that happens right now—today.

Where to Start

A central goal of *Food for Life* is to help you bridge the gaps that exist in your overall approach to nutrition. For many people, these gaps have nothing to do with portion control or butter vs. margarine, but rather the role that food plays in their lives. This book strives to take a different approach to helping you understand and live in harmony with the emotional, psychological and even spiritual aspects of nutrition. In fact, you might coin this as "nutritional homeopathy" because it will deal with the underlying cause of the nutrition imbalance.

Step 1—Identify the Gaps

Before you can bridge the gaps, you need to identify them. Take a moment right now to list some of your negative feelings about certain foods and nutritional practices or concepts. Here are some examples:

- I feel that eating healthy is going to be too hard.
- I can't afford the nutritious diets seen in so many magazines.
- I don't know how to prepare the

ethnic foods that I enjoy most, so I eat out and, many times, eat too much.

Acknowledging our fears and anxieties about food is an important first step. Because eating is something that we all do, it tends to be something that is taken for granted. Now take a minute to turn your negative statements into positive affirmations or personal challenges. Here are some examples:

- I will work hard at improving my approach to nutrition, and I will make sure that I take care of myself in the process. My first goal will be to get enough sleep every night. (Adequate sleep is linked with better weight management control.)
- I will establish and stick to a food budget. The food budget will be designed to make sure I get 3 servings of fruits and vegetables every day. (Your first goal is 3 servings since most Americans get an average of 2½ servings per day. A later goal will be 5 servings a day.)
- I will learn how to cook my favorite ethnic dishes. I will try a favorite ethnic recipe at least twice each month. (If you like these recipes, you can save money by eating out less often and regain control of some of your dining. Studies suggest that most of us have less control over the amount of food we consume when eating in the presence of others. This finding is a double-edged sword. Joyous, relaxed dining is one of the greatest activities we can enjoy. Most of us would agree: It feeds the soul.)

These statements can serve as guides to help you delve into the complex landscape of nutrition and what's typically referred to as the "mind-body connection." When you're faced with choices, these affirmations and statements will remind you of those areas where you are most vulnerable and where you may need to give yourself extra time, more structure, less temptation and so on.

Step 2—Build Better Nutrition Habits & Joyous Dining Skills

Now let's talk about how to cross the river to better nutrition and healthier living! Goal setting is the most typical approach that nutrition and diet manuals offer. It's a linear approach that works for many people. Goals, by definition, need to be measurable. Counting fat grams, calories and carbohydrates will tell a person from day to day whether they are meeting, exceeding or failing at their stated goals.

However, those types of goals don't work as well when it comes to tracking progress against emotional or psychological hurdles. For example, one of the sample statements of negative feelings about nutrition was that healthy eating is "too hard." What does that really mean? It's difficult for the average person to establish a unit of measurement that will quantify how "hard" something is.

Spend just a minute thinking about how you might track whether a struggle is getting easier or harder, and you'll quickly realize that unless you can live in a total vacuum, the events and people in your life will impact your mood and your assessment of life on a daily, if not hourly, basis. This is the phenomenon

that explains why all of a sudden we wake up one day and recognize that we've gotten over a past relationship or can finally take the first step toward achieving something that we've been thinking about for a long time.

Certainly, if you were to review a history of your own life, over the past week, month or year, you would find hours or days of tiny, almost imperceptible ups and downs. You probably would find some moments that stick out in your mind—particularly good or bad days. Yet it would have been hard to predict with any certainty the final outcome (for example, "I'll never love again," or "I'm going to get back up on that horse and try once more"). It would have been even harder to predict when the breakthrough or change in the status quo would occur. This is the limitation of a linear, strictly goals-based approach.

A "Critical Qualities" Approach to Goal Setting

Instead of quantitative goals that are established today, which may or may not be achieved at some later point in time, think about a "critical qualities" approach to transforming your emotional and psychological approach to nutrition and improving your health and life. Close your eyes and think about the qualities of life that you desire related to food and nutrition. If things don't immediately come to mind, think about those people in your life who seem to display positive food interactions that you would like to emulate.

- How do they seem to feel about food?
- How do they talk about the food

they eat and their dining experiences? How do they talk about the food they don't choose to eat?

- Have you ever witnessed one of their negative food experiences? Did they share some background to shed light on the situation?
- How did your parents or grandparents treat food when you were growing up? Are you stuck in their rut?
- Was your family's approach to food the one you would like to have in your own life as it continues to unfold?

Every person's critical qualities are different. The following example might help you begin to identify your own nutrition goals through the "critical qualities" approach.

You will want to customize your list by adding your own unique critical qualities. Now, think for a minute about how important each quality is to you. Give each quality a ranking of 1 through 10, where 1 is the least important and 10 is the most important. Then think about how well you're currently doing at each of these items. Again, give a rating of 1 through 10. Finally, multiply the importance factor by the current success rating to complete the total points column. Add up the total points. Record this number with the current date. This number is a benchmark. Over time, if you use this same process, you should be able to see how your total points increase or decrease. Presumably, you will be more successful at things that are important to you. If your points decrease

Critical Quality	Importance	Current Success Rating	Total Points (Imp. x Success)
Lower anxiety about making the right food choices			
Less late-night emotional eating			
More dinner parties and enjoyment of food			
Build a support network of friends who can socialize while drinking less			

over time, this can be a way to point out the need to refocus. This process helps quantify something that may feel intangible and prioritize the things that are most important to you.

Analyzing the Evaluation Process

Let's take a minute to analyze the evaluation process that went into this example. Item #1 on the list, "lower anxiety about making the right food choices," was the most important quality of life issue for the person in this example. If every food decision has been causing this person anxiety, that's a lot of misspent time and energy. Think of how often we're confronted with food decisions every day.

Item #4 on the list was perhaps an idea that, when thought about more critically, simply can't be controlled. Meeting new people and establishing friendships is something that has to happen over time. In this example, the evaluator determined that the importance was low (only a 2 out of 10). If this person was a recovering alcoholic (as opposed to a person who simply wanted to drink less), this last item might have been rated a 10 for importance. When something is that important, consider more creative solutions—run an ad in a paper, stop by an AA meeting and propose the idea, call family and friends and ask for their support.

By listing the non-scientific qualities about our relationships with food and nutrition (the "feel good" and "feel bad"

Critical Quality	Importance	Current Success Rating	Total Points (Imp. x Success)
Lower anxiety about making the right food choices	8	5	40
Less late-night emotional eating	7	7	49
More dinner parties and enjoyment of food	4	5	20
Build a support network of friends who can socialize while drinking less	2	0	0
TOTAL			109

Critical Quality	Importance	Current Success Rating	Total Points (Imp. x Success)
TOTAL:			

stuff), we are recognizing that these emotions and psychological states are critical to our overall success in a healthy lifestyle change. Just as *Food for Life* empowers you to be smarter about the food choices you make, it is also a tool for building or repairing your overall relationship with food.

■ **Nutrition Activity:** Make several copies of the "Critical Qualities" grid on page 26. Complete the grid and do a self-appraisal every other week for the next 3 months. This exercise will help you keep your most critical qualities front and center in your mind. Further, you'll begin to collect some data about those emotional and psychological barriers that can sabotage your attempts to eat healthier. You'll also be able to tell at a glance whether your energy is being spent on critical or non-critical aspects of food and diet. Some people find it helpful to think of and list all the qualities (not just the highly desired ones) that color their relationship with food. The non-desired qualities will get a low importance rating, but often, people have a hard time redirecting energies that have typically gone to those tasks.

Establish a Vital Foods Framework—Keep Track of What You Eat

Using the principles discussed in this book, think about creating a daily menu framework that ensures the vital nutrients are consumed each day. Vital nutrients are those 40-plus nutrients needed in specific amounts every day by your body. (See the "Food Sources of Spotlighted Vital Nutrients" chart beginning on page 51 in chapter 2 for amounts.) Eating a varied, well-balanced diet can help ensure all vital nutrients are consumed. Once the vital nutrients have been captured, you can round out your daily menu with additional foods you enjoy. Note that the vital nutrients work equally well for vegetarians or those who enjoy meat and dairy.

Build Vital Eating Habits

Once you're familiar with the vital nutrients, you can use the "Vital Eating—Daily Tracker" chart (page 29) to help you determine how much of each food category you need to eat to provide a variety of the 40-plus vital nutrients needed by your body each day.

Think of this tool as help with a lifelong commitment to better personal nutrition and health. Many people find that only through monitoring and reviewing their eating over a period of 2 to 3 weeks can they spot patterns that do not support vital eating. Once you spot the pattern, you can work to build a preferred habit. Remember, most experts say it takes 6 months of directed practice at something before it really becomes a habit. Revisit this tool as often as practical and useful for you, but at least every 6 months.

Daily Vital Nutrient Framework

Meals	Food Categories that Are Sources of Vital Nutrients	Your favorite sources of each nutrient. *Refer to the information throughout the book on each vital nutrient.*
Breakfast	■ Vitamin C-rich ■ Whole grain carbohydrates ■ Lean protein ■ Calcium (dairy or fortified soy)	
Snack	Mixed energy snack—items that are easy to prepare or buy and provide a combination of the following: ■ Lean protein ■ High fiber ■ Healthy fat	
Lunch	■ Lean protein ■ High fiber ■ Healthy fat ■ Deep green- or deep yellow-colored fruits and vegetables ■ Whole grain carbohydrates	
Snack	As noted above	
Dinner	■ Lean protein ■ High fiber ■ Healthy fat ■ Deep green- or deep yellow-colored fruits and vegetables ■ Whole grain carbohydrates ■ Calcium (dairy or fortified soy)	
Snack	As noted above	

Vital Eating—Daily Tracker

Whole Grain Carbohydrates
(6 to 12 servings)

☐ ☐ ☐ ☐ ☐ ☐
☐ ☐ ☐ ☐ ☐ ☐

- ½ cup whole grain cereal or cooked brown rice
- 1 slice of whole grain bread or ½ whole bagel
- ½ hamburger or other bun

★ *Three items each day should be high in fiber.*

Vegetables
(3 to 5 servings)

☐ ☐ ☐ ☐ ☐

- 1 cup lean veggies, like carrots, cabbage, lettuce, green beans or peppers
- ½ cup of starchy veggies, like corn, potatoes or baked beans

★ *One serving should be deep green and leafy or deep yellow.*
★ *Eat beans and legumes at least three times each week.*

Fruit
(2 to 4 servings)

☐ ☐ ☐ ☐

- ½ cup of juice or chopped fresh fruit
- 1 small banana or medium-size apple or other fruit
- ½ cup canned or frozen fruit without extra added sugar

★ *One serving should provide a good source of Vitamin C.*

Calcium (Dairy or Fortified Soy)
(2 to 3 servings)

☐ ☐ ☐

- 1 cup skim or low-fat milk or soy milk
- ½ cup low-fat cottage cheese
- 1 ounce low-fat cheese
- ½ cup yogurt

Lean Protein
(1 to 2 servings—each serving no larger than a deck of cards)

☐ ☐

- Poultry (without the skin), seafood, beef or pork
- Eggs—no more than 3 to 4 per week
- Soy foods
- 1 ounce nuts

★ *Limit red meat to a few portions each week.*

Healthy Fats
(3 to 7 servings)

☐ ☐ ☐ ☐ ☐ ☐ ☐

- 1 teaspoon olive oil or canola oil
- 1 teaspoon non-hydrogenated margarine
- 1 to 2 teaspoons of nuts

★ *Try to limit "unhealthy fats."*

Water
(8 to 10 servings)

☐ ☐ ☐ ☐ ☐ ☐ ☐ ☐ ☐ ☐
- 8 ounces or more water

Use this space to note other things you ate that don't fit the vital eating menu plan.

Put this puzzle together and you will find milk, cheese and eggs, meat, fish, beans and cereals, greens, fruits and root vegetables—foods that contain our essential daily needs.

—Irma S. Rombauer
Joy of Cooking

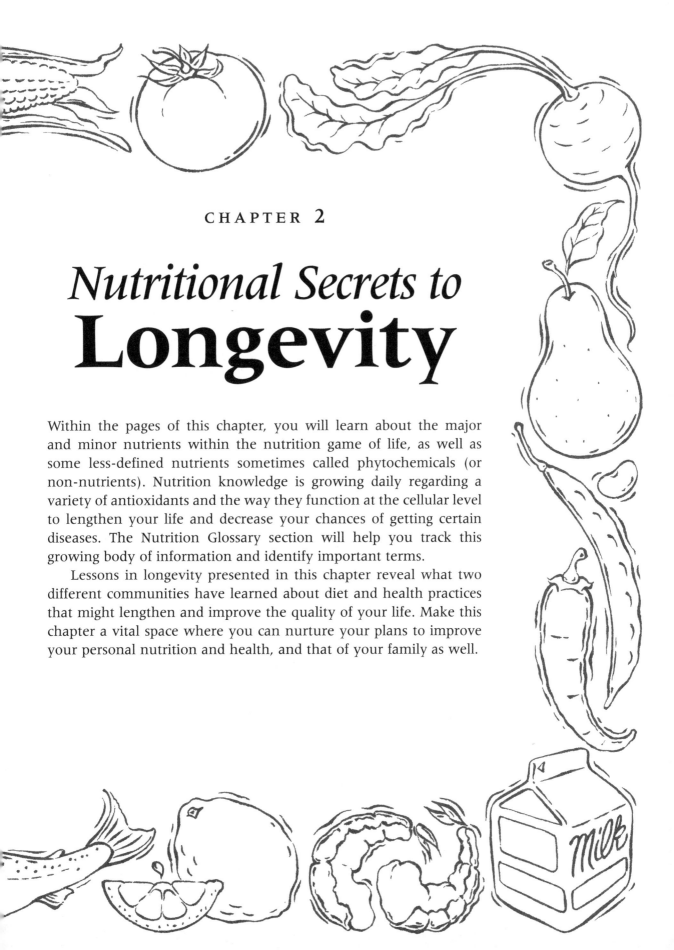

CHAPTER 2

Nutritional Secrets to **Longevity**

Within the pages of this chapter, you will learn about the major and minor nutrients within the nutrition game of life, as well as some less-defined nutrients sometimes called phytochemicals (or non-nutrients). Nutrition knowledge is growing daily regarding a variety of antioxidants and the way they function at the cellular level to lengthen your life and decrease your chances of getting certain diseases. The Nutrition Glossary section will help you track this growing body of information and identify important terms.

Lessons in longevity presented in this chapter reveal what two different communities have learned about diet and health practices that might lengthen and improve the quality of your life. Make this chapter a vital space where you can nurture your plans to improve your personal nutrition and health, and that of your family as well.

Nutrition Glossary

In this glossary, scientific terms have been described in simpler terms. Sometimes these definitions may still seem complicated. The process of explaining health and longevity at the cellular level, which is where it really occurs, is rather in-depth. This glossary, as well as charts throughout the chapter, will help clarify these processes.

Antioxidants: protect other compounds from oxygen by reacting with oxygen, which allows antioxidants to protect cells from free-radical damage, or oxidation. Antioxidants appear to keep your immune system strong and to prevent carcinogens (cancer-forming substances) from forming or gaining access to cells. Common antioxidants include beta-carotene (a precursor to vitamin A), vitamin C, vitamin E, selenium, coenzyme Q10, glutathione and superoxide dismutase (SOD). Vitamin and mineral antioxidants are generally found in fruits, vegetables, whole grains and tea. Herbs that appear to have antioxidant properties include ginkgo biloba, hawthorn (which the FDA lists as an herb of undefined safety) and rosemary.

Antioxidant capacity: the internal and external mechanisms that ensure oxidative balance. The foods we eat have varying capacities to help keep free radicals in control and protect us against cancer.

Ascorbic acid: vitamin C.

Beta-carotene: precursor of vitamin A; star player in the carotenoid family.

Carotenoids: include more than 600 related compounds widespread in nature that form precursors to vitamin A. Found in yellow-orange vegetables and fruits, green leafy vegetables and red fruits, carotenoids contribute to healthy vision and may reduce the risk of cancer and heart disease.

Coenzyme Q10: ubiquinone; made in the liver from precursors of cholesterol, but is also present in foods like mackerel, sardines, salmon, liver, beef and peanuts.

Dietary Reference Intake (DRI): sets an upper level of intake to protect you from the risk of toxicity. Designed by the National Academy of Sciences to do more than protect against deficiency, DRIs also aim to lower your risk of major chronic diseases.

Flavonoids: water-soluble plant pigments that are widespread in the diet. Food sources include tea, berries, apples, tomatoes, broccoli, carrots and onions. Flavonoids in tea may inhibit the early steps leading to cancer. Flavonoids have also been associated with a decrease in cardiac disease and a lower risk of stroke.

Free radical: unstable, reactive oxygen molecule that can potentially damage body cells.

Free-radical damage: oxidative damage that makes us age. Free-radical damage is responsible for the initiation of many diseases, including heart disease and cancer.

Indoles (isothiocynates): nutrients that generate enzyme production to halt damage to DNA by carcinogens. Found in cruciferous vegetables such as broccoli, broccoli sprouts, Brussels sprouts, cabbage, cauliflower, collard greens, kale, kohlrabi, mustard greens, radishes, rutabagas, turnips, watercress and horseradish.

Isoflavones (daidzein and genistein): interfere with estrogen synthesis at the cellular level; may reduce serum cholesterol and decrease risk of breast and ovarian cancer. Found in soy and legumes.

Lycopene: one of the carotenoids found in tomato-rich foods, watermelon, red grapefruit and guava.

Megadose: 10 times the Recommended Daily Allowance (RDA).

Non-nutrients: newly discovered substances that occur naturally in small amounts in fruits, veggies, herbs and grains. Hundreds of non-nutrients have already been discovered. One example of phytochemicals (a class of non-nutrients) are the curcumins found in ginger and turmeric.

Oxidants: see free radicals.

Oxidation: a process that can potentially damage body cells. See also free-radical damage.

Oxidative balance/stress: condition of balance or imbalance (stress) occurring between pro-oxidants and antioxidants.

Phenolic compounds: antioxidants (such as flavonoids) that inhibit cancerous changes in the body.

Phytoestrogens: plant hormones that interfere with the body's production of estrogens; can be helpful or harmful.

Phytonutrients (phytochemicals): made by plants; more are being identified daily. Examples include catechins found in green tea, which appear to help decrease the incidence of some cancers, and lycopene, which is touted to decrease the incidence of prostate cancer.

Polyphenolic compounds: phenolic acids, like those found in red wine, grapes, berries, nuts and whole grains, that act as antioxidants.

Pro-oxidants: factors that play an active role in the enhanced formation of free radicals or other reactive oxygen species, which tend to damage the body's cells.

Recommended Dietary Allowance (RDA): designed by the National Academy of Sciences in 1941 for the War Department to use as a guide for feeding American soldiers, and the basic concept has not changed much since then. If you are a healthy person and eat close to 100 percent of the RDA for the nutrients listed, you probably have a balanced diet.

Synergy: an interrelationship between nutrients.

Tocopherols: vitamin E.

Lessons in Longevity

Clarence Nuti, my grandfather's brother-in-law, is more than 100 years old. His life provides me with a personal lesson in longevity. Although Clarence is short of stature and very lean—as he always has been—his mind and voice remain strong. Clarence and his late wife, Alice, always ate and drank carefully, always maintaining an ideal body weight. Although the Nutis are not a documented research project, I have observed their nutrition behaviors for 40-some years, and I think they have some "longitudinal" strength. Look at members of your own family and see what lessons of longevity and disease you find.

Lessons from Okinawa

Did you know that one secret to long life just might be found in Okinawa? This Japanese island has more than 34 centenarians for every 100,000 islanders—the highest ratio in the world. Its residents expect to live an average of 81.2 years. But here's the rub: Okinawans under age 50 have Japan's highest rates of obesity, heart disease and premature death. Does this point a finger at our modern ways of eating, or what? In this chapter, you will begin to learn more about the nutritional secrets the older Okinawans know and nutritional truths that other cultures have discovered as well.

Traditional diets, like those eaten by the older Okinawans, contribute to the longevity of people around the world, and they are getting a lot of press in recent years. For example, the Mediterranean eating style has gotten more attention recently, with its empha-sis on olive oil and wine in moderation, and daily servings of beans, legumes and nuts, with red meat eaten only a few times a month. These diets are often rich in phytonutrients.

Lessons from the Nuns

The "Nun Study" is an ongoing research program examining aging and Alzheimer's disease in a population of 678 members of the School Sisters of Notre Dame religious order. Participants range in age from 75 to 106. The study finds that:

- Weight loss in the elderly is associated with a high risk of losing both mental function and physical abilities.
- The social importance of meals cannot be overestimated.
- The carotenoid called lycopene showed a strong correlation to physical function in the sisters in Mankato, Minnesota (one mother-house location), and, later, showed a strong link to survival. Sisters with the lowest lycopene levels in their blood more frequently needed help performing self-care tasks such as eating, bathing, dressing, standing and using the toilet. Other studies suggest that lycopene may offer protection against heart disease and cancer of the breast, lung, bladder and prostate.
- Vitamin E seemed to delay institutionalization of Alzheimer's patients.
- Ginkgo biloba had modest effectiveness in stabilizing early-stage Alzheimer's disease and, in some cases, improving cognitive function.

Eating to Improve Your Health & Longevity

Aging occurs when dangerous oxidized molecules called free radicals cause tissue damage within your body. Antioxidants compete for, and react with, oxygen to protect our cells. Free radicals contribute to hardening of the arteries, increased risk of heart attack or stroke and cause damage to your skin—speeding the wrinkling process.

What happens as we age? As many as 30 percent of people at age 65 develop atrophic gastritis, the inability to produce stomach acid. This leads to impaired absorption of certain important nutrients, including folic acid, calcium, iron and vitamin B12. It is estimated that by age 80, up to 40 percent of persons develop atrophic gastritis, which has a significant impact on the bioavailability of some key nutrients. Atrophic gastritis may continue to be inevitable, but a balanced diet can help.

Remember that no single nutrient is a magic bullet in any disease. Nutrients and antioxidants work in concert with other protective nutrients, as part of long-term good eating. The most dramatic health benefits seem to be found in the synergy of the variety of nutrients found in a balanced diet.

Healthcare providers like physicians and registered dietitians often recommend supplements—often to better manage a disease or condition—to help fill in the gaps found in your established eating patterns and preferences, or to make up for specific inadequacies found within your body. It's important to remember that any supplement prescribed beyond 200 percent of the Recommended Dietary Allowance (RDA) for most vitamins and minerals will require additional amounts of other vitamins and minerals. Vitamins usually work as catalysts with equations. They work with other hormones, nutrients and minerals. When you offer your body more of one, you often find the need to have more of another. Check with your healthcare provider to determine the best proportions to consume additional nutrients and antioxidants if you decide to supplement.

The terms *macronutrients* and *micronutrients* refer to whether your body needs a lot (macro) or a little (micro) of that nutrient. The term *non-nutrients* is given to many parts of foods that provide needed substances used at the cellular level, but the exact mechanism is not always yet known or explained.

Antioxidants

An antioxidant is a chemical compound or substance that inhibits oxidation. So how do antioxidants work? They act as circuit breakers; they insert themselves into the free-radical chain reaction. They quench the generation of reactive oxygen species (ROS). They slow down the natural tendency of our cells to age.

Oxygen, the big player in oxidative stress, is vital to breath and life, but can be caustic when it forms free radicals, which have been fingered for causing oxidative stress. Biomarkers of oxidative stress have been detected in people with diabetes, in smokers and in individuals with high cholesterol. Oxidative stress is implicated in the development of cancer, cardiovascular disease (heart disease), diabetes, various eye diseases and neurologic conditions.

Under normal conditions, antioxidants counter the effects of oxidative stress. Food sources rich in antioxidants work cooperatively in your body to help prevent or delay oxidization of your cells. Vitamins E and C and glutathione are the major antioxidants that complement one another in your body. These nutrients work together synergistically: When the antioxidant and the pro-oxidant activities are in balance, your body remains in a steady state.

Americans are living longer and say they want to stay healthier. Scientific literature promotes consuming five to nine servings of fruits and vegetables each day. Diets rich in fruits and vegetables are high in both antioxidants and phytochemicals. Your diet is the best place to get the antioxidants you need. Your elaborate antioxidant defense system depends on two things: the dietary intake of antioxidant vitamins and the endogenous production of antioxidant compounds.

The jury is still out on whether antioxidant nutrients should be taken as supplements or consumed in foods. In fact, results from large, multicenter studies revealed that antioxidant vitamin supplementation was not always effective. Further studies will deal with finding the right dose in healthy vs. high-risk individuals. The safety and efficacy of supplements is usually dose-dependent, even in healthy individuals.

Additional Benefits of Consuming Antioxidants

Besides combating damaging free radicals, antioxidants may be helpful in managing or preventing neurological disorders and diseases involving the immune systems, like Parkinson's disease, Alzheimer's and arthritis. Antioxidants are also one of the most common groups of food additives used to prevent change in color, flavor and rancidity in your foods. Two synthetic antioxidants are BHA and BHT. Antioxidants keep your immune system strong.

Less Commonly Known Antioxidants

Coenzyme Q10 (ubiquinone, or CoQ10) is synthesized in the body from precursors of cholesterol synthesis. The ability to synthesize CoQ10 decreases with age, and there may be an increasing dependence on food to supply the nutrient. The most abundant sources are fresh unprocessed foods, particularly meats, fish, nuts and seed oils. The average daily intake of CoQ10 is approximately 2 mg, but currently there are no data on the amount required for optimal health. Dietary supplementation with CoQ10 increases the resistance of LDL ("bad" cholesterol) to oxidation by free radicals.

Quercetin and rutin (a citrus bioflavonoid), in pharmacological doses, may possibly lower the risk of cardio-vascular disease (CVD). Quercetin is a flavonoid like CoQ10. Flavonoids are parts of plants that are being studied to determine whether they can protect LDL cholesterol from damaging cells, whether they can help lower the risk of stroke, and to learn about their anticarcinogenic properties.

It is believed that the flavonoids in wine and beer, along with ellagic and tannic acid, have been associated with greater decreases of CVD than consumption of spirits. The health benefits attributed to alcohol relate to moderate daily intakes of 20 to 30 grams.

Omega-3 & Omega-6 Fatty Acids

Polyunsaturated fats are found in two forms: omega-3 fatty acids and omega-6 fatty acids. Both are considered essential fatty acids because our bodies can't make them and our diets must include them. Omega-6 sources can be damaging to the body because they are converted to substances that promote inflammation and blood clotting and stimulate other substances called "growth factors." So they can promote

heart disease and cancer as well as help with wound healing. You get these with most vegetable oils, fried foods, crackers and other bakery goods made with these oils, and in grain-fed animals. An intake of 4 to 6 grams of omega-6 is appropriate in your diet.

Since Americans eat many more omega-6 fats than omega-3 fats, you will want to be aware of sources of omega-3s to boost your consumption. They are found in fatty fish (like flounder, salmon and tuna), flaxseeds, flaxseed oil, canola oil, walnuts and many other nuts. Omega-3 fatty acids have an anti-inflammatory and anticlotting effect on our bodies and may suppress the growth of tumors. Try to get at least 2.5 grams

Evaluating Anti-Aging Supplements

Youth-promoting nutrients, or any other nutrients, are always best obtained from their natural sources. Therapeutic diets that limit certain nutrients and calories might just meet your nutrient needs. You might feel that you want to push the limits of safe anti-aging supplements you will take. Never take more than double the RDA/DRI of any nutrient. Recommended Daily Allowances (RDAs) and Dietary Reference Intakes (RDIs) are guidelines designed by the National Academy of Sciences for intakes of certain nutrients.

- **Carotenoids & Vitamin A** are antioxidants that protect and support cells, help reduce abnormal cell growth and tumor formation and protect against certain chemicals. They help prevent common ailments like arthritis, heart disease, cancer and memory loss.
- **Cytokine** is an antioxidant amino acid that is the precursor, along with selenium, of the enzyme glutathione peroxidase, which helps to detoxify and protect your body from chemicals.
- **Fiber** helps the body eliminate waste properly, which is particularly important for the elderly. Fiber also detoxifies chemicals, lowers cholesterol and may protect against certain cancers.
- **Phytonutrients** are the active chemicals in plant foods you eat every day that have been linked to reduced risk of chronic disease.

of omega-3 fatty acids in your diet.

Non-Nutrients

A whole class of non-nutrients is developing within the nutritional community. These substances, and others yet to be discovered, are needed by the body; however, in some cases, nutrition researchers have not yet quantified requirements. In other cases, researchers are daily discovering how non-nutrients interact with other nutrients at our bodies' cellular level to make us ill or to improve our health. Some classes of non-nutrients are better defined below.

Phytochemicals are plant chemicals that protect vegetation from harmful bacteria and viruses. When you eat foods that contain these plant-protecting compounds, they begin to protect you, too. They work to halt the forces that zap health in humans—things like cancer, high cholesterol levels and even the aging process.

Flavonoids, a class of water-soluble plant pigments, are found in a wide range of foods. Some of the best-known flavonoids include genistein in soy and quercetin in onions. Other flavonoids are hesperidin, rutin and citrus flavonoids.

Carotenoids, a group of about 600 nutrients, are converted in the body to vitamin A. The most widely studied carotenoid is beta-carotene. Other key carotenes include lycopene, lutein and zeaxanthin. The exact way that carotenoids work to promote health is not known, but it's thought they protect cells from oxidative damage. Experts believe that carotenoids work best as a team along with phytochemicals and vitamins.

Fiber, an indigestible carbohydrate, is consumed as part of many foods. Most fiber simply passes through the digestive tract because we do not possess the enzymes needed to break it down so that it can be absorbed into the blood. Some fiber parts can be broken down by bacteria in the large intestine to create products that can be absorbed and used as an energy source.

Experts recommend consuming 20 to 35 grams of fiber per day. One-fourth of total fiber should come from soluble fiber (5 to 9 grams) and three-fourths from insoluble fiber (15 to 26 grams). This ratio can be achieved in a diet containing a wide variety of foods. Most Americans need to double their daily intake of fiber to meet the recommended amount. It is important to remember to increase fiber intake gradually.

When you begin to increase your fiber intake, you will also need to increase the amount of fluid you drink each day. Insoluble fiber tends to absorb water and increase in bulk, greatly contributing to the volume of stools (feces). Insoluble fiber speeds the movement of material through the GI tract, especially the colon.

Fiber promotes a feeling of fullness and helps decrease the urge to eat. One study involving more than 12,000 middle-aged men from seven countries found that body fat levels were strongly related to physical activity and dietary fiber intake.

Three things work together to keep

you regular: fiber in your diet, adequate fluid intake (more is needed with greater amounts of insoluble fiber) and physical activity. There are a number of practical ways to add fiber to your diet:

- Choose natural foods such as fiber-rich whole grains, fruits and vegetables.
- Substitute fiber-rich ingredients for processed and refined foods whenever possible.
- Add ethnic choices, which are often rich in fiber.
- Choose snacks of raw vegetables, popcorn, or fresh or dried fruit with the skins on instead of nibbling on "junk food."

Substitute	For
Whole grain flours	White flour
Brown rice	White rice
Bulgur, barley and whole wheat pasta	White pasta
Dried peas, beans and lentils	More processed and less flavorful grains

Fiber

Dietary Fiber is the part of the plant material that cannot be digested and absorbed into the bloodstream. It is a complex carbohydrate. The term *dietary fiber* is often used as a collective term to describe the indigestible residue of the structural components of plants. The chemical components of fiber are: gum, hemicellulose, lignin, mucilage, pectin and cellulose. The most abundant organic chemical on earth, cellulose is found in fruits, vegetables, whole grain cereals, wood, leaves, stems and roots of all plant life. Most foods contain a combination of the various fiber components.

Insoluble Fiber does not dissolve in water and remains relatively unchanged as it moves through the digestive tract. Insoluble fiber promotes regularity. It may assist in preventing certain diseases, such as diverticulitis, and may also reduce the risk of colorectal cancer. Food sources containing insoluble fiber include: fruits, vegetables, barley, legumes, oats and oat bran.

Soluble Fiber dissolves in water. In addition to helping to lower blood cholesterol, soluble fiber has important positive effects on the digestive and absorptive processes. The chemical name for soluble fiber is psyllium hydrophilic mucilloid. Food sources containing insoluble fiber include: fruits, vegetables, cereals, whole wheat products and wheat bran.

Macronutrients

Nutrients fall into six classes plus alcohol. Macronutrients provide energy or calories and come from four of these seven categories: proteins, carbohydrates, fats and alcohol. (The remaining three categories are vitamins, minerals and water.) The few minerals needed by the body in large amounts (calcium, phosphorus and magnesium) are known as macrominerals. Alcohol provides a minimal amount of nutrients but a substantial number of calories.

Energy Nutrients

Carbohydrates are either simple or complex. Both types are found almost exclusively in plant foods. Simple carbohydrates are sometimes called simple sugars. Fruit juice and milk products contain the simple carbohydrates fructose and lactose. Sucrose, the most common simple carbohydrate, is found in sweeteners including honey, corn syrup and white sugar.

The more important complex carbohydrates are also called starches. Complex carbohydrates make up a large part of the world food supply such as rice, wheat and corn. Fruit, vegetables and legumes are also complex carbohydrates. Complex carbohydrates are the premium grade of fuel for your body's energy needs because carbohydrates are easily stored in your muscles. These complex carbohydrates break down more slowly than simple sugars and release their available glucose over time.

Protein helps build and maintain just about everything in your body. From muscles to membranes and blood vessels to bones, protein helps make it and keep it in good repair. Proteins are made of structural units called amino acids, of which there are 22. Nine of these amino acids you can only get from foods. They are called the essential amino acids. Your body makes the other 13 amino acids as needed. All 22 amino acids link together to form chains. You need to eat foods containing the essential amino acids to fill each link in the body's amino acid chains to make them complete. Protein is abundant in all animal foods and is found in smaller amounts in most grains and vegetables.

Fat might not be as bad as we have been taught over the years. Researchers are taking a closer look at fat, which is an essential nutrient needed for good health. Fats are really combinations of many different fatty acids, and each one plays a different role in how your body works. Fat is critical for growth in children, is needed for healthy skin, helps hormone-like substances regulate body processes and is essential for the absorption of fat-soluble vitamins. It is important to note that there is no one best source of fat. Each type of fat (polyunsaturated, monounsaturated and saturated) is important to your health. The key is to limit sources of saturated fat and eat sources of polyunsaturated and monounsaturated fats in moderation.

Macrominerals

Calcium accounts for about 3½ pounds of weight in an adult male and approximately 2¼ pounds in the average female. More than 99 percent of the calcium in your body is in your bones and teeth; however, it is the remaining 1 percent found in blood, lymph fluid and cell structures that is most crucial to your health. When necessary, your body will deplete calcium stores from your bones and weaken them to provide blood calcium levels required for circulation, nerve transmission and muscle contraction.

Calcium absorption will vary widely over your lifespan. Infants absorb about 60 percent of the calcium they take in; following infancy, absorption rates decline dramatically. During puberty, calcium absorption rebounds and then levels off at about 25 percent in early adulthood. Calcium absorption gradually declines with age at about the rate of 0.2 percent a year for postmenopausal women and older men.

Bone is living, growing tissue that is constantly being broken down and rebuilt, just like your hair and nails. About 20 percent of your skeleton is made brand new every year. Bone density tests are the best way to measure the strength of your skeletal system. Calcium also assists in blood clotting and maintenance of cell membranes, and is critical for heartbeat regulation through its effects on the heart muscle. Essential for nerve impulse conduction, calcium also plays a role in the release of neurotransmitters and activates some enzymes that help generate nerve impulses.

Phosphorus is second only to its mineral relative, calcium, in abundance in the body. In the form of phosphates, it is a major component of the mineral phase of bone and is involved in almost all metabolic processes. It also plays an

Phosphorus Thieves

Do you consume soft drinks or take antacids that contain aluminum hydroxide? Check the ingredient list. If you find it listed on the label, you might be disrupting your body's delicate calcium/phosphorus balance. Too much aluminum hydroxide may decrease your absorption of phosphorus, which can lead to weakened bones. Processed foods are another culprit, frequently adding phosphorus-containing preservatives to your diet. Milk provides the best ratio of phosphorus to calcium.

important role in cell metabolism. Phosphorus helps build strong bones and teeth and helps form genetic material, cell membranes and many enzymes. Phosphorus helps release energy from protein, fat and carbohydrate during the digestion of food.

Magnesium works with more than 200 enzymes to help keep things running smoothly. Magnesium functions as both the partner and opponent of calcium. Together, they build strong bones and teeth and also make it possible for muscles to function properly. In the heart tissue, magnesium functions as a calcium channel-blocker preventing the influx of too much calcium into the cells.

About 60 percent of the magnesium in the adult human body finds a home in the bones; the rest either resides in the cells or circulates through the bloodstream. This nutrient helps the body regulate body temperature, cellular glucose metabolism, protein digestion and certain hormone receptor signal transmissions. Magnesium also regulates cellular ion balance, keeping potassium in and sodium out of the cells.

Relatively few people are obviously and seriously deficient in magnesium, but smaller deficiencies are fairly common and uncommonly troublesome. Many Americans aren't meeting the RDA for magnesium, which is 400 mg per day, and it's been estimated that 15 to 20 percent of Americans are chronically deficient. People with chronic magnesium deficiency may be taking too much calcium in their foods and/or supplements, and may not be able to absorb enough of the magnesium they consume. Or there may be problems with the way their bodies use magnesium. Physical and emotional stress may cause their bodies to burn up the magnesium they do take in.

Micronutrients

Micronutrients are identified as vitamins and minerals. Vitamins are essential nutrients, vital to life and indispensable to body functions, but needed in minute amounts. Minerals are inorganic elements that occur naturally. Some minerals are needed in smaller amounts and are called microminerals.

Vitamins

Vitamin A is a family of fat-soluble nutrient compounds called retinoids that are stored in your liver. Vitamin A is found in two forms: preformed vitamin A, also called retinol, is found only in animal foods. Provitamin A, or beta-carotene, is stored in plant foods. Vitamin A is best absorbed in the presence of some dietary fat.

Growth and development of teeth and bones depend on an adequate supply of vitamin A, especially during infancy and the years of rapid growth. Vitamin A helps stimulate the immune system to line your air passages and digestive tract with protective cells that resist infection. Optimal intakes of vitamin A may strengthen the immune system and fend off certain cancers. Vitamin A helps protect body surfaces designed to keep infection and disease out. These special surfaces include your skin and the moist lining of your mouth, throat and digestive tract. Vitamin A is essential for normal growth and healthy development of all body tissues and helps maintain the protective layers of your skin, especially the eyes.

Thiamin, or vitamin B1, is water soluble and functions as part of an enzyme (thiamin pyrophosphate) essential for energy production, carbohydrate metabolism and nerve function. Some thiamin is stored in the heart, liver and kidneys, but these stores do not last long and a continuous intake is necessary to prevent deficiency.

Thiamin, which is found in both plant and animal foods, helps stabilize the appetite by improving digestion, particularly that of sugars, starches and alcohol. Thiamin helps maintain a healthy nervous system and positive mental attitude. Thiamin's coenzyme form is also utilized in the synthesis of acetylcholine, a lack of which causes inflammation of the nerves, and memory loss. Thiamin is also involved with improving learning capacity and is necessary for general growth and development in children.

Riboflavin, vitamin B2, is easily absorbed by your body when it comes from food. But your body captures relatively little riboflavin from supplements, unless they're taken with food. Unlike some other nutrients, riboflavin is not stored in large amounts in the body, so you need to get adequate amounts every day. Excess amounts of riboflavin, especially when taken in supplement form, are excreted in the urine, coloring it a bright yellow.

Riboflavin provides energy at the most basic level—your cells. Every cell needs riboflavin to release energy from protein, carbohydrates and fat. Riboflavin is important in the production of thyroid hormones and in adrenal gland function. Riboflavin aids in the production of infection-fighting immune cells. Nerve development and brain neurotransmitters require the presence of riboflavin. It appears that some migraine sufferers need very large amounts of riboflavin because of a defect in the function of mitochondria, the energy generators for our cells.

Niacin, vitamin B3, is actually the generic name for two similar substances—nicotinic acid and nicotinamide—neither of which are related to the nicotine in cigarettes. Niacin is involved in more than 200 enzyme reactions in your body. Water-soluble niacin is found in foods, but can also be converted from the amino acid tryptophan if you have plenty of iron, riboflavin and vitamin B6 available.

Niacin helps relax and loosen blood vessels. Niacin is required in the formation of a variety of hormones including sex hormones, cortisone, thyroxin and insulin. An abundance of niacin also helps your body quickly notice and respond to insulin released after eating. Niacin plays an essential role in the normal functioning of your brain and nervous system.

Pantothenic acid, also known as vitamin B5, is a member of the water-soluble B-vitamin family. It is an essential ingredient of two substances (coenzyme A and acyl carrier protein), which are needed to metabolize carbohydrates and fats. The name pantothenic acid comes from the Greek word pantos, meaning "everywhere," referring to its wide availability in foods. Therefore, it is easily accessible in the diet.

Pantothenic acid is essential for the release of energy from food. It is used in the manufacture of a compound called coenzyme A, which plays a vital role in the breakdown of fats and carbohydrates. It is also necessary for building cell membranes. Pantothenic acid is necessary for the production of some neurotransmitters, such as acetylcholine, and is essential for normal nervous system function. Pantothenic acid is essential for production of adrenal hormones, such as cortisone, which play an essential part in your body's reaction to stress. The production of other steroid hormones and cholesterol, as well as vitamin A, vitamin D and vitamin B12 requires pantothenic acid. Antibody synthesis requires pantothenic acid; it is also involved in wound healing.

Pyridoxine, or vitamin B6, is a water-soluble vitamin that has three forms: pyridoxine, pyridoxal and pyridoxamine. It performs a wide variety of functions and is essential for overall good health. More than 60 different enzymes depend on B6 for activation.

Vitamin B6 helps make nonessential amino acids or proteins; turn tryptophan—an amino acid—into niacin and serotonin; and produce insulin, hemoglobin and antibodies that fight infection. This nutrient also helps maintain the chemical balance of body fluids and regulates water excretion. Vitamin B6 helps your body maintain normal homocysteine levels that can lower your risk for heart disease. Vitamin B6 is crucial in making key nervous system regulators or neurotransmitters. Vitamin B6 deficiency is extremely rare in humans, but it is seen occasionally in persons with chronic alcoholism. Some healthcare providers recommend supplements of vitamin B6 paired with magnesium during the 2 weeks prior to a woman's period to relieve symptoms of PMS.

Folic acid, or vitamin B9, is a water-soluble nutrient. Folic acid is the synthetic form of folate, which is found naturally in foods. Folic acid has earned the honor of contributing the most striking public health improvement of any vitamin this decade. As more women learn of the link between folic acid and prevention of birth defects, the number of babies born with spina bifida has decreased. Evidence is mounting that optimal levels of folic acid may also help reduce heart disease by controlling the amount of homocysteine in the blood. High levels of homocysteine can damage artery walls and speed the buildup of plaque.

Folic acid helps your body make new cells and hemoglobin and is a vital component of white blood cell manufacturing, which helps the functioning of your immune system. It helps produce the DNA and RNA that are so crucial during the first trimester of pregnancy. Folic acid is involved in the production of neurotransmitters such as serotonin and dopamine, which regulate brain functions including mood, sleep and appetite. Folic acid helps "funnel off" excess homocysteine, which can signal risk of heart disease and heart attack. Strict vegans and the elderly can be at the greatest risk when too much folic acid is taken. This condition can mask pernicious anemia, in which the body's red blood cells can't carry enough oxygen.

Vitamin B12, or cobalamin, is a water-soluble nutrient that binds with a substance called intrinsic factor (a protein produced in your stomach lining) before being absorbed in your intestines. Low levels of stomach acid or too little intrinsic factor can lead to deficiencies of B12. Cobalamin can sometimes be considered a true miracle cure. Picture an elderly woman admitted to the hospital with symptoms of senility. She is frail, but was able to care for herself, carry on intelligent conversations and answer common questions. Gradually, her mental abilities faded to the point that Alzheimer's or senility was considered.

After ruling out these and other serious problems, a simple injection of vitamin B12 led to sudden, dramatic improvements. She's up, walking the halls of her hospital wing, smiling and is "back to normal." That's quite an impact!

How does B12 effect this improvement? As humans age, our bodies naturally make less intrinsic factor, which helps us absorb vitamin B12. Injections or large doses of B12 help stimulate how much can be absorbed and can result in rapid neurological improvement.

The coating of nerve tissue, the myelin sheath, is made with help from vitamin B12. It is also essential in the formation of transmitters that send nerve impulses. Normal red blood cell production and function rely on vitamin B12. Too little vitamin B12 leads to a reduction in the number of white blood cells, which help fight infection.You need vitamin B12 to help metabolize both fat and carbohydrates. B12 helps the formation of amino acid chains to make protein. Rapidly growing cells such as bone marrow and the outer layers of skin need B12 more than other cells.

Vitamin C, also known as ascorbic acid, is a modified sugar molecule that helps reduce oxidation in the watery areas of the body, especially inside the cells. Vitamin C is commonly used as an additive in processed foods.

By working as an antioxidant, this nutrient helps protect other vitamins from harmful oxidation. Vitamin C helps prevent cell damage and may stop the production of cancer-causing nitrosamines in the stomach. Adequate vitamin C intake helps rid the body of toxic levels of stored lead, and vitamin C helps increase iron absorption and helps improve your ability to use folic acid. Vitamin C helps form collagen, which keeps your gums, tendons and ligaments healthy and elastic and prevents bruising. Without sufficient support from vitamin C, the tissues that surround tiny capillaries break and leave black and blue marks caused by blood leaks. Vitamin C helps stimulate the adrenal glands to manufacture cortisone and other hormones that help your body cope with stress. Vitamin C also aids healing of wounds by stimulating antibodies and production of white blood cells that help fight infection and illness.

Vitamin C is commonly used as a dietary supplement, often in megadoses. But your body cannot store vitamin C to use later. There is minimal justification for using megadoses of vitamin C (that is, 200 mg or more per day). Vitamin C does not help prevent colds and respiratory infections, but might help shorten how long they last.

Vitamin D really isn't a vitamin at all; it's a steroid hormone. It was originally misclassified as a fat-soluble vitamin, and to confuse matters even more, it's actually two separate calciferol (calcium-related) compounds: cholecalciferol and ergocalciferol. Exposing your skin to a sufficient amount of sunlight or artificial ultraviolet radiation can create each form of calciferol. But the clothes we wear, pollution, and the need to avoid the sun reduce how much vitamin D our bodies make. Vitamin D's most important role is to regulate calcium levels in your body. The amount needed each day varies with age.

Vitamin D plays a critical role in regulating how much calcium stays in your blood. Calcium is important for the transmission of nerve impulses and is required for muscle contraction. Perhaps the most important muscle that needs calcium to work effectively is your heart. Vitamin D is also essential for helping calcium get into your bones. Without proper levels of vitamin D, you can't absorb enough calcium no matter how much you take in. Too little vitamin D can speed up the development of osteoporosis. Occasionally, a vitamin D deficiency may cause slow, progressive hearing loss. If the bones in the inner ear become too weak or porous, they will not properly transmit sound waves. Sometimes, this special type of hearing loss can be improved with an adequate intake of vitamin D.

Vitamin E is a group of 'fat-soluble compounds that are stored in fatty tissue throughout your body and in the liver. Its main function is the prevention of tissue breakdown. Unfortunately, vitamin E is one nutrient that is difficult to obtain in optimal amounts from moderate-calorie foods.

Vitamin E helps protect the thymus gland and circulating white blood cells from damage. It also helps protect the immune function during chronic viral illness. Working as an antioxidant, vitamin E protects various tissues from destruction by free radicals (see page 32 for more information). Vitamin E has been shown to help prevent age-related damage and deterioration to skin, blood vessels and the eyes. Vitamin E also helps protect immune function during chronic viral illness and helps protect circulating white blood cells from damage. Antioxidants such as vitamin E hold great promise in reducing the risk of stroke, heart disease and Alzheimer's disease.

Vitamin K, which is known for its critical role in blood clotting, is studied by only a handful of researchers worldwide. But with the aging of North America's population, this vitamin may rate a bigger following as its importance to the integrity of bones becomes increasingly clear. Vitamin K is a fat-soluble vitamin. Most Americans consume about three to five times more than the RDA of vitamin K and deficiencies are quite rare.

Vitamin K helps maintain healthy bone tissue and activates at least three proteins involved in bone health. It is also a critical part of the healing process after bone fractures. The most well-known function of vitamin K is the key role it plays in helping control blood clotting by the production of prothrombin.

Biotin is a nutrient that is synthesized by the bacteria in your intestinal tract. You can make all the biotin you need in your intestines, but it is also widely available in small amounts in most common foods. Most people excrete more biotin in waste products than they take in through foods.

Bios is the Greek word for life. Biotin is needed for carbohydrate metabolism and helps in the synthesis of fatty acids. It also helps join amino acids into proteins. Biotin is important to help keep your hair and nails healthy.

Choline, an unofficial vitamin, is manufactured by your body, and you don't have to get it from foods. The Food and Nutrition Board recently set a precedent by classifying choline as a nutrient, even though it's not essential for all people. Research suggests that men and pregnant or breastfeeding women require a dietary source of choline of 500 mg per day. These people have the highest calorie needs and may not be able to make enough of this nutrient in the liver.

Choline helps your brain store memories and keeps your emotions and judgment in line. This vitamin-like compound works as a precursor to the nerve messenger acetylcholine and helps maintain smooth, fluid connections between brain cells. Small quantities are made in your liver with the help of vitamin B12, folic acid and methionine. It's thought that higher amounts than your body makes are required for optimal health. Pregnant women have lots of choline circulating around the placenta, the organ that passes nutrients from the mother to the developing baby. It's been suggested, but not proven, that choline is important for fetal growth.

Minerals

Boron is a trace mineral that was thought to be essential only for plants until recently. Evidence shows that boron might be essential to humans, too. Boron is distributed throughout your body with the highest concentrations in bones and tooth enamel, but the functions of boron are not completely known. Because boron works with calcium, magnesium and phosphorus, it is thought to play a role in the formation of bone tissue. Boron affects the metabolism of steroid hormones and may also have a role in converting vitamin D to its more active form. Boron also may play a role in male sex hormone production.

Chloride is part of sodium chloride, or table salt. Chloride also combines with hydrogen to make hydrochloric acid, or stomach acid, which helps nutrient absorption during digestion. This caustic compound is what helps you break down food so individual nutrients can be absorbed and used by the body.

Chloride is an electrolyte that helps maintain the balance of water between body cells and surrounding fluids. Chloride ions located mainly outside cell walls help monitor and regulate the flow of fluid inside and outside cell walls. Transmission of nerve impulses to the brain and regulation of electrical impulses that travel across nerves are aided by chloride.

Chromium is the same stuff that makes old-fashioned car bumpers shiny. It also helps you shine when you need to work or play hard. Chromium works with insulin to help use glucose and maintain normal blood sugar levels. Because it helps regulate insulin, chromium is important in helping you maintain peak energy under pressure. That doesn't mean it will make you stronger, smarter or capable of more than is normal for you. Other than knowing that it is somehow involved with protein, fat and carbohydrate metabolism, we still don't fully understand the role of chromium. We do know that this mineral is stored in your brain, skin, fat, muscles, spleen, kidneys and testes.

Copper is a brownish red metallic element usually found in foods containing iron. Your liver and brain contain the largest amounts of copper, while small amounts are stored in other organs. The amount of copper found in the human body would probably fit on the head of a pin. But such a tiny quantity doesn't prevent this mighty mineral from performing some impressive feats to promote optimal health. As part of at least 13 enzymes, copper is crucial to a variety of functions.

Bones, joints and connective tissues require copper to help jump-start enzymes that make and maintain these structures. Copper is used to make cell membranes and maintains the protective covering around nerve cells. Copper is part of the copper-zinc team that helps protect against damage by free radicals. The formation of melanin, a natural coloring pigment in your skin and hair, needs a copper-dependent enzyme.

Fluoride's biggest source is usually the local water supply. Half of all U.S. water supplies are fluoridated. Those that aren't are in homes that rely on well water or nonmunicipal water sources. Most bottled water does not contain fluoride. Controlled doses of fluoride are beneficial to the dental health of adults as well as children. Fluoride helps to harden tooth enamel, protects teeth from decay and strengthens all bone tissues.

If you don't know whether your water is fluoridated, call your local water department to find out. A typical amount added is 0.7 to 1.2 mg per liter of water. The American Academy of Pediatrics recommends that all breast-fed infants and babies using reconstituted formula in households where the water is not fluoridated start supplements at 6 months. Many experts recommend continuing with supplements until age 16, especially if you drink and cook exclusively with unfluoridated tap or bottled water. Unlike most nutrient supplements, fluoride is available by prescription from your doctor or dentist. Fluoride mouth rinses are also available for adults and children over the age of six.

Iodine's most significant source in the United States is iodized salt. The average adult body contains between 20 and 50 mg of iodine, most of it concentrated in the thyroid gland. Iodine helps your body form thyroid hormones, which are vital to physical growth and development. Thyroid hormones control metabolism, improve mental functioning and give you healthier hair, skin, nails and teeth.

Iron is the most abundant element on earth, yet is needed in only minute amounts for humans. Iron is found in both animal and plant foods. How much iron you have determines how much oxygen gets to the rest of your body tissues. Thyroid hormones require iron for production, and iron is critical in building and maintaining a healthy immune system.

Manganese, like copper, molybdenum and other minerals, is an essential part of many enzymes. This mineral is present in a wide variety of foods. We don't know much yet about manganese, because few scientists are interested in studying it. What we do know is that manganese helps in the development of bones, teeth and joints. Manganese is also required for female sex hormones and thyroid hormones to work properly.

Molybdenum is the least known of all essential minerals. It's also one of the scarcest elements in the earth's crust. Molybdenum is an essential trace mineral needed for the proper function of certain enzyme-dependent processes.

Potassium is usually supplied in adequate levels through a balanced diet, but potassium supplements seem popular because illness or treatment with certain medicines can dramatically deplete potassium stores in your body. Potassium affects blood pressure by relaxing the artery walls. Relaxed walls allow blood to flow smoothly, which helps keep your blood pressure low.

Selenium is a trace element found to a varying extent in soil. It enters the human diet through plants such as corn and through the meat of animals grazing on vegetation containing selenium. Products from selenium-rich soils of the United States' plains and mountain regions carry proportionately more selenium than those coming from the Upper Midwest, Northeast and Florida, where selenium soil concentration is low. Selenium is being researched heavily to examine the role this mineral may play in reducing your risk of several major diseases, including cancer and heart disease.

Your body's most abundant natural antioxidant is an enzyme that is dependent on selenium. In this form, selenium helps protect red blood cells and cell membranes from free-radical damage. It also works with and helps vitamin E with other antioxidant functions. Selenium is needed to activate thyroid hormones, and it may help protect against some of the damaging effects of ultraviolet light. Selenium is essential for healthy immune functioning. As a result, selenium supplementation has reduced the incidence of hepatitis in deficient populations. In elderly people, selenium has been found to stimulate the activity of white blood cells—primary components of the immune system.

Sodium is the nutrient most frequently associated as a villain in blood pressure. Current research shows some individuals have much greater blood pressure responses to salt than others. About half those individuals who have high blood pressure are "salt sensitive." But only 10 percent of the total American population falls into this category. Since there is no harm in moderately cutting back on dietary sodium, reduction is widely recommended. There's also a theory that high levels of sodium over time may cause rising blood pressure as you age. So if your blood pressure is normal now, cutting back to a reasonable amount of sodium may help keep it that way.

If you ate only unprocessed foods and added no table salt, you'd still get enough sodium to meet normal needs. Just 400 to 500 milligrams of sodium per day is enough to keep your body fluids and blood pressure in balance. Of course, if you are extremely active, have a fever, prolonged diarrhea or vomiting, you need extra sodium. That's why soup, broth and saltine crackers are frequently recommended during illness. Sodium, along with potassium and chloride, help regulate fluid balance and keep your blood pH normal. The best-known function of sodium is to help regulate blood pressure. The electrical current that helps send nerve impulses through your body is stimulated by the positive charge of sodium molecules. Sodium also aids in muscle contraction.

Zinc is essential in the composition or function of at least 59 enzymes involved in digestion and metabolism, although the presence of all have not been demonstrated in humans. Zinc is absorbed in the upper part of the small intestine. About one-third to one-half of the 10 to 15 mg provided in the diet is absorbed. Absorption is increased when blood levels fall, or in the presence of vitamin D. On the other hand, absorption is decreased as the stores of zinc increase or when the diet contains the outer husk of whole grains in which either phytic acid or fiber bind zinc in an insoluble complex. High levels of dietary calcium or copper also result in a lowered absorption of zinc. This is not a problem with normal dietary intakes.

Zinc is important for reproduction, skin health and maintaining our sense of taste. Registered dietitians prescribe extra amounts of zinc to help skin ulcers heal and to restore taste and appetite. It is not recommended to stay on large doses of zinc for long periods of time.

Food Sources of Spotlighted Vital Nutrients

The following chart lists foods that are known sources of important nutrients in your diet. Reliable sources of foods with more than one major nutrient appear on more than one list. By planning menus using the Food Guide Pyramid (see page 229) and by using these lists, your diet will include a variety of foods that provide the 40 or more nutrients your body needs every day. Consider posting these helpful lists in your kitchen. Double-check a given meal or a whole menu against these foods, which are sources of vital nutrients. Choose from the lists the foods you like best. They will help you meet your nutrition goals and save other calories for a treat.

Non-Nutrients	How much do you need every day?	What is its function in your body?	Sources in your diet.
Carotenoids	■ Not known at this time ■ 5 to 9 servings of all fruits and vegetables	■ Intake is associated with a decreased risk of age-related macular degeneration	■ Apricots ■ Broccoli ■ Carrots ■ Colorful fruits and vegetables ■ Dark green leafy vegetables ■ Kale ■ Spinach ■ Tomatoes
Flavonoids	■ Not known at this time ■ 5 to 9 servings of all fruits and vegetables	■ Act as antioxidants, protect LDL ("bad") cholesterol from oxidation ■ Inhibit platelets from sticking together (precursor to stroke) ■ Have anti-inflammatory and antitumor action	■ Apples ■ Arrowroot powder ■ Beans and legumes, cooked (see list on page 53) ■ Broccoli ■ Celery ■ Cranberries ■ Flaxseed ■ Fruits ■ Garlic ■ Grape products ■ Green tea ■ Miso paste ■ Miso soup ■ Onion ■ Soy nuts ■ Soybean sprouts ■ Tofu ■ Wine

Non-Nutrients *continued*	How much do you need every day?	What is its function in your body?	Sources in your diet.
Omega-3 Fatty Acids	■ Eat one or more good sources each day ■ Exact amounts have not yet been discovered, but 2.5 grams daily has been proven effective	■ May help prevent cardiac disease and tumor development	■ Black currant oil ■ Beans (great northern, kidney, navy, soybeans) ■ Canola oil ■ Fish, cooked (bonito, eel, flounder, halibut, "horse" mackerel, mackerel, Pacific saury, salmon, sardines, sea bream, shrimp, tuna, yellowtail) ■ Fish oil capsules ■ Flaxseed, ground ■ Flaxseed oil ■ Omega-3 eggs ■ Omega-3 margarines ■ Pumpkin ■ Soy products or soybean oil ■ Tofu ■ Walnuts, chopped
Alcohol	■ No minimal need ■ Females: one drink per day, but avoid alcohol during pregnancy ■ Males: two drinks per day ■ Certain individuals should avoid alcohol completely	■ Increases blood pressure ■ May stimulate appetite in elderly	■ Beer ■ Spirits ■ Wine

Non-Nutrients continued	How much do you need every day?	What is its function in your body?	Sources in your diet.
Fiber	■ 25 to 35 grams of fiber ■ 3 servings a day of whole grains is recommended (Americans average 1 or fewer servings per day)	■ Intake of whole grains is linked to improved gastrointestinal function, antioxidant protection and intake of phytoestrogens ■ Whole grain foods also contain B vitamins, vitamin E, selenium, copper, zinc and magnesium ■ Insoluble fiber binds to estrogen, which is a factor in breast-cancer risk; fiber can reduce blood levels of estrogen ■ Because soluble fiber stays in your stomach longer than foods low in soluble fiber, you have a greater feeling of fullness and satisfaction, which helps you eat less at your next meal and can improve weight loss ■ Reduces insulin levels; high levels can promote weight gain	**Fruits & vegetables** ■ Apples ■ Berries ■ Broccoli ■ Brussels sprouts ■ Carrots ■ Cauliflower ■ Figs ■ Oranges ■ Pears ■ Peas ■ Potatoes ■ Prunes **Whole grains** ■ Bran muffins ■ Brown rice ■ Cereals, cooked or dry ■ Oatmeal ■ 100% whole wheat bread ■ Wheat bran or miller's bran **Beans & legumes** ■ Black beans ■ Black-eyed peas ■ Cannelini beans ■ Fava beans ■ Garbanzo beans ■ Great northern beans ■ Kidney beans ■ Lentils ■ Lima beans ■ Navy beans ■ Pinto beans ■ Red beans ■ Soybeans

Non-Nutrients *continued*	**How much do you need every day?**	**What is its function in your body?**	**Sources in your diet.**
Water	■ 8 (8-ounce) glasses ■ See page 234 for further information regarding fluid needs	■ Lubricates joints and digestive tract ■ Universal solvent where nutrients and waste products travel ■ Required by cells ■ Holds heat and maintains body temperature	■ Water ■ Juice ■ Milk ■ Soup
Macronutrients			
Carbohydrates	■ 140 to 275 grams each day. Grams of carbohydrate are best eaten in amounts of 5 to 75 grams per meal or snack, with an ideal average of 30 to 60 grams ■ Athletic individuals, larger men and people with special needs will need varying amounts	■ Three major types of carbohydrates are **starch**, **sugar** and **fiber** ■ Stores glucose (simple sugar) as glycogen; splits glucose for energy, literally fueling the body; helps maintain the blood glucose level; converts glucose to fat ■ The kind and amount of carbohydrate plays a role in prevention and/or treatment of tooth decay, diabetes, hypoglycemia (too low and fluctuating blood sugar)	■ Baked goods ■ Beans and legumes (see list on page 53) ■ Breads ■ Breakfast cereals ■ Cereal grains (includes rice) ■ Cookies ■ Crackers ■ Dairy foods ■ Deep-fat coating ■ Desserts ■ Fruit and fruit products ■ Legumes ■ Pasta ■ Potatoes ■ Snack foods ■ Soups ■ Sugars ■ Vegetables ■ Whole grain cereals and breads

Macronutrients *continued*	How much do you need every day?	What is its function in your body?	Sources in your diet.
Proteins	■ Adults need about 0.8 gram of protein per kilogram of ideal body weight (2.2 pounds = 1 kilogram). For individuals 40 and older within normal weight range, this usually totals somewhere between 50 and 63 grams per day *(Note: If you are overweight, you do not use your actual weight in kilograms, because much of that number is not lean body mass. A safe number to use is your ideal body weight in kilograms plus 5%.)*	■ Provide growth and maintenance of body tissues ■ Contribute to acid-base balance ■ Are a source of energy ■ Help with digestion and absorption	■ Animal-based foods ■ Beans and legumes (see list on page 53) ■ Dairy ■ Rice ■ Pasta ■ Potatoes ■ Seafood ■ Vegetables ■ Whole grain cereals and breads

Macronutrients *continued*	How much do you need every day?	What is its function in your body?	Sources in your diet.
Fats	■ 30 to 35 percent of your total calories	■ Storage form of energy ■ Part of essential nutrients like vitamins ■ Protect cell membranes and body organs	■ Butter ■ Canola oil ■ Eel ■ Fat used to deep-fry ■ Fish oil ■ Flaxseed oil ■ Flounder ■ Halibut ■ Hydrogenated fats ■ Kidney beans ■ Mackerel ■ Navy beans ■ Nuts ■ Olive oil ■ Omega-3 eggs ■ Omega-3 margarine ■ Peanut oil ■ Pumpkin seeds ■ Salmon ■ Sardines ■ Shrimp ■ Soy products ■ Trans-free margarine ■ Tuna

Macronutrients *continued*	How much do you need every day?	What is its function in your body?	Sources in your diet.
Calcium	■ Women aged 19 to 50: 1,000 mg/day ■ Women aged 51 and up: 1,200 mg/day ■ Men aged 19 to 50: 1,000 mg/day ■ Men aged 51 and up: 1,200 mg/day ■ During pregnancy: 1,000 mg/day ■ The National Osteoporosis Foundation recommends 1,200 to 1,500 mg of calcium per day for females ages 11 to 24, 1,000 mg per day for women age 25 and over, 1,500 mg daily for post-menopausal women not taking estrogen, and 1,200 to 1,500 mg of calcium daily for pregnant or lactating women	■ May promote a sound night's sleep when taken before bed ■ Supports bone health during and after menopause for prevention and treatment of osteoporosis ■ Reduces muscle cramps and menstrual cramps ■ Prevents tooth decay ■ Assists in blood clotting and maintenance of cell membranes ■ Critical for heartbeat regulation ■ Essential for nerve impulse conduction, plays a role in the release of neurotransmitters and activates some enzymes that generate nerve impulses	■ Almonds ■ Apricots ■ Beet greens ■ Bok choy ■ Brazil nuts ■ Broccoli ■ Cheese ■ Collard greens ■ Dandelion greens ■ Dried figs ■ Ice cream ■ Kale ■ Kelp ■ Milk ■ Molasses (blackstrap) ■ Mustard greens ■ Parsley ■ Peas ■ Pudding or custard ■ Rice milk ■ Salmon with bones ■ Sardines with bones ■ Seaweed ■ Sesame seeds ■ Soy milk, fortified ■ Spinach ■ Tofu ■ Turnip greens ■ Yogurt

Macronutrients *continued*	How much do you need every day?	What is its function in your body?	Sources in your diet.
Phosphorus	■ Women aged 19 and up: 700 mg/day ■ Men aged 19 and up: 700 mg/day ■ During pregnancy: 700 mg/day	■ Helps build strong bones and teeth ■ Helps release energy from calorie-producing nutrients during digestion ■ Helps form genetic material, cell membranes and enzymes ■ Is part of the phospholipid lecithin	■ Carp ■ Chocolate milk ■ Lowfat or nonfat yogurt ■ Mackerel ■ Salmon (canned swordfish)
Magnesium	■ Women aged 19 to 30: 310 mg/day ■ Women aged 31 and up: 320 mg/day ■ Men aged 19 to 30: 400 mg/day ■ Men aged 31 and up: 420 mg/day ■ During pregnancy: 350 to 360 mg/day	■ In conjunction with calcium, magnesium helps build strong bones and teeth ■ Helps regulate calcium within the cells ■ Helps regulate body temperature ■ Helps manage cellular balance among the various ions ■ Regulates cellular glucose metabolism and protein digestion	■ Avocados ■ Bananas ■ Beets ■ Black beans ■ Bran cereal ■ Broccoli ■ Brown rice ■ Dates ■ Dry beans ■ Dry peas ■ Halibut ■ Lentils ■ Nonfat yogurt ■ Nut butters ■ Nuts ■ Raisins ■ Soybeans and lima beans ■ Spinach ■ Sweet potatoes ■ Whole grain breads and cereals

Micronutrients Vitamins	How much do you need every day?	What is its function in your body?	Sources in your diet.
Vitamin A/ Beta-carotene	■ Women aged 19 and up: 700 mcg/day ■ Men aged 19 and up: 900 mcg/day ■ During pregnancy: 770 mcg/day	■ Essential for vision—improves poor night vision—growth, reproduction ■ Assists formation and maintenance of skin mucous membranes; helps treat skin problems, especially acne, and thus increases resistance to infection ■ Has strong anti-oxidant activity and helps prevent development of some kinds of cancers, including skin and lung	**Dark Green Leafy Vegetables** ■ Beet greens ■ Broccoli ■ Carrot tops ■ Chard ■ Chicory ■ Chrysanthemum greens ■ Collard greens ■ Dandelion greens ■ Endive ■ Escarole ■ Kale ■ Mustard greens ■ Romaine lettuce ■ Spinach ■ Turnip greens ■ Watercress **Deep Yellow Vegetables** ■ Carrots ■ Pumpkin ■ Sweet potatoes ■ Winter squash **Other Sources** ■ Apricot nectar ■ Apricots ■ Asparagus ■ Cantaloupe ■ Chile peppers ■ Eggs ■ Mangoes ■ Mixed vegetables ■ Nectarines ■ Peppers ■ Purple plums *continued*

Micronutrients Vitamins cont.	How much do you need every day?	What is its function in your body?	Sources in your diet.
Vitamin A/ Beta-carotene	*See previous page*	*See previous page*	*continued* **Available in specific locations** ■ Amaranth, boiled ■ Garland chrysanthemum ■ Horseradish leaf tips, boiled ■ Japanese persimmon ■ Loquats, raw ■ Plantain, cooked ■ Potherb jute, boiled
Thiamin/ Vitamin B1	■ Women aged 19 and up: 1.1 mg/day ■ Men aged 19 and up: 1.1 mg/day ■ During pregnancy: 1.4 mg/day	■ Used to treat nervous system disorders like Bell's palsy, multiple sclerosis and neuritis ■ May help prevent or slow Alzheimer's disease ■ Functions as part of a coenzyme in carbohydrate metabolism and production of ribose for DNA and RNA formation ■ Promotes normal function of nervous system	■ Breads, fortified ■ Cereals, fortified ■ Ham ■ Pasta, fortified ■ Pompano fish ■ Pork ■ Rice, fortified ■ Sunflower seeds

Micronutrients Vitamins *cont.*	How much do you need every day?	What is its function in your body?	Sources in your diet.
Riboflavin/ Vitamin B2	■ Women aged 19 and up: 1.1 mg/day ■ Men aged 19 and up: 1.3 mg/day ■ During pregnancy: 1.4 mg/day	■ Functions as part of coenzymes that release energy within the cell ■ Essential for maintenance of skin, mucous membranes and nervous system ■ Used in the formation and maintenance of cornea and eye tissues ■ Helpful in relieving stress and fatigue. Increased need by women taking estrogens (for birth control, menopause or after antibiotic use) ■ Used with pyridoxine to help lift mood ■ Part of the treatment for migraine headaches ■ May help to protect against colon cancer	■ Buttermilk ■ Milk ■ Yogurt

Micronutrients Vitamins *cont.*	How much do you need every day?	What is its function in your body?	Sources in your diet.
Niacin/ Vitamin B3	■ Women aged 19 and up: 14 mg/day ■ Men aged 19 and up: 16 mg/day ■ During pregnancy: 18 mg/day	■ Functions as part of a coenzyme involved in fat and carbohydrate metabolism and tissue respiration ■ Essential for growth and hormone production ■ Promotes healthy skin ■ Vitamin B6 is a cofactor in the conversion of the amino acid tryptophan (which is involved in more than 50 metabolic reactions) to niacin ■ Helps lower cholesterol and triglycerides in the body	■ Chicken ■ Lamb ■ Mackerel ■ Mullet ■ Pork ■ Salmon ■ Swordfish ■ Veal

Micronutrients Vitamins *cont.*	How much do you need every day?	What is its function in your body?	Sources in your diet.
Pantothenic acid/ Vitamin B5	■ Women aged 19 and up: 5 mg/day ■ Men aged 19 and up: 5 mg/day ■ During pregnancy: 6 mg/day	■ Functions as a coenzyme involved in gluconeogenesis, synthesis and degradation of fatty acids and synthesis of some hormones ■ Treats fatigue and stress after surgery or during recovery from illness or injury ■ May help prevent and treat some kinds of acne ■ With vitamin C, strengthens skin and promotes healing	***Almost all foods*** ■ Avocados ■ Brewer's yeast ■ Cauliflower ■ Dried beans ■ Egg yolks ■ Fish ■ Green beans ■ Sweet potatoes ■ Whole grain cereals ***Also made by your intestinal bacteria***

Micronutrients Vitamins *cont.*	How much do you need every day?	What is its function in your body?	Sources in your diet.
Pyridoxine/ Vitamin B6	■ Women aged 19 to 50: 1.3 mg/day ■ Women aged 51 and up: 1.5 mg/day ■ Men aged 19 to 50: 1.3 mg/day ■ Men aged 51 and up: 1.7 mg/day ■ During pregnancy: 1.4 mg/day	■ Functions as part of a coenzyme involved in protein and lipid metabolism, and niacin and red blood cell formation ■ It's a cofactor in making niacin (B3) from tryptophan and serotonin ■ Used clinically in a wide variety of conditions: PMS, pregnancy and its associated nausea, carpal tunnel syndrome, problems of nerves and water retention ■ Helps produce insulin, hemoglobin and antibodies that fight infection	■ Avocados ■ Bananas ■ Beans (garbanzo, green, lentils, lima, pinto beans) ■ Beef ■ Cereal, fortified (some) ■ Chestnuts ■ Chicken ■ Eggs ■ Fish (catfish, cod, crab, halibut, herring, mackerel, salmon, sardines, tuna) ■ Green peppers ■ Mangoes ■ Parsley ■ Peanuts ■ Plantains ■ Potatoes ■ Soybeans ■ Spinach ■ Wheat bran ■ Wheat germ

Micronutrients Vitamins *cont.*	How much do you need every day?	What is its function in your body?	Sources in your diet.
Folic Acid/ Vitamin B9	■ Women aged 19 and up: 400 mcg/day ■ Men aged 19 and up: 400 mcg/day ■ During pregnancy: 600 mcg/day	■ Functions as part of a coenzyme for amino acid metabolism ■ Makes new body cells by helping produce DNA and RNA ■ Lowers homo-cysteine levels ■ Promotes red (with vitamin B12) and white blood cell formation ■ Linked to neural tube defects	*Abundantly available in fresh, unprocessed food* ■ Asparagus ■ Black-eyed peas ■ Kidney beans ■ Lentils ■ Oatmeal ■ Orange juice ■ Pinto beans ■ Spinach, cooked
Vitamin B12/ Cobalamin	■ Women aged 19 and up: 2.4 mcg/day ■ Men aged 19 and up: 2.4 mcg/day ■ During pregnancy: 2.6 mcg/day	■ Works closely with folic acid with red blood cells and treats many anemias ■ Helps maintain nerve tissue ■ Requires "intrin-sic factor"—a compound made inside the body— for absorption from the intestinal tract into the bloodstream ■ Helps your body use fatty acids and some amino acids (the building blocks of protein)	*Primarily found in animal-based foods* ■ Eggs ■ Fish ■ Meat ■ Milk ■ Poultry *Contamination (of bacteria and soil) in foods and water (i.e., microorganisms) contribute to B12 intake*

Micronutrients Vitamins *cont.*	How much do you need every day?	What is its function in your body?	Sources in your diet.
Vitamin C/ Ascorbic acid	■ Women aged 19 and up: 75 mg/day ■ Men aged 19 and up: 90 mg/day ■ During pregnancy: 85 mg/day	■ An antioxidant necessary in formation of collagen, strengthening and protecting blood vessels. Protects the tissues and lenses of the eye from free-radical damage that causes cataracts, macular degeneration and loss of vision in older people ■ Promotes wound-healing process, increases resistance to infection and supports immune function ■ Protects from viral disease and reduces the production of cancer-causing nitrosamines in the stomach ■ Aids in absorption of iron ■ Prevents vitamin E from oxidation	■ Asparagus ■ Bean sprouts ■ Bell peppers ■ Black currants ■ Broccoli ■ Brussels sprouts ■ Cabbage ■ Cantaloupe ■ Cauliflower ■ Chard ■ Collard greens ■ Cranberry juice ■ Grapefruit and juice ■ Green chili ■ Guava ■ Honeydew ■ Kiwi ■ Kohlrabi ■ Lemons ■ Limes ■ Mangoes ■ Oranges and juice ■ Papaya ■ Pineapple ■ Potatoes with skins ■ Rose hips ■ Salsa ■ Spinach (fresh and frozen) ■ Strawberries ■ Tangerines ■ Tomatoes and juice ■ Turnips ■ Vitamin C-fortified juice

Micronutrients Vitamins *cont.*	How much do you need every day?	What is its function in your body?	Sources in your diet.
Vitamin D	■ Women aged 19 to 50: 5 mcg/day ■ Women aged 51 to 70: 10 mcg/day ■ Women aged 71 and up: 15 mcg/day ■ Men aged 19 to 50: 5 mcg/day ■ Men aged 51 to 70: 10 mcg/day ■ Men aged 71 and up: 15 mcg/day ■ During pregnancy: 5 mcg/day	■ Proper formation of skeleton and teeth, healing of fractures and prevention of osteoporosis with adequate calcium, phosphorus and exercise ■ Increases intestinal absorption of calcium and helps prevent tooth decay ■ Helps with the function of the heart ■ Has a potential role in reducing cancers of the breast, prostate and colon	■ Cereals, fortified with vitamin D ■ Cod liver oil ■ Custard ■ Egg ■ Herring, kippers ■ Mackerel ■ Margarine, fortified ■ Mazola corn oil ■ Milk, fortified with vitamin D ■ Milkshake (fast food) ■ Mushrooms ■ Pudding ■ Salmon ■ Sardines ■ Soy milk, fortified with vitamin D ■ Sunshine— 20 minutes (without sunscreen), 3 times a week at minimum ■ Tuna ■ Yogurt with vitamin D added

Micronutrients Vitamins *cont.*	How much do you need every day?	What is its function in your body?	Sources in your diet.
Vitamin E	■ Women aged 19 and up: 15 IU/day ■ Men aged 19 and up: 15 IU/day ■ During pregnancy: 15 IU/day	■ Guards against free-radical damage of cells and vessel walls ■ Decreases heart attack risk ■ Improves immunity ■ Decreases cancer risk because it protects the cell's DNA ■ Reduces the risk of dementia	■ Almonds ■ Canola oil ■ Cereals, fortified ■ Hazelnuts ■ Margarine ■ Mayonnaise ■ Olive oil ■ Peanut butter/oil ■ Rice bran oil ■ Safflower oil ■ Shrimp ■ Sunflower seeds and oil ■ Wheat germ ■ Whole grains
Vitamin K	■ Women aged 19 and up: 90 mcg/day ■ Men aged 19 and up: 120 mcg/day ■ During pregnancy: 90 mcg/day	■ Essential for formation of prothrombin (clotting factor in the blood) and other proteins necessary in regulation of blood clotting ■ Required for biosynthesis of some proteins in plasma, bone and kidney ■ Used to counter-act the blood-thinning medicine, Coumadin	■ Asparagus ■ Broccoli ■ Brussels sprouts ■ Cabbage ■ Cauliflower ■ Coffee ■ Collard greens ■ Endive ■ Garbanzo beans ■ Green apples ■ Green tea ■ Kale ■ Lentils ■ Liver ■ Onions (cooked) ■ Red leaf lettuce ■ Seaweed ■ Soybean oil ■ Spinach ■ Swiss chard ■ Turnip greens ■ Watercress

Micronutrients Vitamins *cont.*	How much do you need every day?	What is its function in your body?	Sources in your diet.
Biotin	■ Women aged 19 and up: 30 mcg/day ■ Men aged 19 and up: 30 mcg/day ■ During pregnancy: 30 mcg/day	■ Functions as part of a coenzyme involved in fat synthesis, amino acid metabolism and glycogen formation ■ Assists in maintenance of nerve tissue, skin, hair, blood cells and sex organs ■ Taken by people with diabetes to help support fat and carbohydrate metabolism	Eggs Yeast breads ***Made by your intestinal bacteria***
Choline	■ Women aged 19 and up: 425 mg/day ■ Men aged 19 and up: 550 mg/day ■ During pregnancy: 450 mg/day	■ Taken as a supplement for neurologic disorders, such as Alzheimer's disease, as well as gallbladder and liver problems ■ May help your liver cells regenerate more efficiently ■ Can help your brain store memories and keeps your emotions and judgment in line	■ Brewer's yeast ■ Eggs ■ Legumes ■ Meat ■ Nuts ■ Whole grains

Micronutrients Minerals *cont.*	How much do you need every day?	What is its function in your body?	Sources in your diet.
Boron	■ There is no RDA developed yet for boron ■ Most people get 2 to 5 mg/day from foods, and that appears to be adequate	■ Helps the bones use calcium and prevent bone loss ■ May act on the parathyroid glands to regulate calcium, magnesium and phosphorus balance	■ Avocados ■ Beer ■ Cider ■ Leafy green vegetables ■ Legumes ■ Nuts ■ Wine
Chloride	■ There is no RDA established for chloride ■ Most experts suggest about 750 mg/day (the amount found in ¼ teaspoon table salt) ■ If you exercise, you may need more chloride	■ Helps monitor and regulate the flow of fluid inside and outside cell walls ■ Excess chloride is removed through sweat, urine and feces ■ Combined with hydrogen, helps nutrient absorption during digestion ■ Aids transmission of nerve impulses that travel across nerves	■ Salted foods ■ Table salt

Micronutrients Minerals *cont.*	How much do you need every day?	What is its function in your body?	Sources in your diet.
Chromium	■ Women aged 19 to 50: 25 mcg/day ■ Women aged 51 and up: 20 mcg/day ■ Men aged 19 to 50: 35 mcg/day ■ Men aged 51 and up: 30 mcg/day ■ During pregnancy: 30 mcg/day	■ Works with insulin to help your body use glucose and maintain normal blood sugar levels ■ May influence cholesterol levels by improving its metabolism ■ Crucial to blood sugar and cholesterol metabolism ■ Popular in weight-loss programs	■ Apples ■ Beef ■ Beer ■ Bran ■ Brewer's yeast ■ Corn on the cob ■ Dairy products ■ Eggs ■ Meats ■ Prunes ■ Soy flour ■ Sweet potatoes ■ Wheat germ ■ Whole grains
Copper	■ Women aged 19 and up: 900 mcg/day ■ Men aged 19 and up: 900 mcg/day ■ During pregnancy: 1,000 mcg/day	■ May lower cholesterol levels ■ May improve symptoms of arthritis ■ With zinc, helps protect against free-radical damage ■ Required in formation and maintenance of bones, joints and connective tissues ■ Melanin—a natural coloring pigment in your skin and hair—needs a copper-dependent enzyme ■ Used to make cell membranes and maintains the protective covering around nerve cells	■ Barley ■ Crab ■ Lobster ■ Oysters

Micronutrients Minerals *cont.*	How much do you need every day?	What is its function in your body?	Sources in your diet.
Fluoride	■ Women aged 19 and up: 3 mg/day ■ Men aged 19 and up: 4 mg/day ■ During pregnancy: 3 mg/day	■ Protects the teeth from decay, hardens tooth enamel and may strengthen the bones ■ Used in toothpaste and as fluoride treatments	■ Not widely found in foods; varies with soil content where food is grown ■ Fluoridated tap water ■ Some bottled waters
Iodine	■ Women aged 19 and up: 150 mcg/day ■ Men aged 19 and up: 150 mcg/day ■ During pregnancy: 220 mcg/day	■ Helps thyroid gland make thyroid hormones, which controls physical growth, development, metabolic rate and body temperatures ■ Supports other biochemical reactions	■ Iodized table salt ■ Saltwater fish ■ Seafood

Micronutrients Minerals *cont.*	How much do you need every day?	What is its function in your body?	Sources in your diet.
Iron	■ Women aged 19 to 50: 18 mg/day ■ Women aged 51 and up: 8 mg/day ■ Men aged 19 and up: 8 mg/day ■ During pregnancy: 27 mg/day	■ Rebuilds red blood cells after blood loss ■ Determines how much oxygen gets to the rest of your body tissues through hemoglobin in the blood and myoglobin ■ Critical in maintaining and building a healthy immune system	■ Beef ■ Beef liver ■ Bran ■ Breads, fortified ■ Cereals, fortified ■ Clams ■ Egg yolks ■ Figs ■ Grains, fortified ■ Kidney beans ■ Lamb ■ Leafy green vegetables ■ Lima beans ■ Molasses ■ Nuts ■ Oysters ■ Pasta, fortified ■ Peas ■ Pinto beans ■ Pork ■ Prunes and juice ■ Pumpkin ■ Raisins ■ Soybeans (cooked) ■ Spinach (cooked) ■ Sunflower seeds ■ Wheat germ ■ White rice, fortified

Micronutrients Minerals *cont.*	How much do you need every day?	What is its function in your body?	Sources in your diet.
Manganese	■ Women aged 19 and up: 1.8 mg/day ■ Men aged 19 and up: 2.3 mg/day ■ During pregnancy: 2.0 mg/day	■ Helps in the development of bones, teeth and joints ■ Functions in female sex hormones and thyroid hormones ■ Activates many enzymes in cell metabolism ■ Helps utilize a number of vitamins ■ Helps with protein and amino acid digestion and utilization	■ Kale ■ Lentils ■ Pineapple ■ Strawberries ■ Tea ■ Whole grain
Molybdenum	■ Women aged 19 and up: 45 mcg/day ■ Men aged 19 and up: 45 mcg/day ■ During pregnancy: 50 mcg/day	■ Helps your body use stored iron ■ Helps your body burn fat for energy	■ Breads, fortified enriched ■ Cereals, fortified ■ Dark leafy green vegetables ■ Legumes ■ Milk

Micronutrients Minerals *cont.*	How much do you need every day?	What is its function in your body?	Sources in your diet.
Potassium	■ No minimum levels have been established	■ Provides balance with sodium in controlling blood pressure ■ Helps the body utilize energy ■ Provides a place for electrical impulses to cross cell membranes	■ Acorn squash ■ Apricots (dried) ■ Avocados ■ Bananas ■ Cantaloupe ■ Carrot juice ■ Figs ■ Halibut ■ Honeydew ■ Kidney beans ■ Lima beans ■ Mangoes ■ Molasses ■ Orange juice ■ Pinto beans ■ Potatoes (baked or french fried) ■ Snapper ■ Spinach ■ Tomato juice ■ Trout ■ Yogurt
Selenium	■ Women aged 19 and up: 55 mcg/day ■ Men aged 19 and up: 55 mcg/day ■ During pregnancy: 60 mcg/day	■ An antioxidant that works with vitamin E to reduce free-radical damage ■ Helps protect against the effects of ultra-violet light	■ Brown rice ■ Cereals ■ Garlic meats ■ Haddock ■ Salmon ■ Some seafood ■ Wheat germ ■ Whole grains ■ Yeasts

Micronutrients Minerals *cont.*	How much do you need every day?	What is its function in your body?	Sources in your diet.
Sodium	■ There are no minimum levels	■ Helps regulate blood pressure and muscle contraction ■ Regulates fluid balance and blood pH ■ Important in conducting nerve and cellular impulses	■ Bacon ■ Bologna and other lunch meats ■ Bouillon (canned or dried) ■ Cottage cheese ■ Dill pickles/ pickle relish ■ Garlic salt or other seasoning salts ■ Ham ■ Hot dogs ■ Olives ■ Saladitos (salted prunes) ■ Salted nuts ■ Sauerkraut ■ Smoked meats/fish ■ Soy sauce ■ Table salt ***All foods contain some sodium***

Micronutrients Minerals *cont.*	How much do you need every day?	What is its function in your body?	Sources in your diet.
Zinc	■ Women aged 19 and up: 8 mg/day ■ Men aged 19 and up: 11 mg/day ■ During pregnancy: 11 mg/day ■ About one-third to one-half of the 10 to 15 mg provided by the diet is absorbed. Absorption increases when blood levels fall or in the presence of vitamin D ■ See page 99 in chapter 3 for list of high-phytate foods; foods high in phytate decrease absorption ■ High levels of dietary calcium and copper result in lowered absorption of zinc	■ Important for reproduction, skin health and to maintain the sense of taste ■ Helps protect against damage caused by free radicals ■ Makes essential hormones like testosterone ■ Boosts the immune system ■ Is a component of at least 60 enzymatic actions within the body ■ Maintaining, replicating and using genetic information depends on zinc ■ May be effective in reducing the duration and severity of cold symptoms	■ Beef, cooked, lean ■ Black-eyed peas, cooked ■ Chicken ■ Crabmeat ■ Green peas, cooked ■ Lamb, cooked, lean ■ Legumes ■ Lima beans, cooked ■ Liver, calf, cooked ■ Milk, whole ■ Nuts ■ Oysters, Atlantic ■ Oysters, Pacific ■ Pork ■ Pork loin, cooked ■ Potato, baked, with skins ■ Shellfish ■ Shrimp ■ Tuna, oil-packed ■ Veal ■ Whitefish ■ Yogurt

Life is filled with beginnings. Each beginning brings change from what has been comfortable. Each beginning creates uncertainty for what the future might hold. But change and uncertainty are just stages, a part of human growth.

—Dr. Laura Pawlak
Appetite: The Brain Body Connection

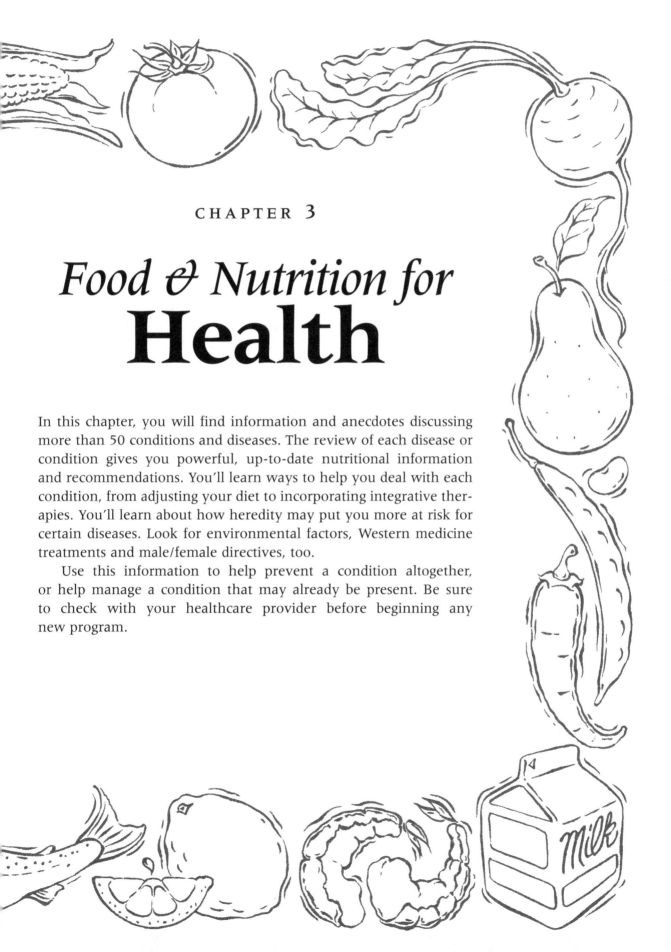

CHAPTER 3

Food & Nutrition for Health

In this chapter, you will find information and anecdotes discussing more than 50 conditions and diseases. The review of each disease or condition gives you powerful, up-to-date nutritional information and recommendations. You'll learn ways to help you deal with each condition, from adjusting your diet to incorporating integrative therapies. You'll learn about how heredity may put you more at risk for certain diseases. Look for environmental factors, Western medicine treatments and male/female directives, too.

Use this information to help prevent a condition altogether, or help manage a condition that may already be present. Be sure to check with your healthcare provider before beginning any new program.

Get All the Facts

It is wonderful to partner with your healthcare provider in solving your own health problems, but make sure you get the rest of the story. Each member of the healthcare team, including the integrative practitioner, has something unique to offer to a customized treatment plan that addresses your particular needs. Review each recommendation carefully, in terms of sound medical and nutritional advice.

About Those Herbs

A number of herbs and natural medicine remedies are mentioned throughout this chapter. Most of the herbal recommendations made in *Food for Life* have been formed using the same rating standards found in *The American Pharmaceutical Association's Practical Guide to Natural Medicines* by Andrea Peirce. Most scientists and clinicians agree on seven different study categories, the first being termed "the clinical gold standard of modern medicine," the only standard accepted by the FDA. It includes large, randomized, placebo-controlled human trials.

Marketing & Medication Mayhem

"Hey, Doc! I was watching TV today and now I wonder if I should be taking Avandia, Lipitor, Zocor, Prevacid, Prilosec, Orlistat, Celebrex, Paxil and Plavix?"

You know what my doc said? "Listen, take an aspirin and call me in the morning."

That old advice about aspirin? Not a bad thought. If you're over the age of 50, you may just want to think about taking aspirin. In fact, it's now considered a standard recommendation for anyone who's had a heart attack or heart event, or if you're at risk for heart disease. If you've had a stroke (caused by a clot, not a bleed) you'll be advised to take a daily aspirin. A daily aspirin is recommended for anyone with diabetes over the age of 40. There is, however, a quick caveat—you shouldn't take aspirin if you are at risk for, or have, a bleeding condition (ulcers, gastrointestinal bleeding or a blood disorder).

There is some controversy about dosage. Should you take a baby aspirin (81 mg), two baby aspirin (160 mg) or a regular aspirin (325 mg)? Coated or not? Generally, if you're taking the aspirin prophylactically (to help keep a condition from happening), a single baby aspirin daily is fine. Coated aspirin may be best for you because it offers a little less irritation to the stomach. In any of the other instances, it's best to clarify the dose with your healthcare provider.

The APA's second category is defined in terms of being large-scale, clinical human trials. The third category no longer includes human trials but rather large, placebo-controlled animal studies. And so on, working down through the remaining four categories. Only herbs meeting the criteria of the top two categories have been recommended in *Food for Life*. All others are either excluded or carry a cautionary warning: "May be harmful."

Inclusion in *Food for Life* was also significantly influenced by information from *The Honest Herbal* by Varro E. Tyler, Ph.D., a top herbal authority. Both references mentioned routinely refer to *The Complete German Commission E Monographs: Therapeutic Guide to Herbal Medicine*. The "E Monographs" are truly regarded as the gold standard of herbal research and reference.

Important reminders when considering and choosing herbal treatments should include the following (as set forth by Peirce):

- Research your information about herbs. Make sure it's solid and fact-based, having strong links to peer-reviewed research conducted by authorities.
- Select high-quality products (the actual quantity of herb or active ingredient contained in the herbal supplement may be small or even missing entirely).
- Beware of herbal products whose use has been documented as causing serious disease-provoking illness or death (for example, kava kava and ephedra).
- Report adverse reactions to the Centers for Disease Control (CDC) at (404) 639-3311 or the Food and Drug Administration (FDA) at (800) 332-1088.
- Don't take unnecessary risks. Most herbs should not be used by pregnant women or small children. Elderly people must also exercise extra caution, because they may have trouble clearing medications and herbs from their systems (especially if any changes occur in liver or kidney function).
- Don't assume that more is better. More is sometimes toxic, even fatal.
- Don't self-treat a serious disease or symptom without consulting your healthcare provider.
- Don't make drug substitutions on your own, and take extra care when selecting an herb that might provide more of the same effect as a medication taken simultaneously. For example, some people have experienced side effects when taking St. John's wort with the prescription drug Prozac.
- Never ignore adverse reactions to a substance. Stop taking it and see your healthcare provider.

Beneficial Herbs with Strong Evidence of Safety

Name	Other names	Claims
Chamomile, German (*Matricaria chamomilla*)	■ Matricaria recutita ■ Chamomilla recutita ■ Hungarian chamomile	Claims to soothe an upset stomach and German authorities endorse tea for peptic ulcers. Rare adverse reaction if allergic to ragweed, asters, chrysanthemums or other members of the Asterasceae family. Literature cites only five reports of allergy between 1887 and 1992.
Echinacea (*Echinacea angustifolia, Echinacea purpurea*)	■ American coneflower ■ Purple coneflower	May stimulate the immune system. CAUTION: A member of the daisy family and may cause reactions if allergic to the sunflower family. Stop taking several weeks before elective surgery because of effect on blood coagulation.
Feverfew (*Tanacetum parthenium*)	■ Wild chamomile	Claims to give headache relief; used with migraine therapy. Main side effect is irritation and possible inflammation of the lining of the mouth.
Garlic (*Allium sativum*)	■ Allium	Claims to reduce blood cholesterol and prevent cancer. Most clinical studies have used the brand name Kwai, and clinical studies on aged garlic extract have used the brand name product Kyolic.
Ginger (*Zingiber officinales*)	■ Jamaican ginger	May reduce chemotherapy-induced nausea. Safe in limited amounts for nausea with pregnancy. Can inhibit blood clotting if taken in large amounts.
Ginkgo (*Ginkgo biloba*)	■ Bai guo ■ Biloba ■ Kew tree ■ Maidenhair tree	Claims to improve memory and other mental functions and treat vascular disease. Problems have been with minor GI distress and, on rare occasions, headache and dizziness.

Beneficial Herbs *continued*

Name	Other names	Claims
Ginseng, Asian, Chinese or Korean (*Panax ginseng*)		Claims to increase vitality, help the body cope with stress, achieve balance and strength, increase endurance, alleviate fatigue and regulate glucose. Prescribed for older adults suffering from fatigue after serious illness. Mexican research suggests that ginseng given with a multivitamin improves the quality of their lives, better than the multivitamin alone. Other studies do not support this claim.
Milk thistle (*Silybum marianum*)	■ Gaertn ■ Our Lady's thistle ■ St. Mary's ■ Silybum	Used for two thousand years in Mediterranean region for liver ailments, digestive system upset, excessive menstrual flow and other conditions. Silymarin is isolated portion of milk thistle fruit believed to be useful to liver functions.
Peppermint (*Mentha piperta*)	■ Black and white mint	Claims to help quell nausea. German authorities endorse use for symptoms of irritable bowel syndrome.
St. John's wort (*Hypericum perforatum*)		Affects certain neurotransmitter levels; should not be taken in conjunction with monoamine oxidase (MAO) inhibitors. This combination can cause your blood pressure to become critically high. In combination with fluoxetine (Prozac), it can cause serotonin syndrome, which can bring on agitation, confusion, tremor and muscle spasms. Fair-skinned persons are advised to avoid direct sunlight after taking this herb.
Valerian (*Valeriana officinalis*)		Claims to have calming effects on emotions. Used in long flights and Alzheimer's units to perpetuate calm. Avoid large doses or taking herb continuously.

Harmful Herbs with Documented Safety Concerns*

Name	Other names	Claims
Aconite (*Aconitum napellus*)	■ Monkshood ■ Wolfsbane	Strong, fast-acting poison. Numerous poisonings, both oral and topical.
Arnica (*Arnica montana*)	■ Wolfsbane ■ Mountain tobacco	Fatal poisonings reported with internal use: cardiac toxicity. External use acceptable, but rashes possible.
Astragalus (*Astragalus membranaceos*)	■ Hunag bai ■ Milk vetch ■ Mongolian milk vetch ■ Yellow leader	Antiviral properties may improve the abilities of the white cells to stimulate the immune system; used in treatment of cancer. May stimulate production of interferon; used with AIDS patients and with cardiac patients. Overdosing may cause suppression of the immune system. No reliable studies on humans.
Belladonna (*Atropa belladonna*)	■ Deadly nightshade	Contains three toxic alkaloids, one of which is atropine. Considered unsafe for use.
Blue cohosh (*Caulophyllum thalictroides*)	■ Squaw root	Potential for toxic effects of heart muscle and intestinal spasms.
Borage (*Borago officinalis*)	■ Bee plant ■ Ox's tongue ■ Starflower	May contain liver toxins and carcinogens. Others argue that borage should be included in food composition tables with the leafy vegetable group. Potassium is the major mineral element and has some iron. German authorities have declined to approve use.
Broom (*Cystisus scoparius*)	■ Broom tops ■ Irish or Scottish broom	Contains toxic alkaloids and tyramine. Danger of mold contamination in flowers. May slow heart rhythm.

***This list is not all-inclusive**

Harmful Herbs *continued*		
Name	**Other names**	**Claims**
Calamus (*Acorus calamus*)	■ Sweet root ■ Sweet flag	Certain types containing beta-isoasarone are carcinogenic. FDA prohibits use in foods.
Cat's claw (*Uncaria tomentosa*)	■ Life-giving vine of Peru	May have low-level antioxidant activity. High in tannins, which may interfere with absorption of nutrients. Adulteration is common, which can lead to harmful effects.
Chaparral (*Larrea divaricata*)	■ Creosote bush ■ Stinkweed	Has been linked to acute liver damage in several North Americans. Responsible for at least six cases of hepatitis, with one person requiring a liver transplant.
Coltsfoot (*Tussilago farfara*)	■ Cough plant, ■ Kuan dong hua	Contains a liver toxin (pyrrolizidine alkaloid called senkirkine), which is also a carcinogen.
Comfrey (*Symphytum officinale*)	■ Blackwort ■ Russian comfrey ■ Slippery root	Contains liver toxins (pyrrolizidine alkaloids) linked to liver disease and possible death. Organ problems and cancer seen in animal studies. Totally inappropriate for pregnant women.
Ephedra (*Ephedra sinica*)	■ Ephedrine ■ Epitonin ■ Ma huang	Stimulant that can induce heart palpitations, high blood pressure, stroke, psychosis and so on. Excessive doses have caused several deaths and hundreds of adverse reactions have been reported to the FDA. The three-herb mixture of ephedra, caffeine and white willow bark (salix alba) creates combined thermogenic effects. *continued on next page*

Harmful Herbs *continued*		
Name	**Other names**	**Claims**
Germander (*Teucrium chamaedrys*)	■ Wall germander ■ Wild germander	Marked as a folk medicine for weight loss. Used in teas, elixirs, capsules or tablets since 1986. At least 27 cases of acute non-viral hepatitis, including one death, associated with commercial products made in France. Linked to cases of liver inflammation, kidney damage and death.
Guarana (*Paullinia cupana*)	■ Brazilian cocoa	Claims to be energy booster. Studies in mice only. Caution because of high caffeine content. Large doses may cause blood pressure and heart rate response, gastro-intestinal distress and diuresis.
Jimsonweed (*Datura stramonium*)	■ Devil's apple ■ Stinkwort	Contains potentially toxic alkaloids, such as atropine. Can cause allergic reactions. High potential for toxicity.
Kava (*Piper methysticum*)	■ Kava kava ■ Ava ■ Awa ■ Intoxicating pepper ■ Kava root or pepper ■ Kawa ■ Kew ■ Rauschpfeffer ■ Sakau ■ Tonga ■ Wurzelstock ■ Yang-ona	Linked to serious toxicity, liver injury, need for liver transplant (as a result of liver damage) and death. Has been approved in several European countries—but not in the United States—for the treatment of anxiety, insomnia and restlessness. It may interfere with the way the body handles dopamine and would never be advised with Parkinson's disease, where there is already a loss of dopamine activity.
Kombucha Tea	■ Champagne of Life	Fermentation of various yeast and bacteria in a mixture of black tea and sugar. Prone to contamination. Has alcoholic content. Is a culture medium for anthrax.

Harmful Herbs *continued*		
Name	**Other names**	**Claims**
Licorice (*Glycyrrhiza glabra*)	■ Sweet root	If used in excess, potential for high blood pressure, low potassium and cardiac arrest.
Lobelia (*Lobelia inflata*)	■ Indian tobacco ■ Wild tobacco	Reports of respiratory depression, rapid heartbeat, low blood pressure, coma, convulsions and death.
Pennyroyal oil (*Hedeoma pulegioides*)	■ American pennyroyal	Especially toxic. Liver damage, convulsions, abortions, coma and death have been reported.
Periwinkle (*Vinca minor*)	■ Common periwinkle	Toxic to liver and other body cells. Contains the chemotherapy agents vincristine and vinblastine. When used with cancer diagnosis, requires physician dosing and monitoring.
Pokeweed root (*Phytolacca americana*)	■ American nightshade ■ American spinach	Extremely toxic. Death, gastroenteritis, low blood pressure and reduced respiration have been reported.
Sassafras (*Sassafras ablidum*)	■ Ague tree ■ Cinnamon wood	Contains a carcinogen, safrole, banned by the FDA for food use, but sold in health food stores as a supplement.
Wormwood (*Artemesia absinthium*)	■ Wermut ■ Absinthe	Extreme mind-altering effects. Convulsions, unconsciousness.
Yohimbe (*Pausinystalia yohimbe*)		Monoamine oxidase inhibitor (MAO), which can increase blood pressure if certain foods are not avoided. Reports include: anxiety, psychoses, hallucinations, paralysis and fatigue. Linked to kidney failure and death.

Alcoholism

Have you ever heard the term "banana bag" used for a certain IV (intravenous) solution? That's the slang used for one of the IVs given to a patient admitted to a hospital with acute alcohol overdose. Why the name? There are lots of B vitamins and potassium in the mixture, and bananas are a rich source of potassium. This is an important need for people suffering from acute alcoholic overdose.

Nutritional Recommendations for Modifying Lifestyle Choices

If you overdrink habitually (or know someone who does), you may know the liver can fail to ably process vitamins from foods, resulting in certain deficiencies. Overdrinking can rob your liver of the ability to use the vitamins in foods, and people with active alcoholism may fail to eat nutrient-rich foods that provide enough vitamins.

The most common vitamin deficiencies in alcoholics are:

- thiamine (vitamin B1), which is associated with a brain disorder called Wernicke's encephalopathy
- riboflavin (vitamin B2)
- niacin (vitamin B3)
- folic acid
- pyridoxine (vitamin B6)
- magnesium
- potassium
- zinc

Up-Close-and-Personal Statistics

Thirteen million Americans abuse alcohol. That's about 10 percent of the population. It is estimated that financial losses of $80 billion occur each year due to excessive alcohol use by Americans. Alcoholism is considered a chronic disease with genetic, psychosocial and environmental factors influencing its development.

When you drink alcohol, it depresses your central nervous system by acting as a sedative or tranquilizer. If your stomach is empty, most of the alcohol is usually quickly absorbed. But having food in your stomach or small intestine, especially solid and fatty foods, slows the emptying action of the stomach and the absorption rate of the alcohol into your bloodstream.

Nearly all of the alcohol is burned as fuel for your body. Your body processes alcohol just as it does other food—metabolizing it in the liver to produce heat and energy. But the food value of alcohol is limited because its calories yield no vitamins, minerals or proteins to help in the basic "upkeep" of your body.

Alternative Treatments

No herbs have been proven effective in treating alcohol abuse. One well-designed study showed that 140 mg of silymarin (milk thistle), 3 times a day, reduced the death rate among people with alcohol-induced cirrhosis. Milk thistle has been shown to be safe with the only side effect being mild diarrhea.

The Morning After

Most of us, on occasion, have wished for a miracle drug to diminish the side effects of overdrinking. There is an herbal remedy called Kudzu that has been identified as a potential hangover helper. It has been used for treating alcoholism and hangovers, but so far, studies have been limited to small animals; no human trials have yet been done.

Other Diseases Related to Alcoholism

Alcoholics develop other medical problems as a direct result of alcoholism, including high blood pressure, increased blood sugar, liver disease, heart disease, gastrointestinal ailments and pancreatitis.

Question/Answer

Q "Is there a concern with foods, drinks and over-the-counter (OTC) products that may supply alcohol to individuals who shouldn't have it?"

A Yes! Many mouthwashes and cold remedies contain alcohol, sometimes as much as 30 percent. Examples include Listerine, Nyquil (no wonder you sleep so well when you take it!) and Vicks Cough, Cold and Flu Relief. Look carefully at liquid cough and cold preparations, or better yet, look for ones labeled "alcohol-free."

Other problems include kidney and bladder problems, as well as impotence in men.

Many other drugs—and alcohol *is* a drug—have potentially dangerous interactions. In short, taking alcohol with other drugs could make you very ill.

Tylenol (acetaminophen) is an important one to think about. Many of us just pop a couple Tylenol without thinking about it. Because it's an over-the-counter (OTC) medicine, we think it's safe. But Tylenol is cleared, or metabolized, through the liver. When the liver is damaged from alcohol abuse, toxic levels of Tylenol can build quickly, and even cause death. You may want to check with your pharmacist to identify drugs that you shouldn't mix with alcohol.

Alcoholism

Reasons to Be Concerned (Inherited Traits and Environmental Factors)	**Family history increases chances of developing alcohol addiction** ■ Alcoholism rate in sons of alcoholic fathers is as high as 25 percent ■ The Irish and Native Americans have an increased incidence ■ Jewish Americans and Asian Americans have a lower risk **Psychosocial factors** ■ Severe depression or anxiety ■ Higher incidence of violence and accidents involving alcoholism **Environmental factors** ■ Often paired with other health-depleting addictions ■ Increases risk of colon cancer and liver disease ■ Can cause cardiovascular disease (leading cause of death), high blood pressure, diabetes, diarrhea, osteoporosis, night blindness, anemia and early death
Western Medicine Recommendations	■ Abstain from alcohol ■ Join Alcoholics Anonymous (AA) ■ Inpatient and outpatient therapy ■ Psychotherapy ■ Antidepressants and antianxiety medications ■ Treat withdrawal symptoms as needed
Integrative Therapy	■ Acupuncture ■ Traditional Chinese medicine ■ Chiropractic ■ Biofeedback training ■ Ayurvedic medicine ■ Homeopaths have common acute remedies ■ Writing therapy ■ Yoga ■ Herbals include: milk thistle for alcohol-induced cirrhosis

Alcoholism *continued*	
Male or Female Directives	■ More than 9 percent of men and almost 2 percent of women are heavy drinkers ■ More than 22 percent of men are binge drinkers and 8.7 percent of women ■ Younger women follow the drinking patterns of their partners—and engage in heavier drinking during their premenstrual period ■ Women do not metabolize alcohol as well as men and are more susceptible to developing alcoholism ■ Women tend to become alcoholic later in life ■ Pregnant women risk miscarriage and babies with birth defects
Best Nutritional Strategies	■ Abstain from alcohol ■ If drinking excessively, consider multivitamin and mineral tablet that meets 100 to 150 percent of the recommended dietary allowance (RDA) ■ Do not exceed 4,000 IU of vitamin A—toxicity can develop ■ Excessive iron intake, especially in males, can lead to heart disease; always monitor hemoglobin/hematocrit when supplementing with iron ■ Stimulate your appetite with small, frequent meals ■ Drink lots of non-caffeinated fluids, especially; coffee and tea interfere with some nutrient absorption
Supplements or Functional Foods to Consider	■ B-vitamin deficiencies in recovering alcoholics may need to be treated ■ National Institutes of Health (NIH) study suggests that increased omega-3 fatty acids are linked to decreased depression, violence and suicide

Alzheimer's Disease (AD)

Don't Be Fooled

How many of you, on a day-to-day basis, forget simple things like a friend's name or the reason you went into a room? And then you say, "I must be getting Alzheimer's." The good news is that Alzheimer's is uncommon in middle age. Very few individuals have the form of the disease that presents a major memory loss at an early age. (If you're really concerned about Alzheimer's, you can be tested for specific linked genes.)

What is your real risk of developing Alzheimer's? The percentages increase as we age. The disease occurs in approximately 4 percent of persons 65 to 74 years old. About 4 million people in the United States are currently diagnosed with it.

If You Are Worried

If you suspect Alzheimer's disease, get a thorough medical and neurological evaluation. Some signs and symptoms may occur with normal aging or be related to another disease. You could even be having an adverse reaction to a prescribed medication. Diagnosis of Alzheimer's in the early stages is crucial and allows you to take advantage of the drugs available to treat Alzheimer's.

Nutritional Recommendations for Modifying Lifestyle Choices

Medications and B vitamins may delay the development of some cases of Alzheimer's, but they cannot alter the course of this dreaded disease. Taking folic acid and other B vitamins may help your body reduce the level of homocysteine in your body; high levels of this amino acid are associated with Alzheimer's disease. The higher the level of homocysteine in the blood, the greater the risk of damage to the artery lining. This same physiologic effect causes additional risk of heart disease. The only difference is that in Alzheimer's, the lining of the small blood vessels in the brain is damaged.

The Stages of Alzheimer's

Alzheimer's disease causes your brain to shrink, your neurons to degenerate and "plaques and tangles" to accumulate in your brain. It has been described as having three to six stages. These stages take a few years or much longer to develop. The bottom line is that you become progressively more dependent on caregivers with every stage. Basic care needs increase, and often the type of food you eat changes.

Persons in the middle stages of Alzheimer's often benefit from a finger food diet. They may not be able to use silverware well, but are happy to pick up sandwiches and chunky, tender-cooked vegetables and fruits.

People with Alzheimer's often keep their sweet tooth and enjoy foods like cookies, bars and ice cream. It is wise to provide these foods throughout the day as snacks. Keep them in places the person can easily see. Some people with Alzheimer's burn up extra calories that need to be replaced. This is because they engage in extra activity and pacing, especially after sundown.

In the later stages of Alzheimer's, persons may not eat whole foods well. It may be best to puree regular foods to an easily swallowed consistency. Make high-protein and high-calorie malts with ice cream, whole or 2% milk and malt powder. You may want to add instant breakfast drinks to increase calories and protein. These malts can be made in large batches and frozen. High-calorie and high-protein malts can be used during any stage of Alzheimer's. They work well for anyone needing a caloric boost in their diet.

Sometimes during the last stages,

Tips for Feeding Folks with Failing Memories

If you are caring for an aging parent, you know that nothing about it is easy. Here are some tips from trained healthcare workers that will help make mealtime a little more manageable.

- Offer small meals and frequent snacks.
- Offer high-calorie, nutrient-dense foods first.
- Provide important nutrient sources, such as protein in meat, poultry, fish, eggs or dairy, at a time when the person is most alert.
- Allow fewer food selections at each meal. Offer one food at a time to avoid further confusing the person.
- Verbally instruct through every step of the eating process. It may take longer for the "memory lost" person to recognize your words. Wait. Repeat the same direction after 30 to 60 seconds.
- Place a utensil in the person's hand and physically guide them in eating. Finger foods are often a wise choice when managing silverware seems impossible.
- Allow sufficient time to eat.
- Avoid distractions and stimulations at meals (for example, television, telephone and conversations).
- Provide simple, colorful table settings at meals and snacks. "Memory lost" persons may be able to see contrasting colors. Modern Fiestaware would be an excellent choice for a plate. Tableware needs to be lightweight. Large-handled silverware may be helpful. Special dishes and cups with added rims to allow better "scooping" will help.
- Add nutritional supplements and homemade malts if needed.

people can only drink their meals and snacks, or they may be fed through a feeding tube (a tube inserted through the nose or into the stomach or lower section of the bowel that gives a nutrient- and calorie-rich mixture that sustains life).

Herbal Therapy

Herbals recommended for Alzheimer's include ginkgo and lecithin. Ginkgo may be safely used, especially in the early stages of Alzheimer's, and recent small-scale studies have shown improved memory. Use caution, however, with

Alzheimer's Disease	
Reasons to Be Concerned (Inherited Traits and Environmental Factors)	■ Family history is a risk ■ Increased risk if you have Down syndrome ■ Lack of physical activity is linked to AD. Get off the sofa! ■ History of a head trauma may contribute ■ Only solid diagnosis is autopsy
Western Medicine Recommen-dations	■ Initial testing includes scales to rate memory function and a neurological exam ■ PET scans can detect the disease accurately in 91 percent of patients in earliest stages ■ In early stages, treated with donepezil, rivastigmine, galantamine and behavioral exercises ■ Small doses of aspirin may be used ■ On the horizon: Human trials are going on to test an Alzheimer's vaccine. In mice, it prevents the formation of the type of tangles and plaques that clog the brains of persons suffering from Alzheimer's ■ Medicine tailored to your genes: Investigation into the human genome may help explain what causes Alzheimer's
Integrative Therapy	■ Stress-reduction techniques help in the early stages ■ Music therapy ■ Herbals include: ginkgo, 80 mg, 3 times a day effective in early stages

lecithin, as studies showing improved memory with lecithin have not been reproducible.

Some homes for people with Alzheimer's use lavender-scented light bulbs to help soothe their residents. You may do something similar with a pot-

pourri pot strategically and safely placed in the home of your loved one.

Alzheimer's Disease *continued*	
Male or Female Directives	■ Half of women over 80 develop a form of dementia ■ Older women who aren't or can't go on hormone replacement therapy (HRT) may be at greater risk for AD
Best Nutritional Strategies	■ Five+-a-day servings of fruits and vegetables—orange juice and fortified grains, good sources of folic acid ■ Consume fish regularly. Eat a diet that's low in saturated fat. ■ Include nuts and seeds for sources of vitamin E (as chewing and swallowing ability allows) ■ Finger-food diet in middle to advanced stages to avoid weight loss and keep calories adequate ■ High-protein and high-calorie malts and drinks ■ Eat often to boost total calories of the diet ■ Provide easily accessible cookies, bars and ice cream as daily snacks (people with AD recognize foods from their past) ■ Weigh at least monthly, more often when weight loss trend occurs ■ Limit coffee to avoid raising homocysteine levels
Supplements or Functional Foods to Consider	■ Multivitamin and mineral supplement (MVI) providing 100 to 150 percent of recommended dietary allowance (RDA) ■ Coenzyme Q10, vitamin B6 and iron restored "mental capacity" in one study ■ Niacin, vitamins C and E and folic acid supplements are used

Anemia
(Iron Deficiency)

In a *Nutrition Today* article, James R. Connor, Ph.D., and John L. Beard, Ph.D., explain that "anemia of chlorosis"—iron deficiency anemia—was first described as nutritional iron deficiency in 1895. Today, we still have iron deficiency anemia with recommendations for iron replacement. But we also have conditions involving too much iron (see page 98). You may wonder why the caution about too much iron is repeated so often in *Food for Life*. Simply stated, there is a growing concern that too much iron may be related to certain diseases like liver cancer, diabetes and heart failure. And because so many processed products are being enriched and fortified today, men, for example, usually would not want to further supplement with iron. Discuss this with your registered dietitian and/or healthcare provider.

But back to deficiency. There are two pools of dietary iron—heme and nonheme iron. Heme iron is primarily

Anemia	
Reasons to Be Concerned (Inherited Traits and Environmental Factors)	■ Typical American diets (below 2,500 calories) do not provide enough absorbable iron ■ Women need 18 mg through age 50 or until menopause ■ Menstruating females, vegetarians and the elderly are at high risk for iron deficiency ■ Strict vegans may have problems ■ People who suffer from alcoholism and gastrointestinal ulcers may also be more prone to iron depletion
Western Medicine Recommendations	■ Labs are part of screening—Hemoglobin/Hematocrit ■ Iron supplements (FeSo4, ferrous sulfate)—usually 3 times per day for treatment ■ Take iron 1 hour before or 2 hours after bran, high-phytate foods, fiber supplements, black tea, herbal tea, cocoa, coffee, dairy products or egg ■ Take antacids, calcium, magnesium, zinc or copper supplements separately from ferrous sulfate by 2 or more hours. High doses of iron decreases zinc absorption. May need zinc supplement. Best absorbed on an empty stomach—but many can't tolerate it without food or drink ■ Ferrous sulfate may cause anorexia (loss of appetite)
Integrative Therapy	None applicable

found in animal products, while non-heme iron is found in plant sources. However, nonheme iron (which accounts for 85 percent of the iron in our average diet) is very poorly absorbed. Its absorption increases two- to fourfold when meat, fish or poultry (all sources of animal protein) is eaten with it. This phenomenon is referred to as "the meat factor." (Nonheme iron is also better absorbed by simultaneously taking in vitamin C.)

Why Am I Anemic?

Hemoglobin is the main component of red blood cells and the first and most direct measure of status, whether it be within normal or deficient limits. It is decreased when you develop anemia, suffer a hemorrhage or become mal-nourished. If your iron level gets too low, you can develop iron-deficiency anemia. You typically feel weak and fatigued.

Anemia *continued*	
Male or Female Directives	■ Babies, toddlers and adolescent girls at risk ■ Premenopausal women who exercise intensely may be at risk ■ Pregnant vegetarians may be at increased risk of anemia ■ Women with heavy menstrual flows
Best Nutritional Strategies	■ Eat a varied diet with foods providing adequate lean red meat—this promotes iron absorption ■ Study nutrition labels—look for iron-fortified foods ■ Pair a vitamin C–rich food or drink with an iron-rich food for better absorption ■ Read labels—iron-enriched foods may improve absorption ■ Use cast-iron cookware to improve absorption ■ Eat an adequate daily source of folic acid (see chapter 2 for a list of folic acid-rich foods)
Supplements or Functional Foods to Consider	■ 200 mg vitamin C with 30 mg iron will increase iron absorption

Nutritional Recommendations for Modifying Lifestyle Choices

Maximize iron absorption from your diet. Check out the list in chapter 2 of iron-rich foods. Remember to pair these foods with a food or drink rich in vitamin C (see chapter 2) because an acid environment promotes iron absorption.

When taking ferrous sulfate (iron preparations), there are several food/drug interactions that can improve the absorption of iron within your body. Review the bulleted list called "Western Medicine Recommendations" found on page 96. High-phytate foods mentioned in the sidebar should be taken 1 hour before or 2 hours after taking iron preparations. You may note differences in the amounts of phytic acid in foods. Phytic acid is a part of plant fiber that binds to substances like calcium and iron and can inhibit the absorption of these nutrients from the gastrointestinal tract. The content of phytic acid can vary according to the plant part and the state of maturity at harvest.

Iron Overload

For about 1.5 million Americans, an iron-rich diet is too much of a good thing. These individuals suffer from hemochromatosis, a genetic disease that causes their bodies to hoard iron. Unchecked, this disease can lead to organ damage and even death from heart attack or liver disease. Symptoms include not only fatigue and weakness, but also abdominal pain, skin discoloration, male impotence and increased susceptibility to infections.

Iron overload is even more common in people with arthritis. Because the symptoms are vague, many people don't know they have the disease until they suffer organ damage. If you experience any of these symptoms, see your healthcare provider and have a blood test done.

All About My Blood

Hematocrit is the ratio of plasma, which is mostly fluid, to the volume of packed blood cells. It is an indicator of circulating water volume within your blood. Blood plasma contains a certain amount of iron bound to the carrier protein transferrin. Decreased levels occur when the blood has too much fluid. Your blood volume enlarges during infancy, childhood, adolescence and pregnancy. Increased levels occur if you are dehydrated or if you suffer blood loss.

Recognizing where iron is stored in your body may help you better understand your lab values. One-third of the iron in your body is stored in the protein compounds ferritin and hemosiderin. Ferritin is the primary storage form for iron in the body found primarily in the liver, spleen and bone marrow. Hemosiderin is a form of iron stored in the liver when the amount of iron in the blood exceeds the storage capacity of ferritin. Both of these protein compounds can be used to synthesize hemoglobin. Two-thirds of the iron in your body is called functional iron and is found in:

- hemoglobin
- transferrin and serum ferritin (in blood)
- myoglobin (in muscle)
- enzymes (in every cell)

High-Phytate Foods

Food Item	Phytic Acid (mg)
Grain/Grain Products	
Barley, whole grain—3.5 oz. (100 gm)	970
Oats, raw—3.5 oz. (100 gm)	943
Wheat bran, crude—1 oz. (28 gm)	843
Barley, pearl, raw—3.5 oz. (100 gm)	491
Wheat germ—1 Tbsp. (6 gm)	244
Corn chips—1 oz. (28 gm)	178
Cereals—1 oz.	
All Bran	679
Shredded Wheat	415
Wheat Flakes	411
Oatmeal, cooked—½ cup	113
Bread, rye—1 slice	235
Nuts, Nut Products and Seeds	
Nuts—3.5 oz. (100 gm)	
Brazil nuts	1,799
Almonds	1,280
Walnuts	760
Peanuts	748
Hazelnuts	604
Coconut, raw	270
Sesame seeds, raw—1 oz. (28 gm)	·1,319
Peanut butter—1 Tbsp. (16 gm)	200
Vegetables—3.5 oz. (100 gm)	
Rice, wild, raw	2,200
Kidney beans, raw	1,200 to 2,060
White beans, raw	1,030
Rice, brown, raw	890
Peas, dried, raw	851
Pinto beans, raw	620 to 1,950
Rice, white, long-grain, raw	340
Garbanzo beans, raw	280
Navy beans, raw	280
Rice, white, short-grain, raw	140
Miscellaneous—3.5 oz. (100 gm)	
Soybean meal	1,400 to 1,600
Soybean protein concentrate	1,240 to 2,170
Soybean protein isolate	430 to 1,170
Cocoa, dry powder—1 Tbsp. (5 gm)	94

Anticoagulant Therapy

How to Eat Well While Taking Blood Thinners

Anticoagulant therapy (using medications to keep the blood thinned and to prevent risk of blood clots) is used to treat and prevent a number of diseases. You'll find healthcare providers prescribing blood thinners for the following reasons:

- atrial fibrillation (the top of the heart not pumping effectively)
- bleeding disorders (like essential thrombocythemia)
- diabetes
- family history of heart disease
- heart disease, or history of heart attack or heart surgery
- history of blood clots
- mitral valve stenosis (narrowing of one of the heart valves)
- post-surgery, when the person will not be walking on his own or with assistance immediately (for example, after some total hip and total knee replacements)
- stroke (or mini-stroke) prevention or treatment

A note of caution, though: Anyone with a history of ulcers or bleeding disorders should not take a blood thinner unless specifically directed to do so by their healthcare provider.

Some Common Anticoagulants

So, what's the most common blood thinner? Surprisingly enough, it's everyday aspirin. Numerous studies have proven that aspirin is a safe, yet effective, blood thinner. In fact, it's now a prevention standard of care for people over 50 with any family history of heart disease, and for those over 40 with diabetes (because the risk of heart attack/heart disease is increased with diabetes).

Other common blood thinners are Coumadin or warfarin, Heparin and Lovenox (both injected), and three antiplatelet drugs: Ticlid, Plavix and Persantine.

What Foods Should I Avoid?

If you're taking a blood thinner, you'll want to limit foods that are high in vitamin K (a natural blood thickener) and those with vitamin E (a natural blood thinner). Chapter 2 has lists of food sources high in these vitamins. We once told people to completely avoid these foods. But today's recommendation is: Don't consume excessive amounts, and don't suddenly change the amount of intake of these foods. In other words, a standard, regular amount of spinach is fine, but you shouldn't eat a whole pound in one day if you are used to eating just one salad a day containing spinach.

There are also herbs and supplements to consider. Ginkgo and ginseng have both been shown to possess blood-thinning properties and need to be regulated while taking anticoagulants.

Another note of caution: Avoid alcohol, herbal teas containing coumarin and vitamins K and E while you are taking blood-thinning medications to help your blood supply remain consistent with regard to its clotting potential.

Watch Out for Vitamin K

If you're taking a blood thinner, you can eat a regular amount of these foods that are high in vitamin K each day, but make sure you don't suddenly change the amount (a lot more or a lot less).

Vegetables

higher concentrations of vitamin K are found in outer leaves and peels

Asparagus
Broccoli
Brussels sprouts
Cabbage (green raw)
Cauliflower
Chayote leaf
Chive (raw)
Collard greens
Coriander leaf
Cucumber peel
Endive

Garbanzo beans
  (chickpeas)
Green tomatoes
Kale
Lentils
Lettuce
Mint
Mung beans
Mustard greens
Nettle leaves
Purslane

Romaine lettuce
Scallions
Seaweed (extremely
  high levels)
Soybeans
Spinach
Swiss chard
Turnip greens
Watercress

Fats and Oils

exposure to fluorescent light and sunlight rapidly destroys vitamin K in oils

Canola oil (rapeseed)
Soybean oil

Other

Algae (purple laver
  and hijiki)
Apples (green)

Beef liver
Chicken liver
Egg yolk

Green tea leaves
Pork liver

Anticoagulant Therapy

Reasons to Be Concerned (Inherited Traits and Environmental Factors)	■ Anticoagulant therapy is used before and after surgery as necessary, in some cases of heart disease and stroke, in some bleeding disorders, and in people with diabetes (over the age of 40) ■ Preventative anticoagulants are recommended with a history of heart disease, or history of heart attack or heart surgery and in history of blood clots, and mitral valve stenosis
Western Medicine Recommendations	■ Aspirin is a very effective blood thinner ■ Coumadin, Plavix, Ticlid, and Persantine Aspirin are common orals ■ Heparin and Lovenox—common injected meds ■ Anticoagulent therapy needs to be discontinued before surgery ■ Check INR (a blood test to measure clotting function) more frequently when taking antidepressants, many of which will cause drug interactions
Integrative Therapy	■ Certain herbals may have blood thinning properties (ginkgo, ginseng and echinacea are good examples); make sure to inform your healthcare provider if you are taking these—or considering taking them. Don't start taking them without checking with a healthcare provider.
Male or Female Directives	■ Heparin: bleeding especially in elderly women and in people with renal disease ■ Coumadin: has decreased effectiveness in women taking oral contraceptives
Best Nutritional Strategies	■ See chapter 2 for list of foods that are high in vitamin K—restrict use of these ■ See page 100 for additional information about anticoagulant therapy
Supplements or Functional Foods to Consider	■ None noted

Anxiety

Anxiety is a general feeling of being worried. We all experience anxiety from time to time as a normal part of life. People with generalized anxiety disorder feel anxious frequently or excessively. This feeling is often not related to a situation.

This leading mental disorder affects approximately 10 million Americans, and can run the gamut in severity of symptoms. Intense physical symptoms such as hyperventilation, heart palpitations, tightness in the chest or gastrointestinal problems definitely have a strong impact on how one feels. The manifestation of a precise physical condition emanating from an emotional source is more and more prevalent today, and continues to gain greater clinical understanding.

No longer are causes of anxiety traced simply to genetic and psychological roots, but now diet and nutritional factors must be regarded as significant determinants. Even exposure to chemicals, toxins, electromagnetic fields and other modern environmental elements plays some role in our overall health, including mental health issues. And the very use of anti-anxiety medications can set up a toxic situation in the user, upsetting certain chemical balances in the nervous system.

In addition to more traditional treatments of psychotherapy and/or drug therapy, more recent alternatives are gathering credence at a brisk pace.

Nutritional Recommendations for Modifying Lifestyle Choices

Certainly, attention to basic common-sense eating habits can be a valuable starting point. For example, you should eat natural foods (for example, fresh vegetables, whole grains), not processed, and foods that are free of pesticides and additives. You should enjoy foods without overeating or bingeing, while including a wide variety in your diet. This can at least help minimize nutritional deficiency and its consequent effects on brain function and state of mind.

Treatment with Integrative Therapy

Similarly, emerging integrative therapy will prove to be more and more beneficial. Such mind-body techniques as meditation, yoga, biofeedback, guided imagery and hypnotherapy can reduce anxiety. "Re-learning" to breathe properly via the diaphragmatic technique, or trying some elements of reflexology, qigong, light therapy, sound therapy or magnetic field therapy, could provide the advances in treatment of anxiety that the new millennium requires.

Then there is the herbal approach to anxiety treatment, as related to aromatherapy. Adding essential oils of jasmine, bergamot or lemon balm to bath water, an atomizer or cotton ball, can have a calming effect on the soul. Other herbal treatment is also worth exploring. But, as with all health matters, it is important to have your problem medically diagnosed before proceeding.

St. John's wort, passionflower, lemon balm and skullcap (among others) all show promise as beneficial in "spirit enhancement" and can be obtained in the forms of dried extracts, glycerites or tinctures for varied applications. Kava, used by some, has, in some cases, been linked to liver abnormalities and cancer. It cannot be recommended unconditionally. In the case of kava and St. John's wort, use them only in tea; avoiding pure dried extract forms. If you are considering St. John's wort, make sure to discuss this with your healthcare provider. It should never be taken in conjunction with other antidepressant medicines. And a word of caution to pregnant women: Herbal preparations are not recommended. They react very

Anxiety	
Reasons to Be Concerned (Inherited Traits and Environmental Factors)	■ Genetics and early life experiences may play a role ■ 30 percent report onset of symptoms before 11 years of age, and 50 percent before 18 years of age ■ Interferes with healing, compromising the immune system and leads to cardiovascular disease ■ Can contribute to alcohol and substance abuse ■ Affects 4.1 to 6 percent of population over a lifetime
Western Medicine Recommendations	■ Psychotherapy ■ Strengthening social support sources ■ OCD (Obsessive Compulsive Disorder) is classed as an anxiety disorder ■ Anti-anxiety medications (Paxil, for example); other antidepressants
Integrative Therapy	■ Massage therapy ■ Biofeedback ■ Chiropractic ■ Guided imagery ■ Yoga ■ Relaxation/breathing retraining ■ Magnetic field therapy ■ Hypnotherapy ■ Light therapy ■ Qigong ■ Reflexology ■ Homeopathy ■ Transcendental meditation

similarly to prepared traditional medications, and combining any medication with an herbal preparation could result in a number of side effects, which include increasing your intake beyond the recommended dose and damage to you or your unborn baby.

Great anxiety can now be met head-on with a holistic approach and individualized treatment.

Anxiety *continued*	
Integrative Therapy *continued*	■ Aromatherapy ■ Music therapy ■ Herbals include: ginkgo, St. John's wort, hops, passionflower
Male or Female Directives	■ Female to male 3:2, but females report it less
Best Nutritional Strategies	■ Fresh vegetables, whole grains and protein nourish the nervous system ■ Avoid caffeine, alcohol and food additives ■ Reduce consumption of refined foods ■ Be aware of common allergen foods (see section in this chapter) ■ Drink a lot of fluids—fruit juice is great ■ Herbal teas can soothe tension (see charts prefacing this section) ■ Coffee and tea interfere with some nutrient absorption
Supplements or Functional Foods to Consider	■ Vitamins B1, B3, B6, B12, folic acid and vitamin C ■ Calcium (1,000 mg/day) ■ Magnesium (400 to 600 mg/day) ■ Alpha-linolenic acid (an essential omega-3 fatty acid) ■ 500 mg glucosamine hydrochloride or sulfate, 3 times a day

Arthritis

A rather sassy widow friend recently told me she starts every morning with Art, Ben and nine gin-soaked golden raisins. At first, I was surprised at her boldness, but she just smiled and explained that it's Arthritis, and that Ben Gay and the raisins (having been soaked in the gin until the gin evaporates) miraculously seem to treat her condition! This humorous friend of mine is typical of such osteoarthritis sufferers seeking relief of any kind.

In fact, many older people have it, but don't realize they have arthritis until it's seen on a routine x-ray. A very common treatment is an anti-inflammatory agent such as Ben Gay or aspirin cream used topically. And I know you're wondering about those raisins. Unfortunately, there aren't any studies to back up the frequently touted "arthritis martini" of gin-soaked raisins, but I guarantee you'll hear about it from someone who swears it works for them!

Osteoarthritis & Rheumatoid Arthritis

There are two common types of arthritis: osteoarthritis and rheumatoid arthritis. Both involve inflammation of joints between bones, and both result in pain in those joints. Osteoarthritis evolves from the wear and tear of normal joint usage (it's also called "wear-and-tear arthritis" and "degenerative arthritis"), and is usually seen in the elderly. Rheumatoid arthritis is an autoimmune condition in which the body's immune system attacks itself, and the disease-fighting cells inflame the joints. It usually occurs between the ages of 20 and 50.

But be sure to get the right diagnosis, because the two disorders require very different treatments. A thorough physical is the first step, including x-rays and lab work. Bone spurs and Heberden's nodes may be seen in osteoarthritis. Blood tests (namely erythrocyte sedimentation rate and rheumatoid factor) can be done to test for rheumatoid arthritis.

How to Treat Arthritis

The most effective treatment for osteoarthritis is exercise, weight control and medication (as needed). Suitable treatment for rheumatoid arthritis takes aim at the ebb and flow of the disease, and includes a proper balance of rest and exercise. When the disease flares up, the following may be necessary:

- rest
- pain reduction/management
- immobilization
- joint replacement surgery (sometimes recommended for severely eroded joints caused by either form of arthritis)

Medications commonly used include aspirin, anti-inflammatory meds, various pain relievers and even steroids such as cortisone or prednisone (injected or taken by mouth).

Almost every natural medicine and herb has some claim to treating arthritis. Why is this? Because arthritis is such a common disease. But only a few such "sure-fire" remedies have actually provided proven positive results based on reproducible human studies.

Glucosamine (a natural compound in the body used to make a gel-like substance that cushions the joints) is a promising new supplement that seems safe, well tolerated and beneficial over the short term. It relieves pain, lessens inflammation and improves mobility. Glucosamine is often combined with chondroitin sulfate (a chemical made in the body) for the treatment of joint disorders.

Another choice is evening primrose oil, a proven-safe supplement for rheumatoid arthritis sufferers. It has been shown to be effective in a well-designed, double-blind study. Peppermint and menthol, with their cooling properties, can numb pain and help relieve inflammation when used externally. A very small study of seven people showed less joint pain and increased movement when treated with oral ginger.

Unproven or unsafe remedies abound. Cod liver oil and shark cartilage, frequently promoted as arthritis "cures," have no scientific basis showing effectiveness. Other natural medicines showing no proven value or conflicting results of effectiveness and safety include: borage, chamomile, echinacea, nettle, New Zealand green-lipped mussel, rehmannia, superoxide dismutase, willow bark and yucca. There is a potential for cancer risk with borage.

Controlling stress is also important in managing life with arthritis. Osteoarthritis pain is worse in times of high stress and during difficult emotional states. Cold weather and a falling barometer can also make the knees hurt. Rheumatoid arthritis, with its ebbs and flare-ups, can worsen with fatigue and high levels of stress. A balance of rest and exercise, accompanied by individualized stress-reduction techniques,

makes living with arthritis more manageable.

Nutritional Recommendations for Modifying Lifestyle Choices

Including all of your vital nutrients each day in your diet is your first line of defense. Another nutrition strategy to assist in managing the pain and inflammation of arthritis is to maintain an ideal body weight, or keep as close to it as possible. If you are overweight, consider cutting portion sizes and reducing total fat intake with an ideal body weight goal in mind. This may make movement a little easier and encourage you to increase your exercise tolerance. Pay special attention to eating foods that provide nutrients that you may be lacking. Indocin, a common drug used with osteoarthritis, depletes your body of thiamin and vitamin C. Methotrexate, used with rheumatoid arthritis, causes an increased need for folic acid. You will want to review the listings of each of these nutrients in the "Food Sources of Spotlighted Vital Nutrients" chart beginning on page 51 in chapter 2.

Osteoarthritis (OA)

Reasons to Be Concerned (Inherited Traits and Environmental Factors)	■ Family history increases risk ■ Genetic tendency for Heberden's nodes—bony lumps found in joints of the fingers ■ Cold weather and dampness may increase arthritic pain ■ Periods of stress and emotional upheaval may increase discomfort
Western Medicine Recommen-dations	■ Hyaluronic acid is a natural lubricant injected into arthritic knees and might even postpone knee replacement in people with severe osteoarthritis ■ Knee or hip replacement operations may be needed when long-term joint deterioration occurs ■ Aspirin is one of the most effective drugs ■ Other drugs—anti-inflammatory medications may be used ■ When inflammation is severe, an injection of a steroid may be recommended (a "cortisone" shot)—usually used in a weight-bearing joint like knee or ankle ■ Discuss prescription medicine with medical care provider that targets the COX-2 enzyme for pain relief—Celebrex is one example.
Integrative Therapy	■ Placebo effect—power of suggestion—may account for much of pain relief that allows patients to put off surgery for awhile ■ Bodywork ■ Chiropractic ■ Acupuncture ■ Ayurvedic medicine ■ Yoga ■ Music therapy for acute and chronic pain ■ Herbals include: glucosamine chondroitin (this may not be appropriate for individuals who have seafood/nut allergies)
Male or Female Directives	■ 10:1 ratio of women to men for Heberden's nodes

Osteoarthritis *continued*

Best Nutritional Strategies	■ Maintain an ideal body weight, or close to it ■ Good nutrition and balanced diet are important ■ Cayenne pepper may help ■ Depletion of thiamin and vitamin C with drug Indocin (consider additional food sources/supplements as necessary)
Supplements or Functional Foods to Consider	■ Calcium and magnesium ■ SAM-e used in Europe to treat arthritis

Rheumatoid Arthritis (RA)

Reasons to Be Concerned (Inherited Traits and Environmental Factors)	■ Affects about 1 percent of adult population who develop this type of arthritis when they are young to middle-aged ■ Tendency to develop this has a genetic basis
Western Medicine Recommendations	■ Knee or hip replacement operations may be needed when long-term joint deterioration occurs ■ Aspirin is one of the most effective drugs ■ Other drugs—anti-inflammatory medications may be used—non-steroidal anti-inflammatory drugs (NSAIDS) like ibuprofen and Naproxen are often used ■ Discuss prescription medicine with medical care provider that targets the COX-2 enzyme for pain relief—example, Celebrex ■ When inflammation is severe, an injection of a steroid may be recommended (a "cortisone" shot)—usually used in a weight-bearing joint like knee or ankle

continued on next page

Rheumatoid Arthritis *continued*	
Integrative Therapy	■ Glucosamine chondroitin (this may not be appropriate for individuals with seafood/nut allergies) ■ Bodywork ■ Chiropractic ■ Acupuncture ■ Ayurvedic medicine ■ Writing therapy ■ Yoga ■ Music therapy for acute and chronic pain ■ Herbals include: evening primrose oil (in one study significantly improved the condition of rheumatoid arthritis); feverfew (avoid feverfew if you have allergies to other plants in the daisy family)
Male or Female Directives	■ Affects twice as many women as men
Best Nutritional Strategies	■ Maintain an ideal body weight, or close to it ■ Good nutrition and balanced diet are important ■ Possible link to decaffeinated coffee—monitor consumption ■ Increase folic acid consumption with methotrexate
Supplements or Functional Foods to Consider	■ Calcium and magnesium ■ Flaxseed or flaxseed oil (see other omega-3 fatty acid sources in chapter 2)

Asthma

There aren't many things that would be worse than not being able to catch your breath. People with asthma give us an exercise to try, so we know what it feels like to have the disease. Run in place for 1 to 2 minutes, as hard as you can. Then take a straw and breathe through it. Breathe only through the straw; don't gasp around it, as you'll really want to do. That's how tight asthmatic breathing can be.

Asthma is an acute process of inflammation in the bronchial tubes of the lungs. It causes mucus buildup, obstruction of the bronchioles and extreme shortness of breath. Wheezing, coughing and chest tightness are common symptoms.

New Occurrences Since September 11, 2001

If you think of asthma as a childhood disease, you're right, but 14 million Americans have the disease. Many more in New York show the symptoms or have developed it since the collapse of the World Trade Center towers and nearby buildings. Fires that couldn't be put out generated noxious dust and gases for many weeks. Rescue workers and New Yorkers complained of diminished lung capacity and "World Trade Center Cough." Fully one-third of the firefighters working at Ground Zero have been diagnosed as having asthma. This disaster has produced the highest levels of certain pollutants ever.

These pollutants consist of both very fine particles (< .001 inch) and larger, coarser particles. Both are deadly. Very fine particles penetrated deep into the lungs of individuals at Ground Zero and the surrounding proximity. Air samples taken in New York in the weeks after September 11 showed unprecedented levels of pollutants such as sulfur and silicon.

A study in the *American Journal of Epidemiology* provides the first definitive link between air pollution and birth defects. About 9,000 babies born from 1987 to 1993 were studied. Pregnant women who were exposed to the highest levels of ozone and carbon monoxide (because their homes were close to busy highways) were three times as likely to have a child with certain heart defects than women breathing the cleanest air. The defects the researchers found were specific: conotruncal heart defects, pulmonary artery/valve defects and aortic artery/valve defects. No other birth defects were linked with pollution.

Diagnosing & Avoiding Attacks

Diagnosing asthma may include:
- a physical exam
- x-rays
- a breathing history
- breathing tests
- allergy testing
- use of a device called a peak flow meter to measure the amount of air you exhale

Keeping a daily log of your lung function can help diagnose the disease and alert you of an impending serious asthma attack.

Attacks vary in length from minutes to days. These are periods of acute breathing difficulty. They range from mild to life-threatening. Most asthma attacks are preceded by a "trigger" of some kind. (See sidebar, this page.) It's been shown that vitamin C, taken 1 hour before exposure to known allergens, may reduce the allergic reaction. Attacks are treated with inhalers and sometimes hand-held nebulizers (medications in mist form to be breathed into the lungs).

Nutritional Recommendations for Modifying Lifestyle Choices

See the nutritional recommendations found in the accompanying chart. When taking corticosteroids (such as prednisone) over a long period of time, you may need additional foods rich in calcium, vitamin D, protein, potassium, vitamin A, vitamin C and phosphorus. If taking methylprednisolone, be aware that you should not take it with grapefruit, grapefruit juice or Seville oranges. The food-drug interaction in a vast majority of cases leads to a reduction in metabolism of this drug and an increase in the amount of drug entering the bloodstream. The effect of grapefruit on intestinal enzymes is irreversible and can persist for up to 72 hours after consumption of the grapefruit, until the body produces more of the drug-metabolizing enzymes.

Common Medications

Medications have been used very effectively to treat asthma. These include metered-dose inhalers, such as Cromolyn (used daily), Albuterol, ipratropium, salmeterol or theophylline, which dilate the bronchial tubes (can be used several times a day, and during attacks).

Corticosteroid inhalers (triamcinalone, beclosmethasone, flunisolide) are also used. These are powerful anti-inflammatory agents and have been found to be more effective than oral corticosteroids in the management of asthma. However, inhaled steroids can cause a yeast infection in the mouth or throat (commonly called "thrush"). Prevention is as simple as washing or rinsing the mouth after usage. A new medication type, leukotriene inhibitors, is effective

Asthma Triggers

- Allergies: pollen, animal dander, insect droppings (like from dust mites); the recent increase in urban asthma may be related to roach droppings
- Molds
- Environmental pollutants and chemicals
- Cigarette smoke
- Smog, natural gas, propane or kerosene, wood smoke and paint fumes
- Viral respiratory infections
- Sensitivity to aspirin or non-steroidal anti-inflammatory agents (like ibuprofen and Naproxen)—true for about 5 percent of people with asthma
- Exercise can produce exercise-induced asthma
- Inhaling cold, dry air

for the 5 percent of people whose asthma is worsened by aspirin.

Exercise-Induced Asthma

Some people have exercise-induced asthma. Their wheezing and shortness of breath occurs only when they vigorously exercise. However, this isn't an excuse to not stay physically fit! Although exercise may induce asthma in some people, regular exercise keeps muscles toned and decreases the workload for the rest of the body, including the lungs. Athletes like Olympic track star Jackie Joyner Kersee help us realize that even high-performance exercise is possible with asthma.

In some women, asthma symptoms can worsen during their menstrual cycle. Standard asthma treatment is not as effective once the "attack" is underway. The treatment in this case is to use medications preventatively in the days before your menstrual period begins.

Changing Your Environment

Environmental changes that you may want to implement if you have asthma include: using air conditioning and keeping windows closed during high pollen times, adding HEPA filters to your furnace, maintaining optimal humidity in the environment, cleaning, sweeping and vacuuming regularly, covering bedding with airtight plastic covers and avoiding feather pillows.

Can we be too clean? The research says it's possible. Experts are studying a phenomenon called the "hygiene hypothesis." This theory, which suggests your environment can be too clean, has been validated in studies from America, Italy and other European countries. The results? Children show less incidence of asthma and allergies when they:

- grow up on farms
- live in large families
- are infected with parasitic worms
- are not taking antibiotics in the first few years of life
- breathe polluted air
- experience more upper respiratory infections when they're young
- don't have indoor plumbing

Apparently, each of these factors helps build the immune system, by exposing the child to pathogens, and thereby turning on the body's natural bug-fighting system.

Herbal Therapy

Natural medicine remedies or treatments with some solid study include: ginkgo, kola (cola, kola nut, guru nut, kola seed) and coltsfoot (fresh or dried). Ginkgo has anti-allergic properties and can limit the allergic response in those with asthma. It may be of help in both early and late bronchospasm. The FDA categorizes kola nut as "Generally Recognized As Safe" (GRAS) for food consumption. The risks associated with kola are the same as those evidenced from other caffeine-containing substances such as black tea. Caffeine has also been touted as an asthma treatment because it dilates (opens up) the bronchial tubes (airways), which swell and start to close during a typical attack. Additionally, kola also contains small amounts of theobromine, which likewise dilates the bronchial tubes. Can't you see the commercial? "Thanks to my inhaler and my Coca Cola, my asthma is virtually gone!"

A suitable application for coltsfoot is to use it as a fresh leaf poultice: 2 tsp. crushed leaves in 1 cup of water. It contains a mucilage that coats and soothes the airways, shields them from irritants that may aggravate asthma and clears mucus from the airways. However, use with caution. Experts believe that all parts of this herb contain toxic alkaloids that can cause cancerous liver tumors, especially when used over prolonged periods of time These coltsfoot-leaf preparations shouldn't be taken for more than 4 to 6 weeks a year. Pregnant women and anyone with liver disease should never take this prepara-

Asthma	
Reasons to Be Concerned (Inherited Traits and Environmental Factors)	■ 20 to 25 percent have a sibling or parent with asthma ■ Childhood asthma is on the increase ■ Exposure to pollutants increases risk; avoid places where very fine particles (less than .001 inches in diameter) of sulfur and silicon exist ■ "World Trade Center cough" coined by New Yorkers and rescue workers ■ Exposure to cigarette smoking increases risk ■ Studies show "too-clean" environments may increase incidence of asthma
Western Medicine Recommendations	■ Avoid "triggers" ■ No smoking ■ Remove allergens ■ Test breathing capacity every day (peak flow meter) ■ Medications: Intal (cromolyn, an anti-inflammatory medication) to reduce inflammation, bronchodilator inhalers like Albuterol, Atrovent and theophylline ■ Theophylline oral pills ■ Corticosteroid inhalers have been found to be much more effective than oral steroids (but can cause a yeast infection in the mouth and/or throat) ■ Cold compresses to the chest may lessen severity of an attack

tion. In fact, pregnant women are ill-advised to take most herbs and will want to discuss this matter with their healthcare provider.

Lastly, let's look at the poppy plant. It supplies us with morphine and codeine (prescription medications). The alkaloid, papaverine, also found in poppy, is prescribed for asthma-related breathing spasms. But exercise strong caution when considering Devil's dung, forskolin (and coleonol) and picrorhiza. Studies are either absent or conflicting regarding their effectiveness and safety.

Asthma *continued*	
Integrative Therapy	■ Homeopathy ■ Hydrotherapy ■ Aromatherapy ■ Acupuncture ■ Massage therapy ■ Meditation and deep breathing exercises ■ Writing therapy ■ Yoga ■ Herbals include: coltsfoot, ginkgo, kola, and poppy (prescription meds derived from poppy)
Male or Female Directives	■ In children, boys are affected twice as many times as girls ■ After puberty women almost twice as likely as men ■ 30 to 40 percent of women have more severe episodes during their menstrual cycle ■ Menopause increases risk of hospitalization for asthma fourfold
Best Nutritional Strategies	■ Increase your intake of whole grains, fruits and vegetables ■ Eliminate foods that you are allergic to
Supplements or Functional Foods to Consider	■ Those with asthma have been shown to have lower levels of B6—consider supplementing ■ Antioxidant vitamin C, E, beta-carotene and selenium ■ Vitamin C, 1 hour before exposure to known allergens, may reduce the allergic reaction ■ Magnesium (200 mg, 2 to 3 times a day) relaxes bronchioles

Cancer

It's probably the scariest of all medical conditions—a diagnosis that none of us wants to hear. Yet millions of people each year are diagnosed with, living with and being cured of cancer.

Take a look at chapter 3 for the leading types of cancer in men and women as well as the leading cancer causes of death in men and women. Are you surprised? Obviously, we have some work to do. Note that the leading cancer cause of death is lung cancer, and we still have a society of smokers. However, there is good news. Recently, for the first time, the number of teenagers who are smoking dropped. But we're not done yet. There's definitely work to do in eliminating the number one risk factor for cancer—smoking. (Refer to the section on Nicotine Addiction in this chapter.)

You've heard about a variety of cancers and risks for these: lung, skin, breast, rectal (or colon) and prostate. Treatments are varied and highly specific to the type of cancer; so are the foods recommended to try in order to avoid a specific cancer. New research is constantly shifting the way we treat the different cancers. Two common treatments are radiation (killing cancer cells with radiation) and chemotherapy (killing cells with strong medicines). Both of these treatments carry a risk of killing normal cells as well as the cancer cells. Other treatments used in cancer care boost the immune system, so you can effectively fight the cancer cells on your own.

Nutritional Recommendations for Modifying Lifestyle Choices

Try not to lose weight while you battle cancer. Weight loss has a direct impact on survival during cancer. Anorexia and cachexia—weight loss in patients with chronic illness—are directly associated with survival rates in patients with cancer. Of people with malignant disease, 87 percent experience weight loss and cachexia. These conditions are involved in 80 percent of all cancer deaths. Cachexia is the cause of death in 22 percent of all cancer patients.

Be aware of unintentional weight loss—losing 10 percent or more of your normal weight—when taking chemotherapy. Monitor your weight regularly. Identify any appetite and weight loss issues before they become significant. Look at some of the tips found in the Alzheimer's and HIV sections of this chapter that deal with maintaining and gaining weight.

Malnutrition can be addressed with medical nutritional therapy from a registered dietitian or other healthcare provider, supplementation to the diet with high-calorie and high-protein foods and drinks, prophylaxis, exercise and drug therapy. Combinations of these interventions can improve survival and have an important impact on your quality of life.

Appetite stimulants such as Marinol (dronabinol) and Megace (megestrol acetate) help you increase your appetite and maintain weight. This helps ensure that you get the nutrients needed to stay healthy.

Prostate Cancer & Lycopene-Rich Foods

"I'll tell you, I'm gonna stop eating sliced tomatoes and start ordering Bloody Marys!"—John, age 52, exclaims upon hearing the benefits of eating more lycopene-rich foods.

As John's dietitian, I would explain to him that first, he's identified a drink rich in lycopene. Bloody Marys have tomato juice in them. They also have alcohol. The downside is, too many alcohol drinks may promote liver cancer. Once again, moderation is a great rule.

Lycopene is a pigment found in tomatoes and cooked or processed tomato products, such as tomato sauce or ketchup. It seems to be involved in preventing prostate cancer.

Laetrile

We can't talk about cancer without hitting on a 30-year-old remedy called Laetrile. Popular in the 1970s and early 1980s, Laetrile has gone from preventing and curing cancer, to "controlling" cancer, to being a part of a bigger treatment plan of metabolic therapy. Despite its appeal at one time, Laetrile has been clinically tested and has had no benefit in treating tumors in animals or in treating cancer in humans.

Similar testing has occurred with shark cartilage, finding no data that supports shark cartilage as an effective cancer therapy. And in this case, there's been legal action against at least three companies marketing the product, with more than $500,000 in penalties assessed.

Integrative Remedies

There are hundreds, if not thousands, of reputed remedies that are alternative, complementary or integrative in the treatment of cancer. Many of these are "quack" remedies, yet they abound, as people search for any option that might help them cure their cancers. The American Cancer Society, in response to this need by so many people, has published the *American Cancer Society's Guide to Complementary and Alternative Cancer Methods*. If you're looking at alternative cures for cancer this is a good resource. A specific listing is included for which "there is not scientific evidence that any of the following can cure or influence the course of any cancer." You may want to check out another Web site called quackwatch.com.

The Effects of Fiber on Development of Colon Cancer

The amount of fiber in the diet determines the stool weight and transit time in the colon. There is an inverse relationship between stool weight and colon cancer, so risk decreases as stool weight increases.

Transit time is still being studied. Things that seem to affect it are exercise, emotional state and hormones. There may be other factors as well. Low stool weight usually corresponds with slow transit time.

Cancer	
Reasons to Be Concerned (Inherited Traits and Environmental Factors)	■ Colon cancer remains the second-leading cause of cancer deaths in the United States. Most colon cancer is diagnosed at age 50 or older, and is preventable ■ In African-Americans and Ashkenazi Jews, colon cancer risk factors include family history of colon cancer, intestinal polyps and inflammatory bowel disease ■ Carcinogens like viruses and chemicals may increase risk ■ Lifestyle factors lead to cancer (especially smoking) ■ Environmental exposure to pollutants increases risk
Western Medicine Recommendations	■ Prevention ■ Early detection and screening ■ Cancer treatment programs ■ Exercise ■ Control risk factors ■ Intervene in cancer at an early stage ■ Smoking cessation ■ Evaluate the environment for toxins, radiation, pollution and possibly even electromagnetic fields ■ Chemotherapy and/or radiation ■ Surgery ■ Much-improved second generation vaccines for cancer—a vaccine that targets a person's unique tumor—show potential for continued clinical success with prostate and kidney cancer ■ Statin drugs (used primarily for treating high cholesterol) appear helpful in decreasing risk of developing colon cancer ■ Medicine tailored to your genes: Investigation into the human genome may help explain what causes cancer
Integrative Therapy	■ Stress reduction techniques like writing therapy and yoga ■ There are a number of immune enhancements (to boost immune system and help fight cancer) ■ Two other herbs are recommended: Take foxglove only with extreme caution and only as part of standardized digitalis preparations. This is a poisonous plant that is a cardiac stimulant. Bugleweed should only be taken under a doctor's supervision. German health authorities recommend that people with an enlarged thyroid avoid this herb

Cancer *continued*	
Integrative Therapy *continued*	■ Macrobiotic diets of any kind are not appropriate for people with cancer
Male or Female Directives	■ Top three cancers for men (incidence): Prostate, lung and colon/rectum. Top three in women: breast, colon/rectum and lung ■ Cancers causing death: Men—lung, prostate and colon/rectum. Women—lung, breast and colon/rectum
Best Nutritional Strategies	■ Maintain the best weight for you and get regular exercise—obesity is linked to breast, colon, gallbladder and uterine cancer ■ Eat a wide variety of foods daily ■ Some foods may decrease certain cancer risks. Some of these are listed in the "Food Sources of Spotlighted Vital Nutrients" chart that begins on page 51 in chapter 2 ■ Limit intake of alcohol to no more than one drink per day for women and two drinks per day per men—liver cancer ■ Eat more cruciferous vegetables (vegetables from the cabbage family)—bladder cancer ■ Choose carrots, citrus fruits, green vegetables—most fruits and vegetables in general, and whole grains—mouth and throat cancer ■ Whole grains, carrots, leafy green vegetables, tea and tomatoes—stomach cancer (garlic and onions may be helpful, too) ■ Folic acid-rich fruits and vegetables and foods fortified with folic acid—avoid large amounts of red meat, which are associated with increased risk for colon and rectal cancer ■ Choose selenium-rich foods ■ Increase intake of fiber to 30 to 35 grams ■ Increasing consumption of whole grains and cereal fiber like whole wheat bread, cereal, pasta, rice and oats—may reduce risk of mouth, stomach, colon, gallbladder and ovarian cancer. Three large-scale Swedish studies found that participants who consumed the most cereal fiber had a 70 percent lower risk of developing stomach cancer *continued on next page*

Best Nutritional Strategies *continued*	■ Carrots may help women with a family history of breast cancer ■ Tomatoes and cooked or processed tomato products (provide lycopene, which can help prevent prostate cancer) ■ A liberal macrobiotic diet may be appropriate for the prevention of cancer—includes whole grains, fish, nuts, seeds, tofu and vegetables ■ Choose a low-fat eating plan (will reduce fat intake and decrease intake of toxins stored in fatty tissue)—breast, colon and prostate cancers ■ Avoid foods grilled at very high temperatures or blackened, especially fatty foods. Trim fat before grilling ■ Limit consumption of smoked foods, salt-cured, pickled and nitrite-cured foods, such as processed luncheon meats and bacon ■ For meat eaters: Conjugated linoleic acid (CLA) is a good type of fat that may help ward off some kinds of cancer. Cattle fed on pasture alone produce meat that contains five times more CLA than grain-fed cattle. The meat from these same animals will have more vitamin E and selenium—powerful antioxidants—than meat from grain-fed animals
Supplements or Functional Foods to Consider	■ Avoid soy supplementation for people with cancer ■ 100 to 150 percent of recommended dietary allowances (RDAs) for those at risk and those who have had cancer ■ Morinda citrifolia, noni juice, may boost the immune system to help in dealing with effects of cancer treatment

Constipation

Is constipation the opposite of being "regular"? No, because "regular" means different things to different people. Constipation is the difficulty that results from having infrequent bowel movements consisting of hard, dry stools. Constipation is the most common gastrointestinal complaint in the United States.

In normal bowel movements, the colon moves the food through via muscle contractions, absorbing water while forming waste products (stool). By the time it reaches the rectum, the stool is solid because it has absorbed most of the water. When the colon (instead of the stool) absorbs too much water, hard, dry stools form—the result of slow, sluggish muscle contractions.

Four-and-a-half million people complain of being constipated most or all of the time. The sidebar identifies some causes of constipation.

Nutritional Recommendations for Modifying Lifestyle Choices

Why the big push on fiber? Fiber increases stool bulk, holds water and acts as a substrate for colonic microflora. The microflora increase bacterial, water and salt content and produce hydrogen, methane and other gases that enhance the bulking effect. Fiber decreases transit time, reduces colonic pressure and produces a softer stool. But you may need to eat more than the American average of 5 to 20 grams a day.

If you are troubled by constipation, you will want to slowly increase the amount of fiber and fluid in your diet and get more exercise. Actually, diet and lifestyle changes will help relieve many symptoms of constipation, as well as help prevent it. For a high-fiber menu, see pages 249–251. Also, the recipes in chapter 5 are analyzed for fiber content. On page 53 in chapter 2 you will find a list of high-fiber foods. Work your way toward a goal of 20 to 35 grams of fiber in your diet each day. Just remember to go slowly.

Common Causes of Constipation

- not enough fiber in diet
- not enough liquids
- lack of exercise
- medications that slow bowel activity, such as pain medications (especially narcotics), antacids containing aluminum, antispasmodics, antidepressants, iron supplements, diuretics, and anticonvulsants (for treatment of epilepsy)
- irritable bowel syndrome (IBS)
- changes in life or routine, including pregnancy, aging and travel
- abuse of laxatives
- ignoring the urge to have a bowel movement
- specific diseases, such as multiple sclerosis and lupus
- problems with the colon and rectum
- problems with intestinal function (chronic idiopathic constipation)

Constipation

Reasons to Be Concerned (Inherited Traits and Environmental Factors)	■ Constipation is more common in elderly people ■ Up to 60 percent of elderly people report laxative use
Western Medicine Recommendations	■ Eat more fruits, vegetables, whole grain breads and cereals ■ Provide sufficient fiber and fluids ■ Increase physical activity ■ Adequate rest and relaxation ■ Regular meals and bowel habits ■ Drink 8 or more glasses of non-caffeinated fluids each day ■ Monitor dehydration status if using laxatives ■ Toilet regularly
Integrative Therapy	■ Individualized stress reduction techniques (stress may cause constipation or diarrhea) ■ Herbals include: aloe vera; apple (not the seeds!) and blueberry
Male or Female Directives	■ Affects men and women equally ■ Women report laxative use more than men
Best Nutritional Strategies	■ Increase high-fiber foods—add prunes/prune juice ■ Set up schedule for toileting (daily, first thing in the morning, warm or hot fluids beforehand) ■ Respond promptly to the urge to defecate ■ Discourage use of mineral oil to avoid fat-soluble vitamin losses
Supplements or Functional Foods to Consider	■ Consider products like Metamucil and Citrucel

Depression

She sits on the couch in her robe. The TV is on, but she's not focused on it at all. If she picks up the remote, it's just to repeatedly click through the channels, never resting on one for long. She's tired; didn't sleep well again. The breakfast dishes sit on the counter, where they've been all morning. The kids ate, but she couldn't bring herself to eat even the piece of toast with peanut butter that her husband made for her when he fed the kids. She feels guilty that she doesn't fix their breakfast and see them off, but she just doesn't have the energy. She hasn't been out for weeks; even her card club friends are calling to wonder about her. Hers is a classic case of depression.

Depression is expected to be the second leading cause of disability worldwide in the 21st century. About 19 million Americans are estimated to experience depression each year. And the treatment? New research shows that a combination of talk therapy and antidepressant drugs is the most effective treatment for people who have long-term depression. And fortunately, nearly 80 percent of this group responds favorably, making significant strides in mood and life adjustment.

Depression is a true physical imbalance. There are more than 60 chemical messengers called neurotransmitters in the brain. Severe mental illness means there has been a chemical mix-up of some sort, often with these neurotransmitters. Researchers are looking for the reasons, which include, but are not limited to:

- virus
- environment (maybe toxins)
- psychological trauma

Treating depression is not as easy as sparing an unborn child a birth defect. All the folic acid in the world will not fix this problem. We don't know exactly how to avoid the problem, either, but treatment with drugs is common. You've probably heard of Prozac. It is just one of a group of selective serotonin-reuptake inhibitors (SSRIs). SSRIs work by increasing levels of serotonin in the brain. Zoloft and Paxil are two other SSRIs. SSRIs work for about two-thirds of depressed people. Older drugs on the market, monoamine

---

Depression Signs & Symptoms

- Having four or more of these eight symptoms (most days for at least 2 weeks) qualifies as a major depressive disorder
- change in appetite
- change in sleep
- feeling highly agitated or very slow
- loss of interest in usual activities or decreased sex drive
- increased fatigue
- feelings of guilt or worthlessness
- slowed thinking or difficulty concentrating
- suicide attempt or thinking about suicide

oxidase (MAO) inhibitors and tricyclics, have also also been used successfully.

Postpartum Depression

We should consider a particular form of this ailment unique to women: the condition called postpartum depression. Up to 12 percent of women experience it after giving birth. Symptoms include feelings of hopelessness, guilt, difficulty in concentrating, poor appetite and thoughts of suicide. The situation may well be exacerbated in cases where women have a prior history of major depression or earlier postpartum problems. Other reasons for increased risk are:

- difficult labor
- birth of a premature baby
- severe PMS
- low self-esteem
- unwanted pregnancy
- lack of social support

Sadly, most cases of postpartum depression go undiagnosed, and thus untreated. This is unfortunate for the new mother as well as any young children in the home. One study showed a greater likelihood of problem behavior and lower scores on standardized tests by children whose mothers suffered from postpartum depression.

The better news is that effective treatments in the form of counseling, support groups and/or antidepressant medications can help restore the joy found in motherhood.

Nutritional Recommendations for Modifying Lifestyle Choices

See accompanying chart for nutrition recommendations.

Depression

Reasons to Be Concerned (Inherited Traits and Environmental Factors)	■ Mechanisms of depression are poorly understood ■ Family history increases risk ■ Weakens your immune system function ■ Leads to increased risk of cancer and earlier death ■ Extremely stressful life events may precede depression (loss of loved one, especially) ■ About half of Alzheimer's patients have serious clinical depression (realizing that their condition and memory function are deteriorating) ■ Odds for clinical depression in people with diabetes are twice that of those who do not have diabetes
Western Medicine Recommendations	■ Psychotherapy (talk therapy) ■ Antidepressant medications ■ SSRIs (newest and most effective) ■ Tricyclics ■ Monoamine oxidase (MAO) inhibitors—(think food/drug interactions when using) ■ PET scans and MRIs may be done ■ Lifestyle changes ■ Stress management ■ Strengthening—developing closer ties with friends
Integrative Therapy	■ Stress management ■ Acupuncture ■ Massage therapy ■ Biofeedback ■ Guided imagery ■ Mind/body techniques ■ Magnetic field therapy ■ Aromatherapy ■ Biological dentistry ■ Hypnotherapy ■ Light therapy ■ Qigong ■ Music therapy for mental health needs application ■ Yoga

continued on next page

Depression *continued*	
Integrative Therapy *continued*	■ Safe and effective herbals: evening primrose oil, ginkgo and St. John's wort (caution—never use St. John's wort while taking another antidepressant)
Male or Female Directives	■ Women are at risk twice as much as men

Best Nutritional Strategies	■ Balanced overall diet with emphasis on complex carbohydrate foods to help boost serotonin levels (see chapter 2 for whole grains choices)
	■ Minimize the amount of sugar in the diet, often found in processed foods
	■ Choose foods that have a blend of protein, complex carbohydrate and/or fat. High-protein foods eaten alone as snacks may lower the tryptophan and serotonin levels in your brain.
	■ Vitamins and minerals of greatest importance to treating and avoiding bouts of depression:
	    ■ Vitamin B6—pyridoxine
	    ■ Folic acid
	    ■ Vitamin B12
	    ■ Calcium
	    ■ Iron
	    ■ Magnesium
	    ■ Selenium
	    ■ Zinc
	    ■ Omega-3 fatty acids

Supplements or Functional Foods to Consider	■ Little-known European drug called tianeptine used there ■ Foods purported to be serotonin rich: avocado, banana, blue-red plums, dates, eggplant, papaya, passion fruit, pineapple, plantain, red plum and tomato ■ Early research from the National Institutes of Health (NIH) suggests that omega-3s might boost serotonin activity and help curb depression, impulsive violence and even suicide. ■ SAM-e used in Europe to treat arthritis

Diabetes Mellitus

Meet the cast of characters for our scenario: Sophia, Josh and Aaron. Sophia Anna Lorenzo is a mom of four and co-owner and chef of a local restaurant. Life has been chaotic and busy, but she finally has made time for her annual (well, it's really been about two years now) physical. Her nurse practitioner (N.P.) orders some standard blood tests, which she's done prior to this meeting.

Sophia is surprised, to say the least, that her fasting blood sugar is 151 mg/dl. Normal fasting sugar is 70 to 110 mg/dl. In fact, her N.P. tells her, a previous fasting sugar had been 134 mg/dl. Because she's had two fasting sugars greater than 126 mg/dl, she's diagnosed with type 2 diabetes. "But how could I have diabetes with absolutely no symptoms? I feel just fine. I'm not sick." Sophia needs to learn how to change her food choices and activity choices to lower her blood sugar. She may need oral medications to control her diabetes.

Compare Sophia to 17-year-old Josh. Josh's mom brings him to the ER; he's complaining of belly pain. His face is flushed. He's breathing hard and fast, and his breath smells like ripe bananas. When completing a history, the nurse finds out that he's been drinking a half gallon of orange juice at a time, probably five or six times a day. "Even then, he'd still be thirsty." And, of course, he was peeing a lot: "Look how much he was drinking." His blood is drawn and his blood sugar comes back at 850 mg/dl. Intravenous fluids are started and insulin is given. Because Josh had a random blood sugar significantly higher than 200 mg/dl *and* symptoms of high blood sugar, Josh is admitted to the hospital with type 1 diabetes. Josh's diabetes will be treated with insulin shots. He'll take them the rest of his life (or until the "inhaler" insulin is available—human studies are being done).

Next is Aaron. He's 66, still working as a barber, and has a strong family history of diabetes. He makes sure his fasting blood sugar is checked every year. (Good job, Aaron!) Last month, he broke his ankle after a fall on the ice and has not been as active as usual. In addition, his weight is creeping up after sitting around and

Types of Diabetes

- Type 1—formerly known as juvenile diabetes, or IDDM (insulin-dependent diabetes mellitus)—usually diagnosed before the age of 30.
- Type 2—formerly known as adult-onset diabetes, or NIDDM (non-insulin–dependent diabetes mellitus)—usually diagnosed after the age of 30.
- Gestational diabetes—diabetes diagnosed during pregnancy in a person who previously has not had diabetes.
- Impaired fasting glucose (IFG)—blood sugars are above normal, but not high enough for diagnosis of diabetes (110 to 125 mg/dl).

enjoying the foods brought in by family, close friends and loyal customers. His fasting sugar today is 121 mg/dl. (Remember that normal is 70 to 110 mg/dl, but diagnosis of diabetes is 126 mg/dl and above). His provider, a physician's assistant, tells him he has impaired fasting glucose. He doesn't have diabetes, yet—but he's definitely at risk. In fact, he's at high risk for developing type 2 diabetes.

Learning about Diabetes

Sophia, Josh and Aaron are all referred to the local diabetes program, where they will meet a dietitian and a nurse to learn more about diabetes and how they will live with their diagnosis. During

their sessions for diabetes education, they may be seen individually or, in many organizations, they'll participate in group programs. Some of the newest research is showing better blood sugar control in people who meet regularly (two to four times a year) as a group, as compared with those who just meet individually with their healthcare provider or diabetes educator. Does this mean you're more motivated to do better for your peers in your group than you are for your doctor? Do others with diabetes motivate you more than those of us who are teachers and healthcare providers? Hmmm.

Finding Excellent Diabetes Care

1. Ask around. Everyone knows someone with diabetes. Where did they get the best education? Where did they really learn about their diabetes?
2. Look for a program that has CDEs (Certified Diabetes Educators). These healthcare professionals have specialized diabetes and adult education knowledge.
3. Meet the educators, either in person or on the phone. Are they the kind of people you can talk to about your concerns and your questions?
4. Find out how comfortable your healthcare provider is with diabetes. Is he or she aggressive in treating this disease? Does he or she have the latest information about diabetes? If not, look to another healthcare provider for your diabetes questions.
5. Ask others who's the best at taking care of diabetes. (See the "Standards of Care" sidebar on page 133.) Which healthcare provider is really staying current with diabetes management through seminars, reading and talking with the experts? That's who you'll want to see.
6. Again, meet with the healthcare provider and make sure that you're comfortable with their style and that you feel comfortable asking questions and being active in your plan of care. If you're not comfortable, look again.

Feel the Burn!
Work that Body!

Our three amigos go on to learn that regular activity (formerly known as exercise) both treats and prevents diabetes. Josh and Sophia learn that regular exercise will lower their blood sugar, increase their sense of well-being and decrease their risk of heart attack and stroke. For Aaron, the newest studies tell us that with regular exercise and a controlled carbohydrate intake (see the next section on nutrition recommendations), even people with a high risk of diabetes may not develop the disease. So, what does that mean? It means you want to engage in 20 to 30 minutes of continuous movement (aerobic is preferred), at least three times a week. More often is better.

"STOP!" Sophia cuts in. She is quick to point out that she probably doesn't have more than 10 to 15 minutes of free time during her day. That's okay, her R.N. Certified Diabetes Educator (C.D.E.) assures her. "Start there. Do what you can. Even 5 minutes a day of walking is better than none at all!"

Nutritional Recommendations for Modifying Lifestyle Choices

What about this diabetes diet? Eating to control diabetes is simply eating a healthy diet: a food plan that almost every person in this country should be following. The meal plan can be individualized to fit each person, including their favorite foods on occasion, being careful about portion sizes. The first step is to learn to count carbohydrates (carbs). Limiting the carb content of each meal to about 60 grams is a general rule of thumb, not a prescription for every person with diabetes. Another 15 to 30 grams of carbs can be used for between-meal snacks. This approach means that the body only produces limited amounts of insulin to cover the carbohydrate taken in. And what's a carbohydrate? Breads, pastas, potatoes, all fruits and other starchy foods (like tortilla shells and starchy vegetables). All

Common Sources of 15 Grams of Carbohydrate

- 1 slice of bread, ½ small bagel
- ½ cup squash, baked beans or mashed potatoes
- 10 oz. of milk
- 1 medium apple or orange, or about 10 grapes
- ½ cup canned fruit (juice removed)
- 4 oz. (½ cup) of most fruit juices (check the label)
- 4 oz. (½ cup) of most carbonated beverages (lemon-lime soda, root beer)
- ½ cup Bran Flakes or Chex
- ½ cup cooked pasta
- 5 gingersnaps or vanilla wafers
- 2 small cookies (check the labels)
- $\frac{1}{16}$ of a sponge cake or angel food cake (no frosting)
- $\frac{1}{12}$, or 3-inch square, of cake (no frosting)

sweets—cookies, cakes, pies and bars are carbohydrate- (and fat-) laden. Limit these choices in your food planning and intake; you don't have to eliminate them.

The key concept with carb counting is: A carb is a carb is a carb. In other words, 15 carb grams of bread is the same as 15 carb grams of fruit and the same as 15 carb grams of chocolate cake. Find a good reference tool that has carbohydrate amounts listed. Once you tackle this concept, it really is easier to manage your blood sugars. A great tool is *The Doctor's Pocket Calorie, Fat and Carbohydrate Counter*, by Allan Borushek.

(Costa Mesa: Family Health Publications, 2002). You may even want to check their Web site at www.calorieking.com.

What about Fiber?

People with or without diabetes need similar amounts of fiber. But some soluble fibers may be capable of delaying glucose absorption from the small intestine. This is the controversial "glycemic index" factor. Some experts feel that foods with a higher glycemic index will cause blood sugars to rise faster than those with a lower glycemic index. When these foods are eaten individually,

Could You Have Diabetes? Take the Test!

Enter the indicated score if you answer yes to the following. Enter a 0 if you answer no.

_____ My body mass index (BMI) is greater than 26 to 27. (See the BMI formula on page 210.) (5 points if yes)

_____ I'm under 65 years of age and get little or no exercise. (5 points if yes)

_____ I'm between 45 and 64 years of age. (5 points if yes)

_____ I'm 65 years of age or older. (9 points if yes)

_____ I have a brother or sister with diabetes. (1 point if yes)

_____ I have a mother or father with diabetes. (1 point if yes)

_____ I am a woman who has had a baby greater than 9 pounds at birth. (1 point if yes)

_____ Total score

If you scored 10 or more points, you are at high risk for diabetes. Make sure you see your healthcare provider and are tested for diabetes on a regular basis.

If you scored 3 to 9 points, you probably are at a low risk for diabetes, for now. If you are overweight, lose weight. Get more active most days. Lower your fat intake and increase your intake of fresh vegetables, fruits and whole grain foods.

Adapted from the American Diabetes Association's Diabetes Alert.
Call 1-800-DIABETES for more information.

this proves true. The controversy comes into play when there is a mix of foods eaten at the same time, which is pretty much any time we eat. Which food's glycemic index wins? Probably, it will be a combination of the glycemic indexes.

Testing, Testing, 1-2-3

Josh, Sophia and Aaron will start monitoring their own blood sugar by poking their fingers several times during the day. This way, they can check in regularly to see how they're doing with food, activity and medication (as appropriate). New blood sugar meters (monitoring devices) are better than ever:

- They take tiny amounts of blood.
- They have memories to keep many test results.
- Some offer testing on the arm, which is much less painful.
- They are easier to use, with only 3 to 4 steps.
- They're getting faster.

I know you're ready to ask: What about the meter that shines a light through your finger to get a reading? It's not here yet. However, there are definitely companies working full-speed-ahead on devices like that.

Medications

As we noted, Josh will have to take insulin injections to live with type 1 diabetes. In type 1 diabetes, the body no longer produces insulin; therefore, shots must be taken. Many people with type 1 diabetes (and even some who have type 2) are candidates for the insulin pump. This device provides a small amount of

Possible Long-Term Complications

Long-term complications of diabetes can be varied. Often, the cause is sugars that are elevated over a long period of time. Tight control (keeping sugars as close as possible to "normal") is the primary way to prevent, or significantly delay, long-term complications including:

- eye changes (retinopathy, glaucoma, cataracts)
- kidney changes (nephropathy)
- heart attack, stroke and atherosclerosis (blood vessel changes)
- changes in cholesterol levels
- high blood pressure
- nerve changes (neuropathy)
- impotence
- decreased awareness of "lows"
- silent heart attacks (no pain)
- leg pain, burning, tingling
- delayed stomach emptying (gastroparesis)
- problems with bladder control (neurogenic bladder)

insulin every hour, all day long, and extra insulin can be taken, as needed, when sugars are high or the person will eat more carbs. The best control for Josh will be several shots a day. At least four will give him the best control with a lesser risk of going too low.

Sophia eventually may need to take medications for type 2 diabetes. These meds are in four basic categories, based on their action. Some stimulate the pancreas to make more insulin (sulfonylureas). Some slow the absorption of carbs in the stomach and bowel (alpha-glucosidase inhibitors). Some "calm" the liver, so it doesn't release sugar (from your stored-up supply) or make new sugars (biguanides). Some work at the cellular level to make the cells more sensitive to the insulin the body already has (thiazolidinediones). Sophia's nurse practitioner also recommends hormone replacement therapy (HRT), because a number of studies show better glucose control with HRT.

Each of them may choose integrative therapies to help in the day-to-day work of taking care of their diabetes as featured in this section. Therapies that are especially valuable include those that reduce levels of stress because increased stress often means increased blood sugar levels. In fact, Christopher Saudek, president of the American Diabetes Association, says that stress management could replace some medication for those who require fewer drugs to begin with.

What about the Future?

Sophia will see her nurse practitioner every 3 to 6 months to evaluate how she's doing with her diabetes. Josh will see his doctor at least every 3 months. They'll have regular blood tests. They'll take special care of their eyes and feet. They'll learn (from the nurse and dietitian) about guidelines for taking care of diabetes for the rest of their lives (see sidebar on page 133). And they'll learn that their risk of long-term complications of diabetes is greatly reduced when they're keeping the blood sugars as close to normal as possible (this is called "tight control").

Antibiotics May Improve Lipids in Type 1 Diabetes—Reducing Cardiovascular Risk

In a study published in *Clinical Nutrition*, people with type 1 diabetes were tested (using a blood test and a special breath test) for a bacteria called *Helicobacter pylori* (commonly found to be the cause of certain ulcers—see section on Peptic Ulcer disease). The 29 people who were found to have this bacteria in their system were treated with antibiotics and Prilosec; 22 of them had the bacteria eradicated and 7 remained infected. Lipid levels were monitored at the beginning of the study and at 3 months. At the end of 3 months, HDL cholesterol in the eradicated group had increased, whereas this change did not occur in the non-eradicated group.

Aaron hopefully will prevent the diagnosis of diabetes for a long time. This will take some effort: watching his carbs, exercising daily and seeing his P.A. regularly.

What's the Big Picture in the United States?

Diabetes rates rose a striking 6 percent among adults in one recent year, according to researchers at the Centers for Disease Control and Prevention (CDC). Prevalence increased among both women and men, and among all ethnic groups, including Caucasians, African-Americans, Hispanics and all others. This is further evidence that diabetes is a major public health threat of epidemic proportions. Currently, more than 16 million Americans have diabetes, and about one-third of those don't

Standards of Care for People with Diabetes

People with diabetes should have the following done yearly:
- lipid tests (cholesterol, HDL, LDL, triglycerides)
- microalbuminuria screening
- dilated eye exam by qualified optometrist or ophthalmologist
- flu shot (pneumonia shot once, repeated as recommended)
- foot exam for any sensation or circulation problems
- complete physical exam

People with diabetes should have the following done twice a year:
- dental visit
- hemoglobin A1C (for well-controlled type 2)
- see your healthcare provider for a diabetes-focused visit for well-controlled type 2

People with type 1 diabetes should have the following done four times a year:
- hemoglobin A1C
- see your healthcare provider for a diabetes-focused visit

At every visit, your healthcare provider should check:
- blood pressure (goal < 130/80)
- activity level and activity goals
- meal plan
- blood sugar records (including how many episodes of too low and too high)
- feet (shoes and socks off at every healthcare visit)
- psyche (odds of clinical depression in people with diabetes are twice that of people who do not have diabetes, regardless of gender and type of diabetes)
- weight

know they have the disease. A study reported in a recent issue of *Diabetes Care* linked the increase in diabetes with the rising rates of obesity, which is a major risk factor for diabetes.

An even newer and more startling trend is the increasing incidence of type 2 diabetes in children, often school-age children. Treating children with type 2 diabetes will continue to be a major health concern for a number of reasons:

- Children have a healthy sense of immortality. They won't care much about "possible" long-term complications of diabetes.
- With no, or minimal, symptoms of high blood sugar, they aren't likely to want to take their medication.
- Their blood sugars may be more erratic because of hormone changes and puberty.
- We have yet to see what "really long-term" use of many of our medications will bring. What will happen when that child is an adult of 70, and has taken these medications for 50 to 60 years?
- What are the cost implications of caring for people with type 2 diabetes and preventing long-term complications? One recent year, an estimated $98 billion was spent on healthcare associated with diabetes.

Diabetes	
Reasons to Be Concerned (Inherited Traits and Environmental Factors)	■ 16 million in U.S. have diabetes mellitus and approximately ⅓ don't know they have the disease ■ Increased risk if you have a parent, brother or sister with diabetes ■ Type 1 is most likely an autoimmune response to a viral infection ■ Type 2 risk increases at age 45, and up more significantly at age 65 ■ Increasing numbers of children are being diagnosed with type 2
Western Medicine Recommendations	■ Exercise (#1) for treatment and prevention ■ Food choices—count carbohydrates for treatment and prevention ■ Monitor blood sugars at home (poking the finger to get blood reading) ■ Sulfonylureas stimulate pancreas to make more insulin ■ Metformin slows the liver's glucose production down and makes cells less resistant to insulin ■ Thiazolidinediaones (TZDs) decrease cellular resistance to insulin ■ Insulin injections

Diabetes *continued*	
Integrative Therapy	■ Traditional Chinese medicine ■ Ayurvedic medicine ■ Massage ■ Reflexology ■ Qigong ■ Yoga ■ Aromatherapy ■ Hydrotherapy ■ Biofeedback training ■ Guided imagery ■ Magnetic field therapy ■ Ozone therapy ■ Hydrogen peroxide therapy ■ Chelation therapy ■ Herbals include: Siberian ginseng, glucomannan and gymnema
Male or Female Directives	■ If you are a woman who had a baby who weighed more than 9 pounds, you have at least one risk factor for diabetes ■ Type 2 is prevalent in people who are obese; women are generally more obese than men within most age groups
Best Nutritional Strategies	■ Eat smaller portions of carbohydrate more often, as opposed to large meals with large carbohydrate load ■ Count carbohydrates—focus on complex carbohydrates rather than refined cereal grains. It is believed that a condition where blood sugar and insulin levels are increased in many people causes a condition known as "hyperinsulinemia." This condition increases the risk of a collection of diseases called "Syndrome X"—type 2 diabetes, high blood pressure, high cholesterol, obesity and harmful changes in blood chemistry. ■ Do not start a high-protein, very low-carbohydrate diet without checking with your healthcare provider
Supplements or Functional Foods to Consider	■ Include adequate food sources of chromium ■ Foods rich in B vitamins ■ You may want to check out the effects of zinc and coenzyme Q10 ■ Vitamins A and C for antioxidant, eye health, but do NOT take megadoses

Diarrhea, Chronic (Colitis/Crohn's/ Irritable Bowel Syndrome)

Irritable bowel syndrome (IBS) is one condition that can cause diarrhea. High-fiber diets can help manage IBS. Some dietary fibers are able to normalize the time it takes for food residues to pass through the body. If you have IBS, you may experience bouts of loose, watery stools interchanged with dry, compacted stools. Soluble fiber sources (see chapter 2) have been shown to alleviate constipation and normalize transit time for people with IBS.

Hydration or Fluid Needs

The amount of fluid needed by each of us to maintain normal daily activities, involving both work and leisure, is considerable. But the fact of the matter is that many people do not recognize thirst and their true fluid needs. Not all fluids are equal. Caffeinated fluids and alcoholic beverages, for example, tend to further dehydrate us. They do not actually replenish us. Fluids that hydrate us include milk, juice, non-caffeinated fluids and, best of all, water.

Usually, if you wait until your body signals its thirst, you are not drinking quite enough fluid to meet your body's basic needs.

Nutritional Recommendations for Modifying Lifestyle Choices

One way you can roughly figure your fluid needs as an adult is to take your weight in pounds and divide it by kilograms. Each kilogram (kg) equals 2.2 pounds. For example, a man named Tony weighs 175 pounds (equal to about 80 kg). Tony is age 50, works as a CPA and enjoys tennis in his leisure time. To figure the actual amount of fluids needed by Tony (with greater amounts needed during heavy physical exercise and periods of illness, such as bouts of diarrhea accompanied by fever), we have a formula to follow. This formula is comprised of several metric factors. The volume of fluid most of us within this age group require ranges between 35 to 45 cubic centimeters (ccs) for each person's weight in kilograms. Older folks and children have a different range standard. And when any of us encounters an illness or engages in more strenuous activity, our fluid needs go up.

What Is Dehydration?

General signs of dehydration include:

- thirst
- less frequent urination
- dry skin
- fatigue
- light-headedness

If you suspect that you are dehydrated, call the doctor immediately. Severe dehydration may require hospitalization.

Tony's body weight in kilograms (80 kg) is then multiplied by 35 to 45 (ccs) per each kilogram of his body weight. In Tony's case, this would equal 2,800 to 3,600 ccs each day. Tony would divide his total fluid needs by the number of ccs in a cup, which is 240. This translates into approximately 12 to 15 cups of fluid each day. For optimum hydration, Tony should consume this amount of fluid over the course of the entire day.

Women of a similar age would use the same equation. Late-life seniors will probably need just a little less fluid each day. And those with special health-care needs may need slightly more or less than the guideline used by Tony to figure his fluid needs.

Diarrhea, Chronic

Reasons to Be Concerned (Inherited Traits and Environmental Factors)	■ Causes: medications, microscopic colitis, long-standing diabetes, irritable bowel syndrome, infections, lactase deficiency (enzyme necessary to break down milk sugar), ulcerative colitis and Crohn's disease and cancer ■ Medications are common offenders with biggest culprits being: non-steroidal anti-inflammatory drugs (NSAIDs), magnesium-containing antacids, antiarrythmics, beta-blockers, quinidine and digoxin ■ 10 percent of HIV/AIDS patients are elderly and a variety of infections including diarrhea from IBS occur ■ Osmotic diarrhea can occur from ingestion of substances like laxatives containing citrate, antacids containing magnesium hydroxide and some sugars such as mannitol, sorbitol and fructose found in antacids, chewing gum, diet candy and fruits ■ African-American and Jewish people are among the 80 percent of world population with primary lactase deficiency—occurs in childhood and cannot be outgrown ■ Bloody or inflammatory diarrhea contains blood and leukocytes such as found in ulcerative colitis and Crohn's disease, cancer of the colon and radiation colitis
Western Medicine Recommendations	■ Simple cases can often be treated with over-the-counter (OTC) Imodium or Pepto Bismol ■ Consult healthcare provider if diarrhea lasts more than 3 days; if you have severe pain in the abdomen or rectum; fever of 102°F or higher; blood occurs in your stool or have black, tarry stools; signs and symptoms of dehydration occur

continued on next page

Diarrhea, Chronic *continued*	
Western Medicine Recommendations *continued*	■ Testing should occur when there are greater than or equal to six stools in 24 hours or bloody diarrhea ■ Fluid and electrolyte replacement may be necessary ■ Antibiotics usually given for infectious diarrhea (may occur with traveler's diarrhea, i.e., Montezuma's Revenge) ■ In the elderly serious diarrhea can lead to hospitalization ■ Laboratory tests and stool samples will be done
Integrative Therapy	■ Herbals include: guarana—avoid large amounts because it contains caffeine; tannins in it may contribute to cancer risk and be hepatotoxic (unsafe for the liver)
Male or Female Directives	■ None noted between sexes—may have slight differences with various specific diseases
Best Nutritional Strategies	■ Stabilize fluid and body weight concerns ■ Provide clear liquid diet (if needed) with appropriate calories—diet is intended for short term use only and does not meet the recommended dietary allowances (RDAs) ■ BRAT diet (Bananas, Rice, Applesauce, Toast without margarine or butter) Banana flakes mixed in foods or drinks may also help ■ Increase fluids and consider drinks like Gatorade, which replace electrolytes ■ Avoid milk products and foods that are greasy, high-fiber or very sweet—these tend to aggravate diarrhea ■ Advance diet to include foods that "feel bland" and sound good to you—besides the BRAT diet, consider boiled potatoes (with minimal or no fat), crackers, cooked carrots and baked chicken without the skin
Supplements or Functional Foods to Consider	■ Pedialyte ■ Osmolite

Irritable Bowel Syndrome

Reasons to Be Concerned (Inherited Traits and Environmental Factors)	■ People describe acute episodes of stress preceding the onset of bowel symptoms ■ Defecation is irregular or varies more than 25 percent of the time ■ Characterized by two or more of the following: altered stool frequency, altered stool consistency (hard or loose or watery stool), altered stool passage (straining or urgency, feeling of incomplete evacuation), passage of mucus and bloating or feeling of abdominal distention
Western Medicine Recommendations	■ Too much fiber may cause irritable bowel syndrome and cause decreased absorption of some minerals—magnesium, calcium, zinc and iron ■ Prelief may help (an over-the-counter drug that takes acid out of food)
Integrative Therapy	■ Herbals include: peppermint
Male or Female Directives	■ More women than men (2:1 to 3:1 ratio) ■ Uncommon in elderly persons ■ Typical intake of fiber for males is 15 grams ■ Typical intake of fiber for females is 10 grams
Best Nutritional Strategies	■ 20 to 25 grams of dietary fiber per day ■ Foods that can make IBS worse: lactose (milk sugar), fatty foods, alcohol, artificial sweeteners and beans
Supplements or Functional Foods to Consider	■ Vitamin B complex ■ Vitamin E and C ■ Bioflavonoids ■ Magnesium

Diverticulosis/ Diverticulitis

Can you imagine inviting your mother-in-law to a dinner that causes her to have a bout of diverticulitis that results in her having a colostomy? Well, I can, because 20-some years ago, that happened to me. Each dietetic student at Clarke College prepared a special meal during the Meal Management class. My entrée had water chestnuts in it. My dear mother-in-law, Marie, was good enough to attend. Within a few days, she developed intestinal inflammation and had to have a colostomy. Thankfully, she was able to reverse it later. And what do water chestnuts have to do with her bowel? Well, Marie had diverticulosis. We're not sure what those chestnuts did to her, if anything, but they may have been an increase in her fiber, or a small piece of one of them may have gotten lodged in a diverticulum.

Thirty million people have diverticulosis. It is associated with a weakening of the intestinal wall caused by the pressure from hard stools. The weakened intestinal wall then develops small outpouchings (called diverticulum) in which fecal material becomes trapped. Diverticulitis is an inflammation of the intestinal wall that develops when these outpouchings become irritated or infected.

During a diverticulitis attack, the weak areas or pouches in the wall of your large intestine become inflamed. They look somewhat like small thumbs poking out of the side of the bowel. These pouches seem to develop more as you age. Inflammation occurs when diverticula become blocked with stool. Sometimes the inflammation can lead to a hole or perforation in the wall of the intestine. If the lining of the abdomen becomes inflamed, you can get peritonitis. This is more serious.

Symptoms of diverticulitis may include:

- alternating diarrhea and constipation
- severe, intermittent cramps in the lower left side of the abdomen
- tenderness in the lower left side of the abdomen
- chills or fever
- rectal bleeding

Nutritional Recommendations for Modifying Lifestyle Choices

Uncomplicated diverticulosis requires a high-fiber diet (refer to page 53 for a list of high-fiber foods). We have to increase fiber in a very gradual manner for people with diverticulosis, especially in people who are older. A slow but regular increase in fiber is really important. And as we increase fiber content, we must increase fluid intake.

Another way to increase fiber is the use of stool softeners with psyllium products. Metamucil and Citracil are common psyllium products. My favorite is Citracil. I mix the Citracil with my morning orange juice so that I get my vitamin C *and* fiber. There are wafer products out there, too.

Acute diverticulitis may hospitalize you. Your medical provider may recommend antibiotics, intravenous fluids and naso-gastric suction, a procedure that relieves pressure in the intestine. In advanced cases, the diseased section of the intestine is removed surgically, connecting the remaining sections. A temporary colostomy is required. A colostomy is an operation to bring part of the large intestine to the abdominal surface to form a new opening for bowel movements.

How to Help Prevent Diverticulosis & Manage Diverticulitis

Review the "Best Nutritional Strategies" found in the chart that follows. The incidence of diverticular disease is associated with consistent consumption of a low-fiber diet. Increasing the intake of insoluble fiber may alleviate the need to exert considerable pressure when passing stools, thereby preventing segmentation of the colon.

Supplementing with 6 to 10 grams of insoluble fiber per day may help relieve the heaviness and distention sometimes associated with diverticular disease. Increased insoluble fiber may not be effective unless constipation is also a problem. Remember, you may not see results for several months of sticking to this schedule.

There are times when a high-fiber diet is not advised. This is certainly true if you are diagnosed with a complicated case of diverticular disease—in other words, if you have intestinal bleeding, perforation or abscess, or when acute diverticulitis occurs. As always, you will want to report these type of changes immediately to your healthcare provider.

Diverticulosis/Diverticulitis	
Reasons to Be Concerned (Inherited Traits and Environmental Factors)	■ Average American diet provides only about 12 to 15 grams of fiber a day ■ Lack of adequate fiber contributes to development of diverticulosis
Western Medicine Recommendations	■ During diverticulitis (inflammation), follow high-fiber diet with no foods with skins, indigestible seeds or strings; avoid nuts (especially peanuts) and whole spices, popcorn, raisins, whole-kernel corn ■ Test for food allergies ■ Get adequate exercise ■ Fiber supplements (psyllium, flaxmeal) *continued on next page*

Diverticulosis/Diverticulitis *continued*	
Integrative Therapy	■ Homeopathy ■ Fasting may be used in diverticulitis to give the bowel a rest
Male or Female Directives	■ No research to indicate a difference
Best Nutritional Strategies	■ 20 to 35 grams of dietary fiber per day to encourage the formation of softer stools ■ 5 a day + servings from the fruits and vegetable groups ■ 6 servings of grains and cereals per day with at least 2 as whole grain or minimally processed ■ Increase fiber slowly with whole grain cereals like 100 percent bran, oats and whole wheat flour ■ Increase fluids—8 or more cups of fluid minimum per day
Supplements or Functional Foods to Consider	■ None noted

Epilepsy (Seizure Disorder)

One of the most frightening things to experience is to witness someone having a seizure, especially a grand mal, full-blown, tonic-clonic contracture seizure. It's the sense of helplessness that is so hard, because you really can't do anything to intervene, except make sure the person suffers no further injury. In other words, you need to clear away sharp objects or furniture. Don't try to insert anything in the mouth—unlike what we've heard for years—to "make sure they don't bite their tongue." As soon as possible, call for emergency help.

For family members of people who have recurrent seizures, in a disease like epilepsy, this experience is relived over and over. Once other reasons for seizures have been ruled out (tumors, scar tissue, brain injury or trauma, brain infection or hemorrhage), treatment with anti-seizure medications is started. Common medications include Gabapentin (which is the newest), Dilantin and Phenobarbital.

Nutritional Recommendations for Modifying Lifestyle Choices

Eating meals regularly is an important aspect of living with a seizure disorder. The added stress of missing a meal may increase the frequency of seizures. You'll want to use special care in the intake of alcohol and caffeine, as these may interfere with your seizure medications. Consult your pharmacist or healthcare provider for assistance in this area. Consider a multivitamin and mineral supplement, and avoid extra folic acid if you have epilepsy or a history of seizure disorders.

You may have heard about a ketogenic diet used in children with epilepsy. While ketogenic diets do work with some children, there are no studies to show effectiveness in adults. In addition, ketogenic diets can be dangerous to your health if not followed closely under the supervision of your healthcare provider and/or dietitian.

See also the recommendations found in the chart that follows on page 144. Some medications used by people with epilepsy may cause increased nutrient needs of these nutrients:

- Calcium and vitamin D (phenytoin—Dilantin). See chapter 2 for recommendations of food sources.
- Biotin (Tegretol)
- Folic acid or vitamin B9 (Tegretol)
- Tegretol, phenytoin and a whole host of other medications besides anticonvulsants have the potential of interacting with grapefruit, grapefruit juice and Seville oranges. Grapefruit affects the metabolism in the intestinal wall, which may lead to a reduction in metabolism. The effect of grapefruit on intestinal enzymes is irreversible and can persist for up to 72 hours after grapefruit or juice is consumed. Take medications like these with other sources of liquid or food.

Epilepsy

Reasons to Be Concerned	■ 70 percent with no known cause ■ 6.5 cases per 1,000 population, peak incidence found in people older than 65 years
Western Medicine Recommen-dations	■ Identify and eliminate cause, if cause can be found ■ Anti-convulsant medication (one or two drugs) ■ Surgery may be an option when medicine fails
Integrative Therapy	■ Fasting ■ Biofeedback ■ Meditation, hypnosis and yoga ■ Acupressure ■ Ayurvedic medicine ■ Bodywork ■ Hydrotherapy ■ Reflexology ■ Chiropractic ■ Craniosacral therapy ■ Traditional Chinese medicine
Male or Female Directives	■ Males slightly more than females
Best Nutritional Strategies	■ Eat a diet from a wide variety of foods ■ Adequate fluids ■ See page 143 for additional nutrient needs when taking anti-convulsants over the long term ■ Need to monitor and adjust the amount of folic acid absorbed by diet (with phenytoin—Dilantin). Very high folic acid intake increases the drug metabolism and may decrease the blood level of folic acid
Supplements or Functional Foods	■ None noted

Erectile Dysfunction (Impotence)

Well, at least Viagra got us talking about it. Erectile dysfunction was previously known as impotence. The clinical definition is a chronic inability to achieve and maintain an erection to complete intercourse or achieve sexual satisfaction.

Approximately 7 million men are affected in the United States, and that number increases to 30 million if the definition includes those who have partial erectile dysfunction. Your risk of experiencing erectile dysfunction is higher as you get older, and the causes are varied. See the sidebar.

Diagnosis of erectile dysfunction occurs if the condition lasts more than 2 months or is a recurring problem. Tests to rule out medical or physical causes include: urine and blood sugar testing to rule out diabetes; measuring the level of male hormones in the blood; testing penile blood flow and pressure. If nighttime or early morning erections are experienced (and this is tested by measuring the nighttime stiffness of the penis using a snap gauge test or a stamp test), psychological causes need to be investigated. When the cause is psychological, treatment with both partners is encouraged. All of these diagnostic tools are prescribed by a healthcare provider.

Elimination of causes is the first and foremost treatment. Other treatments range from testosterone (if levels are low) to medications (taken orally, by injection into the penis or by suppository inserted into the urethra) to vacuum erection devices.

A safe and proven natural medication for erectile dysfunction and impotence is ginkgo. When given to 60 men for 12 to 18 months, ginkgo improved their ability to have erections (presumably from the herb's ability to increase blood flow to blood vessels in the penis). Similar results have not been seen in short-term treatment.

Yohimbe is a commonly, but loosely, recommended treatment for impotence. It should be avoided because the effective dose is very close to the toxic dose. Study data showing improved erectile function and increased blood flow to the penis is limited and inconsistent. The FDA has listed yohimbe as unsafe for over-the-counter (OTC) use. Persons with chronic disease (low blood pressure, prostate, heart, liver or kidney disease) should never take yohimbe. It also reacts with a number of medications (decongestants and antidepressants) as well as wine and cheese.

Causes of Erectile Dysfunction (Impotence)

- medications
- illicit drug use
- chronic diseases like diabetes
- atherosclerosis
- pelvic surgery (especially some prostate procedures)
- stress
- depression
- performance anxiety
- overuse of alcohol

Nutritional Recommendations for Modifying Lifestyle Choices

Increasing fiber and fluids is important for overall general health. Increasing physical activity (if you're fairly sedentary) may increase both libido and sexual function. See the chart that follows for certain foods that you may want to try for intermittent erectile dysfunction, in conjunction with recommendations from your healthcare provider.

Erectile Dysfunction	
Reasons to Be Concerned (Inherited Traits and Environmental Factors)	■ Psychogenic erectile dysfunction, organic impotence and neurogenic causes ■ Medications are commonly the cause—antihypertensives, antidepressants, antipsychotics, histamine blockers, nicotine, alcohol and others
Western Medicine Recommendations	■ Diagnose primary or secondary impotence if condition lasts more than 2 months or is a recurring problem ■ Tests include: urine and blood sugar tests to rule out diabetes; measure testosterone levels (predominantly male hormone) in the blood; test penile blood flow and pressure; measuring nighttime stiffness of the penis with the snap gauge test or stamp test; ruling out psychological problems (and often working with both partners if treatment is needed) ■ Treat Benign Prostatic Hypertrophy (BPH) or enlargement of prostate ■ Treat prostatitis (prostate inflammation or infection) and prostate cancer ■ Check drugs for side effects of impotence ■ Vacuum erection devices ■ Medications to cause erection through vasodilation (Viagra) ■ Injection to cause erection (Alprostadil) ■ MUSE-medicated urethral system for erection (medication in tiny suppository form to be inserted in urethra ■ Sleep clinics can help monitor the occurrence and duration of nocturnal erections

Erectile Dysfunction *continued*

Integrative Therapy	■ Herbals include: ginkgo and yohimbe. Yohimbe should be avoided because it is a monoamine oxidase (MAO) inhibitor that can increase blood pressure. Reports of its use include psychoses, paralysis, fatigue, kidney failure and death ■ Biofeedback training ■ Meditation and yoga ■ Aromatherapy (provocative smells include bread baking—men, pumpkin pie—both men and women, strawberries—women) and many others ■ Hydrotherapy (sitz bath) ■ Chiropractic ■ Homeopathy ■ Hypnosis ■ Magnetic field therapy ■ Traditional Chinese medicine ■ Bodywork ■ Chelation therapy
Male or Female Directives	■ By definition, only in males ■ Nearly 2 percent for men in their 40s, 25 percent for men in their 60s ■ Peak incidence in over-70-year-old men ■ Up to 50 percent of men with diabetes will experience impotence
Best Nutritional Strategies	■ General diet ■ Adequate fiber and fluid ■ Adequate physical activity ■ Oysters are high in zinc as well as nutrients important to the production of semen and testosterone in males ■ Asparagus contains substances that affect hormone production
Supplements or Functional Foods to Consider	■ Foods, spices or herbs believed to be aphrodisiacs: cinnamon, artichokes, asparagus, oysters, figs, truffles, chiles, chocolate, licorice, avocados, cloves, onion, ginseng, garlic, dill, cashews, saffron, endive, carrots, honey and vanilla ■ Avoid high quantities of licorice root extract. Testosterone levels plummeted by 40 percent in just four days. Most licorice candy is artificially flavored, but this ingredient is often found in breath fresheners and cough drops.

Fibromyalgia

"I can't believe the pain that I have in my knees, elbows and hips. I can't have arthritis already, can I? On top of that, I just can't sleep. I saw a rheumatologist and he said I've got 12 of the 18 'trigger points.' Does that mean I have fibromyalgia? Can't they just do a blood test to tell me yes or no?" Answers to the three questions posed: probably not (arthritis), probably (fibromyalgia) and no (blood tests).

If you're a woman aged 35 to 60, you're more likely to have fibromyalgia (or fibromyalgia syndrome, or FMS). This disorder is more common than rheumatoid arthritis, affects about 7 million people in the United States and about 1.5 percent of the world's total population. And it's probably one of the most misunderstood disorders—by healthcare providers and patients alike. Because there are no lab tests to "prove" fibromyalgia, it's sometimes not treated like a real disease, or it becomes a catch-all disease for people with unexplained pain: "Oh, you must have fibromyalgia."

FMS is characterized by musculoskeletal pain, as opposed to joint pain. Other common symptoms include:
- migraines, headaches and jaw pain
- changes in sleep patterns
- fatigue
- irritable bowel syndrome
- numbness and tingling or a feeling of poor blood flow
- eye changes, like dry eyes and trouble focusing
- dizziness and changes in balance
- urinary problems, such as a strong urge to urinate frequently
- bladder and pelvic pain
- depression

Diagnosing & Treating Fibromyalgia

Diagnosing FMS includes a thorough history and physical to rule out other disorders, and applying pressure on the 18 trigger points. Pain at 11 or more sites would indicate a positive for diagnosis, although there is some controversy for the number of sites needed to diagnose. A history of sleep disorders, irritable bowel syndrome and migraines is common. No blood test is available for fibromyalgia at this time.

Treatment with antidepressants and sedatives alleviate sleep disorders and also the pain. Non-steroidal anti-inflammatory drugs (NSAIDs) have not proven effective, nor have injections of cortisone. Physical therapy may be ordered. Exercise, especially aerobic or swimming, is effective. Stretching exercises are commonly recommended. Exercise should be started slowly and gradually increased.

Nutritional Recommendations for Modifying Lifestyle Choices

A healthy diet (low in animal fat and high in fiber) with plenty of fresh fruits and vegetables is recommended. A small study in Finland showed benefits in people following a vegan diet. They experienced less pain and stiffness, as well as improved sleep. They also lowered their weight and cholesterol levels on this diet. Choosing foods with omega-3 fatty acids is a possible plus, as they've been found to be helpful in arthritic pain; this benefit may also be seen in fibromyalgia.

As you can see, there are not a lot of "tried and true" or "miracle" treatments for fibromyalgia in Western medicine, even in nutritional therapy. You might consider mind-body intervention as an option. In one study, 28 patients using a combination of education, meditation techniques and movement therapy (qigong) were assessed using self-reporting tools. After 8 weeks, they reported improvement in their pain, function and mood. Effective? At least hopeful.

Perhaps the best therapy for treating FMS is a mixed bag:

- Increase fiber and decrease fat in meal planning.
- Establish good sleep hygiene (see sidebar below).
- Practice individual stress-reduction techniques.
- Engage in regular aerobic exercise.
- Investigate mind-body therapies and choose what works for you.

Good Sleep Hygiene

- Limit caffeine in the late afternoon and evening.
- Standardize your bedtime.
- Establish a bedtime ritual.
- Use the bedroom only for sleep (eliminate TV, radio, desk, paperwork, reading materials, exercise equipment and so on).
- Eliminate clutter in the bedroom.
- Pay attention to the amount of noise in your environment (too much noise—eliminate pets, avoid snoring sleepmates or noisy equipment; or too little noise—add a small fan or minimal low-level constant noise to induce sleep).

Fibromyalgia	
Reasons to Be Concerned (Inherited Traits and Environmental Factors)	■ 9 to 10 million Americans suffer with fibromyalgia ■ More common with family history ■ Ages 35 to 50 most common time to experience symptoms—risk increases with age ■ About half of patients report symptoms began during or after a flu-like illness ■ Diagnosis aided by identifying pain being present at a number of 18 different "trigger points"
Western Medicine Recommendations	■ Physical therapy ■ Specific anti-depressants and sedatives (tricyclics and SSRIs) used at bedtime help with sleep patterns ■ Flexeril may be used to relax muscle spasms ■ Hormone replacement therapy ■ Anti-inflammatory meds and cortisone injected into trigger points have not been proven effective
Integrative Therapy	■ Stress reduction therapies ■ Deep breathing exercises ■ Meditation ■ Hypnosis ■ Biofeedback ■ Massage therapy ■ Planned exercise, particularly aerobic and swimming seems better than just stretching exercises ■ Establishing good sleep "hygiene" is very important
Male/Female Directives	■ Women are more often affected than men at a ratio of 20:1
Best Nutritional Strategies	■ Foods low in animal fat and higher in fiber ■ Plenty of fresh fruits and vegetables ■ Use oils containing omega-3 fatty acids
Supplements or Functional Foods	■ SAM-e used to treat fibromyalgia patients successfully in a Danish double blind study

Food Allergies

Your lips start swelling. Your tongue feels like it's too big for your mouth. Now you're a little short of breath; you just can't get air. Your nose feels itchy and you start to have a headache and feel queasy in your stomach. What in the world is going on?

If you know even a little about health, you know this sounds like the beginning of an allergic reaction. If it goes on to more shortness of breath, with a rapid heartbeat and faintness or dizziness, you may be having an anaphylactic reaction (a severe allergic reaction) that could cause you to stop breathing, lose consciousness or even die. Foods that have been known to cause this type of an acute allergic reaction are:

- peanuts and peanut butter
- nuts
- shellfish (shrimp, crab, lobster, scallops, clams, oysters)
- eggs

There are many things that people are allergic to, and of course the focus here is on foods. Two out of five people in the United States self-report food allergies, but these may actually just be food intolerance. Two of the most familiar food intolerances occur to wheat (the gluten or protein in wheat) and to dairy products. Only 6 percent of the unpleasant symptoms people report, such as bloating, diarrhea and abdominal cramping, are actually true allergic reactions. In fact, it's estimated that fewer than 2 percent have true food allergies. They are more common in children than adults, affecting almost one in six kids.

Food intolerances may occur in conjunction with other medical conditions, such as gastritis, colitis, gallbladder disease or peptic ulcers. An intolerance to caffeine or alcohol can cause gastrointestinal irritation or other problems. Caffeine or alcohol can cause disturbances in the heart rate or rhythm or a sense of nervousness or agitation.

Another less common "heightened sensitivity" is to the plant chemical solanine, found in the nightshade vegetable family. You may have heard people with arthritis mention that they avoid these vegetables. Eating these foods produces symptoms of arthritis such as joint tenderness, swelling and even warmth to the touch, like real arthritis.

Members of the nightshade (vegetable) family are:

- eggplant
- white potatoes
- tomatoes (the foliage of tomatoes is poisonous)
- bell peppers
- tobacco
- hallucinogenic jimson weed (all parts of the plant contain belladonna alkaloids that are poisonous; ingestion can cause acute anticholinergic poisoning and death)

Who's Got the Real Food Allergy?

So how do you sort the real allergies from those food intolerances? Healthcare providers use dietary therapy, low-risk food challenges (by mouth), skin testing, endoscopy (scope procedure to look into the throat and stomach) and high-risk food challenges as parts of the diagnosing process.

Your dietitian or medical care provider may advise you to eliminate or avoid a food for a substantial period of time, such as 3 weeks. Then you may be asked to reintroduce the food in a controlled setting under the guidance of your doctor. This helps identify and verify allergic or adverse responses to a particular food.

Once the diagnosis is made, and the culprit found (the food you're allergic to), the treatment is prevention. Avoidance of the culprit food(s) is key. If you do happen to be exposed to, or eat, those foods you are allergic to, antihistamines (like Benadryl, Tavist, Claritin or Hismanal) often provide relief for minor symptoms (rash, headache, mild swelling). If you have a history of a severe reaction, you'll usually be given a prescription for an "Epi-pen," a preloaded syringe with a drug called epinephrine (used to treat allergic reactions and prevent anaphylaxis). You'll be taught how to give this injection if symptoms start.

Oh, Nuts!

Many food allergies are related to nuts, and the most prevalent of those is peanuts. There are an increasing number of children and adults being diagnosed with an allergy to peanuts. And that wouldn't be such a problem, if they could just stay away from peanuts and

Foods Most Likely to Cause Allergic Reactions

- peanuts
- tree nuts (walnuts, pecans, almonds)
- milk
- eggs
- soy
- fish
- shellfish (shrimp, crab, lobster, scallops, clams, oysters)
- wheat

peanut butter, but we've become a society of peanut butter and jelly sandwiches. To make matters worse, peanuts and peanut butter are hidden ingredients in many foods. You'll have to specifically ask about peanuts when eating out, and check pre-packaged food labels especially carefully if you, or your child, has this allergy. Here are some common places you might find "hidden" peanuts:

- African, Chinese and Thai foods, especially egg rolls
- baked pastries and cookies
- ice cream, desserts and garnishes
- candy, particularly chocolate products, marzipan and nougat
- enriched cocoa
- chili
- brown gravies
- hydrolyzed plant protein and hydrolyzed vegetable protein

Food Allergies

Reasons to Be Concerned (Inherited Traits and Environmental Factors)	■ One or two adults in 100 (1 to 2 percent) suffer from true food allergies ■ Although children usually outgrow allergies to most foods, they seldom outgrow allergies to peanuts and tree nuts (walnuts, almonds and cashews) ■ Most patients have other types of allergies (to dust or pollen for example) ■ The most common reactions are to: cow's milk, eggs, peanuts, soybeans, wheat, corn, fish, shellfish; peanut and soybean allergies remain throughout adulthood ■ Majority of people with true food allergies are allergic to 3 or fewer foods ■ Flight attendants often no longer hand out peanuts on airplanes because of the increasing incidence of peanut allergies
Western Medicine Recommendations	■ Check with your medical care provider—don't self-diagnose ■ If diagnosed, wear a warning bracelet or necklace ■ Testing for allergies can be: skin testing (indicates a problem—but you may not have an adverse food reaction); RAST—radioallergosorbent test; ELISA—enzyme-linked immunosorbent assay test; food challenge—food placed in capsules must be swallowed; electroacupuncture biofeedback testing and blood tests. Blood tests are IgG ELISA (an antibody test) and FICA (Food Immune Complex Assay) and a "challenge test," food extracts placed under tongue (or injected) ■ Have "Epi-pen" or Ana-Kit available (works like epinephrine)
Integrative Therapy	■ Acupuncture ■ Acupressure ■ Ayurvedic medicine ■ Homeopathy ■ Fasting ■ Guided imagery ■ Aromatherapy ■ Chelation therapy ■ Hypnosis ■ Neuro-linguistic programming continued on next page

Food Allergies *continued*	
Integrative Therapy	■ Bodywork ■ Oxygen therapy ■ Magnetic field therapy ■ Biological dentistry ■ Herbals include: flaxseed and evening primrose oil (anti-inflammatory)
Male or Female Directives	No difference
Best Nutritional Strategies	■ Avoid foods you are allergic to ■ Keep a food diary to help identify the food(s) that cause allergic reactions for you ■ Recognize your need for nutrients that might be skipped when certain foods must be avoided ■ Read food ingredient lists carefully—look for hidden ingredients ■ Recognize that some people report allergy symptoms from a food when raw but not when cooked, or vice versa ■ Avoid cross-contamination of foods ■ Ask questions before tasting foods ■ Dine out with care
Supplements or Functional Foods to Consider	■ Avoid medications like chondroitin if you have a seafood/ nut allergy ■ Consider intake of essential fatty acids (EFAs), which moderate inflammatory response and decrease allergic response

Gallstones

Gallstones. The pain from gallbladder disease closely mimics a heart attack. It may be the worst pain you can imagine.

About one million Americans will be diagnosed this year, joining the estimated 20 million who already have gallbladder disease. Fewer than 20 percent will actually have symptoms, though, and that's good news. The most common treatment for those who have severe symptoms is one-day surgery: laparoscopic removal of the gallbladder. But some experts believe that we wouldn't need most gallbladder surgeries if we were eating healthier (especially avoiding high-fat foods) and identifying food allergies.

Ultrasound, x-ray, CT scan, oral cholecystogram, TC-hIDA scan (a gallbladder scan), ERCP (endoscopic retrograde cholangiopancreatography—a method of evaluating your bile and pancreatic ducts with an endoscope) and PTHC (percutaneous transhepatic cholangiogram) are all tests that may be done to diagnose this condition. A characteristic pain called "Murphy's sign" is present in most people with gallstones (a sudden, sharp pain when the healthcare provider places a hand under your right rib cage and asks you to take a deep breath).

Nutritional Recommendations for Modifying Lifestyle Choices

Treating gallstones can be different in each individual. In the hospital setting, acute problems with gallstones are often referred to as having a "hot gallbladder." A low-fat diet, between 30 and 45 grams, will sometimes appease the situation, or make the time you wait for surgery bearable. I will always remember a patient of mine whose Saturday night ritual involved eating hamburgers and french fries with his wife of many years. Several times, this gentleman landed in our small community hospital after eating this weekend meal he could not seem to forego. In his case, if he could have just sacrificed one of those foods, he may not have made the condition worse. I admit

Scenario

The man in the three-piece suit looked like a pharmaceutical salesperson and asked for a nurse. He wanted a nurse, *now*. His partner, just behind him, could barely stand. He was almost doubling over and was sweating like crazy. When I asked what was wrong, "chest pain" was all he could get out. The pain radiated to his back and both shoulders.

As an ER nurse, all the bells and whistles go off when you start thinking about chest pain and heart attacks. We whisked him to the ER, got the EKG done, an IV in and labs drawn. The pain didn't subside but we fairly quickly ruled out a heart attack. His history revealed very limited cardiac risk factors but he described a generous breakfast of sausage, eggs, toast with butter and, to top it all off, a big cinnamon roll!

feeling frustrated with the situation, but more sorry for this patient who suffered a great deal of pain when he ingested more fat than his body could handle during these gallbladder attacks.

We don't know why, but lettuce or similar foods also seem to play havoc with "hot gallbladders." Consult your registered dietitian for an individualized session of medical nutritional therapy to manage your case.

Additional information to help you identify and quantify the fat in your diet is found on pages 230–231. Nutrient analysis of recipes provides the number of fat grams per serving in chapter 5.

Cool Crystals

Gallstones are actually crystals of cholesterol or bile that range in size from a grain of sand to larger than a golf ball, and people can have from one to hundreds present in their gallbladder. Gallstones cause havoc (and intense pain) when they block a duct—a passageway from one organ to another or to the intestine—and may need to be removed surgically. Non-surgical approaches are only indicated for a few people; half of those people will have a recurrence of gallstones.

Gallstones	
Reasons to Be Concerned (Inherited Traits and Environmental Factors)	■ Overweight people at greater risk ■ More common in people who have rapidly gained or lost a large amount of weight or are overweight; indulge in fatty foods; undergo hormone replacement therapy or take birth control pills ■ 1 in 10 Americans has gallstones but most don't even know it and show no symptoms ■ Gallstones are more common in both Native Americans and Mexican Americans. Native Americans have the highest prevalence.
Western Medicine Recommendations	■ Surgical approach is common in those who have pain ■ Laparoscopic surgery to remove the gallbladder means a short hospital stay and short recovery time and no recurrence of symptoms ■ Non-surgical approaches include oral or injected medicines or shock waves to dissolve small "stones"

Gallstones *continued*	
Integrative Therapy	■ Fasting ■ Yoga ■ Hydrotherapy ■ Colon therapy ■ Magnetic field therapy ■ Neural therapy ■ Acupuncture ■ Detoxification therapy ■ Homeopathy ■ Herbals include: milk thistle; dandelion root is on the FDA's "generally recognized as safe" (GRAS) list. German health authorities warn that people with intestinal blockages or inflammation or occlusion of the bile duct should not use dandelion preparations. They recommend only taking preparations in moderation for limited stretches of time, about 4 to 6 weeks at a time ■ German health authorities do advise anyone with gallstones or a bile duct obstruction to take cynarin (globe artichoke) only under a healthcare provider's advice ■ Enteric coated peppermint oil may help dissolve stones. Those at risk of heartburn, acid reflux and hiatal hernia should note that peppermint oil may make the condition worse
Male or Female Directives	■ Much more common in women between ages of 20 and 60 ■ Women twice as likely to get gallstones as men—1 in 5 will have them ■ Women who work out reduce risk of need for operation to remove gallstones by 31 percent compared to those who are the least active—mechanism may be that working out reduces cholesterol content in bile and stones are less likely to develop ■ More common in pregnant women or women on birth control pills or replacement estrogen therapy
Best Nutritional Strategies	Lower fat, especially saturated fat (meat and dairy products) Lower cholesterol intake Increase fiber
Supplements or Foods	None known

Heart & Circulatory Diseases

What's the leading killer of women in the United States? Breast cancer, you thought? Wrong. It's heart disease. And the leading killer of men? The same. Heart disease—coronary artery disease (CAD), coronary heart disease (CHD), or cardiovascular disease (CVD)—these terms are nearly interchangeable (and you will see them all). Heart disease is a collection of abnormalities in your blood's pumping and transportation system. CVD includes atherosclerosis (hardening of the innermost part of the arteries), dyslipidemias—blood disorders that involve altered levels of lipids, or fats (high cholesterol and other fats like triglycerides—the storage form of fat in your body), and hypertension (high blood pressure—abbreviated HTN). All these ailments can lead to, and are risk factors for, heart attack and stroke.

If you have CVD, or if you're at risk, there are steps you can take to lower your risk of a future heart attack or stroke. Dr. Michael Davidson, in a cardiac symposium in St. Louis, presented the ABCs of CVD treatment and prevention. They are:

- **A**—Aspirin
- **B**—Beta-blockers (blood pressure and heart medications)
- **C**—Cholesterol-lowering therapy
- **D**—Diet
- **E**—Exercise and vitamin E
- **F**—Folate and other B vitamins (vitamins B6 and B12)
- **G**—Glucose control (especially in people with diabetes)

As noted at the beginning of this chapter, aspirin is certainly regaining its popularity. It's recommended for almost anyone in midlife years, but especially for anyone diagnosed with CVD, in doses from 81 to 325 mg, if not contraindicated. Beta-blockers (for example, Atenolol, Metoprolol, Labetolol) are recommended if you're at high risk or if you've already suffered a heart attack (also called myocardial infarction, or MI). This category of medications is also appropriate for treating high blood pressure.

Regular exercise is strongly recommended. Exercise recommendations differ for those who are currently sedentary compared to those who may already be engaging in regularly planned physical activity. If you are not currently exercising, you will want to reach a target goal of 30 minutes, 3 to 4 times a week. Remember to clear any new exercise program with your healthcare provider before beginning. This is extremely important since exertion levels need to be monitored carefully for your age and other risk factors. Trained exercise physiologists, personal trainers and physical therapists will work with your healthcare provider to design the exercise regimen that best meets your needs.

Reduction of Category 1 Risk Factors has been proven to lower cardiovascular disease. Those risk factors are:

- Cigarette smoking (An average smoker dies 3 years earlier than a nonsmoker and 10 to 15 years earlier if other major cardiovascular heart disease risks are present.)
- High-saturated-fat, high-cholesterol diet
- Elevated low-density lipoprotein cholesterol (LDL)
- Hypertension (high blood pressure)
- Left ventricular hypertrophy (thickening of the left ventricle—

the left bottom of the heart that pumps blood to the whole body)

- Thrombogenic factors (another term for things in the blood that make it clot—and especially at dangerously inappropriate and fatal times)

The association between risk of cardiovascular disease and ethnicity cannot be completely explained by differences in socioeconomic status (SES). Most CVD risk factors are more prevalent in African-American and Mexican-American women than in white women.

High levels of homocysteine in your blood damage the linings of your arteries. Drinking five or more cups of coffee a day raises homocysteine levels. Adequate folic acid levels "funnel off" excess levels of homocysteine. Marginal folate deficiency in postmenopausal women may alter your composition of DNA. Women may need more folate than the current Dietary Allowance, as this amount may not be sufficient to prevent an increase in plasma homocysteine levels in postmenopausal women. Intake levels between 286 to 516 micrograms folate per day were needed to reverse DNA hypomethylation and repair DNA.

Nutritional Recommendations for Modifying Lifestyle Choices

Cholesterol-lowering therapy and diet modification is reviewed below. Diet will be addressed in each section as we look at nutritional recommendations for each condition. The American Heart Association (AHA) has established dietary guidelines for reducing your risk of heart disease and total serum choles-

terol. The following is a summary of these standard guidelines:

- Eat a diet that lowers total calories and reduces total fat and cholesterol intake.
- Limit total daily fat intake to no more than 30 percent of total calories.
- Limit cholesterol intake to less than 300 mg each day.
- Include carbohydrates to total 55 to 60 percent of total daily calories.
- Avoid foods high in sugar.
- Increase fiber sources slowly to total 25 to 30 grams of fiber with an emphasis on soluble fiber.
- Use monounsaturated oils, such as olive oil and canola oil.
- Eat five or more servings of fruit and vegetables each day.
- Limit salt intake to less than 5 grams (5,000 mg) a day (if you have hypertension, diagnosed coronary heart disease or congestive heart failure, limit to 3 grams, or 3,000 mg).
- Add antioxidants like vitamin C, beta-carotene and vitamin E in the recommended amounts to help lower homocysteine levels and reverse effects of oxidized LDL.
- Eat a variety of foods to get a greater intake of vitamins and minerals needed by the body.

How Does Atherosclerosis Fit into the Picture?

You have probably heard about "hardening of the arteries." *Arteriosclerosis* is hardening of the arteries, while *atherosclerosis* is the hardening of the innermost part of the arteries. It's thought to be an aging process. Through the years, fatty material that contains cholesterol or calcium builds up on the inside of the walls of your blood vessels. This makes the inside diameter narrower. It can get so narrow that a blood clot, even a very small one, can block the flow of blood to a part of the body. If this blood clot is in one of the arteries supplying blood to the heart muscle, you could have a heart attack (MI, or myocardial infarction). If this blood clot is in one of the arteries supplying blood to the brain, you could have a "brain attack" (a stroke or a cerebrovascular accident).

Treating Atherosclerosis with Herbs

Safe herbs used for treating atherosclerosis include: garlic, Siberian ginseng and onion. High doses of garlic (five cloves a day) lower cholesterol levels, increase clot-busting activity and inhibit blood from clotting, thus reducing cardiac risk. But who can eat five cloves a day? Or perhaps the better question is: Who can stand to be around the person who eats five cloves a day? Controversy still exists regarding whether or not "deodorized" preparations are effective, as the active ingredient (allicin) causes the smell.

Do not take alfalfa, coenzyme Q10, pycnogenol, reishi mushroom or saffron. Studies are either absent or conflicting regarding their effectiveness and safety.

Atherosclerosis	
Reasons to Be Concerned (Inherited Traits and Environmental Factors)	■ Atherosclerotic cardiovascular disease is the number one cause of death in Western nations and rapidly becoming a prominent cause of death in economically underdeveloped countries as well ■ 4,000 to 5,000 genes identified that may affect the risk of CVD ■ Elevated total cholesterol increases risk of atherosclerosis, coronary artery disease and carotid artery disease ■ Extremely high in whites
Western Medicine Recommendations	■ Exercise ■ Smoking cessation ■ Daily aspirin ■ Control blood pressure (less than 135/85) through diet or medication ■ Note: blood pressure goal for diabetes is 130/80 ■ Control lipid levels through diet or medications ■ Consider Estrogen Replacement Therapy (ERT) ■ Treatment with vitamin B6 and folic acid varies with levels of homocysteine

Atherosclerosis *continued*	
Integrative Therapy	■ Stress reduction techniques ■ Yoga ■ Chelation therapy ■ Oxygen therapy ■ Traditional Chinese medicine ■ Ayurvedic medicine ■ Herbals include: garlic, Siberian ginseng—limit intake to one-month rounds—and onion ■ Herbal caution: Excessive doses of ginger might have cardiotonic activity that can interfere with therapy for heart conditions
Male or Female Directives	■ Men between 35 and 65 and women between 45 and 65 should be screened for risk factors of heart disease ■ Women with polycystic ovary syndrome (PCOS) have rich factors for premature Coronary Artery Disease (CAD)
Best Nutritional Strategies	■ Keep saturated fat intake low—⅓ or less of total intake ■ Increase omega-3 fatty acids, especially from fish sources ■ Minimize consumption of refined carbohydrates ■ Increase consumption of soluble fiber, such as oat bran ■ Eat garlic, hot red pepper (chile) and shiitake mushrooms frequently ■ Drink green tea regularly ■ Eat plenty of fresh fruits and vegetables, including leafy greens, beta-carotene–rich and flavonoid-rich fruits and vegetables ■ Eat soy foods and other legumes regularly
Supplements or Functional Foods to Consider	■ Flax and products with flax in them ■ Vitamins B6, B12, C, E ■ Folic acid ■ Coenzyme Q10 ■ Selenium ■ Magnesium ■ Calcium ■ Chromium ■ Potassium ■ Functional foods such as Benecol (a type of margarine) ■ Large doses of aspirin may cause urinary loss of vitamin C

Hyperlipidemias—High Cholesterol, High Triglycerides or Both

When your blood has more fat in it than is healthy, this is called hyperlipidemia (lipid meaning fat).

Weight loss may be more important to overweight men with hyperlipidemia than changes in the dietary fat composition. And blood cholesterol levels drop as much as 33 percent in just 2 weeks when women boost their intakes of produce and watch their caloric intake.

High Cholesterol

Make a date with your healthcare provider to have your lipid panel taken. Fast for 12 hours before. Ask for a copy of the results. Use the "Get to Know Your Lipid Values" form to analyze and record your lipids—total cholesterol, LDL ("bad") cholesterol, HDL ("good") cholesterol and triglycerides. Use the suggestions in the far right column to change your eating habits to reduce or increase certain foods, as your lipid panel indicates.

Nutritional Recommendations for Modifying Lifestyle Choices

The biggest recommendation is switching to a low-fat diet, a major factor responsible for lowering plasma cholesterol levels. Increasing fiber is a great adjunct to low-fat food choices. Just 5 grams to 10 grams of soluble fiber will reduce serum total cholesterol by approximately 5 percent. You'll want to choose low-fat meat and dairy foods because these foods contain higher levels of cholesterol.

Soluble fibers like oat bran help decrease total cholesterol almost twice as well as insoluble fibers such as wheat bran.

Raising Cholesterol

These are additional things that can raise your cholesterol levels:
- coffee
- stress
- sustained tension
- alcohol
- steroids
- oral contraceptives
- Lasix (a common water pill) and other diuretics
- L-Dopa (a medication used for Parkinson's disease)

Get to Know Your Lipid Values

Date: _____

	Lab Value Goals	Lab Values	Foods & Activities that Can Improve Your Labs
Total Cholesterol	■ Less than 200 mg/dl		■ Follow your movement/exercise prescription from your physician or physical therapist
LDL ("bad")	■ Individuals without other identified risks: 130 mg/dl or less ■ Individuals with diabetes and other risk factors: 100 mg/dl or less		■ Reduce saturated fat sources, including deep-fried foods, high-fat dairy, red meats, chocolate, high-fat desserts
HDL ("good")	■ Women: 55 mg/dl or greater ■ Men: 45 mg/dl or greater		■ Eat more foods with monounsaturated fatty acids such as olive oil, canola oil, low-fat soy oil, low-fat peanut oil, peanuts and other nuts, avocado
Cholesterol/ HDL Ratio	■ 4.5 or less (divide total cholesterol by HDL)		■ Eat 5 or more servings of fruits and vegetables every day
Triglycerides	■ Less than 200 mg/dl		■ Follow LDL guidelines above and reduce carbohydrate intake ■ Abstain from alcohol or limit to 1 to 2 drinks or fewer per day ■ Limit juices, simple sugars (like table sugar), desserts and soft drinks with added sugars ■ Eat fish high in omega-3 fatty acids

Hyperlipidemias

Reasons to Be Concerned (Inherited Traits and Environmental Factors)	■ See risk factors in this chapter ■ High-fat diet and sedentary lifestyle increase risk ■ Very high levels of triglycerides—greater than 800 mg/dL—may lead to pancreatitis ■ Genetics is very strong risk factor—1 out of every 500 individuals has a form of or inherited familial hyperlipoproteinemias
Western Medicine Recommendations	■ "Statin" drugs ■ Nicotinic acid ■ Bile acid binders ■ Smoking cessation ■ Exercise ■ Control diabetes (elevated blood sugars)
Integrative Therapy	■ Stress reduction techniques (increased stress levels cause cravings for fats and sugar) ■ Herbals include: barley, evening primrose oil, flax, garlic, glucomannan, oats, onion, psyllium and yogurt ■ Red rice yeast (available in Canada and Mexico) contains a natural "statin"
Male or Female Directives	■ Men have the higher risk until women enter menopause
Best Nutritional Strategies	■ Lose weight (if overweight) ■ Increase physical activity ■ Quit smoking ■ Increase water-soluble fiber sources ■ Increase intake of omega-3 fatty acids—sources of eicosapentaenoic acid (EPA) and docosahexaenoic (DHA)
Supplements or Functional Foods to Consider	■ Benocol, Take Control and Smart Balance (margarines) ■ Visit your local grocer and look for claims to have no or reduced trans fatty acid contents on the labels of the foods you buy

Hypertension— High Blood Pressure

There's an old wives' tale about your blood pressure's top number being 100 plus your age, and people still ask if this is true. It's not! Then the question comes: Which number is more important, the top or the bottom? They're both important. The top number tells you the pressure that the heart is beating against during a contraction or pumping action, and the lower number is the amount of pressure as the heart is in its resting phase, relaxing between contractions.

But what's normal? A normal blood pressure that doesn't require action is 130/85. If you're below that, it's recommended to recheck in 2 years. If you're above either number, check with your healthcare provider.

Nutritional Recommendations for Modifying Lifestyle Choices

Designed to help beat high blood pressure, the DASH eating plan is low in saturated fat, cholesterol and total fat. With an emphasis on fruits, vegetables and low-fat dairy foods, the DASH plan is balanced with whole grains, lean meats and nuts. Suggesting foods that are low in sodium and rich in magnesium, potassium, calcium, protein and fiber, DASH adds foods to your diet rather than taking them away and helps reduce cholesterol levels in addition to controlling blood pressure. Most DASH plan eaters see results within just 2 weeks!

Treating Hypertension with Herbs

Natural medicines often recommended for high blood pressure include garlic, Siberian ginseng, hawthorn and onion. These proven options are safe, for the most part. Studies have documented the blood pressure–lowering effect of garlic, Siberian ginseng and onion. Studies (including a small number of human studies) have shown that hawthorn is able to dilate blood vessels, especially coronary blood vessels, thus lowering blood pressure. However, hawthorn must be used with caution, as high doses can cause dangerously low blood pressure and sedation.

Use caution with barberry, forskolin (and coleonol), kudzu, motherwort, olive leaf and yucca. Studies are either absent or conflicting regarding their effectiveness and safety.

Following the DASH Diet

This DASH eating plan is based on consuming 2,000 calories daily. The number of daily servings in a food group may vary from those listed depending on your caloric needs. This chart can help you plan your menus or do your grocery shopping.

Food Group	Daily† Servings	Serving Sizes	Examples and Notes	Significance of Food Group
Grains and grain products	7 to 8	■ 1 slice bread ■ ½ cup dry cereal* ■ ½ cup cooked rice, pasta or cereal	whole wheat bread, English muffin, pita bread, bagel, cereals, grits, oatmeal	major sources of energy and fiber
Vegetables	4 to 5	■ 1 cup raw leafy vegetable ■ ½ cup cooked vegetable ■ 6 oz. vegetable juice	tomatoes, potatoes, carrots, peas, squash, broccoli, turnip greens, collards, kale, spinach, artichokes, sweet potatoes, beans	rich sources of potassium, magnesium and fiber
Fruits	4 to 5	■ 6 oz. fruit juice ■ 1 medium fruit ■ ¼ cup dried fruit ■ ½ cup fresh, frozen, or canned fruit	apricots, bananas, dates, oranges, orange juice, grapefruit, grapefruit juice, mangoes, melons, peaches, pineapples, prunes, raisins, strawberries, tangerines	important sources of potassium, magnesium and fiber
Low-fat or nonfat dairy foods	2 to 3	■ 8 oz. milk ■ 1 cup yogurt ■ 1.5 oz. cheese	skim or 1% milk, skim or low-fat buttermilk, nonfat or low-fat yogurt, part-skim mozzarella cheese, nonfat cheese	major sources of calcium and protein

†Except as noted

Food Group	Daily† Servings	Serving Sizes	Examples and Notes	Significance of Food Group
Meats, poultry and fish	2 or less	▪ 3 oz. cooked meats, poultry or fish	select only lean; trim away visible fats; broil, roast or boil instead of frying; remove skin from poultry	rich sources of protein and magnesium
Nuts, seeds and dry beans	4 to 5 per week	▪ 1.5 oz. or ⅓ cup nuts ▪ ½ oz. or 2 Tbsp. seeds ▪ ½ cup cooked legumes	almonds, filberts, mixed nuts, peanuts, walnuts, sunflower seeds, kidney beans, lentils	rich sources of energy, magne-sium, potassium, protein and fiber
Fats and oils**	2 to 3	▪ 1 tsp. soft mar-garine ▪ 1 Tbsp. low-fat mayonnaise ▪ 2 Tbsp. light salad dressing ▪ 1 tsp. vegetable oil	soft margarine, low-fat mayonnaise, light salad dressing, veg-etable oil (such as olive, corn, canola or safflower)	DASH has 27 percent of calories as fat, including that in or added to foods
Sweets	5 per week	▪ 1 Tbsp. sugar ▪ 1 Tbsp. jelly or jam ▪ ½ oz. jelly beans ▪ 8 oz. lemonade	Maple syrup, sugar, jelly, jam, fruit-flavored gelatin, jelly beans, hard candy, fruit punch, sorbet, ices	sweets should be low in fat

†Except as noted
  * Equals ½ to 1¼ cup, depending on cereal type. Check the product's nutrition label.
** Fat content changes serving counts for fats and oils: For example, 1 Tbsp. of regular salad dressing equals 1 serving; 1 Tbsp. of a low-fat dressing equals ½ serving; 1 Tbsp. of a fat-free dressing equals 0 servings.

Source: National Heart, Lung, and Blood Institute

Hypertension

Reasons to Be Concerned (Inherited Traits and Environmental Factors)	■ See risk factors in this chapter ■ 50,000,000 Americans with high blood pressure (hypertension) ■ 38 percent of all African Americans, and 29 percent of all Caucasians ■ Only 2 out of 3 with hypertension are diagnosed ■ Of those diagnosed, 75 percent receive medications; about 45 percent receive adequate treatment
Western Medicine Recommendations	■ Weight loss ■ Exercise ■ Many blood pressure medications are prescribed: 　■ Diuretics 　■ Beta-blockers 　■ ACE inhibitors 　■ ARB drugs (Angiotensin Receptor Blockers) 　■ Calcium channel blockers 　■ Vasodilators
Integrative Therapy	■ Yoga ■ Herbals include: garlic, Siberian ginseng, hawthorn and onion ■ Excessive doses might increase or reduce blood pressure, interfering with blood pressure control ■ Detoxification ■ Ayurvedic medicine ■ Traditional Chinese medicine
Male or Female Directives	■ None available
Best Nutritional Strategies	■ Increase fruits and vegetables ■ Increase foods rich in calcium, magnesium and potassium (see chapter 2) ■ Avoid salted and salty foods, such as processed foods ■ Eat garlic regularly, one to two cloves a day or equivalent ■ Moderate alcohol consumption
Supplements or Foods	■ None noted

Congestive Heart Failure (CHF)

How can someone live a healthy life if they have a heart that's failed? Congestive heart failure refers to a failure of the heart to pump blood adequately to either the lungs or to the rest of the body. The most common cause is weakening of the heart muscle from a heart attack or viral or toxic damage. Another cause of failure stems from increased work (due to high blood pressure, valve problems, scarring or fibrosis of the heart muscle). The inability of the heart to pump "up to par" may cause fluid backup in the lungs or in the extremities. Symptoms reflecting this situation are puffy feet and/or shortness of breath.

Medical treatment options include use of diuretics (water pills) to decrease the fluid load, ACE (angiotensin-converting enzyme) inhibitors to reduce pressure that the heart has to work against, cautious use of beta-blockers (may improve prognosis) and use of medications to strengthen the heart's pump (like digoxin).

Nutritional Recommendations for Modifying Lifestyle Choices

See additional recommendations in accompanying chart.

Treating CHF with Herbs

Hawthorn is a natural medicine touted for treatment of congestive heart failure. Human and animal studies have proven it can dilate blood vessels, especially coronary arteries (heart blood vessels). Study participants experienced improvement in heart function, fewer palpitations and less shortness of breath.

Congestive Heart Failure

Reasons to Be Concerned (Inherited Traits and Environmental Factors)	■ See risk factors in this chapter ■ 400,000 new cases diagnosed each year ■ 70 percent mortality rate per 10 years of active disease
Western Medicine Recommendations	■ Cardiac rehabilitation programs increase strength ■ 35 percent risk of death using common beta-blockers (metoprolol/atenolol/labetolol) ■ Weigh at least every third day—increase in weight between 3 and 5 pounds usually indicates regain of fluid; call your healthcare provider ■ Individualized plan for balance between activity and rest
Integrative Therapy	■ Herbals include: hawthorn
Male or Female Directives	■ Not applicable—varies with underlying condition that causes CHF
Best Nutritional Strategies	■ Keep saturated fat intake low ■ Increase omega-3 fatty acids, especially from fish sources ■ Minimize consumption of refined carbohydrates ■ Increase consumption of soluble fiber, such as oat bran ■ Eat garlic, hot red pepper (chile) and shiitake mushrooms frequently ■ Drink green tea regularly ■ Eat plenty of fresh fruits and vegetables, including leafy greens, beta-carotene–rich and flavonoid-rich foods ■ Eat soy foods and other legumes regularly
Supplements or Functional Foods to Consider	■ Visit your local grocer and read nutrition labels to determine the amount of sodium in the foods you buy

Stroke

Half a million people in America suffer a stroke every year. And even more suffer from TIAs (transient ischemic attacks, or mini-strokes). Yet despite this large number and the fact that stroke is the third leading cause of death in the United States, it still seems to be a mystery disease. Thankfully, two-thirds of stroke victims survive, but prompt medical help can greatly reduce side effects.

Many people can't name the signs or symptoms of a stroke. Some people are still a little unsure of what it is. Just as the coronary arteries can become blocked by plaque and cause a heart attack, so the arteries supplying the brain can become blocked, which can cause a stroke.

The symptoms are:

- sudden numbness or loss of function on one side of your body, or in one extremity
- sudden severe headache
- sudden vision change
- sudden inability to speak or to understand what is being said

Clot-Buster Therapy

If you have a sudden onset of any of these symptoms, go to the emergency room immediately. Do not pass go; do not collect $200. There are new medications (clot-buster drugs) that can dissolve blood clots, but they can only be used in the first 3 hours from the start of symptoms. And because a stroke can be caused by a blood clot or an episode of bleeding in the brain, which causes a lack of oxygen to brain tissues, a CT scan must be done to rule out a bleed. Then,

within the proper time frame, the clot-buster drugs can be given to break up the blood clot and, hopefully, lessen the long-term disabling effects of stroke.

The use of early CT scanning and clot-buster drugs has decreased the risk of dying from a stroke to less than half of what it was 20 years ago. Two-thirds of all stroke victims now survive, and many of them do so with limited long-term problems.

Nutritional Recommendations for Modifying Lifestyle Choices

Glucose control is especially important in diabetes and one reason is to lessen your risks of other conditions that develop when blood sugar remains high and uncontrolled. When blood sugars do become high over a significant period of time, your risk for high lipid levels, high blood pressure, heart attack and stroke all increase.

Whole Grain Foods Are Winners

Higher intakes of whole grain foods are associated with a lower risk of ischemic stroke in women, independent of known cardiovascular disease (CVD). A study of 75,521 American women, aged 38 to 63, without previous diabetes mellitus, coronary heart disease, stroke or other CVD in 1984, completed detailed food frequency questionnaires in 1984, 1986, 1990 and 1994. They were followed for 12 years as part of the Nurses' Health Study. Women who had 2.7 servings per day of whole grain had a 43 percent lower risk of ischemic stroke (a lack of oxygen to the brain) compared to the women taking the least whole grains. This association remained unchanged when two other factors—saturated fat and trans fatty acid intake—were compared.

Reduce Those Triglycerides

High triglycerides are not easy to treat. Eat a low-fat, low-cholesterol diet (see page 163) and monitor the amount of carbohydrate and alcohol you eat and drink at meals and snacks. See the information on carbohydrate counting in the section on diabetes to learn how to monitor your carbohydrate count. Even though high triglyceride levels are a problem with a storage form of the fat in your body, there is a second factor to monitor while trying to lower them. Excess carbohydrate plays a factor, and

Stroke	
Reasons to Be Concerned (Inherited Traits and Environmental Factors)	■ Family history a risk factor but no distinct genetic cause identified ■ 2,000,000 persons in the United States—10 to 20 per 100,000 persons older than 65 years of age ■ One year mortality: 28 to 40 percent
Western Medicine Recommendations	■ Antiplatelet therapy—aspirin, clopidogrel (Plavix) or ticlopidine reduces the risk of subsequent stroke ■ ECG ■ Potential for other tests ■ CT scan/MRI or x-ray angiography ■ Statin drugs ■ Labs
Integrative Therapy	■ Hyperbaric oxygen chamber—used in West Germany ■ Cardiologist William Lee Cowden, M.D., provides his patients with a combination of high antioxidants, essential fatty acids and either hyperbaric oxygen therapy or ozone therapy within the first 12 hours after stroke. He believes these treatments reduce symptoms, improve strength and mental clarity, and increase orientation, motor and sensory skills. Treatment includes: vitamin E, beta-carotene, ascorbyl palmitate (a fat-soluble form of vitamin C), pycnogenol (a fat-soluble antioxidant found in pine needles and bark) and essential fatty acids eicosapentaenoic acid (EPA) and docosahexaenoic acid (DHA).

particularly excess carbohydrate eaten at any one time.

If bothered by elevated triglycerides, most of us will want to keep our carbohydrate count at meals and snacks between 30 and 60 grams. Complex carbohydrates like whole grains, starches, fruits and vegetables work well. Avoid having more than one serving of fruit at a time. You can have a second and third fruit portion at another meal or snack.

Limit the amount of alcohol, candy and desserts that you eat. Even these foods can be figured into a carbohydrate pattern.

Even though alcohol is not a carbohydrate, and has just slightly more calories per gram than carbohydrate, you are usually safe in dividing the calories in an alcoholic beverage by 4 and using that number of grams in a similar manner to grams of carbohydrate, for the purpose of counting. Depending on the level of

Stroke *continued*	
Integrative Therapy *continued*	■ Margaret A. Naeser, Ph.D., of Boston University School of Medicine and a licensed acupuncturist, conducted research on the use of low-energy lasers in the treatment of paralysis. Improvements were observed even when treatments were begun 3 or 4 years after the stroke. Other approaches can be found in this source.
Male or Female Directives	■ 30 percent higher incidence in males
Best Nutritional Strategies	■ See additional strategies in this section
Supplements or Functional Foods to Consider	■ Eicosapentaenoic acids (EPAs) ■ Visit your local grocer and read labels for the total fat and preferred sources such as monounsaturated and polyunsaturated; total calories; and sodium content

triglycerides, the diagnosis and severity of the case, you can have one to two drinks—single shots or lite beers—each day, once the triglycerides have returned to a normal range.

Israeli researchers, who followed 11,177 men and women who had coronary heart disease but no history of stroke for 6 to 8 years, had study participants who suffered a total of 487 ischemic strokes. After adjusting for other risk factors, on average, the stroke patients had higher blood triglyceride levels—above 200 mg/dL—and lower high-density lipoprotein (HDL, or "good") cholesterol levels than the non-stroke patients. These study participants had a 27 percent increased risk of stroke compared to those with lower levels. Therefore, high triglyceride levels may directly contribute to blocked arteries and have also been linked to abnormalities in blood clotting.

The American Heart Association recommends keeping blood triglyceride levels below 150 mg/dL. See the earlier section on dyslipidemias for other suggestions to help avoid foods that contribute to the production of triglycerides.

In one of the first large studies of its kind, the eating habits of 75,000 women were scrutinized. Harvard epidemiologist Kaumudi J. Joshipura found that for each daily serving of fruit and veggies study participants had, there was a 7 percent reduction in the incidence of stroke. The majority of strokes are described as ischemic—caused by a clot that blocks the flow of blood to the brain. Fruits and vegetables are packed with a variety of heart-friendly nutrients like fiber, potassium and other B vitamins, not to mention a variety of antioxidants.

Specific foods seemed to have an effect in this study. Participants with the lowest risk ate cruciferous foods like broccoli, cabbage, cauliflower, leafy greens and citrus fruit. Potatoes and legumes did not have a measurable risk-lowering effect. The most benefit was seen when individuals in the study had eaten about 6 servings from the fruit and vegetable category each day. This is considerably more than most Americans eat. Consumption data suggest that most Americans eat between 2.5 and 4 servings of fruits and vegetables each day. The goal, of course, is to get 5 or more servings of fruits and vegetables a day.

Serving size does count when meeting your fruit and vegetable consumption goal, and when limiting carbohydrate sources to better control production of triglycerides. Common sense will usually rule, but ½ cup is often the serving of fresh and frozen (without sugar) fruits and vegetables. Naturally, a serving of dried fruit is less, because it is nutrient-dense; servings of some favorite fruits, such as strawberries and most melons, are larger.

Heartburn/Gastro-esophageal Reflux Disease (GERD)

You eat a really spicy meal. You overeat (again) at a great party. Or … you've chosen tonight as the one night you're gonna go all out—whole hog, as it were—and have a lot of the food that everybody says is bad for you. After all, you've been following a lower-fat diet pretty well. So tonight it's a big, greasy pork chop, baked potato with butter and sour cream, and don't forget the double Tequila Sunrise. You guessed it. An hour later, burning pain goes shooting up under your breastbone (sternum). It can be severe enough to make you think you're having a heart attack. What do you have? Probably heartburn, the most common symptom of GERD (Gastroesophageal Reflux Disease) or, more simply, reflux.

It's Not Acid Rock!

GERD happens when the acid from your stomach backs up into the lower part of your esophagus (the tube that takes food to your stomach and air to your lungs), and causes an irritation to that area. Think about it. You wouldn't put your hand into a bucket of acid because it would hurt. That tissue in the esophagus doesn't like acid either, so it may become inflamed, sore, tender or just plain painful. That's heartburn. If this happens repeatedly for a long period of time, we say that you have reflux disease.

There are also tests to help diagnose reflux:

- recorded symptoms for 24 hours (along with a pH recording)
- esophageal manometry
- standard acid reflux test
- acid clearance tests
- x-rays—upper GI series
- upper GI endoscopy (looking into the throat and stomach with a scope)

Eating Better to Prevent or Treat Heartburn and GERD

- Avoid or limit fat intake and make sure to take in enough protein (see lower-fat foods listed in the section on cholesterol).
- Avoid—or limit—irritants (chocolate, alcohol, mint, carbonated beverages, citrus juices, tomato products, coffee—both decaf and caffeinated).
- Make sure you're sitting in an upright position during eating.
- Stop smoking.
- Loosen your belt or unbutton your pants. Avoid constricting clothes in the abdominal area.
- Don't eat within 3 hours of bedtime.
- Raise the head of your bed about 6 inches.

Nutritional Recommendations for Modifying Lifestyle Choices

Some small changes in your eating can make a big difference in how much heartburn you have. In the examples above, they did almost everything wrong. Many foods (caffeine, citrus, carbonated drinks) act as irritants to already inflamed tissue. See sidebar on guidelines for eating better.

Another way you can feel better is to eat foods that will soothe that inflammation, and even act like an antacid. These foods include common-sense foods that may seem bland:

- skim (nonfat) milk (decreases the pressure on the esophageal sphincter)
- steamed or boiled vegetables
- unbuttered rice, pasta or potatoes (baked or boiled)
- gelatin and puddings
- non-citrus fruits, such as apples, peaches and pears

Treatment with medications can range from drugs like Pepcid AC and Tagament (proton pump inhibitors) to standard antacids (which decrease acid) to cisapride (prokinetic agents). Making the recommended changes in your food choices is especially important because this is a lifelong disease.

Heartburn	
Reasons to Be Concerned (Inherited Traits and Environmental Factors)	■ Heartburn occurs in more than 60 percent of adults ■ More than 80 percent of pregnant women ■ Almost 20 percent of adults use over-the-counter (OTC) H2 blockers or antacids at least once a week ■ Hiatal hernia may be present in well more than half of persons with GERD; however, hiatal hernia may not be identified because it does not cause symptoms ■ Lifestyle modifications must be followed lifelong, since this is generally an irreversible condition—recurrence of reflux is common if treatment is discontinued
Western Medicine Recommendations	■ Pepcid, Zantac, Tagamet, Prilosec, over-the-counter (OTC) antacids (Maalox, Mylanta) ■ Prolonged and untreated GERD probably has a causal relationship with esophageal adenocarcinoma ■ Avoid clothes that may be overly tight and contribute to experiencing GERD

Heartburn *continued*

Integrative Therapy	■ No specific therapies because this is a symptom experienced with multiple diseases
Male or Female Directives	■ No difference between men and women
Best Nutritional Strategies	■ Avoid foods that lower the lower esophageal sphincter (LES) pressure: chocolate, yellow onions, peppermint, spearmint, coffee; fatty or spicy foods (such as pizza), citrus fruits, tomatoes, whole milk and alcohol ■ Some foods like skim milk may help increase the pressure on the LES ■ Eat small, more frequent meals with light snacks between— avoid eating 3 to 4 hours before going to bed ■ Elevate the head of the bed at least 6 inches—bending at the waist increases pressure in the abdomen and stomach and increases reflux
Supplements or Functional Foods to Consider	■ None known

HIV/AIDS

HIV/AIDS certainly demands our attention and concern. Did you know that more and more older people are getting HIV/AIDS? The infection rate among heterosexuals is increasing. Statistics from the Centers for Disease Control and Prevention (CDC) indicate that the cases of HIV/AIDS in the over-50 group have increased 22 percent within 5 years. A greater proportion of older adults may be infected because of underdiagnosis and misdiagnosis. Current estimates are that we are close to the one million mark—one million Americans infected with the HIV virus. Only one in 10 HIV-infected persons know they carry the virus. And remember there is no cure, only treatment.

There's a silly assumption that older adults aren't sexually active. Wrong. Some doctors may be less likely to suspect and advise older folks to test for a sexually transmitted disease (STD). They may have other health problems that mask HIV/AIDS. Cervical cancer and recurrent yeast infections in women may be signs of HIV/AIDS that go unrecognized. HIV infections may occur without symptoms or with a variety of symptoms. They include cough, fever and weight loss. These symptoms are also associated with other conditions, such as tuberculosis, cancer, respiratory infections and pneumonia.

The human immunodeficiency virus (HIV) is the cause of AIDS (Acquired Immune Deficiency Syndrome). HIV attacks and depletes the immune system, leading to the development of an AIDS-defining complication.

HIV is usually transmitted by sexual contact (70 percent of cases) or use of contaminated needles. It is transmitted only rarely through blood transfusions or other means. People who had blood transfusions before 1985 may want to consider being tested. Since then, the U.S. blood supply has been carefully screened for the presence of HIV.

Nutritional Recommendations for Modifying Lifestyle Choices

Because of the magnitude and complexity of HIV/AIDS, we will deal principally with battling lack of appetite and weight loss.

The arsenal of powerful drugs used in HIV/AIDS treatment is overwhelming, and many of these drug therapy treatments may make you sick. They may cause your appetite to wane and your weight to slip away.

Older HIV-positive adults sometimes suffer from lipodystrophy. The definition is evolving and means the fat redistribution syndrome. Alan Lee, R.D., a nutritionist working for a community-based organization in New York City, finds a challenge in drawing the distinction between lipodystrophy and the normal aging process in HIV-positive clients.

It is well established that anorexia and cachexia (weight loss in patients with chronic illness) are directly associated with survival rates in patients with HIV infection. Wasting is the unintentional loss of at least 10 percent of normal weight as often seen in HIV/AIDS patients. In a recent study, 42 percent of the patients experienced clinical wasting while taking highly active antiretroviral therapy.

Weight loss can be a sign that your overall condition is deteriorating.

Wasting syndrome is a very serious condition. Try to identify appetite changes and weight loss early on, before they become significant.

Herbal Therapy for HIV/AIDS

Have you ever put aloe vera on a burn to help it heal? Acemannan, a derivative of that same plant, is now being injected experimentally for patients with HIV/AIDS, and shows some success in improving survival times. Marijuana (yes, smoking marijuana—or taking a capsule of it) has proven beneficial in diminishing nausea and pain in some individuals, as well as stimulating the appetite. The active ingredient, THC, is available in a prescription pill format (marinol).

Do not use the herbs Chinese cucumber and skullcap. Studies are either absent or conflicting regarding their effectiveness and safety. But many other herbs are proving helpful, such as Huang qi, gentian, garlic, milk thistle and acidophilus.

HIV/AIDS	
Reasons to Be Concerned (Inherited Traits and Environmental Factors)	■ HIV has a long "dormant" period (median time from HIV positive to AIDS is 11 years) ■ Persons at most risk for HIV: IV drug users sharing needles, persons selling sexual favors, persons practicing unsafe and unprotected sexual behaviors, receipt of blood transfusion in a country or from an agency that does not test for HIV
Western Medicine Recommendations	■ Treat fever, weight loss and anorexia ■ Exercise ■ Antiretroviral therapies ■ AZT (severe side effects) ■ Antivirals ■ Antibiotics to treat pneumonia ■ Prednisone to decrease inflammation (especially with pneumonia) ■ Amphotericin B with flucytosine (for complication of meningitis) ■ Clotrimazole for oral yeast infections ■ T-cell count monitoring ■ New treatments are allowing HIV/AIDS patients to live longer
Integrative Therapy	■ Anabolic corticosteroids ■ Anticytokine agents ■ Yoga *continued on next page*

HIV/AIDS *continued*	
Integrative Therapy *continued*	■ Herbs such as aloe vera are being injected experimentally ■ Marijuana ■ Acupuncture ■ Hyperthermia (heat therapy) ■ Oxygen therapy ■ Mind/body medicine ■ Massage therapy ■ Biofeedback ■ Guided imagery and meditation ■ Aromatherapy ■ Homeopathy ■ Magnetic field therapy ■ Enzyme therapy ■ Traditional Chinese medicine
Male or Female Directives	■ At the current time, males and females are equally likely to contract this disease
Best Nutritional Strategies	■ Nutritional counseling ■ Two drugs that stimulate appetite are Marinol and Megace ■ Ensure and other similar supplements ■ Advera ■ Supplements with arginine ■ Avert/replete weight loss ■ Prevent/replete lean body mass (LBM) ■ Reduce nausea and diarrhea ■ Improve appetite
Supplements or Functional Foods to Consider	■ None known

Kidney Disease, Chronic (Chronic Renal Failure)

Do you know where your kidneys are? Do you know exactly what they do? Most people, if they're answering honestly, will say "no" to both questions. If you'd ask a few of the rowdier high school students where the kidneys are, though, they'd know, because they've taken a "kidney shot." In other words, someone punched them in the back, about the level of the waistline, on either side of the spine. Ow!

Your kidneys are vital organs and two of the best friends you can have. They filter out much of the "garbage" in your system and control the production of your red blood cells. They regulate your blood pressure while balancing your fluids and electrolytes (things like sodium, potassium and chloride).

What is Chronic Kidney Disease?

Chronic kidney disease (also called chronic renal failure) is the result of some process (infection, trauma, heredity, cysts, diabetes, lupus, hypertension, toxic chemicals) that has caused long-term, and usually irreparable, kidney damage, so the kidneys can't perform one or more of those vital functions. Your doctor can diagnose kidney disease with blood tests, x-ray, ultrasound and imaging procedures. If the damage progresses, you will probably be referred for dialysis.

Dialysis is the procedure of cleaning out the waste in the bloodstream. Either the blood itself is removed, cleaned and recycled, or a fluid solution is flushed through the abdomen and drained out. Remember that dialysis is a temporary treatment (even though some people stay on dialysis for years), and the definitive treatment is really a kidney transplant.

Can Eating the Right Foods Help?

One of the most important aspects of treating chronic kidney disease is what you choose to eat. There are some things that actually add to the amount of waste that's produced in the system, including proteins, sodium, potassium, calcium and phosphorus. However, don't just assume that we'd want to eliminate these important dietary needs. Depending on the treatment used, these nutrients and electrolytes may be encouraged or restricted. You may need to eat fewer calories when receiving abdominal dialysis because your body will retain some of the sugar that's used in the solution.

Often, you'll hear of people needing to cut back on the amount of protein if they have chronic kidney problems. This is a common dietary plan. However, when you limit your protein to less than 50 grams a day, you will get inadequate amounts of these nutrients:

- calcium
- iron
- thiamine
- riboflavin
- niacin
- folic acid

Because protein-energy malnutrition (or low levels of the nutrients listed) has been proven to increase morbidity and mortality risks, supplementation may be needed. In this case, your dietitian may recommend a daily multivitamin that includes folic acid. However, often you won't need extra fat-soluble vitamins (A, E and K). There are even cases of vitamin A toxicity in chronic kidney disease. Taking supplements for calcium and iron is done on an individualized basis, based on lab studies.

Next, it's important to realize that some of the treatments for chronic kidney disease may actually cause more problems for the body. Dialysis drains the body of vitamin B6 and folic acid. The dialysate (dialysis solution) may have extra sugar that's retained in the body, so you may gain weight, or have to reduce your intake of calories. Always check with a registered dietitian when adjusting food intake and vitamin or herbal supplementation if you have chronic kidney disease.

Herbal Therapy

Herbal remedies that are recommended for chronic kidney disease include artichoke, asparagus and birch. The extract from artichoke, called cynarin, has been used to treat kidney inflammation, and some studies have shown it to have a diuretic property (causing the body to get rid of excess fluids). Caution: Asparagus root has been used to prevent kidney stones and treat some inflammatory diseases in the urinary tract, but is not proven as safe for that use. In animal studies, birch was seen to: increase urine output, lessen inflammation and infection and prevent kidney stones from forming. Steer clear of horsetail and nettle. Studies are either absent or conflicting regarding their effectiveness and safety.

Kidney Disease, Chronic

Reasons to Be Concerned (Inherited Traits and Environmental Factors)	■ Some cases of vitamin A toxicity have been reported in renal failure ■ Conditions that can cause this disease: chronic hypertension (high blood pressure); diabetes; polycystic kidney and many others
Western Medicine Recommendations	■ Protein restriction ■ ACEs and ARBs (2 blood pressure medication types) may improve kidney function (especially in diabetes)
Integrative Therapy	■ Herbals include: artichoke, asparagus root (not herb) and birch. Herbal caution—individuals with swelling due to impaired heart or kidney function should not use this preparation) ■ Cranberry has been shown to be effective for urinary tract infections (UTIs), and goldenrod works for acute kidney inflammation, but not chronic disease. (Always drink lots of fluids when taking an herb with diuretic properties. Avoid the herb if you have ever had an allergic reaction to other members of the daisy family, like ragweed.)
Male or Female Directives	■ Equal incidence male and females (49 percent male and 51 percent female)
Best Nutritional Strategies	■ The following may be either restricted or encouraged (depending on treatment used): sodium, potassium, calcium, phosphorus and protein ■ Protein restriction may cause deficiencies in calcium, iron, thiamine, riboflavin, niacin and folic acid
Supplements or Functional Foods to Consider	■ Generally, B vitamin and folic acids are supplemented, especially in dialysis patients ■ Do not supplement the fat-soluble vitamins (A, K, E)

Liver Disease: Chronic Hepatitis & Cirrhosis

There are five identified forms of viral hepatitis: Hepatitis A, Hepatitis B, Hepatitis C, Hepatitis D and Hepatitis E. Hepatitis (or inflammation of the liver) can be acute or chronic, and Hepatitis B and C are the most common causes of chronic hepatitis from infection. Other common causes of chronic hepatitis are alcohol, drugs and toxic chemicals. Your liver acts like a giant filter, cleaning out toxins from your system. When the toxins are more than the liver can handle, the liver can get inflamed; then liver damage can occur. What are common signs and symptoms? Jaundice (yellowing of the skin or whites of the eyes), a brownish/yellow tint in the urine, abdominal pain, unexplained fatigue and flulike symptoms (fever, loss of appetite, nausea and vomiting).

Likely contributing factors in contracting hepatitis include:

- working in healthcare, such as in medical laboratories or in dialysis, or in healthcare situations where needles/sharps are used and the unpredictable is expected, such as working in surgery or in an emergency room
- having a parent, sibling or child infected with hepatitis
- engaging in unprotected sex
- injecting drugs (illicit drug use)
- living in or being exposed to unsanitary conditions
- consuming contaminated food or water
- eating or handling raw shellfish

Cirrhosis is a condition in which liver tissue has been irreversibly and progressively destroyed as a result of infection, poison or some other disease. There are various causes and forms of cirrhosis:

- alcohol-induced cirrhosis
- cryptogenic cirrhosis (also know as post-hepatitis cirrhosis)
- primary biliary cirrhosis (chronic inflammation and scarring of the microscopic bile ducts within the liver)
- secondary biliary cirrhosis (results from prolonged obstruction of the common bile duct or one of its branches)
- hemochromatosis (an inherited disease primarily in men between the ages of 40 and 60 that causes the body to store excessively high amounts of iron)
- Wilson's disease (an inherited disorder in which copper accumulates in various organs of the body)
- deficiencies of enzymes that occur during liver development in infancy (rare)

Cirrhosis is very serious because the damage is irreversible. Each year in the United States, 30,000 people die from alcohol-related liver disorders. And with chronic viral hepatitis being the second leading cause of cirrhosis, great concern over the increasing number of these cases is real. The burden on the healthcare system within the next 15 years cannot be ignored.

Nutritional Recommendations for Modifying Lifestyle Choices

There is no specific diet for acute viral hepatitis. Maintain a well-balanced diet with adequate calories. People with cirrhosis must follow a salt-restricted, low-sodium diet to reduce fluid retention. They must also abstain from using alcohol and avoid other medications broken down in the liver. Vitamin supplements like K, A and D are often recommended. If one develops signs of encephalopathy, a low-protein diet may be prescribed.

Liver Disease: Chronic Hepatitis & Cirrhosis	
Reasons to Be Concerned (Inherited Traits and Environmental Factors)	■ Heavy alcohol users more likely to develop hepatitis and cirrhosis ■ Cirrhosis eleventh leading cause of death in United States. Chronic viral hepatitis progresses to cirrhosis ■ Chronic disease can result from the acute disease process with Hepatitis B, C, D, and E ■ Hepatitis D always has underlying Hepatitis B virus ■ History of blood transfusions increases risk of hepatitis ■ 3 million Americans have cirrhosis ■ IV drug users more likely to have cirrhosis
Western Medicine Recommendations	■ Monitor liver function regularly (blood tests) ■ Cirrhosis involves control of bleeding tendencies ■ Monitor electrolyte and lipid levels regularly ■ Hepatitis treatment includes rest, high fluid intake and well-rounded diet ■ Viral hepatitis is treated with corticosteroids ■ Cirrhosis is treated with medication such as Colchicine, diuretics, neomycin ■ Hepatitis B vaccine as preventive measure (especially in high-risk groups)
Integrative Therapy	■ Massage therapy ■ Acupuncture ■ In treatment of cirrhosis castor oil packs may help reduce swelling used externally—caution if castor oil is used internally—fat-soluble vitamins A, D, E, K may be depleted with long-term use

continued on next page

Liver Disease: Chronic Hepatitis & Cirrhosis *continued*	
Integrative Therapy *continued*	■ Homeopathy ■ Massage therapy ■ Acupuncture ■ Herbals include: aloe vera, milk thistle for alcohol-induced cirrhosis. Evening primrose oil may help protect the diseased liver. For cirrhosis, echinacea may boost immune support. Boldo is not indicated for diseases that involve bile, liver or kidney; do not use the volatile oil at all
Male or Female Directives	■ Hepatitis B and C rates higher in IV drug users who share needles and persons who engage in unprotected sex and sex practices where bodily fluids are shared ■ Hepatitis A (HAV) often affects school children ■ Other viral types most associated with older age groups
Best Nutritional Strategies	■ Lower-protein diet is often recommended to minimize stress on the liver. High-quality dietary protein including soy may be helpful with ascites (abdominal fluid retention) and for repairing muscle mass. There is no restriction on the amount of vegetable protein, such as soy ■ Abstain from the use of alcohol and other medications broken down in the liver ■ Increase amount of fresh fruits and vegetables ■ With cirrhosis manipulate fatty acids (reduce animal fats, increase fish and nuts) ■ During recovery from hepatitis eat small frequent meals controlled for sodium content to reduce fluid retention ■ Iron sources may be restricted in cases of cirrhosis
Supplements or Functional Foods to Consider	■ Omega-3 fatty acid supplements may help protect the diseased liver ■ Cirrhosis: Zinc supplements may reduce frequency and severity of muscle cramps and even help against encephalopathy (disorder in which brain function deteriorates because toxic substances build up in the blood) ■ Iron supplements would not be appropriate ■ May need supplements like vitamins A, D, E and K

Lung Disease, Chronic

It is the fourth leading cause of death in the United States. It affects at least 16 million Americans. Its most common forms are emphysema and chronic bronchitis. What is it? Chronic obstructive pulmonary disease (COPD), or chronic lung disease. Unlike asthma, which normally can be viewed as short-term difficulty with breathing, COPD is living with breathing problems every waking and nonwaking hour of your life, day in and day out.

COPD is really a group of disorders that all cause limited airflow and insufficient exchange of oxygen and carbon dioxide in the lungs. The diagnosis can be made after a thorough physical examination, chest x-rays, blood tests and a history of symptoms. In mild COPD, you might be tired or short of air after very heavy work. As the disease progresses, much less effort can result in a state of near or total exhaustion. Treatment often includes medications to dilate the bronchial and breathing tubes. Home oxygen may be ordered at some point.

Weight Loss Means Increased Risk of Rehospitalization

If you know someone who has COPD, you know that often they are undernourished. Why? Because the effort and energy that's used just for breathing saps all their stored energy. Consider this: A person with COPD actually burns between 430 and 720 calories per day, just in breathing. With so much energy given over to breathing, you can't really enjoy anything else, including eating, and you literally might not be able to eat. In fact, many with COPD suffer from anorexia. If you have COPD, losing weight actually adds to the risk of having to be readmitted to the hospital for your breathing disorder. A study published in *Clinical Nutrition* reported that weight loss during and after a hos-

"Burp" Foods

People with COPD should limit these foods as much as possible because they produce gas, which pushes your diaphragm up against your lungs, making it harder to breathe.

- Dried beans, peas and lentils
- Broccoli and brussels sprouts
- Cabbage and cauliflower
- Corn, cucumbers and leeks
- Melons
- Onions, scallions, peppers and pimientos
- Radishes, rutabagas, shallots and turnips
- Sauerkraut and raw apples
- Carbonated beverages and chewing gum

pital admission for COPD increases the risk for a second admission to the hospital. In other words, if you lost weight during or after an episode of illness, you're quite likely to be sick again soon.

Nutritional Recommendations for Modifying Lifestyle Choices

Let's stop the cycle. We do this with several recommendations:

- Eat a well-balanced diet, with smaller, more frequent meals, and consume higher-calorie and high-protein foods first.
- Avoid "burp" foods (see sidebar).
- Ensure high intake of fluids (2 to 4 quarts per day).
- Watch for weight gain and water retention when you take corticosteroids; see the food-drug caution regarding use of grapefruit juice found in the section on Asthma in this chapter.
- Pay attention to your weight (reduction if overweight; if underweight, stabilize weight loss and regain appropriately).
- Practice the energy-saving tips included in the sidebar.

Maintaining a well-balanced diet can be difficult if you are exhausted from the effort of breathing, or if eating requires too much work for your lungs. Smaller, more frequent meals help. So

Energy-Saving Tips— Eating with COPD

- Plan 30 minutes of rest time between preparing and eating meals.
- Eat during times when you're feeling "up."
- Consider more convenience foods (watch sodium if you are taking steroids).
- Use vegetables that don't require peeling.
- Prepare foods ahead of time and freeze.
- Check into sharing meals at meal sites, local "Meals on Wheels" programs and home meal replacement options (such as those found in your local grocery store).
- Use microwaves, food processors and mixers to save time.
- Keep nutritious snack foods at hand (milk, yogurt, crackers, fresh or dried fruit).
- Sit, instead of standing, to prepare foods (peeling, chopping and so on).

does eating slowly and not including a lot of fluid with your meal (this makes you feel too full). Avoid "burp" foods (again, they increase the feeling of fullness by putting pressure on the diaphragm and on the lungs). If you are underweight or losing weight, concentrate on eating your higher-calorie, higher-protein foods first.

Increasing your fluids to 2 to 4 quarts a day will keep mucus thin and easy to cough up. This is a common problem with COPD. On days when there is more mucus, consider acidic drinks like lemonade, orange juice or diet cola (unless you have an ulcer and these drinks are restricted). Use caution with alcohol and caffeinated drinks. These act as diuretics and increase your urine output, so in the long run, they dehydrate rather than hydrate. Some think that milk increases mucus formation, so they avoid it. Actually, it doesn't make the mucus thicker; it just coats the back of the throat. Rinsing the mouth with water after drinking milk will remedy this problem.

Corticosteroids (like Prednisone and Cortisone) are frequently prescribed in COPD to decrease inflammation in the tissues of the respiratory tract. But they can cause havoc with nutrition. Eat moderate calorie amounts and get regular exercise to stabilize weight and decrease weight gain. Limit salt to decrease water weight gain (puffiness and swelling due to retention). Include good protein sources because steroids can cause loss of body protein and muscle tissue. (See the sections in this chap-

ter on Cancer and Surgery.) Eat a balanced diet and consider supplementation for vitamins and minerals, especially vitamins C, D and B6, folate, calcium and zinc.

Start a Pulmonary Rehabilitation Program

"So, how exactly, would you propose to 'rehab' my lungs, especially if I have chronic lung disease?" This might be your question after you've been diagnosed with, or even if you've been living with, COPD. After all, if it's chronic, how can we rehab? By getting involved with a pulmonary rehabilitation program, that's how.

A pulmonary rehabilitation program is a combination of therapies, provided

Common Educational Components of Pulmonary Rehab Programs

Check your local pulmonary rehab program to see how many of these educational offerings are available.

- Nutrition and eating to reduce risk of lung problems
- Stress and stress-reduction techniques
- Structure and function of the lung and breathing anatomy
- Different lung problems, such as emphysema and asthma, and lung risk factors
- Pharmacy considerations for medications you take
- CPR and its importance
- Home-care equipment choices (for equipment and home oxygen)
- Emotional aspects of lung disease—support groups
- Stopping smoking
- Importance of exercise, and instructions for proper exercise
- Energy conservation
- Integrative therapies

by a team of health experts. Of course, exercising is important, but education about your disease and treatment options is just as important (see sidebar). And one of the biggest benefits is the fact that you are training yourself for a lifelong commitment to exercising regularly. That means you reduce your risk for other health disorders.

The foundation for pulmonary rehab is structured exercise. This means you will exercise while experienced respiratory therapists and physical therapists monitor your vital signs and oxygen level. Aerobic exercises are most commonly used: stationary bikes, recumbent (sitting) steppers, treadmills and arm exercisers. The goal for exercise is to increase the strength of the arms and particularly the legs, so the lungs don't have to work so hard while undergoing activity.

A crucial piece of the pulmonary rehab program is the education component. You'll learn how to prepare foods ahead of time to lessen the work at mealtimes and how to eat with the "most bang for your buck," choosing great nutritional foods so as to prevent having to eat in bulk—and much, much more. Attend as many education sessions as possible.

Lastly, graduates of pulmonary rehab programs simply feel better. Some talk about increased strength, others about less fear and anxiousness, and some sing praises of the camaraderie of being with others who have similar concerns and health issues.

If you've been diagnosed with chronic lung disease, ask your health-care provider about pulmonary rehab programs.

Lung Disease, Chronic

Reasons to Be Concerned (Inherited Traits and Environmental Factors)	■ Affects 16 million Americans, causes 80,000 deaths per year ■ Tobacco abuse is leading cause ■ Occupational exposure (breathing in toxins) ■ Air pollution
Western Medicine Recommendations	■ Stop smoking ■ Review options to be included in a pulmonary rehabilitation program ■ Medications include: bronchodilators (inhalers and oral), steroids (decrease inflammation), antibiotics for bronchitis or pneumonia ■ Oxygen therapy (O_2) as needed—even at home ■ Yearly flu shots and the pneumonia vaccine recommended
Integrative Therapy	■ Meditation and deep breathing exercises ■ Relaxation training ■ Individualized stress reduction techniques ■ Energy-conservation guidelines (see list on page 188)
Male or Female Directives	■ Highest incidence in men over the age of 40

Best Nutritional Strategies	Avoid consuming:
	    ■ Dried beans, peas and lentils
	    ■ Broccoli and brussels sprouts
	    ■ Cabbage and cauliflower
	    ■ Corn, cucumbers and leeks
	    ■ Melons
	    ■ Onions, scallions, peppers and pimientos
	    ■ Radishes, rutabagas, shallots and turnips
	    ■ Sauerkraut and raw apples
	    ■ Carbonated beverages and chewing gum

Supplements or Functional Foods to Consider	■ Products like Pulmocare that provide a higher degree of fat—excessive carbohydrate promotes the production of carbon dioxide and impedes breathing

Macular Degeneration

Did you know that there is a condition of the eye that can cause blindness without causing you any pain? It's called macular degeneration and the typical first symptoms are:

- blurred vision
- a wavy appearance to straight lines
- a dark patch in the middle of words or a page as you read
- a worsening of your color vision

Macular degeneration is damage that occurs to the central part of the retina (light-sensitive tissue at the back of the eye). It's common for many people as they age, usually affecting both eyes. In fact, approximately 25 percent of people aged 65 and older have some signs of this eye disease.

Early detection is important. If you're over age 40, you need to have regular and complete eye examinations. Most doctors will recommend an exam every 2 to 3 years, unless you have diabetes or a family history of eye disease. Then, a dilated eye exam every year would be recommended. You want to do that because early changes may not be noticed or even detected without a complete eye exam. Laser surgery is the most common technique to treat macular degeneration and halt progression of the disease. Multiple laser surgeries may be necessary.

If you're diagnosed with macular degeneration, you will probably be given a chart called an "Amsler Grid." This chart is a graph-like form with intersecting lines, that you would use each day to check for visual distortion. If the lines in the grid all appear straight and you have no areas of blurriness or fading, you've passed your daily test. However, using the Amsler grid is never a replacement for your regular exams with your eye specialist.

Nutritional Recommendations for Modifying Lifestyle Choices

Although larger studies need to be done, there may be some value in increasing your intake of carotenoids (such as spinach and collard greens) and lutein-rich foods (like blueberries and grapes) if you've been diagnosed with, or are at risk for, macular degeneration. A National Institutes of Health (NIH) study showed a 43 percent lower risk of advanced macular degeneration in the people who ate these types of vegetables than in those who ate foods with less carotenoids. Several other small studies link antioxidants to the slowing of the progression of macular degeneration. Therefore, you may want to increase your intake of vitamins E and C, carotenoids, selenium and zinc. It's best if you can use foods that are high in these oxidative ingredients, but you can take a supplement also.

Herbal Therapy

European research has pointed at the use of ginkgo biloba and bilberry as beneficial. Although bilberry appears safe in typically recommended amounts, toxic reactions can occur with prolonged use or high doses of the leaves. Bilberry is used in Germany to treat diarrhea. German authorities endorse the use of the fruits, but not the leaves.

Macular Degeneration

Reasons to Be Concerned (Inherited Traits and Environmental Factors)	■ Leading cause of severe visual loss for people 55 and older ■ Potentials for risk: increases with age, cigarette smoking, family history of macular degeneration, cardiovascular disease, elevated levels of cholesterol, light eye color and excessive exposure to sunlight
Western Medicine Recommendations	■ See vision specialist regularly ■ Laser treatments ■ Using a home-use grid helps you watch for disease progression
Integrative Therapy	■ Biofeedback training ■ Herbals include: ginkgo and bilberry
Male or Female Directives	■ No difference between men and women
Best Nutritional Strategies	■ Lutein-rich diet ■ May be linked to vitamin and mineral deficiencies (limited studies)
Supplements or Functional Foods to Consider	■ Consider antioxidant supplements of vitamin C and vitamin E ■ Zinc

Menopause

My nurse practitioner friend, Pat Udelhofen, always tells her new clients presenting with menopause, that they are going through their second adolescence. Think about it. Hormones are fluctuating. Their cycles are changing. And she stresses to them that this is a natural and expected process. Her goal is to help them analyze their risk factors for a number of diseases as they go into perimenopause (when changes from the normal cycle start taking place) and menopause. Most women worry about their risk of breast cancer, but she points out they also need to think about risk of heart disease, history of Alzheimer's, colon cancer history and vaginal health (it just seems that not too many people are willing to talk about vaginal health).

Your second adolescence, hurray! Right—with hot flashes, changing menstrual cycles, complexion changes, urinating more frequently and difficulty concentrating— who's cheering? On the other hand, some women are thrilled to no longer have the worry and hassle of having periods. In fact, for some women, their sex life improves as they can eliminate the risk of pregnancy as an ongoing concern. And still another friend proclaims that she'd be glad to have the hot flashes—she's been cold all her life!

Just the Facts, Ma'am

Menopause: the end of a woman's reproductive years. Perimenopause: the years of changing menstrual periods before menopause. The average age of onset is 51 (menstrual cycles become less regular between ages 40 and 60),

and menopause lasts about 7 to 10 years, although different sources will give different numbers. It is caused by a gradual decrease in hormones (estrogen and progesterone) because there are fewer functioning follicles in the ovaries where eggs are found. Fluctuations in estrogen and progesterone affect appetite and metabolism—that's right: It's easier to put on extra pounds, and many of us do.

Getting Help

Your best bet, as perimenopause starts, is to find a healthcare provider who will sit down and talk with you about the whole gamut of medical, psychological and emotional changes associated with this process. An excellent resource is the North American Menopause Society (NAMS). They have a Web site that can help you to find recommended providers in your area: http://www.menopause.org.

One goal of treatment should be to help you get through this time "intact as a woman." In other words, keeping your uterus and ovaries, if at all possible. Heavy bleeding, which can occur in menopause, may be associated with hyperplasia (pre-cancerous or cancerous cell growths). Don't assume it's just part of the menopause symptoms. Early treatment of heavy bleeding is essential. In the past, the treatment of choice for chronic heavy bleeding was a hysterectomy, or removal of the uterus and sometimes the ovaries.

What happens if your ovaries are removed? The body's main supply of estrogen and progesterone is removed. Research tells us that estrogen levels in women who've gone through natural menopause are about 30 picograms/nanoliter (pg/nl), whereas the level in women who experience surgical menopause (hysterectomy) is only about 10 pg/nl. Men have approximately 50 pg/nl. Should men really have more estrogen than women?

Hormone Replacement Therapy (HRT)

To HRT, or not to HRT? This is perhaps the biggest question for us as we go through menopause. This decision is not to be made lightly. It is an ongoing process, and one that should be made yearly, if not more often. To make the decision, you and your healthcare provider need to look at the big picture. A complete review of your symptoms, health history (including smoking, alcohol use, exercise and drug use) and risk factors must be considered. Remember that hormone levels are changing—even daily—so blood tests at one isolated time are not really reliable for helping to decide about HRT.

HRT is recommended for a number of reasons. Studies tell us that estrogen:
- helps decrease hot flashes and vaginal changes
- slows bone loss through osteoporosis
- may prevent Alzheimer's and coronary heart disease

But there are risks associated with estrogen. Estrogen increases risk for:
- breast and uterine cancer
- gallbladder disease
- blood clotting

Nutritional Recommendations for Modifying Lifestyle Choices

Soy, 25 to 50 mg per day, is recommended because it contains phytoestrogens and serves as a form of estrogen therapy. It's also been shown to relieve hot flashes and vaginal symptoms and offer protection against osteoporosis and breast cancer.

Menopause	
Reasons to Be Concerned (Inherited Traits and Environmental Factors)	Increased risks for: ■ Osteoporosis ■ Heart disease (see heart section for lipid changes) ■ Cancers of breast, ovary and uterus ■ Mayo Clinic researchers have found an increased risk of developing breast cancer in women who took oral contraceptives before 1975 and have a mother or sister who is a victim of breast cancer ■ Avoid stress—it may contribute to the occurrence of hot flashes—rapid decreases in estrogen levels

continued on next page

Menopause *continued*	
Western Medicine Recommendations	■ Calcium and vitamin D ■ Mammograms and Ductal Lavage for detection of breast cancer ■ HRT where asthma and breast, ovarian and uterine cancers are not of concern ■ Selective estrogen receptor modulators ■ Stop smoking
Integrative Therapy	■ Homeopathy ■ Herbals: black cohosh—which may reduce the incidence and severity of hot flashes—and evening primrose oil; treating hot flashes with supplements is also recommended; a combination of vitamin C (1,200 mg) + hesperidin (900 mg) + hesperidin methyl chalcone (900 mg) is one choice; another is Gamma-oryzanol (300 mg/day—from rice bran oil) ■ Physical medicine ■ Acupuncture ■ Massage therapy ■ Yoga
Best Nutritional Strategies	■ Avoid caffeine, alcohol, spicy foods and hot drinks to lessen hot flashes ■ Soy (25–50 mg of soy or genestein a day); phytoestrogens (natural estrogens) ■ Legumes, seeds and nuts
Supplements or Functional Foods to Consider	■ Vitamin E supplement ■ When taking premarin increase folate sources in diet ■ Flavonoids ■ Argin-Max: combination of ginkgo, ginseng, damiana, L-arginine and 14 vitamins and minerals; Stanford University School of Medicine suggested that this supplement was most effective in women nearing menopause for improved sexual desire and satisfaction

Migraine Headaches

More than 25 million Americans suffer from migraine headaches, as well as nausea and other associated symptoms. They spend more than $20 billion a year looking for relief from migraines, not to mention the dollars, time and pain associated with physician and emergency room visits. The cause remains elusive. Theories include disturbances of serotonin in the brain, irritation of certain nerves or other problems. The cause of the pain is contractions of blood vessels in the brain, setting the migraine in motion.

Alexander Mauskop, M.D., co-author of *What Your Doctor May Not Tell You About Migraines*, recommends a seven-step program for migraine relief. Mauskop suggests reviewing all elements of the program together. Although the program is generally safe, consult your healthcare provider before utilizing the seven steps or prior to embarking on any new program. Certainly check with your healthcare provider before adopting the triple therapy on your own.

Mauskop's seven-step program includes:

1. Getting a proper diagnosis from a medical doctor.
2. Using the triple therapy listed in the chart on page 199.
3. Identifying and avoiding your migraine triggers.
4. Eating to avoid migraines.
5. Taking the edge off (reducing life's stressors as much as possible).
6. Walking it off. Walking may decrease occurrence.
7. Using medicines as necessary.

Nutritional Recommendations for Modifying Lifestyle Choices

See the "Food Sources of Spotlighted Vital Nutrients" chart beginning on page 51 in chapter 2 for sources of riboflavin and magnesium. Magnesium, which does many of the same things that migraine medications do, can act as a medicine for migraines. In combination with riboflavin (which has not had the same in-depth study as magnesium) and feverfew, the "triple therapy" may be used successfully with a medical practitioner's guidance. Excesses of any of these will cause harm. Alexander Mauskop, M.D., director of the New York Headache Center and fellow of the American Academy of Neurology, has directed research and published many studies in this area.

Herbal Therapy

Safe natural medicines recommended for migraine are feverfew and kola (cola). Feverfew is an herb that has been used to prevent (but not treat) migraine pain, nausea and vomiting. The hardest part of getting effective treatment is getting a preparation with the critical ingredient, parthenolide, in the amount needed. Mouth ulcers have been reported as a side effect by 10 to 18 percent of people using feverfew. Kola (cola) contains caffeine and is found in popular cola drinks. However, migraine sufferers usually need about 100 to 200 mg of caffeine for migraine relief, which means 2 to 5 cans of cola.

Migraine Headaches

Reasons to Be Concerned (Inherited Traits and Environmental Factors)	■ Migraines in men up by 34 percent in one modern study ■ Migraines increased for women by 56 percent during same time
Western Medicine Recommendations	■ Oral or injected pain relievers like aspirin or non-steroidal anti-inflammatory drugs (NSAIDs) ■ Ergot derivatives ■ Triptans (Imitrex, Zomig, Amerge) release serotonin in the brain ■ If severe pain, narcotic injections may need to be used ■ Preventative medications may need to be used: propranolol, verapamil, amitriptyline ■ Avoid light and noise ■ Use cold compresses to head ■ Try to sleep ■ Exercise
Integrative Therapy	■ Caution to always use the right substances and high-quality brands of magnesium, riboflavin and feverfew ■ Chinese favor moxa or moxa-bustion ■ Another herbal is kola (caffeine in cola drinks is helpful) ■ Bodywork ■ Relaxation techniques, music therapy, yoga, meditation ■ Biofeedback ■ Hydrotherapy ■ Massage ■ Guided imagery ■ Aromatherapy ■ Acupuncture ■ Chiropractic ■ Craniosacral therapy (also called cranial osteopathy—gentle manipulation with the hands of the skull and lower back) ■ Hypnosis ■ Oxygen therapy ■ Colon therapy ■ Magnetic field therapy

Migraine Headaches *continued*

Male or Female Directives	■ 15 to 20 percent are women and 6 percent are men ■ Half of women with migraines report headaches associated with their menstrual cycle—stress women face ■ During the first 3 months of pregnancy there may be greater frequency
Best Nutritional Strategies	■ Many foods act as "triggers" for migraines—attempt to identify, and avoid, your individual target foods
Supplements or Functional Foods to Consider	■ "Triple Therapy" (300 to 400 mg of magnesium, 400 mg of riboflavin, 100 mg of feverfew per day. Total dosage divided in half taken in doses per day with meals) ■ Migra-Lieve

Nicotine Addiction (Smoking or Tobacco Addiction)

What happens to the arteries when you smoke? The toxins in cigarette smoke damage the endothelium or the inner lining of your arteries. The arterial wall thickens with cholesterol deposits and becomes narrow. Your heart rate increases and your blood pressure goes up. Cigarette smoking lowers high-density lipoprotein cholesterol, which is the good cholesterol, referred to as HDL. At the same time, it raises low-density lipoproteins (LDL), the bad cholesterol. And finally, it promotes the formation of a thrombus, which is a blood clot that may end your life.

Smokers are four times more likely than nonsmokers to get life-threatening blood infections or meningitis from a bacterium that usually causes pneumonia. The more a person smokes, the higher the risk of an infection. Researchers don't know exactly why but think that cigarette smoke makes it harder for the lungs to expel foreign material and easier for bacteria to "stick."

Another interesting fact about smoking is that it stimulates gastric acid production. Therefore, smokers have a higher risk for a number of stomach disorders such as ulcers, heartburn and GERD (Gastroesophageal Reflux Disease). If your healthcare provider directs you to use non-steroidal anti-inflammatory drugs (NSAIDs), like Motrin, Advil or Aleve, do so with caution because these drugs may increase the risk of gastric (stomach) bleeding.

Secondhand Smoke

Living with a smoker is known to increase heart disease risk by 30 percent. A study published in the *Journal of the American Medical Association* documented that just 30 minutes of exposure to secondhand smoke slows the flow of blood in the arteries of the heart. The restrictive blood flow that a smoker experiences when the endothelium is damaged is a result of arteries that cannot flex and dilate properly. This condition is called atherosclerosis, and exposure to secondhand smoke for even a short time may put you at increased risk. In addition, secondhand smoke may increase the risk of infections in nonsmokers—although not as much as in smokers.

Smoking Cessation (Quitting)

When you quit smoking, your body recognizes it immediately. After 1 year of abstinence, the ex-smoker's heart disease risk is reduced by 50 percent compared to those who continue to smoke.

See the sidebar for recommendations that may help you prevent weight gain during your smoking cessation program.

Nutritional Recommendations for Modifying Lifestyle Choices

See recommendations found in this chapter about being overweight. Additional tactics to improve nutrition during smoking cessation include increasing fluids and increasing vitamin C sources in the diet.

Lifestyle Changes

- Avoid caffeine, as it may trigger a craving for a cigarette.
- Avoid other situations or substitute another activity for one that would normally signal the occasion to light up. For example, many people light a cigarette when making a phone call. Of course, it may be impossible to stop making or taking phone calls.
- Physical activity (paired with healthy eating) helps decrease weight gain during smoking cessation.

General Recommendations to Manage Weight

- Ongoing social support during smoking cessation is a key to weight maintenance and a sustained healthy lifestyle. It also helps combat relapse and promotes wellness. Check out a smoking cessation program in your area.
- Since weight gain appears most likely within the first 2 years, you may want to be extra-vigilant of your caloric intake during that period.
- The good news is, even though you may have a relapse, possibly because of weight gain, your chances of successfully quitting smoking increase every time you attempt to quit.

Special Tips for Women

- Combination of behavioral weight control programs with smoking cessation helps women stop smoking and control weight.
- Smoking cessation programs focused on reducing concern about weight gain significantly improve smoking cessation results.

Special Tips for All Smokers

- Substitute low-calorie, healthy snacks for high-fat, high-calorie choices. Choose snacks that are less than 100 calories per serving. A medium serving of fresh fruit falls within this guideline. Read labels on the back of packages for other types of food.
- Recognize that your taste buds are no longer being coated. You may have smoked to satisfy hunger in the past, but now food will taste and smell better. When it does, you may want to eat more, which could lead to increased weight gain. Average weight gain due to smoking cessation is less than 20 pounds. In fact, ⅓ of those who quit smoking gain weight, ⅓ lose weight and ⅓ stay the same. You may need to learn new tricks to deal appropriately with your hunger.
- You may feel tired when you quit smoking because you are losing the nicotine stimulant. But don't lie down on the couch too often; get out and take a walk to help burn more calories and curb that tired-out feeling. This is an opportunity to substitute another activity for smoking.

Nicotine Addiction

Reasons to Be Concerned (Inherited Traits and Environmental Factors)	■ Smokers are likely to have poorer nutrient intakes ■ Detrimentally affects many body systems over time, including respiratory systems, cardiac and vascular systems and skin
Western Medicine Recommendations	■ Smoking cessation programs ■ Nicorette, Nicoderm patches (be sure to use under supervision of healthcare provider) ■ Antidepressants such as Zyban/Wellbutrin (avoid herbal St. John's wort, may contribute to decreased appetite or weight loss, or even have the opposite effect; may decrease cravings for chocolate)
Integrative Therapy	■ Yoga ■ Meditation
Male or Female Directives	■ Women are more likely to be concerned with weight gain following smoking cessation
Best Nutritional Strategies	■ A well-balanced and diverse diet—to avoid weight gain, you may need to reduce calorie consumption to 1300 to 1500 calories per day ■ Limit alcohol consumption ■ Healthy eating combined with physical activity during cessation leads to less weight gain and helps repair damage from years of smoking
Supplements or Functional Foods to Consider	■ A high alkaline diet may help withdraw from nicotine more slowly while an acidic diet may clear nicotine from the system much more quickly

Osteoporosis

If you're an underweight male or female aged 55 or more, sitting around all day smoking and alternating between your black coffee and your rum and Coke, you're a virtual time bomb for osteoporosis. If you're female, menopausal or post-menopausal and not taking estrogen, look out! Osteoporosis afflicts 9 out of 10 females aged 75 and older, and it's becoming more and more prevalent in men. In men, impaired gonadal functioning leads to subnormal testosterone levels in 68 percent of men who have had hip fractures, and this is now being recognized as a risk factor for osteoporosis.

Bone density loss (or bone thinning) is normal with age, but osteoporosis is an acceleration of the process. Osteoporosis, as it sounds, literally makes your bones more porous ("honeycombed") as the amount of calcium stored in the bone decreases. This can cause the skeleton to weaken and bone fractures to occur. The most severe fracture is that of the hip, resulting in significant suffering. As many as 20 percent of women won't survive a hip fracture.

The standard ways of diagnosing osteoporosis can involve x-ray, CT scan, laboratory studies and bone density tests. However, bone density testing is not routinely recommended for all women. If you have specific risk factors or diseases, or are taking medications that affect bone density, you may want this test. Medicare and most insurances now pay for bone density testing for specific instances. Make sure to ask your healthcare provider about this special testing.

The Best Treatment Is Prevention

The best treatment for osteoporosis is prevention. Prevention is a two-step process. First, increase both your intake of calcium (wear the milk mustache proudly!) and the amount you exercise. Second, avoid smoking and limit caffeine and alcohol. Maintaining an adequate intake of calcium during adolescence and young adulthood is crucial. This is when your body accumulates much of the bone stores (hydroxyapatite—a component of bones and teeth composed of calcium and phosphate).

Adequate calcium intake will help avoid or diminish the risk of osteoporosis in later life, but this may be easier said than done. With such a strong

---

Calcium Supplement Choices

If you aren't into the "milk mustache," here are some milk alternatives. Always check with your healthcare provider when using these supplements on a long-term basis.

Calcium carbonate alternatives include VIACTIV Soft Calcium Chews, CalBurst (Calcium Soft Chews), Rolaids and TUMS. Citracel is one calcium citrate alternative.

Keeping Your Bones Dense

Here are some insights on (and techniques for) maintaining strong bones.

1. Include calcium-rich foods or a supplement to equal 1,000 mg/day in your diet. Women who are post-menopausal and not on estrogen replacement therapy (ERT) should take 1,500 mg/day.
2. Participate in regular weight-bearing exercise (20 to 30 minutes, 3 to 4 times a week).
3. Stop smoking.
4. Limit caffeine intake.
5. Limit alcohol intake to no more than one drink a day for women and two drinks a day for men.

The average American diet provides excess daily protein because of the consumption of meat and seafood, eggs and dairy products, as well as vegetable sources. Studies have documented that excessive amounts of protein, usually accomplished by overconsumption of animal products, significantly increases the amount of calcium lost in the urine. Other studies have documented that much lower protein consumption, with smaller amounts of calcium ingestion than we might expect, have not caused excessive calcium loss in the urine.

A second group of foods that might be called "calcium bandits" are caffeinated soft drinks, coffees and teas. These increase the urinary excretion of calcium and increase secretion of calcium into the gut, where it is expelled through the feces. Phytic acid or phytate, described in the section on iron deficiency anemia, and oxalic acid are two other concerns for maintaining strong bones.

Foods that seem to be good sources of calcium but are high in oxalic acid include:

- rhubarb
- spinach
- berries
- chocolate
- cola
- teas (not herbal teas)

Sodium sources—and excessive use of table salt—rob calcium from our bodies. Another way is a diet that is too high in phosphorus.

That's quite a balancing act our bodies are doing every day—so cheerfully, and so well. You can see how making the best choices in your daily diet can help.

emphasis on weight in our society—often on an unhealthy and unnatural low weight—many women are choosing lower-calorie alternative drinks over milk. We are drinking more water, and this is usually helpful. Some flavored waters add calories. Non-calorie types of water are preferred, but drinking any type of water is better than not drinking water at all.

There is such a variety of beverages available today, it's no wonder milk may be skipped. Lunch counters and delis are teeming with drinks such as cappuccino, iced frappuccino, sports energy drinks, fruit drinks and carbonated beverages, to list just a few, and milk consumption continues to decline. One substantial reason for this is the dramatic increase in the consumption of carbonated beverages or soft drinks.

The Activity Factor

Weight-bearing exercise is highly important for women—before, during and after menopause—and for men. Experts note that any activity combining body movement with stress on your arms and/or legs, such as walking, climbing stairs or grocery shopping, is beneficial. Weight training definitely helps.

I'll never forget the dramatic example presented at an osteoporosis seminar I attended. The speaker showed x-rays of a Milwaukee Brewers baseball player's pitching arm and compared it to his non-pitching arm. The actual bones were larger in the pitching arm. This is the power of regular exercise! Resistance training (using weights to do arm and leg exercises) is also powerful. It's appropriate for all ages, even the elderly, to increase their muscles and strengthen bones.

A particular group at risk is teenage girls. They are drinking more and more soda, and skipping milk products because they don't want added calories and weight. If they are choosing Mountain Dew and cola products, they're also inadvertently increasing their caffeine intake. Add to this the fact that smoking is increasing in this population and we potentially have a whole generation of women with osteoporosis.

Estrogen replacement therapy (ERT) at menopause is an important treatment and prevention tool. During the first 3 to 5 years after menopause, you lose about 3 percent of your bone mineral each year. Estrogen replacement slows this process, but is becoming more and more controversial.

Another prevention tip for those who are older, or caring for older family members, is to make the house more "fall-resistant." Eliminate throw rugs, consider handrails on stairs and in bathrooms, keep rooms and halls well lit, and consider non-skid mats for the bathtub and shower.

Medications commonly used in treating osteoporosis include Fosamax (which thickens bones, decreases risk of fractures and decreases risk of height loss) and Miacalcin (which thickens bones).

Nutritional Recommendations for Modifying Lifestyle Choices

See the nutritional recommendations found in the accompanying chart.

The first and most important recommendation is increasing your calcium intake to match recommendations for your age and sex. A superb source of calcium is fortified soy, with the added benefit of being good for your cardiovascular health and even for coping with perimenopause and menopause. Next, avoid very large amounts of fiber, which tends to bind with calcium, and avoid large amounts of protein in your diet.

Osteoporosis

Reasons to Be Concerned (Inherited Traits and Environmental Factors)	■ There is some genetic advantage to being African-American, with Caucasian and Asian women being at a higher risk ■ Nicotine use ■ Excessive use of coffee/tea ■ Early menopause ■ Not having a diet with enough calcium in it ■ Being underweight ■ Family history of osteoporosis ■ Eating disorders, such as anorexia or bulimia ■ Lack of physical exercise
Western Medicine Recommendations	■ Stop smoking—soon! ■ Estrogen supplements (estrogen replacement therapy) at menopause onset—controversial ■ Fosamax: decreases bone resorption
Integrative Therapy	■ Weight-bearing exercise ■ Limit caffeine to equivalent of 3 cups of coffee or less per day
Male or Female Directives	■ Women twice as likely to have ■ 1 in 4 Caucasian women older than 45, and 9 of 10 older than 75 will be afflicted
Best Nutritional Strategies	■ Avoid very large amounts of fiber (binds with calcium) ■ Avoid very large amounts of protein ■ Vitamin K lowers the risk of hip fracture among middle-aged and older women.
Supplements or Functional Foods to Consider	■ Calcium-rich food or a supplement (1,000 mg/day) ■ 1,200 mg/day for 51+ years ■ 1,500 mg/day for men >age 55 to 60 ■ Vitamin D supplements to total of 600 to 800 IU/day

Overweight

One in five Americans is obese, weighing 20 percent or more above an ideal body weight (IBW). There has been a 57 percent increase in obesity from 1991 to 1999. But even though this disease is reaching epidemic proportions in America, many are adopting lifestyle changes that keep weight off permanently.

Personal Fulfillment & Weight Management

You can measure your true weight management success by your personal fulfillment. Weight management attempts are more successful if you experience an emotional, behavioral, physical and spiritual transformation.

Before you plunge into another diet, why not evaluate what's going on with your weight history? I always ask my clients to relate their weight history, just like you would describe a relationship—when it started, how it was in the middle and how it ended,

if it did. And my clients learn to recognize what factors influenced each of these stages.

You, too, will want to consider any non-genetic contributors. Were you subtly reinforced with food when you were little? When you recognized hunger as a child, what choices of food were available? Were you shy and self-conscious about how you looked?

Reasons Women Gain Weight

There are three times during a woman's life when weight is gained easily—infancy, adolescence and the third trimester of pregnancy. I quit weighing myself when I was expecting James, our 24-year-old son. I remember the scale saying 186 pounds, and I quit looking at the numbers on the scale after that. (I weighed all of 132 pounds in my wedding dress.) I was a lucky one: I lost that pregnancy weight within 6 months after my son's birth, but many women don't.

Avoid Being Shipwrecked by a Low-Calorie Diet

- Too-low-calorie diets in women have been associated with the inability to sustain attention. This also may be an early sign of iron deficiency, even when iron intake appears adequate.
- Check out the references throughout *Food for Life* for nutrient levels you need, whether male or female. When calorie levels become too low, it is difficult or impossible to meet these needs.
- Check out the food tracker tools and ideas for identifying some stress-eating habits that may be sabotaging your progress. These are found in chapter 1, and menu-planning tips are found in chapter 4.

Weight-Loss Methods That Work

Here are a variety of weight-loss strategies and techniques. Pick, choose and use ones that might work for you.

- Keep a food and activity journal. Monitor your progress.
- Plan daily and weekly meals ahead. Use the menu planning form found in chapter 4.
- Change your environment. Get organized. Get counseling. Look for spiritual sustenance. Step back and look at your life, then face the matters that may be sabotaging your weight loss efforts. There is no one way to lose weight and you may want to use a variety of methods until you succeed.
- Comprehensive changes may be easier for you to make than moderate ones. Dr. Dean Ornish, in *Eat More, Weigh Less,* believes that needed changes, even though they may feel drastic, should be made in an all-or-none fashion.
- Attend a weight loss retreat to cement your commitment to your new weight-conscious lifestyle.
- Figure out your true motivation

What Is a Realistic Weight-Loss Goal?

Healthy and realistic goals for the weight you want to attain can be found in this chart. Beyond this chart, ask yourself some personal questions to help establish a weight loss goal. *Can I ascend two flights of steps without becoming winded? Can I participate in activities like hiking, softball and swimming with family and friends? Am I satisfied and comfortable with my clothes size? Does my current weight prevent me from doing the things I love the most?*

Suggested Weights for Adults

Height	19-34 years	35 years and older
5' 0"	97-128	108-138
5'1"	101-132	111-143
5'2"	104-137	115-148
5'3"	111-146	122-157
5'4"	114-150	126-162
5'5"	118-155	130-167
5'6"	121-160	134-172
5'7"	125-164	138-178
5'8"	129-169	142-183
5'9"	132-174	146-188
5'10"	136-179	151-194
5'11"	140-184	155-199
6'0"	144-189	159-209
6'1"	148-195	164-210
6'2"	152-200	168-216
6'3"	156-205	173-222
6'4"	160-211	177-228
6'5"	164-216	182-234

and develop a positive attitude for your personal weight management.

- Be realistic with your self-talk. Be positive about your image and set realistic goals for weight loss and increased activity.
- Be action-oriented and develop specific strategies to reach your goal. Be clear about the rewards you will give yourself upon reaching a mini-goal or a major goal. Don't sabotage your own progress by failing to give yourself the reward you have earned. (I don't recommend food rewards unless they are within a very controlled setting.) The best weight management plans encourage you to eat small amounts of foods you like every day.
- Keep data in addition to your weight. Measure your body mass index (BMI), an indicator of your percent of body fat for your height. Excess body fat will be reflected in a higher BMI, predicting more negative health outcomes. See page 210 for calculation instructions.

How Many Calories Can I Eat & Still Lose Weight?

If I could answer that question exactly, I would feel like a character from one of my favorite movies, "The Wizard of Oz." Since I can't answer it, I will give you a guide to calorie requirements. Total calorie intake together with calorie or energy expenditure, in large part, still determines body weight.

If you are 50 years or older and are able to do some exercise, use the following equation to figure your calorie needs.

Figure about 30 calories (cal) for each kilogram (kg) of weight. (To determine your weight in kg, divide your weight in pounds by 2.2. One kg=2.2 pounds.) The equation assumes you are engaged in light activity. Most desk jobs without additional daily exercise would fit this bill, too.

Multiply 63 kg (138 pounds) times 30 cal/kg to equal about 1,890 calories per day to maintain your weight. If you are physically active or have a disease that burns calories, like a chronic lung disease, the amount of calories you need to maintain your weight will be higher. If you have an altered metabolism because of too much yo-yo dieting, or if you take medications that cause you to be hungry and gain weight, your daily caloric need may be lower.

How Much Less Should I Eat to Lose Weight?

Let's use the same example; let's call her Deb. Deb has set a reasonable weight loss goal of ½ to 1 pound per week. Without increasing her activity (which she is also willing to do), Deb will need to eat between 250 and 500 fewer calories most days to meet her weight loss goal. Without increasing her activity level, Deb will want to follow a balanced diet of 1,390 and 1,640 calories each day.

Since Deb is also interested in improving her overall cardiac health, she plans to exercise for 30 minutes, 3 to 4 times per week. This will help her body burn calories more efficiently and further meet her weight loss goal.

Calculating Body Mass Index (BMI)

A couple of simple calculations can determine your BMI. This sample calculation is from a 27-year-old woman.

1. Convert your body weight to kilograms:
Body weight (pounds) ÷ 2.2 = Body weight (kilograms)
Example: 136 pounds ÷ 2.2 = 61.8 kilograms

2. Convert your height to meters:
Height (inches) ÷ 39.37 = Height (meters)
Example: 65 inches ÷ 39.37 = 1.65 meters

3. Calculate your body mass index:
Your weight (kilograms) ÷ Your height (meters)^2 = Your BMI
Example: 61.8 kilograms ÷ 1.65 meters x 1.65 meters = 22.7 BMI

BMI	Risk for Health Problems Related to Body Weight
20 to 25	Very low risk
26 to 30	Low risk
31 to 35	Moderate risk
36 to 40	High risk
41+	Very high risk

A BMI higher than 27 suggests that one is overweight. A BMI of 32 or more suggests health-threatening obesity.

Overweight	
Reasons to Be Concerned (Inherited Traits and Environmental Factors)	■ 97 million adults in the U.S. are overweight or obese (more than 20 percent above ideal body weight) ■ Obesity is the second leading cause of preventable death in the U.S. ■ Obesity is more prevalent in African- and Hispanic-American women compared to non-Hispanic white men and women ■ A combination of dietary factors and sedentary activity patterns account for at least 300,000 deaths each year ■ Obesity increases pain and symptoms of arthritis

Overweight *continued*	

Western Medicine Recommendations	■ Obesity is self-evident on physical examination
	■ X-ray imaging studies are available in diagnosis of obesity but many are often non-specific and unnecessary
	■ Other tests measure:
	   ■ Total body water
	   ■ Total body potassium
	   ■ Bioelectrical impedence
	   ■ Dual-energy x-ray absorptiometry
	■ Treatment aimed at weight reduction and risk factor modification such as diabetes, elevated lipids, high blood pressure
	■ Xenical (Orlistat)—weight control medication that prevents fat breakdown, people taking this medication may experience fecal urgency or incontinence and fatty stools. May also decrease absorption of fat-soluble vitamins
	■ Meridia (Sibutramine)—suppresses appetite, may also increase good cholesterol while lowering the bad (avoid taking with St. John's wort)
	■ Surgery to reduce size of stomach (controversial)

Integrative Therapy	■ Yoga ■ Green tea may give your metabolism a boost—and may help you lose weight
Male or Female Directives	■ U.S. women with low incomes or education are more likely to be obese than women of higher socioeconomic status
Best Nutritional Strategies	■ See information detailed in pages 208–209
Supplements or Functional Foods to Consider	■ Multitudes of remedies exist—most with limited success, many with the potential for great harm

Peptic Ulcer Disease (PUD)

Take a minute to compare the medical treatment of ulcers from 20 years ago to today. If Ward Cleaver had developed an ulcer, he'd have been told to decrease his stress on the job, drink milk and cut back on those two or three martinis he had every night when he came home to June. He surely would have had a roll of Rolaids in his pocket and in his desk at work. Today, Regis may have a high-pressure lifestyle, but he'd be asked about how many aspirin or ibuprofen he was taking to treat his sore "tennis" knees. And he might have a biopsy or even a breath test to find out if bacteria was causing his ulcer. If so, he'd be treated with an antibiotic. Oh, and he'd still be encouraged to avoid alcohol and stop smoking (if he smoked).

Ulcers have been the butt of many jokes, especially in the high-stress crowd of people with Type A personalities. Ulcers were once thought to be caused primarily by stress. However, the medical community has now proven that today's ulcers are commonly caused by an infection or by certain medications. You're more at risk if you take non-steroidal anti-inflammatory drugs (NSAIDs) regularly or if you take glucocorticoids.

And what about that infection? A bacteria called Helicobacter pylori causes infection that can cause an ulcer. Treatment of this ulcer will include antibiotics plus one of the ulcer drugs, like Prilosec, Prevacid or Zantac.

Ulcers can occur in the stomach or in the top part of the small intestine, called the duodenum. In fact, the ratio of duodenal to gastric (stomach) ulcers is four to one.

Nutritional Recommendations for Modifying Lifestyle Choices

Foods that stimulate gastric acid secretion and irritate the gastric mucosa (lining) of the esophagus, stomach or duodenum will delay healing of the ulcer. There are some things you can do to help reduce the pain and discomfort of peptic ulcer:

- Limit or avoid coffee, decaffeinated coffee, caffeine-containing beverages and alcoholic beverages.
- Individualize meal sizes and specific food selections. What may seem like too much food to one person, and further irritate the ulcer, may be just right to another. Each of us can determine which foods irritate this condition. Avoid those foods, especially during the healing phase.

Many of us are tempted to return to previous eating habits when a peptic ulcer no longer bothers us. This is probably a mistake, because those foods and meal sizes that irritated or contributed to the ulcer at first will usually cause discomfort again.

Peptic Ulcer Disease

Reasons to Be Concerned (Inherited Traits and Environmental Factors)	■ Often runs in families ■ Untreated, PUD can be life-threatening and lead to cancer ■ Being elderly ■ Having a history of peptic ulcer ■ Having diseases that require the use of regular NSAIDs—such as chronic low back pain, fibromyalgia, any arthritic condition—causes an increased potential for PUD ■ Alcohol abuse ■ Stress and psychological factors make us more susceptible to all major ulcers
Western Medicine Recommendations	■ Avoid aspirin and non-steroidal anti-inflammatory drugs (NSAIDs) ■ Biopsy of ulcer may show Helicobacter pylori—a bacteria best treated with combination of antibiotics and ulcer medications (Zantac, Prevacid, Prilosec) ■ In "non H. pylori," patients use Histamine-2 receptor antagonists or proton pump inhibitors
Integrative Therapy	■ Herbals include: chamomile, honey, licorice and slippery elm ■ Yoga ■ Meditation ■ Biofeedback ■ Hypnosis ■ Acupuncture ■ Ayurvedic medicine
Male or Female Directives	■ Men have twice the risk for ulcers as women do ■ Duodenal ulcers tend to occur first at around age 25 and continue to age 75 ■ Gastric ulcers peak in people between the ages of 55 and 65
Best Nutritional Strategies	■ Limit fats ■ Avoid alcohol and caffeine ■ Avoid foods that bring on pain ■ Not recommended: frequent milk ingestion (as in older Sippy diet)—ingest normal amounts of dairy in regular portions
Supplements or Functional Foods	■ None recommended

Pregnancy—Advanced Maternal Age

In the eyes of the medical profession, if you are having a baby later in life—at age 40 years or older—you will be referred to as pregnant with "advanced maternal age." Oh well, you are probably thrilled to be having this baby, so don't let the terminology sway you. And what's another year or two anyway? Most people in medicine believe that what counts is the true age of your body, and your agility—not your chronological age.

The majority of women who do give birth after 40 manage to have happy, healthy babies. As you can see in our accompanying chart, page 215, there are some additional risks to postponing motherhood.

Older mothers face an increased risk of a variety of things that may go wrong.

This is because the eggs in an older woman's body are more likely to have chromosomal problems than the eggs of a younger woman. Marginal folate deficiency in postmenopausal women may alter your composition of DNA. Women may need more than the 180 micrograms of folate recommended by the Dietary Allowance. This amount may not be sufficient to prevent an increase in plasma homocysteine levels in postmenopausal women. Intake levels between 286 and 516 micrograms of folate per day were needed to reverse DNA hypomethylation and repair DNA. Be sure to have adequate folic acid intake for several months prior to conception and during gestation.

A woman who gives birth at age 40 or older is four times as likely to develop gestational diabetes as a woman in her 20s. Gestational diabetes is that type of altered blood sugar situation that sometimes occurs when you are pregnant. It usually goes away after pregnancy, but not always. The concern is twofold: There is concern for you and for your baby. The baby is at greater risk when blood sugars are not maintained within normal limits, which are 70 to 110 mg/dL.

You may not want to hear this, but older moms are more likely to become pregnant with multiples. In fact, women over the age of 45 are 10 times as likely to become pregnant with multiples than women in their 20s. Oh well, if you get started later in life, this may work into the grand plan as well.

Remember, most older moms have safe deliveries. You will want to review how you should eat and how much you will gain during this very exciting period of your life.

Stacking the Deck with Baby-Friendly Nutrients

See recommendations in the accompanying chart for information on what to eat while trying to conceive. You will want to include each day:

- 4 servings from the dairy group
- 2 to 3 oz. from the meat group or a protein equivalent
- 1 rich source of vitamin A (see chapter 2)
- 2 rich sources of vitamin C
- 5 or more servings from the fruit and vegetable group
- 4 or more servings from the whole grain and cereal group—probably between 7 and 11 servings
- Adequate sources of healthy fat

found in all three kinds of fatty acids—saturated, monounsaturated and polyunsaturated. Corn oil, olive oil and canola oil will work well. Just as the rest of us are trying to decrease our intake of trans fatty acids—those saturated fats that masquerade as less harmful fats, and are not even available to us on nutritional labels—you will want to limit them in your diet.

■ Additional calories from favorite foods that are nutrient-dense to help stack the deck in baby's favor. Consult with your healthcare provider about individual needs and the use of a multivitamin- and mineral tablet.

Women of normal weight should gain 24 to 27 pounds during pregnancy. You may only need to increase calories by 200 to 300 beyond your normal daily caloric intake to meet the baby's growing needs.

Pregnancy—Advanced Maternal Age

Reasons to Be Concerned (Inherited Traits and Environmental Factors)	■ Increased maternal risks: hypertension, diabetes, miscarriage, placental problems, bleeding ■ Increased fetal risks: Down syndrome and other chromosomal abnormalities ■ Smokers have higher risk of poor micronutrient intake ■ Increased body mass index associated with risk for proteinuria, hypertension and pre-eclampsia
Western Medicine Recommendations	■ Folate ■ Pre-pregnancy checkup and regular prenatal visits ■ Visit high-risk OB if problems are anticipated ■ Tests: ultrasound, triple maternal serum screen, amniocentesis, chorionic villus sampling ■ Moderate exercise—brisk walking 3 or 4 times a week can decrease the risk of having a low-birth-weight baby. Don't go overboard—too much exercise causes problems more often than too little exercise
Integrative Therapy	■ Herbals include: glucomannan for bowel irregularity/constipation (insufficient reliable information: avoid using during pregnancy and lactation), ginger for morning sickness (ginger should be taken with caution because large doses have been associated with damage to the central nervous system) *continued*

Pregnancy—Advanced Maternal Age *continued*	
Integrative Therapy *continued*	■ Moderate exercise, including yoga or comparable activity ■ Macrobiotic and alternative treatment literature gives a wide variety of foods to avoid which appear perfectly fine to ingest during times when you and your partner are seeking to become pregnant. Review the description found on page 17 regarding definitions of macrobiotic diets.

Best Nutritional Strategies	■ Eat a variety of nutritious foods
	■ Attain the proper weight for your height before getting pregnant
	■ No alcohol
	■ No smoking
	■ Take no drugs of any kind without consulting your physician
	Those hoping to conceive will want to get good amounts of whole foods rich in:
	    ■ Folate—up to 800 micrograms (mcg) per day—usually in supplement form (helps avoid neural tube defects in the developing fetus)
	    ■ Vitamins A, E, C and D
	    ■ Calcium, iron and zinc
	    ■ Essential fatty acids as found in safflower oil and other vegetable oils

Supplements or Functional Foods to Consider	■ Oral contraceptives increase need for consumption of foods containing vitamin B6, vitamin B12, folate, vitamin C
	Foods you may want to limit or avoid while attempting to conceive:
	    ■ Alcohol
	    ■ Artificial sweeteners
	    ■ Food coloring
	    ■ Ginger, ginger ale, ginger beer
	    ■ Quinine—key ingredient in tonic water
	    ■ Caffeine (chocolate, sodas, coffee, tea, and some pain and cold remedies)
	    ■ Monosodium glutamate (MSG), BHA and other food additives
	    ■ Partially cooked or uncooked foods (this would not include fresh fruits and vegetables)
	    ■ Contaminated food or water
	    ■ Crash, fad or high-fat diets
	    ■ Non-food items include some medications

Premenstrual Syndrome (PMS)

PMS is characterized by moodiness, anxiety, depression, food cravings and a bloated feeling experienced by many women during the 7 to 10 days before their period. Any menstruating female is a candidate for this, and almost half of all women in their childbearing years experience symptoms to differing degrees.

Sometimes lifestyle factors contribute to PMS. Some of these are stress, lack of activity outdoors and diets high in sugar and refined carbohydrates, salt, fat, alcohol and caffeine. Not surprisingly, women who work full-time and are between the ages of 24 and 44 and have a higher education seem most at risk.

If you feel you are suffering with symptoms of PMS, talk it over with your healthcare provider. Also, see other related sections, including osteoporosis, where you will learn about "calcium bandits" in your diet, and strategies to deal with anxiety and depression, in their respective sections.

Nutritional Recommendations for Modifying Lifestyle Choices

See the nutritional recommendations found in the accompanying chart.

Premenstrual Syndrome	
Reasons to Be Concerned (Inherited Traits and Environmental Factors)	■ Affects at least ⅓ of premenopausal women ■ Women seeking treatment for PMS symptoms are normally in their 30s or 40s ■ May affect relationships or impair normal activities
Western Medicine Recommendations	■ Exercise ■ Adequate rest ■ Well-balanced diet ■ Oral contraceptives or other hormonal treatment ■ Pain relievers ■ Antidepressants may be used to treat Intractable PMS or Premenstrual Dysphoric Disorder (PMDD)
Integrative Therapy	■ Herbals include: black cohosh, chaste tree berry and evening primrose oil (rich source of gamma-linolenic acid, or GLA) ■ Homeopathy ■ Traditional Chinese medicine *continued on next page*

Premenstrual Syndrome *continued*	
Integrative Therapy *continued*	■ Ayurvedic medicine ■ Craniosacral therapy ■ Meditation, relaxation and yoga ■ Acupuncture ■ Biofeedback training ■ Guided imagery ■ Hypnosis ■ Bodywork
Best Nutritional Strategies	■ Fiber-rich fresh fruits and vegetables, whole grains, legumes, nuts, seeds and fish ■ Avoid refined sugars (less than 3 teaspoons per day), large amounts of protein, dairy products, fats, salt, tobacco and caffeine ■ Include 1 to 2 tablespoons safflower oil per day ■ About 1,200 mg calcium a day can ease bloating by reducing water retention ■ Magnesium paired with vitamin B6 and cobalamine given 2 weeks prior to a woman's period helps relieve symptoms of PMS ■ Physical activity as tolerated
Supplements or Functional Foods to Consider	None noted

Sleep Apnea

Sleep apnea is a condition characterized by periods when breathing stops while sleeping. Sometimes physical or structural problems cause breathing passages to become obstructed, thus bringing breathing to a halt. With this cessation, which can happen repeatedly, the "sleeper" is forced to wake up and take necessary breaths. This cycle of interrupted sleep continues, and the sleep apnea patient has to go without a sound night's sleep, and then get excessively sleepy during the day.

Researchers speculate that the lack of oxygen in the blood may also trigger headaches. This is a serious condition that can cause fatal heart problems. Without sleep lab testing, many people are not aware they have sleep apnea.

Signs & Symptoms of Sleep Apnea:

- Loud, irregular snoring, then quiet periods of at least 10 seconds when breathing stops; these episodes can happen up to 100 times or more each hour
- Daytime sleepiness, always feeling tired
- Morning headaches, sore throat, dry mouth, cough
- Feeling depressed, moody, irritable
- Inability to concentrate
- Possible impotence
- High blood pressure
- Bed wetting

Nutritional Recommendations for Modifying Lifestyle Choices

See the bulleted suggestions for nutritional management in the accompanying chart. Strategies for weight loss and management reviewed on pages 207–211 stress eating and goal-setting.

Sleep Apnea	
Reasons to Be Concerned (Inherited Traits and Environmental Factors)	■ Sometimes runs in families ■ Likely to be overweight and snore loudly ■ Drugs such as alcohol, sleeping pills, antihistamines, tranquilizers and heart medication can trigger apnea

continued on next page

Sleep Apnea *continued*	
Western Medicine Recommendations	■ If you're overweight, lose weight ■ Avoid smoking or exposure to other irritants such as dust or perfume ■ Develop regular sleep habits and make sure you get enough sleep at night ■ Use an air humidifier at night ■ Raise the head of your bed by placing bricks under the headboard ■ Overnight testing at sleep clinic may be helpful (will check oxygen levels) ■ Treat allergies, colds and sinus problems ■ CPAP may be used (a special mask that helps you breathe through the night) ■ May be worse when sleeping on your back—devices sometimes used that force people to sleep on their side ■ Morbidly obese may benefit from surgery to treat obesity ■ People with life-threatening sleep apnea may benefit from a tracheostomy
Integrative Therapy	■ Homeopathy ■ Acupuncture ■ Avoid mucus producing foods for 2 weeks (dairy and bananas)—reintroduce them and see if there is a difference
Male or Female Directives	■ Common to all age groups and sexes ■ More than half of all cases of sleep apnea diagnosed in people age 40 and older, slightly higher frequency in men
Best Nutritional Strategies	■ Weight reduction (see overweight—this chapter) ■ Exercise ■ Choose foods higher in essential fatty acids (EFAs)—often low in obese people
Supplements or Functional Foods to Consider	■ Medications usually ineffective ■ Gargle with salt water (without swallowing) to temporarily shrink the size of your tonsils before going to bed

Surgery

Nutritional Preparation for Surgery & Eating to Recover

You've been told you need to have surgery and you have some time to prepare. First, take a few minutes and refer to the accompanying chart on pages 222–223. A major concern that you face before surgery—elective or emergency—is: "Am I in the best possible nutritional health going into this surgery?"

To answer this, your healthcare provider will work with you and may perform a variety of tests. A relatively new approach to pre-operative care is to assess your nutritional risk with laboratory measures of albumin (or similar tests) and review other potential risk factors. These tests will help screen for your individual malnutrition risk. A diagnosis of malnutrition may mean a higher risk of complications both during and after surgery.

Questions to Ask Before an Elective Surgical Procedure

Obviously, if you're having an emergency operation, there won't be much time for questions and a thorough review of all the possible angles of your treatment. But if it's been recommended for you to have an elective procedure, there are a number of questions you may want to ask first. Some of these are included.

- What are the consequences if I don't have this surgery?
- What are some alternatives to this surgery?
- What are the most common complications to this surgery?
- Who will my surgeon be?
- How many of these surgeries does this surgeon do per month or year?
- What are the infection rates at the hospital?
- What are the surgeon's infection rates if this can be shared?
- How long would I expect to stay after the surgery (days, hours)?
- Is this a procedure that could be done as day-surgery?
- Are there any herbs I shouldn't take before surgery?
- Are there any medications I should stop in the days or week before surgery?
- Is it likely that I would need a blood transfusion? And if so, can I donate my own blood ahead of time?
- What about my regular medications (if you take any)? Should I take these the morning of surgery, or not at all the day of surgery? (This is particularly important with diabetes.)
- Will I need therapy of some kind afterward?
- Will I need any special home equipment or help after surgery?

People with certain other conditions share similar malnutrition concerns. Check out the nutrition recommendations found in the sections on Alzheimer's, HIV/AIDS and cancer in this chapter. There are a variety of helpful suggestions to increase the protein and calorie content of your diet to halt further weight loss and maybe regain a portion of your usual body weight prior to surgery. Planning your foods wisely and getting as much physical activity as possible will help you regain true muscle weight, and not fat.

Keep in mind that sometimes you'll want to encourage appetite by having many small, nutrient-dense meals each day instead of larger, less frequent meals. You may need to rely on supplemental liquid nutrition (such as Ensure and Boost; Glucerna—especially for people with diabetes; or Pulmocare—especially for people with breathing problems) to boost your overall nutritional intake.

Aspects to be considered regarding nutritional status include:

- how you eat
- whether you have easy access to food sources
- your ability to conduct activities of daily living (like cleaning, cooking, dressing)
- whether you have had a significant weight loss or gain within the last 6 months (A loss of 5 to 10 percent of your usual body weight within a short period of time could signal a need to reconsider elective surgery at this time.)

There are a number of questions you may want to pose before you head into elective surgery. (See the sidebar.) When your questions are all answered and your nutrition is in tip-top shape, you're ready for that elective surgery.

Surgery: Before the Procedure	
Reasons to Be Concerned (Inherited Traits and Environmental Factors)	■ Supervised acute weight loss prior to surgery to reduce complications with morbidly obese
Western Medicine Recommendations	■ Stop taking aspirin, any aspirin products and any blood thinners prior to surgery ■ Follow physician prescribed directives for fasting and other eating behaviors prior to surgery ■ Do not drink alcohol or take other non-prescribed drugs prior to surgery. They may interfere with anesthesia. Check with your healthcare provider

Surgery: Before the Procedure *continued*	
Integrative Therapy	■ Herbal caution: Stop taking ginkgo, turmeric, chamomile and echinacea for several weeks before elective surgery ■ Refer to list of possible blood thinning supplements/herbs under anticoagulent therapy ■ Inform surgeon or healthcare provider of your use of vitamins/supplements and whether you are stopping them ■ Music therapy ■ Hypnosis and meditation may decrease anxiety ■ Massage and reflexology
Male or Female Directives	■ Does not apply
Best Nutritional Strategies	■ Maintain a well-balanced diet with adequate fluids ■ Have malnutrition risk assessed: albumin status, a measure of visceral protein, can be measured. A low-protein status may indicate need to postpone and replenish stores. Low albumin is associated with increased morbidity (risk of illness/disease/complications) and mortality ■ To improve malnutrition risk, eat well-balanced diet with extra servings of high protein foods (see chapter 2). Refer to sections regarding Alzheimer's, HIV/AIDS and cancer for other suggestions to maintain or improve nutrition status
Supplements or Functional Foods to Consider	■ Increased vitamin C, zinc and protein for wound healing

After Surgery

After some surgeries, you may have a series of diets as you are "advanced" through a diet progression to regular foods at regular meals. This plan varies from hospital to hospital, and especially regarding the specific surgery you have. For example, if you have a surgery that retires the use of one of your gastrointestinal organs, for a time, you may need to be fed with a feeding tube.

During that period, you will receive a completely balanced diet, though it may be a little shy on fiber.

Working with your healthcare provider and registered dietitian, you will be able to progress back toward foods you are used to eating. In the case of diverticulosis or some liver diseases, you may always want to pay special attention to foods and food groups that offend.

Surgery: After the Procedure

Reasons to Be Concerned (Inherited Traits and Environmental Factors)	■ Decreased physical activity and immobility may cause constipation, pressure ulcer development, weight gain ■ Inability to shop and prepare food can lead to further inactivity ■ Inactivity may increase bone calcium loss and osteoporosis
Western Medicine Recommendations	■ Assess person's ability to recognize need for fluid ■ Provide access to fluids, especially water at all times ■ Taste perception may improve with adequate chewing, oral hygiene and smoking cessation ■ Provide adequate lighting and comfortable environment in which to dine ■ Monitor potential food/drug interactions that alter taste or cause dry mouth (ask your dietitian and/or pharmacist) ■ Follow physician-prescribed directives for fasting and other eating behaviors after surgery

Integrative Therapy	■ Therapeutic touch
	■ Gentle yoga and meditation with deep breathing
	■ Aromatherapy with lavender/neroli oils reduces stress and improves sleep
	■ Herbs:
	    ■ Bromelain and turmeric: reduction of swelling, bruising, healing time and pain
	    ■ Gotu kola: promotes connective tissue repair

Integrative Therapy *continued*	■ Herbs (*continued*): 　■ Coneflower/goldenseal: prevents infection 　■ St. John's wort: relief of nerve pain 　■ Aloe vera: pain relief and healing 　■ Marigold/plantain: salve used on "clean" wounds can speed healing
Male or Female Directives	■ Applies to large variety of diseases
Best Nutritional Strategies	■ Encourage small frequent meals ■ Serve meals/snacks in attractive, colorful and flavorful manner ■ Vary texture, color, flavor and temperature of meal parts and snacks to find something that "tastes good" ■ Allow ample time for meal consumption ■ Monitor food intake for texture or other intolerance ■ Experiment with textures, seasonings and flavorings to promote better intake ■ Use sugarless gum or candy to stimulate salivary flow and relieve discomfort ■ Consider artificial saliva if dryness is severe ■ May have a decreased tolerance to fat—avoid fried foods; choose lean meats and low-fat milk and dairy products
Supplements or Functional Foods to Consider	■ Vitamin A ■ Beta-carotene ■ Vitamin E ■ Coenzyme Q10 ■ L-carnitine ■ Calcium citrate ■ Magnesium citrate ■ Folate ■ Essential fatty acids eicosapentaenoic acid (EPA) and docosa-hexaenoic acid (DHA) ■ Vitamin C for wound healing ■ "Seacure": easily absorbable protein for wound healing

We should all think about returning to the sanctity of the table where we can rebuild our families, heal spiritually and physically and reconnect with those we love.

—Art Smith
Back to the Table

226

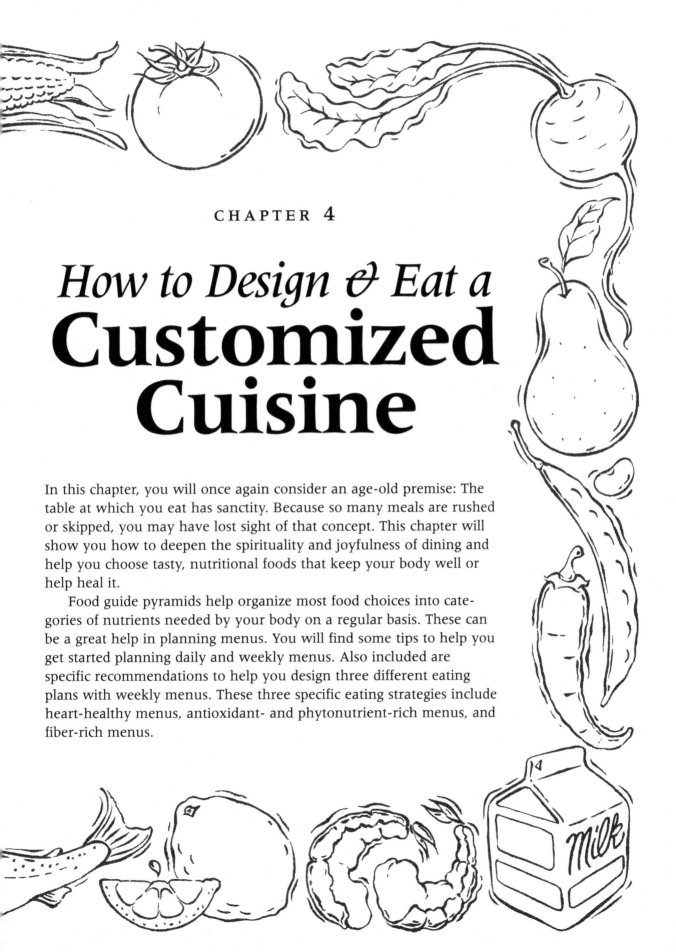

How to Design & Eat a
Customized Cuisine

In this chapter, you will once again consider an age-old premise: The table at which you eat has sanctity. Because so many meals are rushed or skipped, you may have lost sight of that concept. This chapter will show you how to deepen the spirituality and joyfulness of dining and help you choose tasty, nutritional foods that keep your body well or help heal it.

Food guide pyramids help organize most food choices into categories of nutrients needed by your body on a regular basis. These can be a great help in planning menus. You will find some tips to help you get started planning daily and weekly menus. Also included are specific recommendations to help you design three different eating plans with weekly menus. These three specific eating strategies include heart-healthy menus, antioxidant- and phytonutrient-rich menus, and fiber-rich menus.

Carbohydrate-Controlled and Heart-Healthy Menus (pages 241–243) can help you manage diabetes, lose weight and lower cholesterol and triglyceride levels of your blood.

Each meal or snack provides a balance of carbohydrates, the right sources of fat—more monounsaturated sources than saturated—and is controlled for calories.

Limited amounts of alcohol may be included each day, depending on your particular health needs or limitations. Both red wine and tea provide flavonoids and are considered heart-healthy drinks you may want to include daily.

Combined with adequate exercise and weight control, these menus will help you improve blood sugar levels (especially in type 2 diabetes) and maintain or continue to lose weight. If your activity levels and eating plan allow more calories, you can increase portions of specific foods or add more menu choices.

Antioxidant- and Phytonutrient-Rich Menus (pages 244–246) are ideal for lowering your risk of lung, oral, esophageal, stomach and colon cancers, and decreasing your risk of developing cardiac disease.

Each meal or snack provides abundant sources of fruits and vegetables that are rich in vitamins, minerals, newly discovered phytonutrients and fiber. Each day's menu recommends choices of soy, flax, grains and fruits and vegetables. You may further increase your nutrient intake by drinking calcium-fortified juices and eating fortified and enriched grain products. Caution: You will want to avoid megadoses of vitamins and

minerals, especially if you get more than adequate sources from your diet.

Here are two more ways to substitute soy-based products for meat-based products found in these menus:

- Eat ½ cup cooked beans, tofu, tempeh or textured vegetable protein (TVP) with meals
- Mix 3 to 4 tablespoons soy protein powder in your milk, juice or smoothies

Strict vegetarians will need to be especially vigilant to include daily servings of calcium and iron-rich foods and may want to consider supplementing with vitamin B12.

These menus are less carefully controlled for calories than the Carbohydrate-Controlled and Heart-Healthy menus. Most individuals getting between 30 and 60 minutes of daily exercise will find them appropriate.

Fiber-Rich Menus (pages 249–251) will help you lower your risk of developing or further manage diabetes, heart disease, diverticulosis and constipation. Remember to increase your fluid consumption as you increase your fiber intake. This is essential in preventing constipation.

Each day's menu will provide between 25 and 35 grams of fiber from both soluble and insoluble sources. Increased fiber intake helps your body move fecal material through the intestinal tract at a more rapid rate. This may further protect you from substances produced during normal breakdown of wastes that linger.

The highest level of nutrition actualization combines parts of each of these three eating strategies. You will probably want to focus on one strategy and sample from the others while you design your own daily and weekly menu plans.

Food Guide

The USDA's Food Guidance System emphasizes variety, proportionality, moderation and activity. MyPyramid (www.MyPyramid.gov) represents specific recommendations for making healthy choices that meet your personal needs. These recommendations are interrelated and are meant to be used together for maximum benefit. The five major food groups—and oils—are symbolized by six bands of the Pyramid. Each food group provides some, but not all, of the nutrients you need. Food in one group can't replace foods in another. No individual food group is more important than another; for good health, you need them all.

• **Activity** is represented by the steps and the person climbing them, as a reminder of the importance of daily physical activity.

• **Moderation** is represented by the narrowing of each food group from bottom to top. The wider base stands for foods with little or no solid fats or added sugars. These should be selected more often. The narrower top area stands for foods containing more added sugars and solid fats. The more active you are, the more of these foods can fit into your diet.

• **Proportionality** is shown by the different widths of the food group bands. The widths suggest how much food a person should choose from each group. The widths are just a general guide, not exact proportions. Check www.MyPyramid.com to find out how much is right for you.

• **Variety** is symbolized by the Pyramid's six color bands representing the five food groups plus oils. (From left to right, the bands symbolize grains, vegetables, fruits, oils, milk, and meat & beans.)

MyPyramid.gov
STEPS TO A HEALTHIER YOU

This illustrates that foods from all groups are needed each day for good health.

Taste Reigns

Taste will always be the most important factor influencing you. Many of us have an inborn taste preference for sweetness. We learn preferences for fat as babies and young children. Our brains recognize when our diets have more fat, which in turn abates hunger and provides a feeling of satiety. Satiety is that pleasant just-full feeling when your meal has nourished both your body and your soul; it is most easily conveyed through foods in the meal that are partially comprised of fat.

One of the reasons that satiety occurs with adequate fat present in the meal is that fat is metabolized last, lingering longest in the intestinal tract. Our brain signals this "satisfied" feeling when all of the components of a meal or snack meld together to yield this feeling, and our brain isn't easily fooled. Adequate

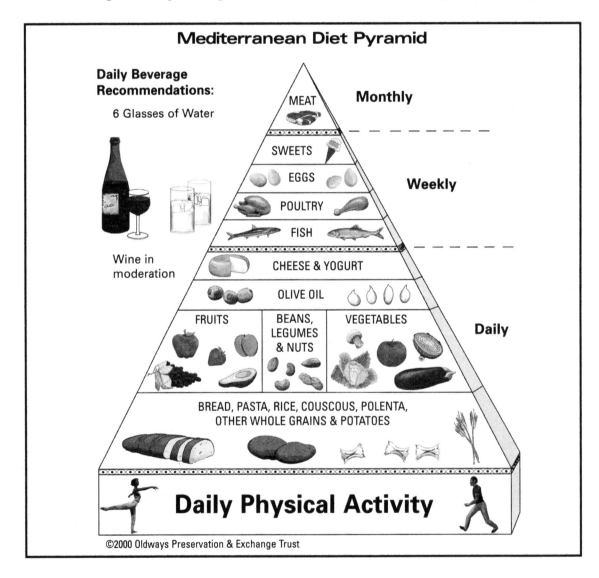

Mediterranean Diet Pyramid

Daily Beverage Recommendations:

6 Glasses of Water

Wine in moderation

MEAT — **Monthly**

SWEETS

EGGS

POULTRY — **Weekly**

FISH

CHEESE & YOGURT

OLIVE OIL

FRUITS

BEANS, LEGUMES & NUTS

VEGETABLES — **Daily**

BREAD, PASTA, RICE, COUSCOUS, POLENTA, OTHER WHOLE GRAINS & POTATOES

Daily Physical Activity

©2000 Oldways Preservation & Exchange Trust

calories and a mixture of food groups with fat represented satisfy our physical need to "rub our belly," you might say, and walk away from the table with a physiological and emotional feeling of satisfaction.

Sample the Mediterranean Flair

As you develop your personal nutrition style, consider the health benefits of the Mediterranean diet. Olive oil, a source of monounsaturated fatty acid, is one of the staples of the Mediterranean diet. It was already being produced 5,000 years ago. Ancient accounts of "The Great Flood" include a dove returning with an olive branch in tow.

The Mediterranean diet is linked to decreased cardiac risk and better weight control. It pays more attention to the *kind* of fat in the diet rather than simply the *amount*. It uses plenty of fruits and vegetables, is higher in fat, is relatively low in easily digested carbohydrates and has a relatively low impact on blood sugar fluctuations.

The Mediterranean diet has been associated with much lower incidence of obesity, cardiovascular disease and can-

> ## Basic Benefits of the Mediterranean Diet
> - Has a great variety of tastes that appeal to people of many different cultures.
> - Includes lots of whole grain products instead of the refined carbohydrates found in the Western diet, reducing the glycemic load.
> - Contains mostly monounsaturated fat and at least one good source of omega-3 (n-3) fatty acids from fish, flaxseed oil, canola oil and walnuts.
> - Provides less meat and poultry than the Western diet and more fish and legumes.
> - Includes some cheese and yogurt.
> - Has a great variety of fruits and vegetables, including low–glycemic index choices that also provide fiber and protective phytochemicals.
> - Puts an emphasis on fresh foods.
> - Uses familiar ingredients that can be adapted to locally available ingredients.
> - Is relatively easy to prepare.
> - Replaces saturated fats with unsaturated fats as a safe, proven and delicious way to cut the rates of heart disease.
> - Reduces or eliminates sources of trans fatty acids in the diet.
>
> You will probably benefit most from picking and choosing from the best of both the USDA and the Mediterranean pyramids to develop your own healthy eating strategy.

cer than have most diets found in Europe and the West. People in the Mediterranean also get more physical activity than most Americans and enjoy strong social and family bonds centered around meals. Eating together and taking pleasure in food are central to these healthy societies.

Plenty of vegetables and whole

Getting Active to Balance Out Calories & Fat Grams

Fewer than 40 percent of adults are physically active. Did you know that persons who exercise regularly have more energy and a better sex life? Individuals who exercise regularly can also work longer hours than those who do not.

While you're marking the calendar for planned activity times, pencil in all of your daily activity needs. You may wish to track some of these as well and monitor how well you are meeting those goals.

Take a look at the estimated daily energy requirements, translated to calories, based on various levels of activity.

Caloric Requirements

New dietary guidelines issued estimate daily energy requirements, in calories, for people of various sizes and levels of activity.

	Activity Level	Calories
5-foot-1-inch, 98 to 132 lbs.		
Women	Sedentary	1,688 to 1,834
	Active	2,104 to 2,290
Men	Sendentary	1,919 to 2,167
	Active	2,104 to 2,290
5-foot-5, up to 150 lbs.		
Women	Sedentary	1,816 to 1,982
	Active	2,267 to 2,477
Men	Sendentary	2,068 to 2,349
	Active	2,490 to 2,842
5-foot-9, 125 to 169 lbs.		
Women	Sedentary	1,948 to 2,134
	Active	2,434 to 2,670
Men	Sendentary	2,222 to 2,538
	Active	2,683 to 3,078
6-foot-1, 139 to 188 lbs.		
Women	Sedentary	2,083 to 2,290
	Active	2,605 to 2,869
Men	Sendentary	2,382 to 2,736
	Active	2,883 to 3,325

Source: Institute of Medicine/National Academy of Sciences

grains and relatively little meat means a relatively low energy density. The abundance of vegetables and whole grains, as well as the relatively high percentage of fat (30 to 45 percent of calories, mainly from olive and other vegetable oils) make for mild effects on blood sugar. Just as important, this kind of diet is open to creative interpretation. You can incorporate cuisines from around the world, as well as your own creations, into an eating pattern with enough variety and pleasure to last a lifetime.

Review the nutrition, activity and wellness concepts in chapter 3 and translate them into an action plan for your personal eating style. Go back to the "Vital Eating Tracker" you completed in chapter 1. Plan one meal or a week of meals that include the goals you have set for improving your nutritional status. Determine which days include meals eaten out and which ones are focused on meals in your home. Then begin to take a broader view, for even a month or so.

Mark the Calendar & Go For It!

Begin with any week, but let's think of the menu week as running from Monday through Sunday, and I'll tell you why. When I began managing kitchens, the menus were often set up to reflect a typical calendar week, Sunday through Saturday. That may work in some quantity kitchens, but I quickly learned that we were better served by thinking of a week as you might in your own home. The work week really seems to begin on Monday, when most of us go back to our "weekday world." I apply this same concept in my kitchen, and possibly you will choose to as well.

In quantity food service, the same cooks usually work every second or third weekend, often both Saturday and Sunday. A great cook or chef is preparing the meal you're eating today with an eye on what meat or poultry needs to be thawed three days from now, and what foods need to be "prepped" today to complete tomorrow's menu.

The cooks I served appreciated having those back-to-back weekend days staring at them from the same menu page. Hopefully you will not be cooking all weekend like they might be, but most activities on Saturday and Sunday seem to be linked together like salt and pepper (of course, this will vary within some religious beliefs).

You will want some easy-to-read road maps to help plan your first *Food for Life* meal—or your 99th. The lists and menus in this chapter give you the guidelines and basics, and the lists of foods that maximize vital nutrient consumption can be found in chapter 2. You can add ethnic choices and personalize them to best suit your needs. Your personal health profile and concerns about developing a specific disease will help round out your unique eating recommendations list.

Eating is fun. Guides are just that—helpful when needed. You will want to sample many foods that aren't included in the lists provided. Go ahead! Remember, all foods fit.

How Do We Begin?

Remember to refer often to chapter 2 as you interpret the following guidelines. Foods that supply each of the nutrients are listed for you.

Category	Guidelines	A Place to Begin	Advanced Healthy Eating
Eating & Drinking Habits	■ Eat or drink something that supplies calories every 4 hours. ■ Choose "mixed energy snacks" that are easy to buy or prepare, provide a sense of comfort or fulfill the need to crunch while providing vital nutrients. Snacks keep us from getting too hungry between meals. It's best to eat or drink at least every 4 hours. The preferred snack provides a lean protein source, high-fiber carbohydrate, and healthy fat. When snacking, less is always better. You may even prefer to have smaller amounts every 2 hours. ■ Stay hydrated. Drink fluids every 1 to 2 hours. Don't wait to feel thirsty.	■ Choose "mixed energy snacks." The preferred snack provides a lean protein source, high-fiber carbohydrate, and healthy fat. It's best to eat or drink at least every 4 hours. When snacking, less is always better. You may even prefer to have smaller amounts every 2 hours. ■ Minimal fluid need for adults is 8 (8-ounce) glasses of fluids per day—a great proportion of this should be water.	■ Choose "mixed energy snacks." The preferred snack provides a lean protein source, high-fiber carbohydrate, and healthy fat. It's best to eat or drink at least every 4 hours. When snacking, less is always better. You may even prefer to have smaller amounts every 2 hours. ■ Individuals who become dehydrated easily will need to rely on juices and sports drinks to provide needed electrolytes that the body uses to keep balance.

Category	Guidelines	A Place to Begin	Advanced Healthy Eating
Vitamin C	■ Include vitamin C–rich foods every day.	■ Include one vitamin C–rich food every day.	■ Include one or more vitamin C–rich foods every day.
Fruits & Vegetables	■ Eat deep green, leafy and deep yellow fruits and vegetables.	■ Eat deep green, leafy and deep yellow fruits and vegetables at least every other day. ■ Serve spinach at least once a week. Daily salads can include smaller amounts of fresh spinach leaves. Romaine and dark leaf lettuce will add to the nutrient density of your salad.	■ Eat deep green, leafy and deep yellow fruits and vegetables daily. ■ Serve spinach at least 2 or 3 times a week. Daily salads can include smaller amounts of fresh spinach leaves. Romaine and dark leaf lettuce will add to the nutrient density of your salad.
Legumes, Beans & Lentils	■ Eat legumes, beans and lentils often.	■ Eat legumes, beans and lentils 1 or 2 times per week.	■ Eat legumes, beans and lentils 2 to 3 times per week.

Category	Guidelines	A Place to Begin	Advanced Healthy Eating
Grains	■ Eat whole grain and enriched cereals and breads at each meal.	■ Eat whole grain and enriched cereals and breads at each meal. Enriched products are especially helpful for individuals whose palate is less diverse. ■ If you eat enriched and fortified foods while taking megadoses of vitamins and minerals, you may be consuming too much!	■ Experiment with an "old world" whole grain or cereal in a new and different ethnic bread or vegetable dish 1 time per week. ■ Continue to eat whole grain and enriched cereals and breads at each meal.
Dairy	■ Consume adequate dairy and/or soy products for your age. Individuals with lactose intolerance or a dairy allergy will want to take daily supplements of calcium (and possibly vitamin D).	■ Consume adequate dairy and/or soy products for your age. Individuals with lactose intolerance or a dairy allergy will want to take daily supplements of calcium (and possibly vitamin D).	■ Consume adequate dairy and/or soy products for your age. Individuals with lactose intolerance or a dairy allergy will want to take daily supplements of calcium (and possibly vitamin D).

Category	Guidelines	A Place to Begin	Advanced Healthy Eating
Meat & Protein	■ Meat-eaters should consume portions of red meat, poultry and fish that are the size of a deck of cards. Men should stop at 7 oz. per day (2 decks of cards); women at 5 oz. (about 1½ decks of cards). Less may be suitable for you. ■ Vegetarians should boost their protein intake with ½ cup cooked beans, tofu, tempeh, textured vegetable protein (TVP); 2 to 3 oz. of meat substitute; 2 Tbsp. nuts, seeds, nut or seed butter; 1 cup fortified soy or rice milk; 1 cup cow's milk; 1 cup yogurt.	■ Meat-eaters should consume portions of red meat, poultry and fish that are the size of a deck of cards. Men should stop at 7 oz. per day (2 decks of cards); women at 5 oz. (about 1½ decks of cards). Less may be suitable for you. ■ Vegetarians should boost their protein intake with ½ cup cooked beans, tofu, tempeh, textured vegetable protein (TVP); 2 to 3 oz. of meat substitute; 2 Tbsp. nuts, seeds, nut or seed butter; 1 cup fortified soy or rice milk; 1 cup cow's milk; 1 cup yogurt.	■ Meat-eaters may want to consider substituting several of their meat choices with a non-meat choice as described below. Portions of red meat, poultry, fish or meat substitute should be the size of a deck of cards (3 oz). Men should stop at 7 oz. per day (2 decks of cards); women at 5 oz. (about 1½ decks of cards). Less may be suitable for you. ■ Vegetarians should boost their protein intake with ½ cup cooked beans, tofu, tempeh, textured vegetable protein (TVP); 2 to 3 oz. of meat substitute; 2 Tbsp. nuts, seeds, nut or seed butter; 1 cup fortified soy or rice milk; 1 cup cow's milk; 1 cup yogurt.

Category	Guidelines	A Place to Begin	Advanced Healthy Eating
Fats	■ Choose foods and recipes that have primarily mono-unsaturated and polyunsaturated sources. Limit the amount of fat in each meal or snack to 10 to 20 grams, at most. ■ Be aware of trans fatty acids in many processed foods. Look for the words "hydro-genated" and "partially hydro-genated." Recognize that most hydrogen-ated fats are larger sources of trans fatty acids.	■ Choose foods and recipes that have primarily mono-unsaturated and polyunsaturated sources. ■ Be aware of trans fatty acids in many processed foods. Look for the words "hydro-genated" and "partially hydro-genated." Recognize that most hydro-genated fats are larger sources of trans fatty acids.	■ Choose foods and recipes that have primarily mono-unsaturated and polyunsaturated sources. ■ Be aware of trans fatty acids in many processed foods. Look for the words "hydro-genated" and "partially hydro-genated." Recognize that most hydrogen-ated fats are larger sources of trans fatty acids.
Develop Your Own Customized Guidelines			

Menu Planning Tools

Planning meals gives you and your family a sense of control over eating. It helps you meet the nutrition goals you may have set for yourself and plan ahead to include specific nutrients. For example, if you need three or four glasses of milk each day, you have to plan carefully to meet that goal.

Attention to taste will keep you interested in your nutrition and overall health and wellness goals. Review this list as you begin to develop menu plans and start grocery shopping:

■ Recognize that taste is a personal matter. Flavors appeal and please because of several things—physiologic, psychologic and cultural variables. Choose foods that are fresh and full-flavored. Recognize that we eat first with our senses of sight and smell. Only later do we taste the beautiful food that is presented at our joyful table. And finally, the sounds of conversation and laughter further stimulate digestion.

■ Menu planning includes varying the texture, shapes and color presented during the same meal or snack. This ensures visual and palate appeal.

■ Always begin with foods you know you like, and then push the boundaries just a little, to include foods from different ethnic groups, a new herb or spice, and even a food you've never tried before.

■ Foods like garlic, onions, citrus fruits and ripe berries provide a lot of flavor for their size. None of these add significant calories and all contain only trace amounts of fat.

■ Experts in flavor, like Susan Schiffman of Duke University, recommend an extra blast of flavor to help you stick

with a low-fat diet or eating plan. Foods that help do this are salsa, vinegars, horseradish and a variety of herbs and spices.

■ If you are looking to better control your blood sugar, fruits with a lower glycemic index (GI) will help balance other higher-GI foods. Low-GI fruits include apples, apricots, cherries, grapefruit, grapes, oranges, pears, peaches and plums.

■ Breads made with whole or coarsely ground grains and whole wheat are wise choices. Use homemade, baked croutons in cold salads with cruciferous vegetables and carrots for an antioxidant sampling of all sorts.

■ Semolina pastas made with durum wheat—also called hard wheat—are digested more slowly than potato dishes and refined-flour breads. The skin of the potato offers fiber, and in the case of red, round potatoes, some flavonol benefit.

■ Not all rices are equal. Brown rice has a higher fiber content than most rices. Other "healthier" rice choices are long-grain, converted and basmati.

Week-at-a-Glance Menu Worksheet

	Breakfast	Lunch	Dinner	Snacks	Do-Ahead
Monday					
Tuesday					
Wednesday					
Thursday					
Friday					
Saturday					
Sunday					

Carbohydrate-Controlled & Heart-Healthy Menus

For people with diabetes or at risk for diabetes, those attempting to control weight and people with elevated cholesterol and triglycerides.

If you are carbohydrate counting with diabetes or while you are losing weight, work with your healthcare provider to determine the correct number of carbohydrate grams for your meals and snacks. The number of carbohydrates to consume daily varies for each person. A range to consider is 30 to 70 grams of carbohydrate at each meal and 15 to 45 grams at each snack. Your size, activity, sex, medication, type of diabetes and degree of control also influence this number.

Recipes included in this book have serving sizes to help you count carbohydrates and fat grams as well as sodium.

Day 1

Breakfast
Cold breakfast cereal (made from whole
    wheat, oats, barley or other grains)
Whole wheat bagel with low-fat cream cheese
100% cranberry juice
Skim or soymilk

Lunch
Wisconsin Cheesy Vegetable Soup (page 278)
Lean hamburgers with low-calorie buns
Condiments of choice
Carrot & Snow Pea Salad (page 297)
Skim or soymilk

Dinner
Red Pepper Turkey Stroganoff (page 330)
Whole wheat noodles
French-style green beans
Frozen vanilla yogurt with chocolate topping
Skim or soymilk

Snacks
100% fruit or vegetable juice
Roasted pumpkin seeds
Red wine or tea

Day 2

Breakfast
Low cholesterol whole grain popovers
Non-hydrogenated margarine or butter
Fruit spread
Grapes
Apple juice
Skim or soymilk

Lunch
Turkey Salad in a Wrap (page 290)
Fruit, Nuts & Rice (page 256)
Low-calorie butterscotch pudding
Skim or soymilk

Dinner
Slow-Cooked Kraut with Ham & Bacon
    (page 320)
Marjoram & Basil Tomato Bread (page 266)
Rock Star Brownies (page 354)
Skim or soymilk

Snacks
100% fruit or vegetable juice
Carrots, broccoli and cauliflower
Red wine or tea

continued on next page

Day 3

Breakfast
Cold breakfast cereal (made from whole
    wheat, oats, barley or other grains)
Whole wheat english muffin with non-
    hydrogenated margarine or butter
Papaya
Skim or soymilk

Lunch
Ginger Hawaiian Chicken Salad (page 303)
Buttered peas
Jalapeño & Sage Whole Wheat Cornbread
    (page 268)
Non-hydrogenated margarine or butter
Reduced sugar syrup
Skim or soymilk

Dinner
Open-Faced Roast Beef Sandwiches
    (page 288)
M.J.'s Sinless Parsley Scalloped Corn
    (page 311)
Carrot Marinade (page 296)
Sherbet
Skim or soymilk

Snacks
Grape juice
Hardtack
Red wine or tea

Day 4

Breakfast
Cold breakfast cereal (made from whole
    wheat, oats, barley or other grains)
Bran muffin with non-hydrogenated
    margarine or butter
Strawberries
Skim or soymilk

Lunch
Spaghetti Squash Salad (page 301)
Rachel's Vegetarian Sauce with Fennel
    (page 314)
Pears
Skim or soymilk

Dinner
Louisana Rice & Fish Stew (page 283)
Ginger-Roasted Acorn Squash (page 310)
Blueberry Nutmeg Soufflé (page 355)
Skim or soymilk

Snacks
100% fruit or vegetable juice
Parmesan, Crab & Artichoke Appetizer
    (page 343)
Red wine or tea

Day 5

Breakfast
Sausage & Potato Frittata (page 331)
Fresh muskmelon
Whole wheat toast and margarine* or butter
Skim or soymilk

Lunch
Italian Meat Loaf (page 318)
Mashed potatoes with margarine* or butter
Stewed tomatoes
Low-calorie chocolate pudding
Skim or soymilk

Dinner
Sesame Soy Cod (page 322)
Low-cholesterol twice-baked potatoes
Fat-free coleslaw
Crusty warm dinner rolls with margarine*
    or butter
Skim or soymilk

Snacks
100% fruit or vegetable juice
Homemade Low-Fat Granola (page 346)
Red wine or tea

Day 6

Breakfast
Buttermilk pancakes with margarine* or butter
Sugar-reduced syrup
Tangerines
Skim or soymilk

Lunch
Layered Mexican Chicken Casserole (page 329)
Vegetable and lettuce salad
Choice of low-fat/low-calorie salad dressing
Low-fat strawberry ice cream
Skim or soymilk

Dinner
Marinated Salmon on the Grill (page 324)
Gourmet Potatoes on the Grill (page 257)
Artichoke Salad (page 292)
Skim or soymilk

Snacks
Cardamom Chocolate-Orange Shake
    (page 348)
Vanilla wafers
Red wine or tea

Day 7

Brunch
Veggie Baked Omelet for Brunch (page 336)
Pumpernickel toast with margarine* or butter
Honeydew melon
Tomato juice
Skim or soymilk

Afternoon Snack
Chili
Whole grain crackers
Skim or soymilk

Dinner
Salmon Pasta Salad with Cucumber Dressing
    (page 304)
Colby Cobb Salad (page 300)
Warm potato rolls with margarine* or butter
Skim or soymilk

Snacks
100% fruit or vegetable juice
Sweet & Sour Meatballs (page 344)
Whole grain crackers
Red wine or tea

*Margarine should be non-hydrogenated

Antioxidant- & Phytonutrient-Rich Menus

Your diet is the best place for you to get the antioxidants and phytonutrients you need. Your elaborate antioxidant defense system depends on two things: your dietary intake of antioxidant vitamins and your body's production of antioxidant compounds. Diets rich in fruits and vegetables contain both antioxidants and phytonutrients. (Remember to consume at least five servings of fruits and vegetables daily.) The "Food Sources of Spotlighted Vital Nutrients" chart beginning on page 51 in chapter 2 lists many sources of antioxidants and phytonutrients.

The following menus focus on antioxidant- and phytonutrient-rich dishes. The "Cancer-Fighting Foods" chart on pages 247–248 focuses on antioxidant- and phytonutrient-rich fruits and vegetables that may help prevent the development of cancer.

Day 1

Breakfast
Oat bran muffins with blueberries
Non-hydrogenated margarine or butter
Jelly or jam
Pineapple juice
Skim or fortified soymilk/soy beverage

Lunch
Garden Delight Stuffed Peppers (page 315)
Cloves & Allspice Pumpkin Bread (page 265)
Strawberry Tofu Smoothies (page 350)
Skim or fortified soymilk/soy beverage

Dinner
Chicken Broccoli Divan (page 328)
Arugula Nasturtium Salad (page 302)
Crusty rolls
Non-hydrogenated margarine or butter
Chocolate brownie
Skim or fortified soymilk/soy beverage

Snacks
100% fruit or vegetable juice
Red wine or tea

Day 2

Breakfast
Cold breakfast cereal (made from whole
    wheat, oats, barley or other grains)
Whole wheat bagel with low-fat cream
    cheese
Cranberry juice
Skim or fortified soymilk/soy beverage

Lunch
Tangy Broccoli Soup (page 276)
Garlic Fennel Pork Chops (page 321)
Apricot Stuffing for Pork Chops (page 255)
Zesty Anise Apple Crunch (page 353)
Skim or fortified soymilk/soy beverage

Dinner
Sweet & Sour Stir-Fry Shrimp (page 325)
Watermelon and honeydew slices
Herbed breadsticks
Skim or fortified soymilk/soy beverage

Snacks
100% fruit or vegetable juice
Red wine or tea

Day 3

Breakfast
Pumpkin Pancakes (page 334)
Apple Raisin Compote (page 335)
Margarine* or butter
Skim or fortified soymilk/soy beverage

Lunch
Italian Fish Kabobs (page 323)
Savory Rice Pilaf (page 259)
Tomatoes
Skim or fortified soymilk/soy beverage

Dinner
Italian Meatball Hero Sandwich (page 287)
Wild Rice for Picnics (page 261)
Sweet Skillet Carrots (page 310)
Gramma Gren's Sweet Woodruff Winey Fruit
    (page 309)
Skim or fortified soymilk/soy beverage

Snacks
100% fruit or vegetable juice
Red wine or tea

Day 4

Breakfast
Cold breakfast cereal (made from whole
    wheat, oats, barley or other grains)
Bran muffin with margarine* or butter
Strawberries
Skim or fortified soymilk/soy beverage

Lunch
Veggie Burritos (page 335)
Vegetables
Rosemary & Basil Salsa (page 339)
Pumpkin pie
Skim or fortified soymilk/soy beverage

Dinner
Shrimply Wonderful Italian Dinner (page 326)
Peg's Parsley Mediterranean Rice Pilaf
    (page 258)
Gazpacho (page 342)
Skim or fortified soymilk/soy beverage

Snacks
100% fruit or vegetable juice
Red wine or tea

Day 5

Breakfast
Papaya & Kiwi Froth (page 349)
Vegetable stuffed quiche
Toasted whole wheat muffins
Margarine* or butter
Skim or fortified soymilk/soy beverage

Lunch
Beef Burgundy Stew (page 282)
Carrot Sandwiches on Whole Grain Bread
    (page 285)
Crunchy Wild Rice Salad (page 307)
Skim or fortified soymilk/soy beverage

Dinner
Hawaiian Pizza on Cajun Crust (page 270)
Basil & Garlic Summer Squash Stir-Fry
    (page 313)
Skim or fortified soymilk/soy beverage

Snacks
100% fruit or vegetable juice
Red wine or tea

continued on next page

Day 6
Breakfast
Cold breakfast cereal (made from whole
wheat, oats, barley or other grains)
Whole wheat english muffin with margarine*
or butter
Papaya
Skim or fortified soymilk/soy beverage

Lunch
Vegetable Chowder with Turkey (page 277)
Sweet potatoes
Orange & Clove Ambrosia (page 308)
Skim or fortified soymilk/soy beverage

Dinner
Rump Roast with Beer & Tomato Velvet Gravy
(page 319)
Vegetable Stuffing (page 260)
Mediterranean Herby Greens with Mustard
Greens (page 312)
Fresh peaches
Baking powder biscuits
Skim or fortified soymilk/soy beverage

Snacks
100% fruit or vegetable juice
Easy Veggie Pizza (page 272) on Whole
Wheat Pizza Crust (page 271)
Red wine or tea

Day 7
Breakfast
Cold breakfast cereal (made from whole
wheat, oats, barley or other grains)
Apricot muffin
Non-hydrogenated margarine or butter
Apple juice
Skim or fortified soymilk/soy beverage

Lunch
Low-Calorie Turkey-Spinach Lasagna
(page 262)
Crunchy Broccoli Salad (page 294)
Gingerbread cookies
Skim or fortified soymilk/soy beverage

Dinner
Crab cakes
Carrot Lentil Salad (page 295)
Assorted fresh fruits with pink fruit dip
Hot dinner rolls
Megan's Cinnamon Chocolate Chip Oatmeal
Cookies (page 352)
Skim or fortified soymilk/soy beverage

Snacks
Salsa Ranch Dip (page 338)
Raw vegetable dippers
Reduced-fat tortilla chips
Red wine or tea

Cancer-Fighting Foods *Choose five or more servings of fruits and vegetables, with daily emphasis on rich sources of vitamin C and beta-carotene (vitamin A).*			
Food	**What Nutrient in the Food Appears to Be Preventive?**	**Foods Rich in the Respective Nutrient**	**How We Think It Prevents the Development of Cancer**
Allium, or allicin, vegetables (well-known members of the lily family)	■ Organic sulfur compounds called allicin and diallyl sulfate	■ Asparagus ■ Chives ■ Garlic ■ Leeks ■ Onions ■ Scallions ■ Shallots	■ Increases enzyme activity involved in detoxification of cancer-causing substances
Cruciferous vegetables	■ Sources of isothiocyanates, indol-3-carbinol (indoles), diathiolthiones and nitriles	■ Broccoli ■ Brussels sprouts ■ Cabbage ■ Cauliflower ■ Collard greens ■ Kale ■ Kohlrabi ■ Mustard greens ■ Radishes ■ Rutabaga ■ Turnips ■ Watercress	■ Increases enzyme activity involved in detoxification of cancer-causing substances ■ Indol-3-carbinol affects estrogen metabolism and may protect against estrogen-related cancers, such as breast and endometrial cancers
Green, orange and yellow fruits and vegetables	■ Lutein, carotenoid and xanthophylls (antioxidants); and beta-carotene (which can be metabolized to vitamin A)	■ Cantaloupe ■ Carrots ■ Kale ■ Lettuce ■ Mango ■ Mustard greens ■ Papaya ■ Pumpkins ■ Spinach ■ Sweet potatoes ■ Winter squash	■ Associated with a decreased risk of age-related macular disease *continued on next page*

Cancer-Fighting Foods *continued*

Food	What Nutrient in the Food Appears to Be Preventive?	Foods Rich in the Respective Nutrient	How We Think It Prevents the Development of Cancer
Red fruits and vegetables	■ Lycopene (a rich red pigment)	■ Raspberries ■ Red bell peppers ■ Tomatoes	■ Significant antitumor activity associated with decreased risk of prostate cancer
Citrus fruits	■ Coumarins, limonene	■ Grapefruit ■ Lemons ■ Limes ■ Oranges ■ Tangerines	■ Protects cell membranes and DNA from oxidative damage. ■ Increases the activity of other detoxifying enzymes.
Soybeans	■ Isoflavones, genistein ■ Soybeans contain protease inhibitors—saponins, phytosterols and other compounds—that have been shown to stop cancer in animal studies	■ Soybeans	■ Current data insufficient to overwhelmingly state that dietary consumption inhibits estrogen-promoted breast cancer ■ Saponins may exert a preventive effect against colon cancer by binding bile acids and cholesterol in the colon
Legumes	■ Fiber, folate and protease inhibitors	■ Alfalfa sprouts ■ Beans ■ Peas ■ Soybeans	■ May offer some protection against cancer and heart disease

Fiber-Rich Menus

Take time to review the recommendations in chapters 2 and 3 for consuming fiber in your diet. Scientific literature continues to support consuming at least five servings of fruits and vegetables each day (nine servings is ideal), which contributes to your fiber intake. Diets rich in fruits and vegetables contain a triple bonus: antioxidants, phytonutrients and abundant fiber.

Day 1

Breakfast
Cold breakfast cereal (that supplies at least 5 grams of fiber and is made from whole wheat, oats, barley or other grains)
Whole wheat toast
Non-hydrogenated margarine or butter
Orange juice
Skim or soymilk

Lunch
Black Bean Tostadas (page 254)
"Customized" Spinach & Carrot Pâté (page 340)
Whole grain crackers
Red grapes
Skim or soymilk

Dinner
Bayou Fish Stew (page 280)
Green beans
Oyster crackers
Strawberry sorbet
Skim or soymilk

Snacks
100% fruit or vegetable juice
Dried prunes or figs
Hummus

Day 2

Breakfast
Hawaiian Breakfast Sandwich (page 332)
Mango
Orange juice
Skim or soymilk

Lunch
Chili
Cornbread biscuits
Non-hydrogenated margarine or butter
Apple slices with the peel
Skim or soymilk

Dinner
Stromboli (page 289)
Curried Couscous Lentil Salad (page 298)
Watermelon slices
Skim or soymilk

Snacks
100% fruit or vegetable juice
Fruit Pizza (page 345)

Day 3

Breakfast

Cold breakfast cereal (that supplies at least 5
grams of fiber and is made from whole
wheat, oats, barley or other grains)

Pumpernickel toast

Non-hydrogenated margarine or butter

Orange or grapefruit juice

Skim or soymilk

Lunch

Hot Weather Spaghetti (page 263)

Skim or soymilk

Dinner

Peg's Asparagus-Potato Soup (page 275)

Mint & Ginger Apricot Banana Bread
(page 269)

Blueberries in milk topped with pecans

Skim or soymilk

Snacks

100% fruit or vegetable juice

Dried prunes or figs

Day 4

Breakfast

Banana nut muffins

Non-hydrogenated margarine or butter

Papaya slices

Skim or soymilk

Lunch

Roast beef

Mashed potatoes

Non-hydrogenated margarine or butter

Black Bean & Jicama Salad (page 293)

Mixed fruit (pineapple, red grapes, bananas
and apples)

Skim or soymilk

Dinner

Creamy Cucumber Soup (page 274)

Stuffed Tomatoes with Smoked Turkey & Orzo
(page 305)

Allspice Apricot Crunchies (page 351)

Skim or soymilk

Snacks

100% fruit or vegetable juice

Day 5

Breakfast
Cold breakfast cereal (that supplies at least 5 grams of fiber and is made from whole wheat, oats, barley or other grains)
Orange oatmeal muffins
Grape juice
Skim or soymilk

Lunch
Beef & Barley Stew (page 281)
Multigrain bread
Skim or soymilk

Dinner
Hot & Cheesy Italian Sub Sandwich (page 286)
Red & Green Pea Salad (page 299)
Chocolate almond cookies
Skim or soymilk

Snacks
100% fruit or vegetable juice
Dried prunes or figs

Day 6

Breakfast
Ham slices
Tropical Fruit Topping (page 335)
Skim or soymilk

Lunch
Greek Tuna & Pasta Salad (page 306)
Cooked cabbage with walnuts
Strawberry Pie (page 356)
Skim or soymilk

Dinner
Native American Stew (page 279)
Apple Cardamom Bread (page 264)
Fresh fruit of the season
Skim or soymilk

Snacks
100% fruit or vegetable juice
Jane's Caraway Reubens (page 341)

Day 7

Breakfast
Pecan-Stuffed French Toast (page 333)
Maple syrup
Apple cups
Skim or soymilk

Lunch
Yellow, Red & Green Chili (page 284)
Crusty French bread
Wedges of cantaloupe
Non-hydrogenated margarine or butter
Skim or soymilk

Dinner
Caribbean Lime Chicken on the Grill (page 327)
Corn on the cob
Sliced tomatoes
Zucchini Brownies (page 357)
Skim or soymilk

Snacks
100% fruit or vegetable juice
Jalapeño Black Bean Dip (page 338)
Vegetable dippers
Low-fat snack chips

CHAPTER 5

Food for Life
Recipes

You will find a world of nutrition information with every recipe here. Actually, there may be more facts than you need or want. Remember, you're planning meals for enjoyment, taste and nutrition. All foods fit into a healthy eating scheme. Prioritize your nutrition goals and begin with one recipe or one simple menu. The rest will fall in line. You will have met one goal.

Each recipe has been analyzed with the Nutritionist PRO-2002 and First Data Bank. Many recipes have one or more "star nutrients." These meet 25% or more of your daily need. "Noteworthy nutrients" provide 15 to 24% of your daily need.

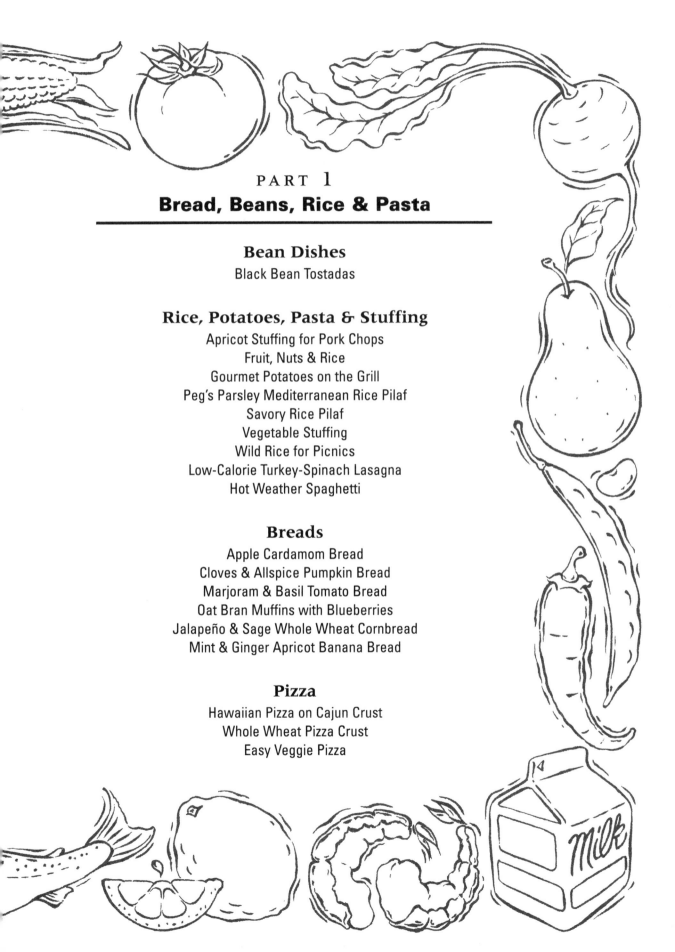

PART 1
Bread, Beans, Rice & Pasta

Bean Dishes
Black Bean Tostadas

Rice, Potatoes, Pasta & Stuffing
Apricot Stuffing for Pork Chops
Fruit, Nuts & Rice
Gourmet Potatoes on the Grill
Peg's Parsley Mediterranean Rice Pilaf
Savory Rice Pilaf
Vegetable Stuffing
Wild Rice for Picnics
Low-Calorie Turkey-Spinach Lasagna
Hot Weather Spaghetti

Breads
Apple Cardamom Bread
Cloves & Allspice Pumpkin Bread
Marjoram & Basil Tomato Bread
Oat Bran Muffins with Blueberries
Jalapeño & Sage Whole Wheat Cornbread
Mint & Ginger Apricot Banana Bread

Pizza
Hawaiian Pizza on Cajun Crust
Whole Wheat Pizza Crust
Easy Veggie Pizza

Black Bean Tostadas

Consider serving Black Bean Tostadas with a green salad topped with low-calorie ranch dressing, spiced pears and grape juice.

- 1 **(16-oz.) can refried beans with chiles**
- 1 **(16-oz.) can black beans, drained**
- 1 **cup chunky salsa**
- 8 **large (10-inch) flour tortillas**
- 8 **oz. Mexican-style cheese blend**

1. Heat oven to 400°F.

2. In mixing bowl, combine refried beans, black beans and salsa; spread mixture over tortillas; place on two large baking sheets. Sprinkle with cheese. Bake 15 minutes.

8 servings.
Preparation: 5 minutes
Ready to serve: 20 minutes

Per serving: 320 calories, 12 g total fat (1 g monounsaturated fat, 7 g saturated fat), 15 g protein, 36 g carbohydrate, 25 mg cholesterol, 1095 mg sodium, 7 g fiber
Star nutrients: Calcium (28%). **Noteworthy nutrients:** Iron (17%).

Apricot Stuffing for Pork Chops

Filled with nutrients … and flavor, too!

4 oz. dried apricots, diced
¼ cup brandy or red wine
⅓ cup hot water
1 small onion, chopped
2 tablespoons margarine, melted
2 teaspoons fennel seeds
½ teaspoon white pepper
½ teaspoon ground nutmeg
2 teaspoons finely grated orange peel
2 eggs or ½ cup liquid egg substitute
1 (8-oz.) pkg. croutons
8 (4-oz.) bone-in pork chops
¼ cup apricot preserves
¼ cup reduced-sodium chicken broth

1. Soak dried apricots in brandy 10 minutes or up to 24 hours. In large mixing bowl, combine marinated apricots, water, onion, margarine, fennel seeds, white pepper, nutmeg, orange peel, eggs and croutons.

2. Heat oven to 350°F. Trim pork chops well. Make a pocket in each chop by slicing horizontally toward bone halfway up thickness of chop. Stuff each with spoonful of stuffing mixture.

3. Spray 13x9-inch baking dish with nonstick cooking spray. In small bowl, combine preserves and broth. Spread evenly over bottom of dish; top with stuffed chops. Spoon any remaining stuffing mixture in and around chops. Cover with aluminum foil; bake 20 minutes. Remove foil; bake 20 minutes more.

8 servings (1 pork chop plus 1 cup stuffing).
Preparation time: 20 minutes
Ready to serve: 1 hour

Per serving (with eggs): 425 calories, 19 g total fat (8 g monounsaturated fat, 6 g saturated fat), 29 g protein, 32 g carbohydrate, 120 mg cholesterol, 325 mg sodium, 3 g fiber.
Star nutrients: Vitamin A (27%), Vitamin B6 (28%), Niacin (38%), Phosphorus (32%), Riboflavin (27%), Thiamin (74%). **Noteworthy nutrients:** Iron (17%), Zinc (16%). **Antioxidants:** 2,636 mcg Beta-Carotene, 7 mcg Lutein (+ Zeaxanthin), 123 mcg Lycopene.

Fruit, Nuts & Rice

The hint of walnuts and dried cranberries gives this side dish (or meatless main dish!) a crisp flavor. Remember, walnuts provide omega-3s and cranberries inhibit microbial growth in the bladder.

2	cups no-added-salt chicken broth
⅔	cup wild rice
2	green onions, finely chopped
1	rib celery, finely chopped
2	tablespoons chopped fresh parsley
2	tablespoons chopped walnuts
¼	cup dried cranberries or raisins

1. In saucepan, bring broth to a boil. Add rice; reduce heat. Simmer 20 minutes.

2. Meanwhile, spray skillet with nonstick cooking spray. Add green onions, celery and parsley. Sauté over medium heat 5 minutes; add to rice. Simmer rice and vegetables 20 minutes. Mix in walnuts and dried cranberries during last 10 minutes of cooking.

4 (¾-cup) servings.
Preparation time: 10 minutes
Ready to serve: 55 minutes

Per serving: 160 calories, 3 g total fat (1 g monounsaturated fat, 0 g saturated fat), 7 g protein, 29 g carbohydrate, 0 mg cholesterol, 205 mg sodium, 3 g fiber.
Noteworthy nutrients: Vitamin C (22%), Magnesium (16%), Phosphorus (16%).
Antioxidants: 145 mcg Beta-Carotene, 375 mcg Lutein (+ Zeaxanthin).

Gourmet Potatoes on the Grill

Wrap these up as a side dish for summer meats.

- 2 **large potatoes, scrubbed, quartered, cut into thin wedges**
- 1 **tablespoon olive oil**
- 1 **teaspoon minced garlic**
- ½ **teaspoon salt**
- ½ **teaspoon dried rosemary**
- ½ **teaspoon freshly ground pepper**
- 2 **tablespoons wine vinegar**

1. In mixing bowl, combine potatoes, olive oil, garlic, salt, rosemary, pepper and vinegar; stir to coat potatoes with seasonings.

2. Wrap potatoes in two (12-inch) square aluminum foil pouches, carefully sealing edges.

3. Grill over medium flame 15 to 18 minutes or until potatoes are tender when pierced with fork.

4 (½-cup) servings.
Preparation time: 10 minutes
Ready to serve: 25 minutes

Per serving: 65 calories, 3 g total fat (2 g monounsaturated fat, 0 g saturated fat), 2 g protein, 7 g carbohydrate, 0 mg cholesterol, 300 mg sodium, 2 g fiber.
Star nutrients: Vitamin C (29%). **Antioxidants:** 6 mcg Beta-Carotene, 33 mcg Lutein (+ Zeaxanthin).

Peg's Parsley Mediterranean Rice Pilaf

Wild rice gives this wonderful pilaf a special nutty flavor. Wild rice is not really a rice at all but rather an aquatic grass seed.

¼ **cup olive oil**
1¼ **cups chopped celery**
1¼ **cups chopped carrots**
1¼ **cups chopped fresh parsley**
¾ **cup chopped dry shallots**
3 **cups wild rice**
1 **tablespoon chopped fresh marjoram or 1 teaspoon dried**
6 **cups reduced-sodium chicken broth**

1. Heat oven to 350°F. Coat 3-quart casserole with nonstick cooking spray; set aside.

2. In nonstick skillet, heat olive oil over medium heat; sauté celery, carrots, parsley, shallots, rice and marjoram about 10 minutes.

3. Meanwhile, in medium saucepan, bring broth to a boil. (Or microwave at High until boiling.)

4. Place vegetable mixture in casserole; pour boiling broth over mixture. Bake uncovered 45 to 60 minutes, stirring after 30 minutes.

12 (¾-cup) servings.
Preparation time: 10 minutes
Ready to serve: 1 hour

Per serving: 205 calories, 5 g total fat (3 g monounsaturated fat, 1 g saturated fat), 7 g protein, 35 g carbohydrate, 0 mg cholesterol, 30 mg sodium, 3 g fiber.
Star nutrients: Vitamin A (81%). **Noteworthy nutrients:** Vitamin C (19%), Magnesium (20%), Niacin (15%), Phosphorus (19%), Zinc (17%). **Antioxidants:** 1 mg Alpha-Tocopherol (vitamin E), 1,472 mcg Beta-Carotene, 708 mcg Lutein (+ Zeaxanthin).

Savory Rice Pilaf

No time to cook rice? Try this quick and easy microwave side dish.

1 **cup long-grain rice**
2 **cups water**
1 **teaspoon seasoned salt, such as Morton's® Nature's Blend Seasoning**
1 **teaspoon margarine**
1 **cup frozen carrots and peas**
   Chopped green chiles or pimientos, for garnish (optional)

1. In microwave-safe steamer or container with very tight-fitting lid, combine rice, water, seasoned salt, margarine and frozen carrots and peas.

2. Microwave, covered tightly, at High 12 minutes. Uncover; stir. If rice seems tender, replace cover; let stand 3 minutes. If rice seems hard, cook 3 minutes more or until tender. Garnish as desired.

6 (½-cup) servings.
Preparation time: 5 minutes
Ready to serve: 20 minutes

Per serving: 130 calories, 1 g total fat (0 g monounsaturated fat, 0 g saturated fat), 3 g protein, 27 g carbohydrate, 0 mg cholesterol, 280 mg sodium, 1 g fiber. Star nutrients: Vitamin A (45%).
Noteworthy nutrients: Folate (20%), Thiamin (15%). **Antioxidants:** 4 mcg Beta-Carotene.

Vegetable Stuffing

Here's how to add interest, taste and pizzazz to vegetables … and make them a family favorite instead of a nutritional obligation.

  1 **tablespoon margarine, melted**
  1 **(12-oz.) pkg. herbed stuffing mix**
  2 **cups broccoli, cabbage or zucchini, cut into bite-size pieces**
  3 **carrots, finely shredded**
  1 **medium onion, chopped**
  1 **cup no-added-salt chicken broth**

1. Heat oven to 350°F.

2. Reserve 1 cup stuffing mix from package.

3. In 3-quart oven-safe casserole, combine margarine, remaining stuffing, broccoli, carrots, onion and broth. Pat evenly into casserole; sprinkle with reserved stuffing.

4. Bake 45 minutes, turning twice during cooking. Alternatively, microwave at High 20 minutes, turning twice during cooking.

8 (1-cup) servings.
Preparation time: 10 minutes
Ready to serve: 1 hour

Per serving: 205 calories, 3 g total fat (0 g monounsaturated fat, 2 g saturated fat), 6 g protein, 38 g carbohydrate, 0 mg cholesterol, 675 mg sodium, 5 g fiber.
Star nutrients: Vitamin A (134%), Vitamin C (32%). **Noteworthy nutrients:** Thiamin (18%). Antioxidants: 2,121 mcg Beta-Carotene, 328 mcg Lutein (+ Zeaxanthin).

Wild Rice for Picnics

This salad is perfect for picnics and hot summer days, and the nutty flavor of the wild rice gives everything a rustic and wholesome flair.

2	cups water
½	cup wild rice
½	cup trimmed chopped scallions (tender onions can be substituted)
8	oz. fresh mushrooms
½	lb. asparagus
3	medium carrots
1	teaspoon plus 2 tablespoons canola oil, divided
¼	cup vinegar
2	teaspoons sugar
1½	teaspoons dry packaged Lemon and Herb Dressing Mix

1. In saucepan, bring water to a boil; add wild rice. Cook 25 minutes. Rinse with cold water; drain well.

2. Meanwhile, slice scallions, mushrooms, asparagus and carrots. Place 1 teaspoon of the canola oil in 2-quart microwave-safe baking dish. Place sliced vegetables in oil; cover. Microwave at High 6 minutes. Uncover; stir to cool.

3. Combine remaining 2 tablespoons oil, vinegar, sugar and dressing mix in shaker container.

4. Place drained rice and cooled vegetables in 2-quart salad bowl; chill at least 1 hour. Just before serving, toss with dressing.

4 (1-cup) servings.
Preparation time: 10 minutes
Ready to serve: 1 hour, 25 minutes

Per serving: 210 calories, 9 g total fat (5 g monounsaturated fat, 1 g saturated fat), 7 g protein, 28 g carbohydrate, 0 mg cholesterol, 335 mg sodium, 5 g fiber.
Star nutrients: Vitamin A (265%), Folate (26%). **Noteworthy nutrients:** Vitamin C (23%), Vitamin E (16%), Copper (23%), Niacin (24%), Riboflavin (24%), Thiamin (15%).
Antioxidants: 4,371 mcg Beta-Carotene, 744 mcg Lutein (+ Zeaxanthin).

Low-Calorie Turkey-Spinach Lasagna

This recipe is an excellent way to use leftover turkey. In fact, your family may even begin to prefer turkey prepared this non-traditional but delicious and healthful way.

 3 **(10-oz.) pkg. frozen chopped spinach, thawed, squeezed dry**
16 **oz. low-fat ricotta cheese**
 2 **cups chopped cooked turkey**
 1 **(15-oz.) jar spaghetti sauce**
 8 **oz. low-fat mozzarella cheese, sliced**
¼ **cup grated nonfat Parmesan cheese**

1. Heat oven to 350°F. Lightly spray 11x13-inch casserole with nonstick cooking spray.

2. Place about one-third of the spinach in bottom of casserole. Spread half of the ricotta cheese over spinach. Cover with half of the turkey. Spoon on half of the spaghetti sauce. Top with half of the mozzarella cheese. Repeat layers using another third of the spinach and the remaining ricotta cheese, turkey, spaghetti sauce and mozzarella cheese. Top with the remaining third of the spinach; sprinkle with Parmesan cheese. Bake 45 to 50 minutes or until browned.

8 servings (⅛ of lasagna)
Preparation time: 30 minutes
Ready to serve: 1 hour, 15 minutes

Per serving: 260 calories, 10 g total fat (1 g monounsaturated fat, 4 g saturated fat), 30 g protein, 12 g carbohydrate, 50 mg cholesterol, 846 mg sodium, 4 g fiber.
Star nutrients: Vitamin A (177%), Vitamin C (47%), Calcium (65%), Folate (33%).
  Noteworthy nutrients: Iron (18%), Magnesium (18%), Phosphorus (22%), Riboflavin (21%).
  Antioxidants: 5,252 mcg Beta-Carotene.

Hot Weather Spaghetti

You'll find this chilled spaghetti dish especially refreshing on a hot summer day, but the flavor is good enough to enjoy any time of year.

4	**large ripe tomatoes**
2	**tablespoons red wine vinegar**
1	**tablespoon canola oil or sunflower oil**
3	**tablespoons chopped green onions**
1	**teaspoon dried basil**
1	**teaspoon dried oregano**
¼	**teaspoon fennel seeds**
⅛	**teaspoon plus ¼ teaspoon salt, divided**
⅛	**teaspoon freshly ground pepper**
3	**quarts water**
8	**oz. spaghetti**

1. Peel tomatoes; chop or process in food processor until chunky.

2. For dressing: In mixing bowl, combine chopped tomatoes, vinegar, canola oil, green onions, basil, oregano, fennel seeds, ⅛ teaspoon of the salt and pepper; chill.

3. Meanwhile, in large saucepan, bring water to a boil; add the remaining ¼ teaspoon of the salt and spaghetti. Boil 8 minutes. Drain; rinse with cold water.

4. Serve spaghetti with cold tomato dressing.

8 servings (1 cup pasta and dressing)
Preparation time: 15 minutes
Ready to serve: 25 minutes

Per serving: 135 calories, 2 g total fat (1 g monounsaturated fat, 0 g saturated fat), 4 g protein, 24 g carbohydrate, 0 mg cholesterol, 117 mg sodium, 1 g fiber.
Noteworthy nutrients: Vitamin C (21%), Folate (19%), Thiamin (22%). **Antioxidants:** 251 mcg Beta-Carotene, 129 mcg Lutein (+ Zeaxanthin), 1,860 mcg Lycopene.

Apple Cardamom Bread

This flavorful bread tastes best served just warm. After storing, tweak it with the microwave before serving. You and your family will appreciate the extra flavor created when you serve it hot.

2	cups all-purpose flour
1	teaspoon baking soda
1	teaspoon ground cinnamon
1	teaspoon ground cardamom
½	teaspoon salt
½	teaspoon baking powder
¾	cup packed brown sugar
¼	cup plain yogurt
¼	cup low-fat margarine
¼	cup orange juice
1	teaspoon grated orange peel
1	teaspoon vanilla
2	eggs or ½ cup liquid egg substitute
2	cups chopped apples
⅓	cup chopped walnuts

1. Heat oven to 350°F. Lightly coat two small (8½x4½x2½-inch) loaf pans with nonstick cooking spray.

2. In bowl, mix together flour, baking soda, cinnamon, cardamom, salt and baking powder; set aside.

3. In another bowl, mix together brown sugar, yogurt, margarine, orange juice, orange peel, vanilla and eggs. Add dry ingredients to mixture. Fold in apples and walnuts.

4. Turn batter into pans. Bake 50 minutes. Insert toothpick. When it comes out clean it is done. Let cool 5 minutes before serving.

20 servings.
Preparation time: 15 minutes
Ready to serve: 1 hour, 10 minutes

Per serving (with eggs): 110 calories, 3 g total fat (1 g monounsaturated fat, 1 g saturated fat), 3 g protein, 18 g carbohydrate, 20 mg cholesterol, 285 mg sodium, 1 g fiber.
Antioxidants: 4 mcg Beta-Carotene, 10 mcg Lutein (+ Zeaxanthin).

Cloves & Allspice Pumpkin Bread

This autumn-oriented pleaser is a rich source of monounsaturated fatty acids, which help maintain levels of "good" (high-density lipoprotein) cholesterol. Serve this delicious, moist loaf warm and fresh from the bread machine.

2	eggs, well beaten, or ½ cup liquid egg substitute
1	cup canned pumpkin
½	cup packed brown sugar
½	cup unsweetened applesauce
⅓	cup canola oil
1⅔	cups all-purpose flour
1	teaspoon baking soda
½	teaspoon salt
¼	teaspoon baking powder
1	teaspoon ground cinnamon
½	teaspoon ground allspice
¼	teaspoon ground cloves
¼	cup chopped pecans

1. Heat oven to 350°F. Coat loaf pan with nonstick cooking spray.

2. In bowl, combine eggs, pumpkin, brown sugar, applesauce and canola oil; set aside.

3. In another bowl, combine flour, baking soda, salt, baking powder, cinnamon, allspice and cloves. Add dry ingredients to pumpkin mixture, mixing well. Fold in pecans.

4. Bake 50 to 55 minutes or until toothpick inserted in middle of loaf comes out clean. Cool 30 minutes before slicing.

20 servings.
Preparation time: 10 minutes
Ready to serve: 1 hour, 30 minutes

Per serving (with eggs): 105 calories, 5 g total fat (3 g monounsaturated fat, 1 g saturated fat), 2 g protein, 13 g carbohydrate, 20 mg cholesterol, 265 mg sodium, 1 g fiber.
Star nutrients: Vitamin A (55%). Antioxidants: 850 mcg Beta-Carotene, 3 mcg Lutein (+ Zeaxanthin).

Marjoram & Basil Tomato Bread

To use this bread as bruschetta, slice it and reheat it with a topping of fresh tomatoes and Parmesan or provolone cheese.

1	(14½-oz.) can no-added-salt whole tomatoes
1½	cups all-purpose flour
¼	cup packed brown sugar
1	teaspoon baking soda
1	teaspoon baking powder
½	teaspoon salt
2	tablespoons plus 2 teaspoons diced onion
1	tablespoon chopped fresh marjoram or 1 teaspoon dried
1	tablespoon chopped fresh basil or 1 teaspoon dried
¼	teaspoon dried oregano
¼	cup low-fat margarine
2	eggs, well beaten, or ½ cup liquid egg substitute
1	teaspoon Schilling® California Style Blend garlic powder

1. Heat oven to 350°F. Coat loaf pan with nonstick cooking spray. Drain tomatoes well, reserving 1 cup of juices. Chop tomatoes; set aside.

2. In bowl, mix flour, brown sugar, baking soda, baking powder, salt, onion, marjoram, basil and oregano.

3. Melt margarine in microwave; combine with eggs, tomatoes and reserved tomato juices. Combine with flour mixture.

4. Place batter in pan; sprinkle with garlic powder. Bake 50 to 55 minutes or until toothpick inserted in bread comes out clean. Cool 15 minutes before sampling.

16 servings.
Preparation time: 10 minutes
Ready to serve: 1 hour, 15 minutes

Per serving (with eggs): 105 calories, 2 g total fat (1 g monounsaturated fat, 1 g saturated fat), 3 g protein, 18 g carbohydrate, 25 mg cholesterol, 480 mg sodium, 1 g fiber.
Antioxidants: 3 mcg Lutein (+ Zeaxanthin).

Oat Bran Muffins with Blueberries

A hearty, tasty muffin. It's difficult to eat just one!

1   cup oat bran cereal
¾   cup all-purpose flour
¼   cup whole wheat flour
½   cup packed brown sugar
4   teaspoons baking powder
¼   teaspoon salt
1   cup nonfat milk
⅓   cup canola oil
1   egg or ¼ cup liquid egg substitute
1   teaspoon vanilla
1   cup drained blueberries

1. Heat oven to 400°F. Grease muffin cups or line with paper baking cups.

2. In mixing bowl, combine cereal, all-purpose flour, whole wheat flour, brown sugar, baking powder and salt. Stir well; set aside.

3. In another bowl, use eggbeater to combine milk, canola oil, egg and vanilla. Pour into dry ingredients. Add blueberries; stir just until moistened.

4. Spoon batter into muffin cups; bake 20 minutes.

12 muffins.
Preparation time: 10 to 15 minutes
Ready to serve: 25 minutes

Per muffin (with egg): 145 calories, 7 g total fat (4 g monounsaturated fat, 1 g saturated fat), 3 g protein, 19 g carbohydrate, 20 mg cholesterol, 215 mg sodium, 1 g fiber.
Antioxidants: 4 mcg Beta-Carotene, 7 mcg Lutein (+ Zeaxanthin).

Jalapeño & Sage Whole Wheat Cornbread

This cornbread with a kick goes very well with any of your favorite Mexican dishes.

- ⅔ cup all-purpose flour
- ⅔ cup whole wheat flour
- ⅔ cup cornmeal
- 2 teaspoons baking powder
- ½ teaspoon dried sage
- ½ teaspoon salt
- ¼ cup low-fat margarine
- ¼ cup packed brown sugar
- 1 cup nonfat milk
- 1 egg or ¼ cup liquid egg substitute
- ¼ cup jalapeño peppers, drained, finely chopped

1. Heat oven to 375°F. Spray 8-inch square pan with nonstick cooking spray.

2. In bowl, combine all-purpose flour, whole wheat flour, cornmeal, baking powder, sage and salt. Set aside.

3. In medium mixing bowl, beat margarine and brown sugar until light and fluffy. Add milk and egg; stir well. Spoon into dry ingredients. Add jalapeños; stir well.

4. Spoon into pan. Bake 30 minutes. Remove from oven; cover with aluminum foil. Let sit 15 minutes before serving.

16 servings.
Preparation time: 10 minutes
Ready to serve: 55 minutes

Per serving (with egg): 75 calories, 1 g total fat (0 g monounsaturated fat, 0 g saturated fat), 3 g protein, 15 g carbohydrate, 15 mg cholesterol, 205 mg sodium, 1 g fiber.
Antioxidants: 6 mcg Beta-Carotene, 79 mcg Lutein (+ Zeaxanthin).

Mint & Ginger Apricot Banana Bread

Flavors of mint, ginger and apricot blend together to make this a most unusual and delightful banana bread.

⅓	cup low-fat margarine, softened
⅓	cup packed brown sugar
8	packets sugar substitute or ⅓ cup sugar
2	eggs, well beaten or ½ cup liquid egg substitute
1	cup (about 3) ripe bananas, mashed
¼	cup buttermilk
¼	teaspoon mint extract
1¼	cups all-purpose flour
1	teaspoon baking powder
½	teaspoon baking soda
½	teaspoon salt
½	teaspoon ground ginger
1	cup chopped dried apricots
¾	cup Fiber One® cereal

1. Heat oven to 350°F. Coat two small (8½x4½x2½-inch) loaf pans with nonstick cooking spray; set aside.

2. In mixing bowl, beat margarine, brown sugar and sugar substitute until light and fluffy. Add eggs, bananas, buttermilk and mint extract. Set aside.

3. In another bowl, combine flour, baking powder, baking soda, salt and ginger. Add dry ingredients to egg mixture. Fold in dried apricots and cereal.

4. Turn batter into pans. Bake 40 to 45 minutes or until toothpick inserted in middle of loaf comes out clean. Cool about 30 minutes.

16 servings.
Preparation time: 15 minutes
Ready to serve: 1 hour, 30 minutes

Per serving (with eggs): 120 calories, 3 g total fat (1 g monounsaturated fat, 1 g saturated fat), 3 g protein, 24 g carbohydrate, 25 mg cholesterol, 335 mg sodium, 3 g fiber.
Noteworthy nutrients: Vitamin A (16%). Antioxidants: 1,449 mcg Beta-Carotene, 3 mcg Lutein (+ Zeaxanthin), 71 mcg Lycopene.

Hawaiian Pizza on Cajun Crust

An interesting, light and satisfying alternative to traditional pizza! The topping's spicy crust and subtle sweetness will make this one of your favorite recipes.

Cajun Pizza Crust
- 1 cup plus 2 tablespoons lukewarm water
- 2 tablespoons canola oil
- 3 cups bread flour
- ¾ teaspoon sugar
- ¾ teaspoon salt
- 2 teaspoons cayenne pepper
- ¼ teaspoon garlic powder
- ¼ teaspoon freshly ground pepper
- ⅛ teaspoon paprika
- 2 teaspoons bread machine yeast

Hawaiian Sauce
- 8 oz. no-added-salt tomato sauce
- 6 oz. no-added-salt tomato paste
- ½ teaspoon dried minced onion
- ½ teaspoon Mexican oregano
- ¼ teaspoon onion powder
- ¼ teaspoon Mrs. Dash® spice blend
- ¼ teaspoon dried tarragon
- ¼ teaspoon paprika

Toppings
- 3½ oz. Canadian bacon, cut into small chunks
- 2 cups fresh pineapple, cut into small pieces
- 1 lb. shredded nonfat mozzarella cheese

1. For crust, add crust ingredients to bread machine according to manufacturer's directions. Select dough cycle; press start.

2. For sauce, in 2-quart bowl, combine tomato sauce, tomato paste, minced onion, oregano, onion powder, spice blend, tarragon and paprika. Stir well.

3. When dough cycle is complete, place dough on lightly floured surface. Knead in enough flour to make dough easy to handle. Coat 14-inch pizza pan with nonstick cooking spray. Heat oven to 425°F.

4. Roll out dough; place on or pat in pan. Top with sauce, Canadian bacon, pineapple and mozzarella cheese. Bake 20 to 25 minutes.

12 servings.
Preparation time: 25 minutes
Ready to serve: 40 minutes

Per serving: 250 calories, 4 g total fat (2 g monounsaturated fat, 0 g saturated fat), 16 g protein, 38 g carbohydrate, 5 mg cholesterol, 680 mg sodium, 2 g fiber.
Star nutrients: Riboflavin (16%), Thiamin (27%). **Noteworthy nutrients:** Vitamin A (16%), Vitamin C (22%), Calcium (22%), Folate (19%), Niacin (20%). **Antioxidants:** 176 mcg Beta-Carotene, 24 mcg Lutein (+ Zeaxanthin), 4,157 mcg Lycopene.

Whole Wheat Pizza Crust

Use this wonderful and hearty crust with any of your favorite pizza toppings.

1	cup warm water (105°F to 115°F)
2	teaspoons sugar
1	pkg. fast-acting dry yeast or active dry yeast
1	teaspoon salt
1	cup all-purpose flour
1	tablespoon canola oil
2	cups whole wheat flour

1. In large bowl, combine water, sugar and yeast. When yeast is dissolved, add salt and all-purpose flour. Add canola oil, reserving ½ teaspoon of canola oil to smear on top of dough in Step 2 below. Mix until smooth; add whole wheat flour. Knead until elastic, about 5 minutes.

2. Place dough in greased bowl; grease top of dough with reserved canola oil. Cover; let rise until doubled in size, about 45 minutes. (It will rise faster if you set it in warm place.)

3. Heat oven to 450°F. Divide dough into two balls. Pat and stretch onto two (12-inch) pizza pans. Let rest 10 minutes before baking.

4. If using for Easy Veggie Pizza (page 272), bake 10 to 12 minutes or until brown. If using with another pizza recipe, add favorite sauce and toppings. Reduce heat to 425°F and bake for 20 to 25 minutes or until brown.

12 servings.
Preparation time: 15 minutes
Ready to serve: 40 minutes

Per serving: 120 calories, 2 g total fat (1 g monounsaturated fat, 0 g saturated fat)`, 4 g protein, 23 g carbohydrate, 0 mg cholesterol, 195 mg sodium, 3 g fiber.

Easy Veggie Pizza

Another great alternative to what we usually think of as pizza!

> 1 cup nonfat sour cream
> ¾ cup low-fat mayonnaise
> 1 tablespoon onion powder
> 1 tablespoon dill weed
> 1 teaspoon garlic powder
> 1 (12-inch) Whole Wheat Pizza Crust, prebaked (page 271)
> 1½ cups cauliflower florets
> 1½ cups broccoli florets
> 1½ cups chopped carrots
> 8 to 10 cherry tomatoes, halved, or 1 medium tomato, thinly sliced
> 1 cup (4 oz.) shredded nonfat mild cheddar cheese

1. In bowl, combine sour cream, mayonnaise, onion powder, dill weed and garlic powder; spread over crust.

2. Fill large microwave-safe bowl half-full with water; microwave until boiling. Add cauliflower, broccoli and carrots. Microwave 2 to 3 minutes or until vegetables are crisp-tender. Arrange cauliflower, broccoli, carrots and tomatoes over sour cream mixture; sprinkle with cheddar. Refrigerate at least 1 hour before serving.

12 servings.
Preparation time: 20 minutes
Ready to serve: 1 hour, 20 minutes

Per serving (without crust): 105 calories, 7 g total fat (3 g monounsaturated fat, 2 g saturated fat), 4 g protein, 7 g carbohydrate, 10 mg cholesterol, 225 mg sodium, 1 g fiber.
Star nutrients: Vitamin A (94%), Vitamin C (34%). **Antioxidants:** 1,428 mcg Beta-Carotene, 308 mcg Lutein (+ Zeaxanthin).

PART 2
Soups, Sandwiches & More

Soups

Creamy Cucumber Soup
Peg's Asparagus-Potato Soup
Tangy Broccoli Soup
Vegetable Chowder with Turkey
Wisconsin Cheesy Vegetable Soup

Stews & Chili

Native American Stew
Bayou Fish Stew
Beef & Barley Stew
Beef Burgundy Stew
Louisiana Rice & Fish Stew
Yellow, Red & Green Chili

Sandwiches

Carrot Sandwiches on Whole Grain Bread
Hot & Cheesy Italian Sub Sandwiches
Italian Meatball Hero Sandwich
Open-Faced Roast Beef Sandwiches
Stromboli
Turkey Salad in a Wrap

Creamy Cucumber Soup

A smooth, cool soup that is perfect for a hot summer day ... or superb as a "different" kind of treat to begin (or star in) any meal.

1   cup nonfat milk
1   cup (8 oz.) nonfat sour cream
1   cup (8 oz.) low-fat plain yogurt
1   tablespoon lemon juice
2   cucumbers, peeled, seeded, chopped
1   green onion, chopped
1   tablespoon minced fresh dill weed
½   teaspoon salt
¼   teaspoon white pepper
    Dash hot pepper sauce
    Fresh dill weed sprigs, for garnish (optional)

1. In blender or food processor, combine milk, sour cream, yogurt, lemon juice, cucumbers, onion, dill weed, salt, white pepper and hot pepper sauce; cover. Process just until smooth. Chill thoroughly, at least 1 hour.

2. Stir well before serving. Garnish with dill weed sprigs.

4 (1-cup) servings.
Preparation time: 30 minutes
Ready to serve: 1 hour, 30 minutes

Per serving: 120 calories, 1 g total fat (0 g monounsaturated fat, 1 g saturated fat), 8 g protein, 20 g carbohydrate, 10 mg cholesterol, 450 mg sodium, 1 g fiber.
Star nutrients: Calcium (27%). **Noteworthy nutrients:** Phosphorus (23%), Riboflavin (18%).
Antioxidants: 59 mcg Beta-Carotene, 415 mcg Lutein (+ Zeaxanthin).

Peg's Asparagus-Potato Soup

You can prepare this soup so quickly! Its wonderful taste belies how easy it is to make, though!

1	(13¾-oz.) can reduced-sodium chicken broth
3	medium potatoes, chopped
⅓	cup chopped onion
¼	teaspoon salt
¼	teaspoon ground nutmeg
8	oz. frozen asparagus
1 ½	cups nonfat milk
5	oz. nonfat cream cheese

1. In saucepan, combine broth, potatoes, onion, salt and nutmeg; bring to a boil. Reduce heat. Cover; simmer 5 to 8 minutes or until potatoes just become tender. Add asparagus; return to a boil. Reduce heat; simmer 5 minutes or until vegetables are tender.

2. Blend milk and cream cheese together; stir into soup mixture until melted. Do not boil.

6 (1-cup) servings.
Preparation time: 30 minutes
Ready to serve: 30 minutes

Per serving: 80 calories, 1 g total fat (0 g monounsaturated fat, 0 g saturated fat), 9 g protein, 10 g carbohydrate, 5 mg cholesterol, 370 mg sodium, 3 g fiber.
Star nutrients: Vitamin C (46%), Folate (26%). **Noteworthy nutrients:** Phosphorus (23%). **Antioxidants:** 4 mcg Beta-Carotene, 22 mcg Lutein (+ Zeaxanthin).

Tangy Broccoli Soup

A bowl of this soup makes a great meal in itself. Pair up with a hearty, whole grain bread.

¼	cup low-fat margarine
4	cups chopped fresh broccoli
½	cup chopped onion
½	cup chopped green bell pepper
3	cups reduced-sodium chicken broth
2	cups nonfat milk
½	cup all-purpose flour
½	teaspoon crushed red pepper
1	cup grated nonfat cheddar cheese
1	cup grated mozzarella cheese

1. In 4-quart saucepan, melt margarine; sauté broccoli, onion and bell pepper 5 to 7 minutes or until tender. Add broth; simmer 35 minutes.

2. Blend milk and flour in shaker container. Add milk mixture to saucepan; stir until smooth. Add crushed red pepper, cheddar cheese and mozzarella cheese. Heat until cheeses melt, stirring often.

6 (1-cup) servings.
Preparation: 30 minutes
Ready to serve: 40 minutes

Per serving: 190 calories, 6 g total fat (2 g monounsaturated fat, 2 g saturated fat), 14 g protein, 18 g carbohydrate, 10 mg cholesterol, 760 mg sodium, 2 g fiber.
Star nutrients: Vitamin A (34%), Vitamin C (126%), Calcium (36%), Phosphorus (13%).
   Noteworthy nutrients: Vitamin D (9%), Folate (16%). **Antioxidants:** 1 mg Alpha-Tocopherol (vitamin E), 482 mcg Beta-Carotene, 1,422 mcg Lutein (+ Zeaxanthin).

Vegetable Chowder with Turkey

Here's an excellent way to use leftover turkey. Of course, once you serve it they won't want to wait for leftover turkey to have this chowder again!

6	slices bacon
1	cup no-added-salt chicken broth
2	cups finely chopped potatoes
1	cup shredded carrots
½	cup chopped onion
½	teaspoon curry powder
⅛	teaspoon freshly ground pepper
1	(12-oz.) can evaporated nonfat milk
1	cup chopped cooked turkey

1. Broil bacon until crisp; tear into pieces.

2. Meanwhile, in 3-quart kettle, combine broth, potatoes, carrots and onion; simmer until tender.

3. Stir in curry powder, pepper, evaporated milk, turkey and bacon pieces. Heat through over medium heat, about 10 minutes. Do not boil.

4 (1-cup) servings.
Preparation time: 25 minutes
Ready to serve: 55 minutes

Per serving: 295 calories, 8 g total fat (3 g monounsaturated fat, 3 g saturated fat), 24 g protein, 31 g carbohydrate, 40 mg cholesterol, 440 mg sodium, 2 g fiber.
Star nutrients: Vitamin A (161%), Calcium (29%), Niacin (24%), Phosphorus (31%), Riboflavin (26%), Zinc (16%). **Noteworthy nutrients:** Vitamin C (24%), Vitamin D (17%), Iron (17%), Thiamin (21%). **Antioxidants:** 2,173 mcg Beta-Carotene, 72 mcg Lutein (+ Zeaxanthin).

Wisconsin Cheesy Vegetable Soup

A cheesy soup that is very satisfying and also so good for you.

2	green onions, finely chopped
1	large carrot, grated
1	large rib celery, finely chopped
1	tablespoon water
1	tablespoon margarine
⅓	cup all-purpose flour
2	cups nonfat milk
1½	cups no-added-salt chicken broth
4	oz. Wisconsin cheddar cheese, shredded
	Paprika, for garnish

1. In microwave-safe dish, combine green onions, carrot, celery and water. Cover; microwave at High 3 minutes.

2. In 2-quart saucepan, melt margarine over medium heat. In shaker container, combine flour and milk; slowly whisk into margarine, stirring and blending until smooth. Add broth, vegetables and cheddar cheese, stirring until cheese melts. Do not boil.

3. Ladle into bowls; garnish with paprika.

4 (1-cup) servings.
Preparation time: 15 minutes
Ready to serve: 1 hour

Per serving: 190 calories, 8 g total fat (1 g monounsaturated fat, 4 g saturated fat), 14 g protein, 17 g carbohydrate, 15 mg cholesterol, 555 mg sodium, 1 g fiber.
Star nutrients: Vitamin A (53%), Calcium (40%). **Noteworthy nutrients:** Vitamin C (17%), Phosphorus (21%). **Antioxidants:** 605 mcg Beta-Carotene, 199 mcg Lutein (+ Zeaxanthin).

Native American Stew

The flavor of this hearty stew improves with time. Prepare it ahead of time and keep for five days, taking a serving or two for reheating and eating as you go.

- ½ cup lentils, rinsed
- ½ cup navy beans, rinsed
- 2 cups chopped onions
- 2 cups chopped celery
- 5 carrots, chopped in 1-inch pieces
- ¼ cup packed brown sugar
- 1 cup pearl barley
- 1 teaspoon chopped garlic
- 1 teaspoon freshly ground pepper
- ½ teaspoon chopped fresh thyme
- 2 bay leaves
- ½ cup red cooking wine
- 1 quart low-sodium tomato-based vegetable juice
- 2 cups water
  Salt (optional)*

1. Combine lentils, navy beans, onions, celery, carrots, brown sugar, barley, garlic, pepper, thyme, bay leaves, wine, vegetable juice and water in slow cooker; cook 4 to 5 hours on high or 8 to 10 hours on low or medium. Beans are done when cooked tender. Remove bay leaves before serving.

10 (1-cup) servings.
Preparation time: 15 minutes
Ready to serve: 4 hours, 30 minutes

Per serving: 205 calories, 1 g total fat (0 g monounsaturated fat, 0 g saturated fat), 9 g protein, 40 g carbohydrate, 0 mg cholesterol, 95 mg sodium, 11 g fiber.
Star nutrients: Vitamin A (193%), Vitamin C (53%), Folate (25%). **Noteworthy nutrients:** Copper (16%), Iron (17%), Magnesium (17%), Phosphorus (17%), Thiamin (20%). **Antioxidants:** 2,732 mcg Beta-Carotene, 2,732 mcg Lutein (+ Zeaxanthin).

TIP * If more salt is desired, add at end of cooking time to avoid toughening the beans.

Bayou Fish Stew

Fish stew is full of nutrients. Made this way, it's full of great taste, too.

  4 oz. fresh mushrooms, sliced
  2 trimmed scallions, chopped
  1 small zucchini, sliced
  1 green bell pepper, chopped
  1 lb. white fish (such as haddock, cod or trout), thawed, cut into 1-inch cubes
1½ cups chunky tomatoes
  1 cup instant rice
  1 teaspoon dried basil
  ½ teaspoon garlic powder
  ½ teaspoon ground cumin
  1 (8-oz.) can no-added-salt tomato sauce
  1 teaspoon Worcestershire sauce
     Cayenne pepper to taste

1. Spray Dutch oven with nonstick cooking spray; sauté mushrooms, scallions, zucchini and bell pepper until crisp-tender. Add fish, tomatoes, rice, basil, garlic powder, cumin, tomato sauce, Worcestershire sauce and cayenne pepper; simmer 30 minutes. Or, microwave at High uncovered in 3-quart microwave-safe casserole 15 minutes.

4 (1½-cup) servings.
Preparation time: 10 minutes
Ready to serve: 40 minutes

Per serving: 240 calories, 2 g total fat (0 g monounsaturated fat, 0 g saturated fat), 27 g protein, 29 g carbohydrate, 65 mg cholesterol, 340 mg sodium, 5 g fiber.
Star nutrients: Vitamin B6 (25%), Vitamin C (64%), Niacin (29%), Phosphorus (27%).
  Noteworthy nutrients: Vitamin A (15%), Magnesium (15%). **Antioxidants:** 289 mcg Beta-Carotene, 1407 mcg Lutein (+ Zeaxanthin).

Beef & Barley Stew

You can prepare this hearty, satisfying stew in less than half an hour. Almost unbelievable!

1   **lb. lean ground beef**
1   **(19-oz.) can beef barley soup**
1   **(1-lb.) pkg. frozen mixed vegetables**
1   **teaspoon dried basil**
1   **teaspoon dried dill weed**

1. In large, deep skillet or stockpot, cook ground beef over medium-high heat 4 to 6 minutes or until no longer pink. Tip pan, draining meat drippings into container and discard.

2. Add barley soup, mixed vegetables, basil and dill weed; cook uncovered over medium-high heat 12 to 15 minutes.

6 (1-cup) servings.
Preparation time: 10 minutes
Ready to serve: 25 minutes

Per serving: 275 calories, 14 g total fat (6 g monounsaturated fat, 6 g saturated fat), 21 g protein, 18 g carbohydrate, 60 mg cholesterol, 260 mg sodium, 4 g fiber.
Star nutrients: Vitamin A (94%). **Noteworthy nutrients:** Vitamin C (15%), Iron (16%), Niacin (23%), Phosphorus (15%), Riboflavin (16%), Zinc (23%).

Beef Burgundy Stew

This very special stew tastes so rich and full, it makes you forget how good-for-you it is!

1	lb. boneless beef chuck or round, cut into 1½-inch pieces
½	teaspoon minced garlic or 2 garlic cloves, minced
2	tablespoons all-purpose flour
1	cup reduced-sodium beef broth
½	cup Burgundy wine
2	tablespoons tomato paste
8	oz. baby carrots
2	large red potatoes, peeled, cut into wedges
1	small onion, sliced into thin wedges
2	tablespoons chopped fresh parsley
½	teaspoon dried thyme
2	fresh basil leaves
1	cup water

1. Heat oven to 350°F.

2. In large oven-safe stockpot, brown beef and garlic over medium heat.

3. In small mixing bowl, combine flour, broth, wine and tomato paste. Use whisk to stir mixture until smooth. Pour flour mixture over browned meat. Add carrots, potatoes, onion, parsley, thyme, basil leaves and water; stir to blend. Cover; bake 2 to 2½ hours.

4 (1-cup) servings.
Preparation time: 15 minutes
Ready to serve: 2 hours, 15 minutes

Per serving: 280 calories, 6 g total fat (1 g monounsaturated fat, 1 g saturated fat), 28 g protein, 22 g carbohydrate, 65 mg cholesterol, 495 mg sodium, 2 g fiber.
Star nutrients: Vitamin A (89%). **Noteworthy nutrients:** Vitamin B6 (22%), Vitamin C (20%), Niacin (16%), Phosphorus (17%), Zinc (15%). **Antioxidants:** 2,164 mcg Beta-Carotene, 205 mcg Lutein (+ Zeaxanthin), 1,203 mcg Lycopene.

Louisiana Rice & Fish Stew

Health and flavor meet in this Cajun-inspired masterpiece.

- **1½ cups instant rice**
- **1 cup frozen Bird's Eye® Farm Fresh Pepper Stir Fry,
  or ½ cup each fresh bell pepper and onion**
- **1 lb. frozen cod pieces**
- **1½ cups water**
- **1 tablespoon Worcestershire sauce**
- **1 (14-oz.) can Cajun-stewed tomatoes**
- **2 teaspoons grated Parmesan cheese**

1. In large saucepan, combine rice, frozen vegetables, cod, water, Worcestershire sauce and tomatoes. Heat over medium heat 15 minutes or until cod is opaque and can be flaked with fork. Ladle into bowls; sprinkle with Parmesan cheese.

4 (1½-cup) servings.
Preparation time: 5 minutes
Ready to serve: 25 minutes

Per serving: 260 calories, 1 g total fat (0 g monounsaturated fat, 0 g saturated fat), 24 g protein, 37 g carbohydrate, 45 mg cholesterol, 355 mg sodium, 1 g fiber
Star nutrients: Vitamin B6 (26%), Vitamin C (44%). **Noteworthy nutrients:** Vitamin A (15%), Phosphorus (22%).

Yellow, Red & Green Chili

A cornucopia of color, flavor and healthy things.

- **1 lb. reduced-fat seasoned pork sausage or ground pork**
- **2 tablespoons chili powder**
- **2 (16-oz.) cans diced tomatoes with onion and green pepper**
- **1 (16-oz.) can chili beans in sauce**
- **1 (16-oz.) can whole kernel corn**

1. In large stockpot, cook pork and chili powder over medium-high heat until pork is no longer pink. Transfer meat to strainer; discard drippings.

2. Return meat to stockpot; add tomatoes, chili beans and corn. Cook 15 minutes over medium-high heat.

8 (¾-cup) servings.
Preparation time: 5 minutes
Ready to serve: 30 minutes

Per serving: 315 calories, 13 g total fat (6 g monounsaturated fat, 5 g saturated fat), 21 g protein, 33 g carbohydrate, 55 mg cholesterol, 605 mg sodium, 7 g fiber.
Star nutrients: Vitamin A (32%), Vitamin C (30%), Iron (48%), Thiamin (34%).
   Noteworthy nutrients: Vitamin B6 (23%), Phosphorus (21%), Zinc (16%).
   Antioxidants: 17 mcg Beta-Carotene, 501 mcg Lutein (+ Zeaxanthin).

Carrot Sandwiches on Whole Grain Bread

My mother and I developed this recipe for the inn we operate, the Parson's Inn Bed and Breakfast in Glen Haven, Wisconsin.

¾	cup water, divided
2	cups chopped carrots
½	cup chopped onion
¼	cup low-fat mayonnaise
¼	cup low-fat cream cheese or Neufchâtel
4	teaspoons dried dill weed
1	teaspoon Mrs. Dash® salt-free seasoning
½	teaspoon Beau Monde® seasoning or celery salt
12	slices whole wheat bread
6	lettuce leaves
	Red radish peel, for garnish

1. Place ½ cup of the water in blender. Gradually add carrots. Chop; drain well. Set aside. Place the remaining ¼ cup of the water in blender. Add onion. Chop; drain.

2. In bowl, blend carrots, onion, mayonnaise and cream cheese. Add dill weed, salt-free seasoning and Beau Monde seasoning. Refrigerate 1 hour to blend flavors.

3. Trim crusts from bread. (If this is done more than 10 minutes before serving, cover bread to avoid drying.) Place ⅓ to ½ cup filling on each of 6 bread slices. Place 1 lettuce leaf on each sandwich; top with second slice of bread. Cut into quarters. Garnish with radish peel.

12 servings (½ of sandwich).
Preparation time: 15 minutes
Ready to serve: 1 hour, 15 minutes

Per serving: 90 calories, 1 g total fat (0 g monounsaturated fat, 1 g saturated fat), 3 g protein, 19 g carbohydrate, 5 mg cholesterol, 150 mg sodium, 6 g fiber.
Star nutrients: Vitamin A (116%). **Noteworthy nutrients:** Vitamin B6 (22%), Zinc (16%).
Antioxidants: 1,848 mcg Beta-Carotene, 143 mcg Lutein (+ Zeaxanthin).

Hot & Cheesy Italian Sub Sandwiches

A quick way to warm up kids of all ages.

- 1 (16-inch) loaf French bread
- 2 tablespoons creamy Italian salad dressing or light ranch or cucumber dressing
- 8 oz. precooked turkey slices
- 8 oz. thin honey ham
- 8 oz. sliced regular or light processed cheese spread loaf

1. Heat broiler. Cut French bread in half lengthwise; spread top of both halves with dressing. Layer turkey and ham over both halves of bread; top with cheese.

2. Place open-faced subs on baking sheet; broil 6 inches from heat source 4 to 6 minutes, watching carefully so cheese does not burn. Cut into 6 pieces to serve.

6 servings.
Preparation time: 10 minutes
Ready to serve: 20 minutes

Per serving: 390 calories, 11 g total fat (2 g monounsaturated fat, 5 g saturated fat), 31 g protein, 42 g carbohydrate, 60 mg cholesterol, 1575 mg sodium, 2 g fiber.
Star nutrients: Calcium (32%), Thiamin (26%). **Noteworthy nutrients:** Folate (18%), Niacin (18%), Riboflavin (15%).

Italian Meatball Hero Sandwich

There are a few steps in making this tasty sandwich, but it's well worth the effort.

1	tablespoon olive oil	⅔	lb. lean ground beef
1	small onion, finely chopped		Salt
1	garlic clove, crushed		Freshly ground pepper
2	teaspoons dried oregano, divided	5	tablespoons plus 1 teaspoon
1	(8-oz.) can tomatoes, drained,		low-fat margarine, divided
	chopped	6	oz. mozzarella cheese, sliced
1	tablespoon tomato paste		Fresh watercress sprigs,
1	(16-inch) loaf French bread		for garnish

1. To prepare tomato sauce, heat olive oil in medium saucepan. Add onion, garlic, 1 teaspoon of the oregano, tomatoes and tomato paste. Cook 10 minutes or until thick, stirring occasionally. Meanwhile, heat oven to 375°F.

2. Slice bread lengthwise, cutting halfway through loaf. (Do not cut loaf in half.) Remove soft bread from center of halves, leaving shell intact. Prepare 2 tablespoons bread crumbs from soft bread by chopping finely with sharp knife. In medium bowl, combine bread crumbs and ground beef. Season with salt and pepper; mix well. Form mixture into 12 balls.

3. Spray medium skillet with nonstick cooking spray. Heat over medium-high heat; add meatballs. Cook 6 to 8 minutes or until set and golden. Test for doneness using meat thermometer, ensuring temperature is 160°F. Drain on paper towels.

4. Spread inside of bread shells with 3 tablespoons of the margarine; add half of the tomato sauce. Fill bread shells with meatballs; spoon the remaining half of the tomato sauce over meatballs. Cover with half of the mozzarella cheese. Press bread shells together. Spread the remaining margarine over outside of bread shells; cover with the remaining half of the mozzarella cheese and the remaining 1 teaspoon of the oregano. Completely wrap sandwich in greased aluminum foil. Bake 20 minutes. Unwrap foil to expose sandwich; bake 8 to 10 minutes more or until crisp. Cut into 8 pieces. Garnish with watercress or other lively green.

8 (2-inch) slices.
Preparation time: 30 minutes
Ready to serve: 1 hour

Per slice: 360 calories, 17 g total fat (7 g monounsaturated fat, 6 g saturated fat), 18 g protein, 33 g carbohydrate, 40 mg cholesterol, 625 mg sodium, 2 g fiber.
Noteworthy nutrients: Calcium (20%), Folate (16%), Iron (15%), Niacin (24%), Phosphorus (22%), Riboflavin (21%), Thiamin (23%), Zinc (18%). **Antioxidants:** 1 mg Alpha-Tocopherol (vitamin E), 78 mcg Beta-Carotene, 15 mcg Lutein (+ Zeaxanthin), 3,353 mcg Lycopene.

Open-Faced Roast Beef Sandwiches

Although people often think of sandwiches as strictly lunch fare, these roast beef sandwiches make a great, satisfying and easy main course for dinner too.

1 tablespoon butter-flavored margarine, melted
3 tablespoons reduced-sodium soy sauce
1 large red onion, thinly sliced
¼ cup minced fresh parsley
1 (1-lb.) loaf Italian bread
1 lb. roast beef, thinly sliced
2 tablespoons Romano cheese

1. Heat broiler. In small bowl, thoroughly blend margarine and soy sauce, reserving 2 tablespoons. In another small bowl, pour remaining soy sauce mixture over onion and parsley; stir to coat.

2. Cut bread into 8 slices. Lightly brush both sides of bread with reserved soy sauce mixture. Place slices of bread on baking sheet; broil 1 minute on each side.

3. Drain onion mixture. Cover each bread slice with roast beef, onion mixture and Romano cheese. Broil 3 minutes. Serve immediately.

8 sandwiches.
Preparation time: 15 minutes
Ready to serve: 20 minutes

Per sandwich: 240 calories, 5 g total fat (2g monounsaturated fat, 1 g saturated fat), 16 g protein, 32 g carbohydrate, 20 mg cholesterol, 1010 mg sodium, 2 g fiber.
Noteworthy nutrients: Folate (15%), Iron (15%), Thiamin (19%). **Antioxidants:** 101 mcg Beta-Carotene, 194 mcg Lutein (+ Zeaxanthin), 0 mcg Lycopene.

Stromboli

Serve with Artichoke Salad (page 292) and a glass of nonfat milk for a wonderfully tasty and healthy meal.

½ **lb. lean ground beef**
1 **medium onion, thinly sliced**
4 **oz. fresh mushrooms, sliced**
2 **garlic cloves, minced (½ teaspoon)**
¼ **teaspoon freshly ground pepper**
1 **cup prepared spaghetti sauce**
1 **(1-lb.) loaf French bread, cut in half lengthwise**
½ **cup (2 oz.) shredded mozzarella cheese**

1. Heat oven to 350°F.

2. In large skillet, brown ground beef. Drain well; remove from skillet. In same skillet, sauté onion, mushrooms, garlic and pepper. Stir in beef and spaghetti sauce. Heat until bubbly.

3. Spread meat mixture over French bread halves; sprinkle with mozzarella cheese. Bake 10 minutes. Slice to serve.

4 servings.
Preparation time: 15 minutes
Ready to serve: 25 minutes

Per serving: 535 calories, 17 g total fat (7 g monounsaturated fat, 6 g saturated fat), 26 g protein, 71 g carbohydrate, 45 mg cholesterol, 1120 mg sodium, 6 g fiber.
Star nutrients: Folate (29%), Iron (28%), Niacin (46%), Riboflavin (38%), Thiamin (45%).
 Noteworthy nutrients: Calcium (22%), Copper (19%), Phosphorus (24%), Zinc (23%).

Turkey Salad in a Wrap

Serve this light, refreshing lunch with Easy Fat-Free Coleslaw (page xx), fresh strawberries and nonfat milk.

8 oz. deli turkey breast, diced or cut into thin strips
⅓ cup fat-free salad dressing
¼ cup chopped walnuts
¼ cup golden raisins or dried cranberries
½ teaspoon dried dill weed
4 (10-inch) flour tortillas

1. In bowl, stir together turkey, salad dressing, walnuts, raisins and dill weed. Divide turkey salad among tortillas; roll up to serve.

4 servings.
Preparation time: 15 minutes
Ready to serve: 20 minutes

Per serving: 260 calories, 8 g total fat (2 g monounsaturated fat, 1 g saturated fat), 18 g protein, 29 g carbohydrate, 25 mg cholesterol, 1120 mg sodium, 2 g fiber.
Star nutrients: Niacin (30%). **Noteworthy nutrients:** Phosphorus (21%), Thiamin (15%).

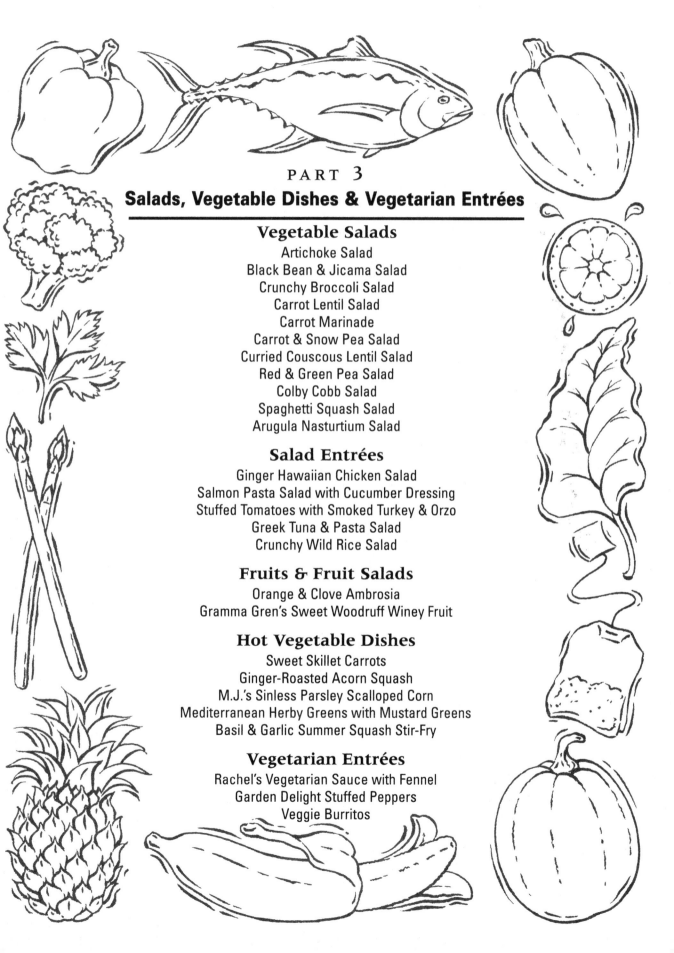

PART 3
Salads, Vegetable Dishes & Vegetarian Entrées

Vegetable Salads
Artichoke Salad
Black Bean & Jicama Salad
Crunchy Broccoli Salad
Carrot Lentil Salad
Carrot Marinade
Carrot & Snow Pea Salad
Curried Couscous Lentil Salad
Red & Green Pea Salad
Colby Cobb Salad
Spaghetti Squash Salad
Arugula Nasturtium Salad

Salad Entrées
Ginger Hawaiian Chicken Salad
Salmon Pasta Salad with Cucumber Dressing
Stuffed Tomatoes with Smoked Turkey & Orzo
Greek Tuna & Pasta Salad
Crunchy Wild Rice Salad

Fruits & Fruit Salads
Orange & Clove Ambrosia
Gramma Gren's Sweet Woodruff Winey Fruit

Hot Vegetable Dishes
Sweet Skillet Carrots
Ginger-Roasted Acorn Squash
M.J.'s Sinless Parsley Scalloped Corn
Mediterranean Herby Greens with Mustard Greens
Basil & Garlic Summer Squash Stir-Fry

Vegetarian Entrées
Rachel's Vegetarian Sauce with Fennel
Garden Delight Stuffed Peppers
Veggie Burritos

Artichoke Salad

Artichokes offer dietary fiber, vitamin C and folate. Fresh artichokes will keep for up to a week. Their peak season is April and May. If you purchase them in spring and summer, expect an even green color. In fall, fresh artichokes may have touches of light brown on their outer leaves.

- 1 **small head Boston lettuce**
- 1 **(16-oz.) can artichoke hearts in water, drained**
- 2 **ribs celery, thinly sliced**
- ½ **cup sliced radishes**
- 1 **tablespoon chopped red onion**
- ¼ **cup reduced-calorie Italian dressing**

1. Wash and drain lettuce; tear into bite-size pieces.

2. In mixing bowl, combine artichokes, celery, radishes, onion and dressing.

3. Divide lettuce among 4 serving plates; spoon salad over top.

4 (1-cup) servings.
Preparation time: 15 minutes
Ready to serve: 15 minutes

Per serving: 60 calories, 1 g total fat (0 g monounsaturated fat, 1 g saturated fat), 4 g protein, 10 g carbohydrate, 0 mg cholesterol, 520 mg sodium, 1 g fiber.
Noteworthy nutrients: Vitamin C (22%), Folate (10%). **Antioxidants:** 31 mcg Beta-Carotene, 48 mcg Lutein (+ Zeaxanthin).

Black Bean & Jicama Salad

Jicama is also known as the Mexican potato. This root vegetable has a thin brown skin and white crunchy flesh. Jicama tastes good raw or cooked. Here we use it raw, and the results are delicious.

1½   **cups matchstick-size strips jicama (⅛x⅛x2-inch)**
1½   **cups cubed honeydew melon, ½-inch cubes**
1   **(16-oz.) can black beans, drained, rinsed**
¼   **cup freshly chopped cilantro**
2   **tablespoons chopped fresh lemon verbena**
2   **tablespoons lime juice**
1   **teaspoon honey**
1   **teaspoon grated lime peel**
¼   **teaspoon salt**

1. In bowl, mix jicama, honeydew, beans, cilantro, lemon verbena, lime juice, honey, lime peel and salt. Cover; refrigerate 1 to 2 hours or until chilled.

10 (½-cup) servings.
Preparation time: 15 minutes
Ready to serve: 1 hour, 15 minutes

Per serving: 70 calories, 0 g total fat (0 g monounsaturated fat, 0 g saturated fat), 3 g protein, 15 g carbohydrate, 0 mg cholesterol, 200 mg sodium, 4 g fiber.
Star nutrients: Vitamin C (29%). **Noteworthy nutrients:** Vitamin A (17%). **Antioxidants:** 92 mcg Beta-Carotene.

Crunchy Broccoli Salad

Crunchy salads fill us up and meet our "chew" needs. This salad also boosts your vitamin A and vitamin C intake, and walnuts offer monounsaturated fat, which helps balance the bacon's saturated fat.

6 cups precut broccoli or 1 large head broccoli, stemmed,
    cut into bite-size pieces
1 small red onion, cut into thin wedges
½ cup dark or golden raisins
½ cup chopped walnuts
4 strips bacon, broiled crisp, drained between paper towels, crumbled

Dressing*
½ cup reduced-fat sour cream
⅓ cup reduced-fat or nonfat mayonnaise
2 tablespoons cider vinegar
¼ cup sugar or equivalent sugar substitute

1. In large salad bowl, mix together broccoli, onion, raisins, walnuts and bacon. This mixture keeps covered in refrigerator for up to 4 days.

2. In shaker container, combine sour cream, mayonnaise, vinegar and sugar; shake well. (Or whisk in small bowl until smooth.) Pour dressing over salad 1 to 4 hours before serving; toss. Refrigerate, covered, before serving. Food safety alert: Remember to keep salads in a cooler when transporting to potlucks and picnics.

8 (1-cup) servings.
Preparation time: 15 minutes
Ready to serve: 1 hour, 15 minutes

Per serving: 190 calories, 11 g total fat (4 g monounsaturated fat, 2 g saturated fat), 6 g protein, 20 g carbohydrate, 10 mg cholesterol, 150 mg sodium, 1 g fiber.
Star nutrients: Vitamin A (34%), Vitamin C (85%), Calcium (55%).

TIP * No time to make dressing? Just use 1 cup prepared coleslaw dressing.

Carrot Lentil Salad

Lentils are a whole-grain substitute for meat, and serve as a staple throughout the Middle East and India. These legumes need no soaking, and cook relatively quickly.

1½	cups diced carrots
1	cup lentils, rinsed
1	bay leaf
¼	cup finely chopped fresh parsley or 1 tablespoon dried
2	tablespoons dried celery flakes
½	teaspoon salt
½	teaspoon dried thyme
¼	teaspoon freshly ground pepper
2	garlic cloves, minced
¼	cup lemon juice
2	tablespoons olive oil

1. In 2 quart casserole, combine carrots, lentils and bay leaf. Cover with 1 inch of water. Bring to a boil; simmer 15 to 20 minutes or until lentils are tender. Remove bay leaf; drain and cool 15 minutes.

2. To make dressing, combine parsley, celery flakes, salt, thyme, pepper, garlic, lemon juice and olive oil. Pour over lentil mixture. Cover; refrigerate at least 3 hours.

6 (¾-cup) servings.
Preparation time: 30 minutes
Ready to serve: 3 hours, 30 minutes

Per serving: 170 calories, 5 g total fat (3 g monounsaturated fat, 1 g saturated fat), 9 g protein, 23 g carbohydrate, 0 mg cholesterol, 210 mg sodium, 11 g fiber.
Star nutrients: Vitamin A (172%), Folate (36%). **Noteworthy nutrients:** Vitamin C (17%), Copper (15%), Iron (19%). **Antioxidants:** 1 mg Alpha-Tocopherol (vitamin E), 2682 mcg Beta-Carotene, 79 mcg Lutein (+ Zeaxanthin).

Carrot Marinade

Feel free to substitute any member of the onion family for scallions, which have a milder flavor than immature onions. Members of the allium (onion) family are touted for their health benefits.

1½	lb. carrots, cut into coins
1	tablespoon water
½	green bell pepper, finely chopped
1	trimmed scallion, finely sliced
1	(8-oz.) can no-added-salt tomato sauce
2	tablespoons vinegar
1	teaspoon Worcestershire sauce
1	teaspoon prepared mustard
2	tablespoons packed brown sugar
½	teaspoon celery seed

1. In microwave-safe 2-quart dish, combine carrots and water. Cover with plastic wrap; microwave at High 3 minutes. Drain well.

2. Transfer carrots to 2-quart salad bowl. Add bell pepper and scallion.

3. In shaker container, combine tomato sauce, vinegar, Worcestershire sauce, mustard, brown sugar and celery seed. Pour over vegetables, tossing to coat. This salad keeps well in refrigerator for up to 4 days.

8 (¾-cup) servings.
Preparation time: 20 minutes
Ready to serve: 25 minutes

Per serving: 60 calories, 0 g total fat (0 g monounsaturated fat, 0 g saturated fat), 1 g protein, 14 g carbohydrate, 0 mg cholesterol, 68 mg sodium, 3 g fiber.
Star nutrients: Vitamin A (481%), Vitamin C (29%). **Antioxidants:** 7,537 mcg Beta-Carotene, 313 mcg Lutein (+ Zeaxanthin).

Carrot & Snow Pea Salad

Snow peas are a sweet, crisp legume whose French name means "eat it all." They are an essential vegetable in Chinese cooking.

- ¼ **lb. snow peas**
- 3 **large carrots, cut into matchstick-size strips (⅛x⅛x2-inch)**
- 1 **tablespoon water**
- ¼ **cup white wine vinegar**
- 1 **teaspoon Dijon mustard**
- 1 **teaspoon honey**
- 1 **green onion, chopped**

1. In 2-quart microwave-safe dish, combine peas and carrots. Sprinkle with water. Cover; microwave at High 4 minutes. Immediately uncover; drain in colander. Cool 5 minutes.

2. In large salad bowl, mix together vinegar, mustard, honey and onion. Add cooled vegetables; toss to serve.

4 (1-cup) servings.
Preparation time: 10 minutes
Ready to serve: 15 minutes

Per serving: 45 calories, 0 g total fat (0 g monounsaturated fat, 0 g saturated fat), 1 g protein, 9 g carbohydrate, 0 mg cholesterol, 50 mg sodium, 2 g fiber.
Star nutrients: Vitamin A (258%), Vitamin C (37%). **Antioxidants:** 4,057 mcg Beta-Carotene, 198 mcg Lutein (+ Zeaxanthin).

Curried Couscous Lentil Salad

Turmeric is a major ingredient in curry powders. Store your curry in the dark, as it is very sensitive to light.

- **1 cup nonfat plain yogurt**
- **2 tablespoons lemon juice**
- **1 tablespoon chopped fresh mint or 1 teaspoon dried**
- **2 teaspoons curry powder**
- **⅛ teaspoon white pepper**
- **1 garlic clove, crushed**
- **1 cup chopped red bell pepper**
- **1 cup dry couscous, cooked according to pkg. directions**
- **1 cup dry lentils, cooked according to pkg. directions**
- **1 cucumber, peeled, seeded and sliced**
- **½ teaspoon salt (optional)**
- **½ cup (2 oz.) shredded nonfat mozzarella cheese**

1. In large mixing bowl, combine yogurt, lemon juice, mint, curry powder, white pepper and garlic; stir well. Add bell pepper, couscous, lentils, cucumber and salt; stir well. Spoon into serving dish; sprinkle with mozzarella.

10 (¾-cup) servings.
Preparation time: 40 minutes
Ready to serve: 40 minutes

Per serving: 80 calories, 0 g total fat (0 g monounsaturated fat, 0 g saturated fat), 6 g protein, 14 g carbohydrate, 0 mg cholesterol, 70 mg sodium, 3 g fiber.
Star nutrients: Vitamin C (55%). **Noteworthy nutrients:** Vitamin A (18%). **Antioxidants:** 376 mcg Beta-Carotene, 1,080 mcg Lutein (+ Zeaxanthin).

Red & Green Pea Salad

The first salads go way back to the Middle Ages. Wheat, beans, peas, turnips, onions, radishes and cabbage were staples of even older ancestors—the primitive Europeans.

½ **cup nonfat mayonnaise**
¼ **cup reduced-fat Italian dressing**
½ **red onion, finely chopped**
1 **(16-oz.) pkg. frozen peas, thawed, drained**
2 **ribs celery, finely chopped**
2 **slices bacon, cooked, crumbled, or ¼ cup bacon bits**

1. In salad bowl, combine mayonnaise and dressing. Add remaining ingredients; mix lightly.

4 (1-cup) servings.
Preparation time; 15 minutes
Ready to serve: 15 minutes

Per serving: 145 calories, 3 g total fat (1 g monounsaturated fat, 1 g saturated fat), 7 g protein, 22 g carbohydrate, 5 mg cholesterol, 660 mg sodium, 6 g fiber.
Star nutrients: Vitamin C (38%). **Noteworthy nutrients:** Vitamin A (17%), Folate (17%), thiamin (22%).
Antioxidants: 393 mcg Beta-Carotene, 1,974 mcg Lutein (+ Zeaxanthin).

Colby Cobb Salad

If you are from Wisconsin as I am, you are expected to send cheese ahead (or arrive with it in your suitcase) as a hostess gift any time you travel out of state. The Dairy State is very proud of its great-tasting cheese such as the cheddar and Swiss cheeses featured in this recipe. Just remember, one ounce of cheese is one inch cubed.

1	bag salad greens
1	small carton cherry tomatoes
2	oz. 2-year-old cheddar cheese, cut into matchstick-size pieces (⅛x⅛x2-inch)
2	oz. Swiss cheese, cut into matchstick-size pieces (⅛x⅛x2-inch)
½	cup cooked bacon pieces

1. In salad bowl, combine salad greens, tomatoes, cheddar cheese, Swiss cheese and bacon; top with favorite salad dressing.

4 (2-cup) servings.
Preparation time: 10 minutes
Ready to serve: 10 minutes

Per serving: 175 calories, 12 g total fat (4 g monounsaturated fat, 6 g saturated fat), 14 g protein, 4 g carbohydrate, 40 mg cholesterol, 575 mg sodium, 2 g fiber.
Star nutrients: Vitamin A (62%), Calcium (25%). **Noteworthy nutrients:** Vitamin C (21%), Phosphorus (16%). **Antioxidants:** 12 mcg Beta-Carotene.

Spaghetti Squash Salad

Serving this distinctive squash gives a unique twist to everyday dinners or special occasions alike.

- 1 small spaghetti squash (2 lb.)
- 2 tomatoes, seeded, chopped
- 1 cucumber, peeled, chopped
- 1 green bell pepper, diced
- 1 yellow bell pepper, diced
- 1 green onion, chopped
- ½ cup reduced-fat Italian dressing

1. Cut squash in half lengthwise; remove seeds. Place squash, cut-side down, in Dutch oven with 2 inches of water. Cover; bring to a boil. Reduce heat; simmer 20 minutes or until tender. Drain squash; cool at least 15 minutes.

2. Remove spaghetti-like strands from squash using fork; drain again. Transfer to large salad bowl. Add tomatoes, cucumber, green bell pepper, yellow bell pepper and onion; mix lightly. Add dressing; toss.

8 (½-cup) servings.
Preparation time: 15 minutes
Ready to serve: 55 minutes

Per serving: 45 calories, 1 g total fat (0 g monounsaturated fat, 0 g saturated fat), 1 g protein, 9 g carbohydrate, 0 mg cholesterol, 225 mg sodium, 1 g fiber.
Star nutrients: Vitamin C (107%). **Noteworthy nutrients:** Calcium (24%). **Antioxidants:** 196 mcg Beta-Carotene, 447 mcg Lutein (+ Zeaxanthin), 930 mcg Lycopene.

Arugula Nasturtium Salad

Arugula's nutty, peppery taste pairs perfectly with pork. Serve this salad with pork roast or pork chops.

1	bunch arugula
10	button mushrooms, sliced (1½ cups)
2	small red onions, sliced, divided into rings (about ½ cup)
1	medium tomato, cut into wedges
12	nasturtium blossoms*
3	tablespoons white wine vinegar
1	tablespoon Dijon mustard
¼	teaspoon salt
¼	teaspoon coarsely ground pepper
2	tablespoons olive oil

1. Wash and dry arugula. Tear by hand; place in salad bowl. Add mushrooms, onions and tomato. Toss briefly. Divide among six salad bowls.

2. Add nasturtium blossoms to salads, using as garnish. Refrigerate until time to serve.

3. For dressing, whisk together vinegar, Dijon mustard, salt and pepper. Slowly add olive oil, whisking until combined. Pour into cruet to serve with salad.

6 (1-cup) servings.
Preparation time: 25 minutes
Ready to serve: 25 minutes

Per serving: 70 calories, 5 g total fat (3 g monounsaturated fat, 1 g saturated fat), 2 g protein, 4 g carbohydrate, 0 mg cholesterol, 120 mg sodium, 1 g fiber.
Antioxidants: 1 mg Alpha-Tocopherol (vitamin E), 81 mcg Beta-Carotene, 27 mcg Lutein (+ Zeaxanthin), 620 mcg Lycopene.

TIP   * Nasturtiums, like other edible flowers, can be picked from your own flowerbed or garden and used in a salad. You will want to avoid using fertilizers and chemicals that would be harmful if ingested; this requires some planning. You could purchase nasturtiums or other edible flowers from a florist or other source. In that case, ingest only those grown organically. (This means that substances harmful to human ingestion have not been used on the soil for a period of years.)

Ginger Hawaiian Chicken Salad

My grandfather had a seed corn test plot on Kauii. He always tried to bring back several fresh pineapples for us to sample. We got good at "dissecting" them with an electric knife. After dissecting your own pineapple, here's a way to put it to good use!

3	cups diced cooked chicken
1½	cups diced celery
1½	cups green grapes, halved, seeded
1½	cups pineapple chunks, drained
1	cup mandarin orange sections, drained
½	cup water chestnuts, drained, sliced
2	teaspoons minced fresh ginger or ½ teaspoon ground
1	cup nonfat yogurt
½	cup nonfat mayonnaise
½	teaspoon lemon juice
⅛	teaspoon salt or to taste

1. In large bowl, combine chicken, celery, grapes, pineapple, mandarin oranges, water chestnuts, ginger, yogurt, mayonnaise, lemon juice and salt; refrigerate at least 2 hours before serving.

8 (1-cup) servings.
Preparation time: 30 minutes
Ready to serve: 2 hours, 30 minutes

Per serving: 165 calories, 2 g total fat (1 g monounsaturated fat, 1 g saturated fat), 19 g protein, 17 g carbohydrate, 45 mg cholesterol, 245 mg sodium, 1 g fiber.
Star nutrients: Vitamin C (31%), Niacin (37%). **Noteworthy nutrients:** Vitamin B6 (19%), Phosphorus (18%). **Antioxidants:** 38 mcg Beta-Carotene, 59 mcg Lutein (+ Zeaxanthin).

Salmon Pasta Salad with Cucumber Dressing

This recipe will help you meet your omega-3 fatty acid quota. You should eat fish 2 to 3 times a week to adequately meet your omega-3 needs.

1	lb. canned salmon
1	teaspoon lemon juice
8	oz.rotini or spiral-shaped pasta
1	large cucumber, peeled, seeded, finely chopped
½	cup reduced-calorie creamy cucumber dressing
4	cups fresh salad greens

1. Drain salmon; remove skin and bones. Place in 3-quart salad bowl; sprinkle with lemon juice. Refrigerate.

2. Cook pasta according to package directions; rinse under cold water. Drain well.

3. Add cucumber to salmon in bowl; stir in pasta and dressing. Serve on bed of greens.

4 (1-cup) servings.
Preparation time: 10 minutes
Ready to serve: 15 minutes

Per serving: 448 calories, 8 g total fat (0 g monounsaturated fat, 0 g saturated fat), 36 g protein, 58 g carbohydrate, 0 mg cholesterol, 210 mg sodium, 5 g fiber.
Star nutrients: Vitamin A (40%), Vitamin C (58%), Folate (48%), Iron (29%). **Antioxidants:** 22 mcg Beta-Carotene, 6 mcg Alpha-Carotene, 168 mcg Lutein (+ Zeaxanthin).

Stuffed Tomatoes with Smoked Turkey & Orzo

The first time I tasted this dish was a boat trip on the Mississippi River with our dear Dr. Downy of Guttenberg, Iowa. M.J. Smith was testing the recipe on us. We gobbled them up, and you will, too!

8	medium tomatoes
4	cups no-added-salt chicken broth
1½	cups orzo
8	oz. smoked turkey, cut into thin strips
2	tablespoons sunflower seeds
2	green onions, finely chopped, tops reserved for garnish
⅔	cup low-fat buttermilk ranch dressing

1. Wash tomatoes; cut off top ½ inch of each. Scrape seeds and flesh from tomatoes.

2. In medium saucepan, bring broth to a boil; add orzo and cook until tender, about 12 minutes. Drain well; rinse with cold water. Drain again.

3. In medium bowl, combine orzo with turkey, sunflower seeds, onions and dressing, stirring to blend.

4. Stuff tomatoes with orzo mixture; garnish with finely chopped green onion tops.

8 servings.
Preparation time: 15 minutes
Ready to serve: 30 minutes

Per serving: 238 calories, 7 g total fat (2 g monounsaturated fat, 1 g saturated fat), 12 g protein, 34 g carbohydrate, 15 mg cholesterol, 740 mg sodium, 3 g fiber.
Star nutrients: Vitamin C (55%), Folate (25%), Thiamin (27%). **Noteworthy nutrients:** Vitamin A (16%), Niacin (20%). **Antioxidants:** 498 mcg Beta-Carotene, 239 mcg Lutein (+ Zeaxanthin), 3,721 mcg Lycopene.

Greek Tuna & Pasta Salad

Feta cheese was originally made of sheep's or goat's milk. Today, large commercial producers often make it with cow's milk. Feta is often referred to as pickled cheese because it's cured and stored in its own salty whey brine.

- ½ **cup orzo or other small pasta**
- 2 **(6½-oz.) cans light tuna packed in water, drained**
- 2 **medium tomatoes, peeled, chopped**
- 2 **oz. feta cheese, crumbled**
- ⅔ **cup reduced-calorie herb vinaigrette dressing**

1. Cook pasta according to package directions; rinse under cold water. Drain.

2. In large salad bowl, gently toss pasta with tuna, tomatoes, feta cheese and dressing. Cover; chill until serving time.

4 (1-cup) servings.
Preparation time: 5 minutes
Ready to serve: 15 minutes

Per serving: 269 calories, 6 g total fat (2 g monounsaturated fat, 3 g saturated fat), 29 g protein, 23 g carbohydrate, 40 mg cholesterol, 493 mg sodium, 1 g fiber.
Star nutrients: Vitamin B12 (50%), Niacin (72%), Phosphorus (25%). **Noteworthy nutrients:** Vitamin B6 (23%), Vitamin C (21%), Folate (17%), Iron (15%), Magnesium (12%), Phosphorus (24%), Riboflavin (20%), Thiamin (22%), Zinc (10%). **Antioxidants:** 242 mcg Beta-Carotene, 80 mcg Lutein (+ Zeaxanthin), 1,860 mcg Lycopene.

Crunchy Wild Rice Salad

Clean wild rice thoroughly before you cook it. Wild rice can take up to 60 minutes to cook, and has a nutty flavor and a chewy texture. Avoid overcooking or you will get mushy, starchy tasting rice.

1	cup brown and wild rice blend
¼	teaspoon seasoned salt
2	cups diced cooked meat of choice (chicken is especially good)
1½	cups green grapes, halved
1	(8-oz.) can sliced water chestnuts, drained well
2	ribs celery, thinly sliced
2	tablespoons minced fresh basil
¾	cup reduced-fat mayonnaise
1	tablespoon lemon juice
1	teaspoon sugar

1. Cook rice according to package directions. Drain well; fluff with fork. Cool to room temperature.

2. In large salad bowl, combine cooled rice, salt, meat, grapes, water chestnuts, celery and basil.

3. In small mixing bowl, blend together mayonnaise, lemon juice and sugar; fold into rice mixture. Serve immediately or chill until serving time.

8 (1-cup) servings.
Preparation time: 15 minutes
Ready to serve: 30 minutes

Per serving: 245 calories, 9 g total fat (5 g monounsaturated fat, 1 g saturated fat), 13 g protein, 28 g carbohydrate, 30 mg cholesterol, 235 mg sodium, 1 g fiber.
Star nutrients: Niacin (30%). **Noteworthy nutrients:** Vitamin B6 (17%). **Antioxidants:** 27 mcg Beta-Carotene, 45 mcg Lutein (+ Zeaxanthin).

Orange & Clove Ambrosia

I first learned about ambrosia in the 1950s, when I began reading my grandmother's cookbooks.

- **2 oranges**
- **1 pink grapefruit**
- **½ cup frozen, unsweetened, pitted Bing cherries**
- **⅛ teaspoon ground cloves**
- **⅛ teaspoon ground nutmeg**
- **1 cup unsweetened cranapple juice**
- **2 tablespoons finely shredded coconut**

1. Peel and section oranges and grapefruit. Cut sections in half; place in bowl. Add cherries.

2. In another bowl, stir cloves and nutmeg into cranapple juice. Pour over fruit; stir well. Refrigerate 30 minutes, stirring every 10 minutes.

3. Serve in Champagne flutes on dessert plates. Lightly sprinkle each serving with coconut.

6 (½-cup) servings.
Preparation time: 10 minutes
Ready to serve: 40 minutes

Per serving: 70 calories, 1 g total fat (0 g monounsaturated fat, 1 g saturated fat), 1 g protein, 15 g carbohydrate, 0 mg cholesterol, 14 mg sodium, 2 g fiber.
Star nutrients: Vitamin C (87%). **Antioxidants:** 270 mcg Beta-Carotene, 87 mcg Lutein (+ Zeaxanthin), 599 mcg Lycopene.

Gramma Gren's Sweet Woodruff Winey Fruit

Sweet woodruff makes the perfect complement for berries, strawberries, rhubarb and fruit mixtures, especially when teamed up with sparkling wine. Sweet woodruff smells like new-mown hay, one of my late father's favorite aromas.

¼   **watermelon, cubed (4 cups)**
½   **cantaloupe, cubed (2 cups)**
½   **honeydew melon, cubed (2 cups)**
1   **lb. green grapes, halved, seeded if necessary (about 1½ cups)**
1   **lb. red grapes, halved, seeded if necessary (about 1½ cups)**
3   **medium plums, chopped (1 cup)**
2   **tablespoons sweet woodruff (blossom and stem), minced,**
      or 2 teaspoons dried sweet woodruff*
24   **oz. zinfandel wine or nonalcoholic Champagne**
2   **cups diet lemon-lime soft drink**

1. Place watermelon, cantaloupe, honeydew, green grapes, red grapes and plums in large bowl.

2. Mix sweet woodruff with wine; pour over fruit. Marinate 6 hours in refrigerator. Add soft drink just before serving.**

16 (¾-cup) servings.
Preparation time: 30 minutes
Ready to serve: 6 hours, 30 minutes

Per serving: 85 calories, 0 g total fat (0 g monounsaturated fat, 0 g saturated fat), 1 g protein, 14 g carbohydrate, 0 mg cholesterol, 15 mg sodium, 1 g fiber.
Star nutrients: Vitamin C (36%). **Noteworthy nutrients:** Vitamin A (17%). **Antioxidants:** 453 mcg Beta-Carotene, 61 mcg Lutein (+ Zeaxanthin), 1,850 mcg Lycopene.

TIPS * Sweet woodruff, like all herbs, can be purchased from a florist or other supplier. Best harvested when the little white flowers appear, sweet woodruff may be an herb to plan in your garden in the early season and cultivate for recipe use after several weeks or months, depending on the growing season.
    ** Excess liquid can be used for storing remaining fruit for several days.

Sweet Skillet Carrots

Grated lemon peel and dill weed bring out the sweetness of these skillet carrots.

1 teaspoon margarine	1 tablespoon fresh lemon juice
1 tablespoon packed brown sugar	6 medium carrots, sliced into coins
1 tablespoon grated lemon peel	2 teaspoons dried dill weed

1. In large skillet, combine margarine, brown sugar, lemon peel, lemon juice, carrots and dill weed. Cook over medium heat 15 minutes until liquid evaporates and carrots are crisp-tender.

4 (1-cup) servings.
Preparation time: 5 minutes
Ready to serve: 20 minutes

Per serving: 60 calories, 1 g total fat (0 g monounsaturated fat, 0 g saturated fat), 1 g protein, 12 g carbohydrate, 0 mg cholesterol, 45 mg sodium, 3 g fiber.
Star nutrients: Vitamin A (516%). **Noteworthy nutrients:** Vitamin C (20%). **Antioxidants:** 8,091 mcg Beta-Carotene, 238 mcg Lutein (+ Zeaxanthin).

Ginger-Roasted Acorn Squash

Crystallized ginger was really the very first candy, and it surely sweetens this acorn squash recipe.

2 medium acorn squash, halved, seeded
8 pieces crystallized ginger
¼ teaspoon ground nutmeg

1. Coat shallow dish with nonstick cooking spray. Place squash in single layer, pulp-side up, in dish. Press 2 pieces crystallized ginger in each squash half; sprinkle with nutmeg. Cover; microwave at High 12 to 15 minutes. Or bake uncovered in 400°F oven 1 hour or until squash pierces easily with fork.

4 servings.
Preparation time: 5 minutes
Ready to serve: 20 minutes

Per serving: 280 calories, 0 g total fat (0 g monounsaturated fat, 0 g saturated fat), 2 g protein, 71 g carbohydrate, 0 mg cholesterol, 15 mg sodium, 5 g fiber.
Star nutrients: Vitamin C (40%). **Noteworthy nutrients:** Vitamin B6 (17%), Vitamin A (15%), Magnesium (17%), Thiamin (20%).

M.J.'s Sinless Parsley Scalloped Corn

This dish travels well to a neighborhood get-together, holiday celebration ... or from your microwave to a hungry, waiting family!

> 2   cups whole kernel corn or 1 (16-oz.) pkg. frozen corn, thawed
> ¼   cup chopped onion
> ¼   cup nonfat milk
> 1   egg or ¼ cup liquid egg substitute
> 1   tablespoon chopped fresh parsley or 1 teaspoon dried
> ¼   teaspoon freshly ground pepper
> 5   wheat crackers with unsalted tops, crushed

1. Heat oven to 350°F. Spray 1-quart microwave-safe casserole with nonstick cooking spray. Put corn in dish. Add onion, milk, egg, parsley, pepper and crackers; stir well.

2. Microwave on High 15 minutes or until mixture is thick. Or, bake in 350°F oven 45 minutes. This dish freezes well.

4 (¾-cup) servings.
Preparation time: 10 minutes
Ready to serve: 25 minutes

Per serving (with egg): 145 calories, 3 g total fat (1 g monounsaturated fat, 1 g saturated fat), 6 g protein, 28 g carbohydrate, 55 mg cholesterol, 40 mg sodium, 3 g fiber.
Noteworthy nutrients: Vitamin C (16%). **Antioxidants:** 50 mcg Beta-Carotene, 104 mcg Lutein (+ Zeaxanthin).

Mediterranean Herby Greens
with Mustard Greens

Greens provide beta-carotene (which becomes vitamin A in your body) and fiber. Make a resolution to try a new green each month. The choices include mustard greens, spinach, nettles and Swiss chard.

3	**cups water**
4	**cups greens (purple kale, spinach or collard greens work well)**
1	**tablespoon olive oil**
3	**garlic cloves, minced**
¼	**cup all-purpose flour**
½	**teaspoon salt**
¼	**teaspoon freshly ground pepper**
¼	**cup fresh mustard greens, chopped**
	Nonfat milk as needed

1. In 2-quart saucepan, heat water to a boil. Meanwhile, trim and wash greens in cool water. Chop greens coarsely by hand or use food processor. Blanch greens in boiling water about 5 minutes. Drain greens, reserving water. (By reusing this liquid in cooking, you retain some of the water-soluble nutrients lost in the cooking process.)

2. In 12-inch skillet, heat olive oil over medium heat until hot; sauté garlic. In small bowl, combine flour, salt and pepper. Mix about 1¼ cups of reserved liquid with flour mixture, stirring until lumps dissolve. Add to garlic in skillet. Cook, stirring constantly, over medium heat until bubbles appear, 3 to 5 minutes. Stir in greens and mustard greens, cooking 2 to 3 minutes more. If sauce seems too thick, thin with milk or additional reserved liquid.

6 (¾-cup) servings.
Preparation time: 10 minutes
Ready to serve: 20 minutes

Per serving: 47 calories, 2 g total fat (2 g monounsaturated fat, 0 g saturated fat), 2 g protein, 5 g carbohydrate, 0 g cholesterol, 259 mg sodium, 1 g fiber.
Star nutrients: vitamin A (40%), vitamin C (60%). **Noteworthy nutrients:** folate (19%).

Basil & Garlic Summer Squash Stir-Fry

Try this stir-fry when you have guests around, or plenty of family helpers in the house. They will love to help chop or slice vegetables!

1   tablespoon canola oil
1   garlic clove, minced
1   large onion, thinly sliced, separated into rings
4   cups thinly sliced zucchini
4   cups thinly sliced yellow crookneck squash
2   tomatoes, cut into wedges
1   tablespoon chopped fresh basil or 1 teaspoon dried
½   teaspoon salt
¼   teaspoon freshly ground pepper
½   cup (2 oz.) shredded nonfat cheddar cheese

1. In skillet or wok, heat canola oil until hot. Add garlic; stir briefly. Add onion; cook 1 to 2 minutes. Add zucchini and yellow squash; cook several minutes or until crisp-tender. Add tomatoes, basil, salt and pepper. Heat. Sprinkle cheddar cheese over vegetables; stir just until cheese starts to melt. Serve immediately.

8 (¾-cup) servings.
Preparation time: 20 minutes
Ready to serve: 35 minutes

Per serving: 60 calories, 2 g total fat (1 g monounsaturated fat, 0 g saturated fat), 3 g protein, 8 g carbohydrate, 0 mg cholesterol, 230 mg sodium, 3 g fiber.
Star nutrients: vitamin C (29%). **Antioxidants:** 411 mcg Beta-Carotene, 1,428 mcg Lutein (+ Zeaxanthin), 930 mcg Lycopene.

Rachel's Vegetarian Sauce with Fennel

Serve over spaghetti, noodles or spaghetti squash.

1	teaspoon olive oil
½	cup chopped onion
2	garlic cloves, minced
4	cups canned no-added-salt diced tomatoes
3	cups water
1	cup thinly sliced fresh mushrooms
½	cup chopped green bell pepper
1½	teaspoons dried basil
1½	teaspoons chili powder
1	teaspoon dried oregano
½	teaspoon salt
½	teaspoon fennel seeds
½	teaspoon paprika
¼	teaspoon freshly ground pepper
1	(12 oz.) can no-added-salt tomato paste

1. Spray large saucepan with nonstick cooking spray. Heat oil until hot; sauté onion and garlic. Add tomatoes, water, mushrooms, bell pepper, basil, chili powder, oregano, salt, fennel seeds, paprika, pepper and tomato paste; stir well. Bring mixture to a boil; reduce heat. Simmer about 1½ hours, stirring occasionally. Sauce will thicken as it cooks.

12 (½-cup) servings.
Preparation time: 15 minutes
Ready to serve: 1 hour, 45 minutes

Per serving: 50 calories, 0 g total fat (0 g monounsaturated fat, 0 g saturated fat), 2 g protein, 11 g carbohydrate, 0 mg cholesterol, 160 mg sodium, 3 g fiber.
Star nutrients: Vitamin A (25%), Vitamin C (41%). **Antioxidants:** 3 mcg Beta-Carotene, 92 mcg Lutein (+ Zeaxanthin), 8315 mcg Lycopene.

Garden Delight Stuffed Peppers

These stuffed peppers will earn you return guests and plenty of compliments. It is also a great way to boost your fiber intake for the day (23%)!

4	green bell peppers
1	(16-oz.) can whole kernel corn, well drained
1	small onion, finely diced
1	(13-oz.) can tomato soup
1	tablespoon chili powder
4	oz. Monterey Jack cheese, shredded

1. Heat oven to 375°F. Remove tops and seeds from peppers.

2. In bowl, mix together corn, onion, tomato soup and chili powder. Carefully stuff peppers. Place on baking sheet; sprinkle with Monterey Jack cheese. Bake 45 minutes.

4 servings.
Preparation time: 15 minutes
Ready to serve: 1 hour

Per serving: 165 calories, 3 g total fat (0 g monounsaturated fat, 2 g saturated fat), 9 g protein, 28 g carbohydrate, 10 mg cholesterol, 340 mg sodium, 6 g fiber.
Star nutrients: Vitamin C (181%). **Noteworthy nutrients:** Vitamin A (20%), Vitamin B6 (16%), Thiamine (17%). **Antioxidants:** 299 mcg Beta-Carotene, 833 mcg Lutein (+ Zeaxanthin).

Veggie Burritos

These low-calorie burritos are a rich source of vitamins A and C. But it's the taste that will make them a popular entree to you and your guests.

- **1 small head cauliflower or bunch broccoli, washed, stemmed and finely chopped**
- **2 large carrots, grated**
- **½ cup nonfat ricotta cheese**
- **4 oz. reduced-fat cheddar cheese, shredded**
- **½ cup reduced-fat creamy Italian dressing**
- **8 (10-inch) flour tortillas**

1. Heat oven to 350°F.

2. In large bowl, combine cauliflower, carrots, ricotta cheese, cheddar cheese and dressing.

3. Lay tortillas flat on work surface; spoon filling on one side of tortillas. Roll tortillas from filled side, folding outside edges over on bottom. Place on baking sheet. Bake 15 minutes or until heated through.

8 servings.
Preparation time: 15 minutes
Ready to serve: 30 minutes

Per serving: 170 calories, 5 g total fat (1.5 g monounsaturated fat, 2.0 g saturated fat), 10 g protein, 22 g carbohydrate, 10 mg cholesterol, 495 mg sodium, 2.5 g fiber.
Star nutrients: Vitamin A (92 %), Vitamin C (45%). **Noteworthy nutrients:** Calcium (22%).
Antioxidants: 1,348 mcg Beta-Carotene, 40 mcg Lutein (+ Zeaxanthin).

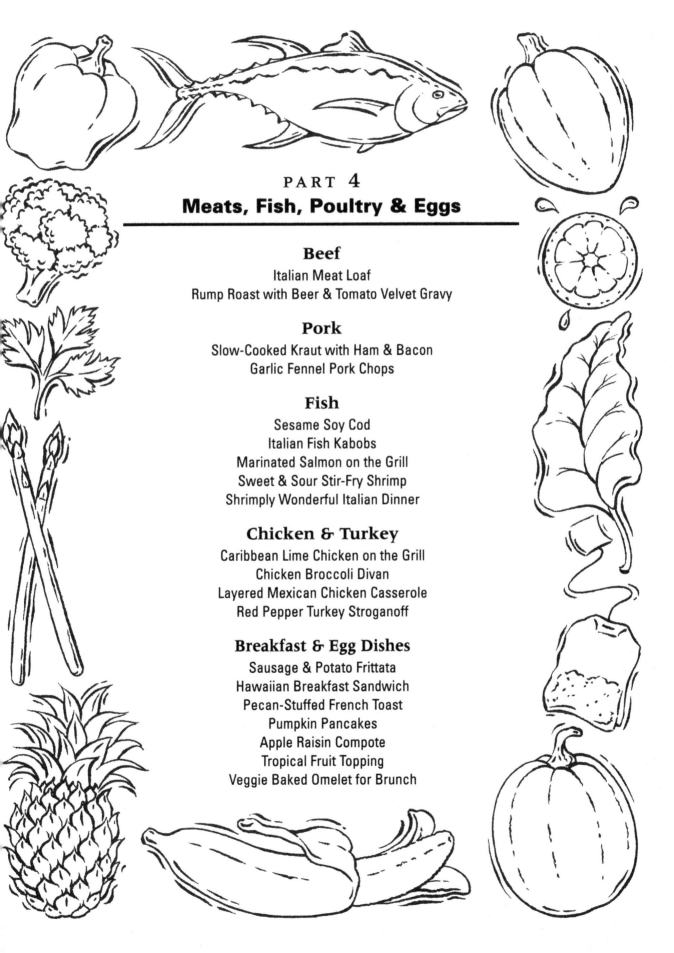

PART 4
Meats, Fish, Poultry & Eggs

Beef
Italian Meat Loaf
Rump Roast with Beer & Tomato Velvet Gravy

Pork
Slow-Cooked Kraut with Ham & Bacon
Garlic Fennel Pork Chops

Fish
Sesame Soy Cod
Italian Fish Kabobs
Marinated Salmon on the Grill
Sweet & Sour Stir-Fry Shrimp
Shrimply Wonderful Italian Dinner

Chicken & Turkey
Caribbean Lime Chicken on the Grill
Chicken Broccoli Divan
Layered Mexican Chicken Casserole
Red Pepper Turkey Stroganoff

Breakfast & Egg Dishes
Sausage & Potato Frittata
Hawaiian Breakfast Sandwich
Pecan-Stuffed French Toast
Pumpkin Pancakes
Apple Raisin Compote
Tropical Fruit Topping
Veggie Baked Omelet for Brunch

Italian Meat Loaf

Spice up an old standby with provolone cheese, basil and tomato.

- ½ cup canned chunky tomatoes
- ½ cup ketchup
- 1 egg or ¼ cup liquid egg substitute
- 1 cup plain dry bread crumbs
- ½ cup chopped fresh basil or 1 tablespoon dried
- ½ cup (2 oz.) shredded sharp provolone cheese
- ½ teaspoon minced garlic
- 1 lb. lean ground beef
- 1 medium onion, chopped

1. Heat oven to 350°F.

2. In medium bowl, combine tomatoes, ketchup, egg, bread crumbs, basil, provolone cheese, garlic, ground beef and onion. Spread mixture in 9x5-inch loaf pan. Bake 1 hour. Let stand 5 to 10 minutes before slicing.

8 servings.
Preparation time: 20 minutes
Ready to serve: 1 hour, 25 minutes

Per serving (with egg): 185 calories, 9 g total fat (4 g monounsaturated fat, 4 g saturated fat), 11 g protein, 11 g carbohydrate, 48 mg cholesterol, 301 mg sodium, 1 g fiber.
Noteworthy nutrients: Vitamin B12 (15%). **Antioxidants:** 73 mcg Beta-Carotene, 2 mcg Lutein (+ Zeaxanthin), 1701 mcg Lycopene.

Rump Roast with Beer & Tomato Velvet Gravy

Cooking with alcohol always lends distinctive flavor. There is minimal alcoholic content left after cooking.

1	teaspoon canola oil
3	lb. boneless rump roast, USDA Select or Choice grade, trimmed of fat
⅔	cup chopped onion
2	teaspoons packed brown sugar
1	teaspoon ground ginger
1	teaspoon ground cinnamon
½	teaspoon salt
	Dash freshly ground pepper
1	large bay leaf
2½	cups water
1	tablespoon vinegar
2	(8-oz.) cans no-added-salt tomato sauce
1	(12-oz.) can light beer

1. Heat oven to 350°F.

2. Spray large skillet with nonstick cooking spray. Heat canola oil over medium-high heat until hot. Brown roast on all sides, about 7 minutes total.

3. Place roast on roasting pan with rack. In bowl, combine onion, brown sugar, ginger, cinnamon, salt, pepper, bay leaf, water, vinegar, tomato sauce and beer; pour over roast. Bake 2 hours. Roast is done when internal temperature reaches 160°F.

4. Remove bay leaf. Thicken juices to make low-fat gravy if desired.

12 servings (3 oz. meat plus 3 tablespoons gravy)
Preparation time: 10 minutes
Ready to serve: 2 hours, 15 minutes

Per serving: 220 calories, 10 g total fat (4 g monounsaturated fat, 4 g saturated fat), 25 g protein, 4 g carbohydrate, 65 mg cholesterol, 180 mg sodium, 1 g fiber.
Star nutrients: Vitamin B6 (28%), Zinc (27%). **Noteworthy nutrients:** Niacin (22%), Phosphorus (21%).

Slow-Cooked Kraut with Ham & Bacon

This one-dish meal is great for any cool fall day.

4	**slices bacon**
1	**cup chopped onion**
1	**(32-oz.) jar sauerkraut, drained, rinsed**
1	**large apple, peeled, chopped**
1	**large potato, peeled, shredded**
½	**cup no-added-salt chicken broth**
2	**tablespoons sweet white wine**
¼	**cup packed brown sugar or equivalent brown sugar substitute***
¼	**teaspoon dried thyme**
¼	**teaspoon freshly ground pepper**
¼	**lb. lean ham, cut into chunks**

1. Cut bacon into small pieces; place on microwave broiling rack. Cover with paper towel. Cook at High 3 minutes. Drain bacon; place in 3-quart slow cooker.

2. Add onion, sauerkraut, apple, potato, broth, wine, brown sugar, thyme, pepper and ham. Cook in slow cooker at High at least 4 hours.

3. Or microwave bacon as directed in step 1; drain. Place in microwave-safe casserole. Add onion, sauerkraut, apple, potato, broth, wine, brown sugar, thyme and pepper. Cook uncovered at High 15 minutes. Stir in ham. Cook at Medium 3 minutes. Serve.

4 (2-cup) servings.
Preparation time: 10 minutes
Ready to serve: 4 hours, 15 minutes

Per serving: 230 calories, 6 g total fat (3 g monounsaturated fat, 2 g saturated fat), 11 g protein, 32 g carbohydrate, 20 mg cholesterol, 1945 mg sodium, 7 g fiber.
Star nutrients: Vitamin B6 (27%), Vitamin C (71%), Iron (25%). **Noteworthy nutrients:** Copper (20%), Folate (17%), Phosphorus (16%), Thiamin (21%).

TIP   * Individuals who want to reduce simple sugars in their diet can use brown sugar substitute in this slow-cooked entree.

Garlic Fennel Pork Chops

The licorice taste and aroma of fennel marries well with these chops.

- 1 **tablespoon olive oil**
- 5 **boneless center loin pork chops (about 3 oz. meat on each)**
- ½ **teaspoon ground nutmeg**
- ¼ **teaspoon freshly ground pepper**
- 1 **(16-oz.) can light apricot halves, drained, juice reserved**
- 1 **cup orange juice**
- 1 **tablespoon barbecue sauce**
- 1 **teaspoon sweet vermouth**
- ¼ **teaspoon hot pepper sauce**
- 1 **tablespoon packed brown sugar**
- 1 **teaspoon Shilling® California Style Blend garlic powder**
- 1 **teaspoon fennel seeds**
- 2 **tablespoons quick cooking tapioca**
- ½ **teaspoon curry powder**

1. Heat oven to 350°F. Coat 15x13-inch glass baking dish with nonstick cooking spray.

2. In 12-inch nonstick skillet, heat olive oil until hot; brown both sides of pork chops, turning once. While browning, sprinkle nutmeg and ground pepper on both sides. Remove from heat.

3. In saucepan, cook reserved apricot juice, orange juice, barbecue sauce, vermouth, hot pepper sauce, brown sugar, garlic powder and fennel seeds over medium heat, stirring occasionally, 3 to 5 minutes. Add tapioca to juice mixture; stir well.*

4. Remove pan from heat. Place pork chops in single layer in baking dish. Layer apricot halves on top; cover with juice mixture. Sprinkle with curry powder. Bake 30 minutes or until internal temperature of pork reaches 165°F.

5 servings (1 pork chop plus ¼ cup sauce)
Preparation time: 20 minutes. Ready to serve: 45 minutes

Per serving: 325 calories, 14 g total fat (7 g monounsaturated fat, 4 g saturated fat), 25 g protein, 24 g carbohydrate, 70 mg cholesterol, 80 mg sodium, 2 g fiber.
Star nutrients: Vitamin A (324%), Vitamin C (50%), Niacin (25%), Thiamin (65%). **Noteworthy nutrients:** Vitamin B6 (22%), Phosphorus (23%), Riboflavin (16%). **Antioxidants:** 2 mcg Beta-Carotene, 18 mcg Lutein (+ Zeaxanthin).

TIP * Never boil tapioca.

Sesame Soy Cod*

This is a true crowd-pleaser. Sometimes I cut the fish into bite-size pieces and serve as a hot hors d'oeuvre. Almost any type of white-fleshed fish can be substituted for cod.

½ cup water
½ cup cider vinegar
½ cup ketchup
¼ cup orange juice concentrate
2 tablespoons soy sauce
1 tablespoon light or dark sesame oil
½ cup packed brown sugar
1½ lb. cod, cut into 6 (1-inch-thick) pieces
1½ tablespoons sesame seeds (optional)

1. In bowl, combine water, vinegar, ketchup, orange juice concentrate, soy sauce, sesame oil and brown sugar. Reserve ¼ cup marinade for basting; refrigerate in separate container.**

2. Place fish in shallow, round, non-aluminum pan; pour marinade over fish. Alternatively, use zip-top plastic bag to marinate fish. Cover pan or seal bag; refrigerate 2 to 3 hours, turning several times and spooning marinade over top of fish.

3. Heat broiler. Spray broiler-pan rack with nonstick cooking spray. Broil fish about 6 inches from heat source 4 to 5 minutes per side. Baste fish with marinade after turning.

4. Sprinkle fish with sesame seeds.

6 servings.
Preparation time: 10 minutes
Ready to serve: 2 hours, 15 minutes

Per serving: 200 calories, 4 g total fat (1 g monounsaturated fat, 1 g saturated fat), 18 g protein, 24 g carbohydrate, 40 mg cholesterol, 635 mg sodium, 1 g fiber.
Star nutrients: Vitamin C (36%). **Noteworthy nutrients:** Vitamin B6 (16%), Phosphorus (23%). **Antioxidants:** 146 mcg Beta-Carotene, 3402 mcg Lycopene.

TIPS * This recipe makes enough marinade for up to 3 pounds of fish.
    ** For food safety reasons, do not save, baste with, or reuse marinade that has been in contact with fish.

Italian Fish Kabobs

A quick, easy and delicious way to prepare fish.

- **1 lb. halibut, thawed**
- **8 oz. cherry tomatoes**
- **8 oz. fresh mushrooms, wiped clean, stemmed**
- **1 green bell pepper, cut into 1½-inch squares**
- **1 cup zesty Italian dressing, divided**

1. Heat broiler. Thread halibut, tomatoes, mushrooms and bell pepper on 4 (18-inch) skewers. Place on broiling pan. Pour ½ cup of the dressing slowly over kabobs.

2. Broil 6 minutes. Turn kabobs over; slowly pour the remaining ½ cup of the dressing over fish and vegetables. Continue broiling 6 to 8 minutes or until fish is opaque.

4 servings.
Preparation time: 15 minutes
Ready to serve: 30 minutes

Per serving: 435 calories, 32 g total fat (7 g monounsaturated fat, 5 g saturated fat), 27 g protein, 12 g carbohydrate, 35 mg cholesterol, 530 mg sodium, 2 g fiber.
Star nutrients: Vitamin B6 (29%), Vitamin C (62%), Vitamin D (181%), Vitamin E (36%), Magnesium (26%), Niacin (47%), Phosphorus (34%). **Noteworthy nutrients:** Vitamin A (15%), Copper (16%), Riboflavin (22%). **Antioxidants:** 3 mg Alpha-Tocopherol (vitamin E), 59 mcg Beta-Carotene, 208 mcg Lutein (+ Zeaxanthin).

Marinated Salmon on the Grill

Your heart will love the omega-3 fatty acids in salmon. Your tastebuds will love the flavor treat of this fine-tasting salmon.

- ⅓ **cup lime juice**
- 1 **teaspoon Old Bay® seasoning**
- 4 **(4-oz.) salmon fillets**
- 1 **green onion, finely chopped**
- 1 **tablespoon water**
- 1 **tablespoon honey**

1. In 10x8-inch shallow glass baking dish, combine lime juice and Old Bay seasoning. Place salmon in dish to marinate, turning once to coat.* If time allows, cover and refrigerate at least 30 minutes. If not, salmon can be grilled at once.

2. Grill salmon 6 inches from medium-heat source (on grill or under broiler) 5 to 7 minutes per side.

3. Meanwhile, in small mixing bowl, combine onion, water and honey. Pour over salmon during last 2 minutes of cooking.

4 servings.
Preparation time: 5 minutes
Ready to serve: 25 minutes

Per serving: 155 calories, 4 g total fat (1 g monounsaturated fat, 1 g saturated fat), 23 g protein, 7 g carbohydrate, 60 mg cholesterol, 480 mg sodium, 0 g fiber.
Antioxidants: 15 mcg Beta-Carotene, 79 mcg Lutein (+ Zeaxanthin).

TIP   * For food safety reasons, do not save, baste with, or reuse marinade that has been in contact with fish.

Sweet & Sour Stir-Fry Shrimp

Although shrimp has ample cholesterol, it is also low in saturated fat, so it's a heart-healthy food you can enjoy at up to one meal weekly.

4	cups enriched, instant or regular long-grain rice
1	teaspoon canola oil or olive oil
1	green bell pepper, diced ½ inch
1	bunch green onions, diced ½ inch
1	lb. shelled, deveined fresh or thawed frozen shrimp
⅔	cup sweet-and-sour sauce
1	tablespoon reduced-sodium soy sauce
1	(8-oz.) can pineapple tidbits or chunks, drained well*

1. If using regular rice, prepare this first. Follow package directions, measuring water and rice carefully.**

2. In large nonstick skillet, heat canola oil over medium-high heat 1 minute. Add bell pepper and green onions. Cook just until bell pepper turns bright green, about 2 minutes.

3. Add shrimp; continue cooking just until shrimp become opaque and are no longer translucent. (They begin to curl in about 3 minutes.) Stir in sweet-and-sour sauce, soy sauce and pineapple. Cook 3 minutes more.

4. Serve over hot rice. *Hint:* To prepare rice in a hurry, use instant rice following package directions exactly.

4 (1½-cup) servings.
Preparation time: 5 minutes
Ready to serve: 20 minutes

Per serving (using instant rice and olive oil): 360 calories, 9 g total fat (1 g monounsaturated fat, 2 g saturated fat), 25 g protein, 46 g carbohydrate, 120 mg cholesterol, 895 mg sodium, 0 g fiber.
Star nutrients: Phosphorus (28%). **Noteworthy nutrients:** Calcium (16%).

TIPS * Avoid stirring rice while cooking, as stirring results in sticky rice.
** Mix drained pineapple juice with sugar-free lemon-lime soft drink for a beverage treat.

Shrimply Wonderful Italian Dinner

Take a look at this rich source of lycopene, the antioxidant that appears to help men decrease their risk of developing prostate cancer. All tomato products are good for us, but cooked tomato products are especially rich in lycopene. Combine the marinara sauce with spinach fettuccine and you have a real winner!

½ **lb. shelled, deveined frozen cooked shrimp**
1 **(15-oz.) can or jar marinara sauce**
9 **oz. eggless spinach fettuccine**
½ **cup freshly grated Parmesan cheese**

1. In medium saucepan, combine shrimp and marinara sauce. Cook over medium-high heat about 7 minutes, until shrimp thaw and begin to curl. Reduce heat to lowest setting; cover and cook another 3 minutes.

2. Meanwhile in large saucepan, bring 3 to 4 quarts water to a rolling boil; add fettuccine. Cook uncovered 8 minutes; drain.

3. Transfer fettuccine to large shallow bowl. Pour shrimp sauce over fettuccine; sprinkle with Parmesan cheese.

6 (1½-cup) servings.
Preparation: 15 minutes
Ready to serve: 20 minutes

Per serving: 265 calories, 5 g total fat (1 g monounsaturated fat, 2 g saturated fat), 17 g protein, 38 g carbohydrate, 80 mg cholesterol, 520 mg sodium, 26 g fiber.
Star nutrients: Folate (25%), Thiamin (26%). **Noteworthy nutrients:** Calcium (15%), Iron (17%), Niacin (20%). **Antioxidants:** 312 mcg Beta-Carotene, 113 mcg Lutein (+ Zeaxanthin), 11,333 mcg Lycopene.

Caribbean Lime Chicken on the Grill

You'll love the tang that comes with this great chicken recipe.

1 **lime, cut into 4 wedges**
4 **boneless skinless chicken breasts**
3 **tablespoons prepared mustard**
2 **tablespoons honey**
1 **teaspoon ground coriander**

1. Rub lime over entire surface of chicken, squeezing lime to produce juice.

2. Grill chicken over medium-hot coals 6 to 8 minutes per side.

3. In bowl, stir together mustard, honey and coriander; spread over chicken during last 2 minutes of grilling. Chicken is done when juices run clear. Do not overcook chicken; it will be tough and dry.

4 servings.
Preparation time: 5 minutes
Ready to serve: 20 minutes

Per serving: 140 calories, 2 g total fat (1 g monounsaturated fat, 0 g saturated fat), 20 g protein, 11 g carbohydrate, 50 mg cholesterol, 180 mg sodium, 1 g fiber.
Star nutrients: Niacin (48%). **Noteworthy nutrients:** Vitamin B6 (24%), Phosphorus (18%).

Chicken Broccoli Divan

Broccoli remains a favored child of the vegetable family, and here's how to pair it perfectly with chicken for a potential one-dish meal.

- 3 **cups frozen diced boneless skinless chicken**
- 2 **cups fresh broccoli florets**
- 1 **cup brown or white instant rice**
- 1 **teaspoon curry powder**
- 1½ **cups water**
- 1 **(10-oz.) can no-added-salt cream of chicken soup**

1. In skillet, sauté chicken over medium heat 8 to 10 minutes or until chicken is no longer pink; remove from skillet.

2. In same skillet, combine broccoli, rice, curry powder, water and soup. Bring to a boil over high heat, stirring constantly. Cover; reduce heat to medium. Cook 8 to 10 minutes before stirring in sautéed chicken. Reduce heat to medium-low; cook 3 minutes more.

4 (2-cup) servings.
Preparation time: 10 minutes
Ready to serve: 40 minutes

Per serving: 205 calories, 3 g total fat (0 g monounsaturated fat, 1 g saturated fat), 13 g protein, 29 g carbohydrate, 35 mg cholesterol, 415 mg sodium, 0 g fiber.
Star nutrients: Vitamin A (30%), Vitamin C (88%). **Noteworthy nutrients:** Niacin (20%).

Layered Mexican Chicken Casserole

A casserole that is just right for any weekend supper ... and perfect for weeknights when you have some time to let it bake.

- 1 (14-oz.) can diced tomatoes
- 1 (11-oz.) can diced white meat chicken
- ¼ cup fresh parsley
- ¼ teaspoon garlic powder
- 6 (6-inch) corn tortillas
- 1 cup (4 oz.) shredded reduced-fat Monterey Jack cheese
- 1 (3-oz.) can diced green chiles
  Chopped lettuce, for garnish (optional)

1. Heat oven to 375°F. Coat a shallow 2-quart casserole with nonstick cooking spray; set aside.

2. In bowl, combine tomatoes, chicken, parsley and garlic powder.

3. Place 2 corn tortillas in bottom of casserole. Spoon half of the chicken mixture over tortillas; top with 2 corn tortillas. Spoon remaining half chicken mixture over tortillas; top with remaining 2 corn tortillas.

4. Sprinkle with Monterey Jack cheese and chiles; cover. Bake 45 minutes. Remove from oven; let sit 5 minutes. Cut to serve. Offer lettuce on the side.

4 servings.
Preparation time: 15 minutes
Baking time: 45 minutes

Per serving: 290 calories, 10 g total fat (3 g monounsaturated fat, 5 g saturated fat), 28 g protein, 23 g carbohydrate, 75 mg cholesterol, 680 mg sodium, 3 g fiber.
Star nutrients: Vitamin C (43%), Calcium (37%), Niacin (35%), Phosphorus (39%). **Noteworthy nutrients:** Vitamin B6 , Folate (15%), Zinc (16%). **Antioxidants:** 201 mcg Beta-Carotene, 388 mcg Lutein (+ Zeaxanthin).

Red Pepper Turkey Stroganoff

This is a second edition of one of my earliest recipes. Twenty-plus years ago, I made it with ground beef; you can still substitute lean ground beef if you want. If you are in a real hurry, purchase ground beef crumbles. These are new products (there are vegetarian crumbles too) that are pre-browned or precooked to save you time.

1	tablespoon olive oil
1	red bell pepper, chopped
½	cup minced onion
1	teaspoon crushed garlic
1	lb. ground turkey
2	tablespoons all-purpose flour
¼	teaspoon salt
¼	teaspoon freshly ground pepper
1	lb. mushrooms, sliced, or 1 (8-oz.) can sliced mushrooms, drained
1	(10½-oz.) can low-fat, low-sodium cream of chicken soup
¼	cup nonfat sour cream
	Fresh parsley

1. In skillet, heat olive oil over medium heat; sauté bell pepper, onion and garlic. Stir in turkey to brown. Stir in flour, salt, ground pepper and mushrooms. Cook 5 minutes.

2. Stir in soup; simmer uncovered 10 minutes. Fold in sour cream. Serve with rice or noodles. Garnish with parsley.

8 (¾-cup) servings.
Preparation time: 10 minutes
Ready to serve: 45 minutes

Per serving: 185 calories, 10 g total fat (4 g monounsaturated fat, 3 g saturated fat), 14 g protein, 11 g carbohydrate, 50 mg cholesterol, 310 mg sodium, 2 g fiber.
Star nutrients: Vitamin A (55%), Vitamin C (145%). **Noteworthy nutrients:** Vitamin B6 (20%), Copper (15%), Niacin (23%), Phosphorus (19%), Riboflavin (21%). **Antioxidants:** 1 mg Alpha-Tocopherol (vitamin E), 1,062 mcg Beta-Carotene, 3,035 mcg Lutein (+ Zeaxanthin).

Sausage & Potato Frittata

This breakfast frittata is just the recipe you need for a big-breakfast morning, or a brunch.

- 1 (1-lb.) pkg. frozen diced potatoes with onions
- 1 medium green bell pepper, diced
- 4 oz. reduced-fat smoked sausage, quartered lengthwise, cut into small pieces*
- 4 eggs or 1 cup liquid egg substitute
- ¼ teaspoon freshly ground pepper
- ½ cup (2 oz.) shredded reduced-fat Monterey Jack cheese

1. Spray 12-inch skillet with nonstick cooking spray; heat over medium heat. Add potatoes and bell pepper; cook 10 minutes, stirring occasionally. Add sausage; cook 5 minutes more, stirring until vegetables are tender.

2. In medium mixing bowl, beat together eggs and ground pepper. Slowly pour eggs over potato mixture. Cook 7 to 10 minutes or until eggs are firm. Sprinkle with cheese.

4 servings.
Preparation time: 5 minutes
Cooking time: 25 minutes

Per serving (with eggs): 235 calories, 9 g total fat (2 g monounsaturated fat, 4 g saturated fat), 15 g protein, 24 g carbohydrate, 235 mg cholesterol, 465 mg sodium, 2 g fiber.
Star nutrients: Vitamin C (50%). Noteworthy nutrients: Phosphorus (17%), Riboflavin (20%).
  Antioxidants: 59 mcg Beta-Carotene, 236 mcg Lutein (+ Zeaxanthin).

TIP   * To reduce sodium, substitute lean cooked pork for the sausage.

Hawaiian Breakfast Sandwich

With a component from almost every food group, this breakfast sandwich is a great way to start the morning!

    1   (12-inch) loaf French bread (not baguette)
    ⅓   cup low-fat plain yogurt
    1   tablespoon honey mustard
    10 oz. farmer's cheese, shredded
    6   oz. ham, sliced
    ¼   cup crushed pineapple, drained

1. Heat oven to 350°F.

2. Cut bread in half lengthwise. In bowl, stir together yogurt, honey mustard and cheese. Spread on bottom half of bread. Arrange ham slices over cheese mixture, cutting to fit. Spread pineapple over ham. Cover with top half of bread. Wrap in foil. Bake 15 to 20 minutes. Cut into 6 (2-inch) slices to serve.

6 servings.
Preparation time: 15 minutes
Ready to serve: 30 minutes

Per serving: 325 calories, 12 g total fat (4 g monounsaturated fat, 7 g saturated fat), 22 g protein, 31 g carbohydrate, 45 mg cholesterol, 895 mg sodium, 2 g fiber.
Star nutrients: Calcium (36%), Phosphorus (35%), Riboflavin (25%), Thiamin (33%).
   Noteworthy nutrients: Niacin (21%), Zinc (17%).

Pecan-Stuffed French Toast

This is a lower fat version of a favorite at the Victorian Swan on Water Bed-and-Breakfast in Stevens Point, Wisconsin. The original recipe is found in Laura Zahn's Wake Up and Smell the Coffee *cookbook.*

4   oz. nonfat cream cheese, cut up
1   teaspoon vanilla
3   tablespoons coarsely chopped pecans
2   tablespoons sugar, divided
1   (18-inch) loaf day-old French bread
¼   cup nonfat milk
3   eggs or ¾ cup liquid egg substitute
    Ground cinnamon and/or nutmeg

1. In small bowl, blend together cream cheese, vanilla, pecans and 1 tablespoon of the sugar.

2. Slice bread lengthwise, cutting halfway through loaf. (Be careful not to cut loaf in two.) Spread cream cheese mixture evenly in pocket. Cut bread in 1½-inch slices.

3. In bowl, mix milk, eggs and the remaining 1 tablespoon of the sugar. Dip bread into mixture, letting slices soak a few minutes.

4. Cook bread on griddle over medium heat or in frying pan sprayed with nonstick cooking spray until both sides are golden brown. Thicker French toast slices will take 8 to 10 minutes per side.

5. Sprinkle with cinnamon. Serve with maple syrup or fruit spread. Cut into 12 (1½-inch) slices and serve.

12 servings.
Preparation time: 15 minutes
Ready to serve: 45 minutes

Per serving (with eggs): 145 calories, 4 g total fat (2 g monounsaturated fat, 1 g saturated fat), 7 g protein, 21 g carbohydrate, 55 mg cholesterol, 300 mg sodium, 1 g fiber.
Noteworthy nutrients: Thiamin (15%). **Antioxidants:** 7 mcg Lutein (+ Zeaxanthin).

Pumpkin Pancakes

These pancakes are great any time, but of course they really suit Halloween guests. This is an unusual way to get extra beta-carotene. Pumpkin pancakes will freeze for up to 2 weeks; just microwave for a few seconds (not too long!) to reheat.

1½	cups all-purpose flour
2	tablespoons packed brown sugar
1	teaspoon baking powder
¾	teaspoon ground cinnamon
¼	teaspoon ground ginger
¼	teaspoon ground nutmeg
1	cup nonfat milk
½	cup cooked or canned pumpkin
2	tablespoons canola oil
1	egg or ¼ cup liquid egg substitute
½	cup chopped pecans

1. In mixing bowl, stir together flour, brown sugar, baking powder, cinnamon, ginger and nutmeg.

2. In another mixing bowl, combine milk, pumpkin, canola oil and egg. Add to flour mixture all at once. Stir mixture just until blended but still slightly lumpy. Fold in pecans.

3. Pour about ¼ cup batter onto medium-hot griddle that has been lightly sprayed with nonstick cooking spray. Flip pancakes over when bubbles appear in center and first side has become golden brown. Serve hot with *Apple Raisin Compote* (page 335).

6 servings (2 pancakes each).
Preparation time: 30 minutes
Ready to serve: 30 minutes

Per serving (with egg): 260 calories, 12 g total fat (7 g monounsaturated fat, 1 g saturated fat), 7 g protein, 32 g carbohydrate, 35 mg cholesterol, 495 mg sodium, 2 g fiber.
Star nutrients: Vitamin A (93%), Phosphorus (27%). **Noteworthy nutrients:** Calcium (22%), Folate (15%), Riboflavin (15%), Thiamin (20%). **Antioxidants:** 1,417 mcg Beta-Carotene, 5 mcg Lutein (+ Zeaxanthin).

Apple Raisin Compote

This compote is excellent served with pancakes in place of margarine and syrup. Freeze this breakfast fruit dish in a covered container for up to 1 month.

½ cup raisins	2 tablespoons sugar
1 cup apple juice or water	1 teaspoon ground cinnamon
2 cups unsweetened applesauce	

1. In microwave-safe bowl, microwave raisins in apple juice 3 minutes at High. Drain; cool. In another bowl, combine applesauce, sugar and cinnamon; fold in raisins.

5 (½-cup) servings.
Preparation time: 10 minutes
Ready to serve: 10 minutes

Per serving: 105 calories, 0 g total fat (0 g monounsaturated fat, 0 g saturated fat), 1 g protein, 28 g carbohydrate, 0 mg cholesterol, 5 mg sodium, 2 g fiber.

VARIATION Warm Compote
In microwave-safe bowl, combine raisins, water, applesauce, sugar and cinnamon. Mix well; cover loosely. Microwave at Medium 3 minutes or until hot. Let cool slightly.

Tropical Fruit Topping

This pancake topping is great on ice cream and yogurt, too.

½ cup fresh pineapple chunks	3 tablespoons lime juice
½ cup papaya chunks	1 tablespoon honey
2 kiwi fruit, peeled, chopped	¼ teaspoon grated lime peel

1. In bowl, combine pineapple, papaya, kiwi fruit, lime juice, honey and lime peel. Refrigerate 1 to 3 hours or until well chilled. Serve with French toast, pancakes or waffles.

4 (¼-cup) servings.
Preparation time: 20 minutes
Ready to serve: 1 hour, 20 minutes

Per serving: 65 calories, 0 g total fat (0 g monounsaturated fat, 0 g saturated fat), 1 g protein, 15 g carbohydrate, 0 mg cholesterol, 5 mg sodium, 2 g fiber.
Star nutrients: Vitamin C (92%).

Veggie Baked Omelet for Brunch

I love making this omelet. My guests oooh and ahhh when I present it for brunch at the Parson's Inn.

2 cups stir-fry or San Francisco blend frozen vegetables
½ lb. reduced-fat pork sausage, cooked, drained well
1 (4-oz.) can diced green chiles, drained
2 cups nonfat cottage cheese
4 oz. nonfat cheddar cheese, shredded
6 eggs or 1½ cups liquid egg substitute
¼ cup all-purpose flour
1 teaspoon baking powder
½ teaspoon freshly ground pepper
¼ teaspoon salt
Red apple rings or slices, for garnish

1. Heat oven to 350°F. Spray 13x9-inch pan with nonstick cooking spray. Spread frozen vegetables in bottom of pan. Sprinkle sausage and chiles over vegetables.

2. In large mixing bowl or food processor, blend cottage cheese, cheddar cheese, eggs, flour, baking powder, pepper and salt until smooth. Pour over sausage and vegetables. Bake uncovered 35 to 40 minutes.

3. Let rest at room temperature 5 minutes; cut into 8 (3x4-inch) squares. Remove servings with spatula; serve vegetable-side up. Garnish with apple rings.

8 servings.
Preparation time: 15 minutes
Ready to serve: 1 hour

Per serving (with eggs): 185 calories, 5 g total fat (2 g monounsaturated fat, 2 g saturated fat), 20 g protein, 13 g carbohydrate, 175 mg cholesterol, 675 mg sodium, 1 g fiber.
Star nutrients: vitamin C (28%). **Noteworthy nutrients:** calcium (17%), riboflavin (15%).
Antioxidants: 21 mcg Lutein (+ Zeaxanthin).

Per serving (with egg substitute): 165 calories, 3 g total fat (1 g monounsaturated fat, 1 g saturated fat), 21 g protein, 13 g carbohydrate, 15 mg cholesterol, 715 mg sodium, 1 g fiber.
Star nutrients: Vitamin A (26%), Vitamin C (28%). **Noteworthy nutrients:** Calcium (17%).

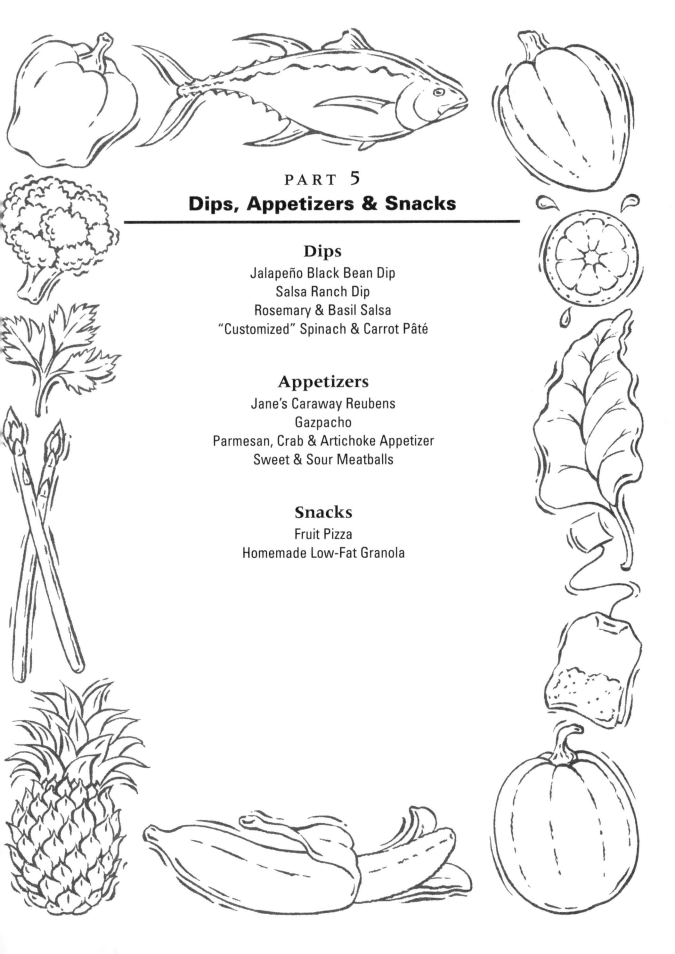

PART 5

Dips, Appetizers & Snacks

Dips

Jalapeño Black Bean Dip
Salsa Ranch Dip
Rosemary & Basil Salsa
"Customized" Spinach & Carrot Pâté

Appetizers

Jane's Caraway Reubens
Gazpacho
Parmesan, Crab & Artichoke Appetizer
Sweet & Sour Meatballs

Snacks

Fruit Pizza
Homemade Low-Fat Granola

Jalapeño Black Bean Dip

Black beans offer a rich, earthy taste and a soft texture.

- **1** **(14-oz.) can black beans, undrained**
- **¼** **cup chopped onion**
- **3** **tablespoons chopped jalapeño pepper**
- **¼** **cup nonfat sour cream**
- **2** **tablespoons salsa**
- **1** **cup shredded (4 oz.) nonfat Monterey Jack or mozzarella cheese, divided**

1. Heat oven to 350°F. Spray 9-inch square pan with nonstick cooking spray.In mixing bowl, mash beans with their liquid. Stir in onion, jalapeño pepper, sour cream, salsa and ½ cup of the cheese. Pour mixture into pan. Bake 25 minutes.

2. Remove pan from oven. Top with the remaining ½ cup of the cheese; bake 5 minutes more. Serve with low-fat chips or vegetables.

32 (2-tablespoon) servings.
Preparation time: 10 minutes. Ready to serve: 40 minutes

Per serving: 20 calories, 0 g total fat (0 g monounsaturated fat, 0 g saturated fat), 2 g protein, 3 g carbohydrate, 0 mg cholesterol, 80 mg sodium, 1 g fiber.
Antioxidants: 2 mcg Beta-Carotene.

Salsa Ranch Dip

Serve this dip with raw vegetables or reduced-fat tortilla chips.

- **1** **(1-oz.) pkg. ranch-style dressing mix**
- **2** **cups nonfat sour cream**
- **½** **cup thick-and-chunky salsa**

1. In small mixing bowl, mix dressing mix, sour cream and salsa together. Refrigerate at least 30 minutes to blend flavors.

10 (¼-cup) servings.
Preparation time: 5 minutes. Ready to serve: 35 minutes

Per serving: 55 calories, 0 g total fat (0 g monounsaturated fat, 0 g saturated fat), 2 g protein, 11 g carbohydrate, 5 mg cholesterol, 505 mg sodium, 1 g fiber.

Rosemary & Basil Salsa

You can use salsa in many ways—as a base for dips, as a flavoring in egg dishes or as a condiment. This salsa recipe feeds a crowd and is rich in lycopene and monounsaturated fatty acids, which are especially good to your heart.

2	(15-oz.) cans no-added-salt stewed tomatoes (drain 1 can)
2	(4-oz.) cans diced green chiles
6	tomatoes, diced
2	bunches green onions, chopped, green part included (about 1½ cups)
¼	cup cider vinegar
2	tablespoons olive oil
2	teaspoons reduced-sodium soy sauce
	Hot pepper sauce to taste
2	tablespoons minced fresh basil or 2 teaspoons dried
1	tablespoon minced fresh rosemary or 1 teaspoon dried
1	teaspoon salt
1	teaspoon dried oregano
1	teaspoon freshly ground pepper
½	teaspoon garlic powder

1. In large bowl, mix stewed tomatoes, chiles, diced tomatoes, green onions, vinegar, olive oil, soy sauce, hot pepper sauce, basil, rosemary, salt, oregano, pepper and garlic powder together; marinate in refrigerator overnight.

2. Serve with low-fat taco chips and/or fresh vegetables.

24 (⅓-cup) servings.
Preparation time: 20 minutes
Marinating time: 12 hours
Ready to serve: 13 hours

Per serving: 35 calories, 1 g total fat (1 g monounsaturated fat, 0 g saturated fat), 1 g protein, 5 g carbohydrate, 0 mg cholesterol, 150 mg sodium, 1 g fiber.
Noteworthy nutrients: Vitamin C (19%). **Antioxidants:** 145 mcg Beta-Carotene, 171 mcg Lutein (+ Zeaxanthin), 930 mcg Lycopene.

"Customized" Spinach & Carrot Pâté

This pâté tastes great spread on low-fat breads and crackers, and also makes a wonderful lasagna filling. If serving as a true pâté, place in bread bowls, or pumpkin or squash bowls nestled in a basket of herbs. If serving with an Italian dish, shred or crumble mozzarella cheese over the top. Just remember: Most of these presentations add a bit of sodium.

- 1 cup (10 oz.) frozen chopped spinach, thawed, drained
- 1 cup grated carrots
- ¼ cup chopped onion
- 2 tablespoons chopped fresh garlic, bell pepper, basil, oregano, parsley, cilantro, dill, sage or other favorite herbs
- 2 (15-oz.) containers nonfat ricotta cheese
- 1 (15-oz.) can garbanzo beans, drained, rinsed

1. In bowl, mix all ingredients thoroughly; refrigerate at least 1 hour. Flavors marry better if pâté is made ahead of time.

10 (¼-cup) servings.
Preparation time: 15 minutes
Ready to serve: 1 hour, 15 minutes

Per serving: 120 calories, 1 g total fat (0 g monounsaturated fat, 0 g saturated fat), 15 g protein, 13 g carbohydrate, 8 mg cholesterol, 322 mg sodium, 3 g fiber.
Star nutrients: Vitamin A (113%), Vitamin C (15%), Calcium (43%). **Noteworthy nutrients:** Riboflavin (15%). **Antioxidants:** 2,269 mcg Beta-Carotene, 29 mcg Lutein (+ Zeaxanthin).

Jane's Caraway Reubens

Sauerkraut is made from cabbage, which helps protect against some cancers.

36 slices party rye bread
¼ cup nonfat Thousand Island dressing
2 (6-oz.) pkg. corned beef
8 oz. (1 cup) sauerkraut, well drained
6 oz. low-fat Swiss cheese, thinly sliced
1 tablespoon caraway seeds

1. Heat oven to 400°F or heat broiler. Place bread on broiler pan. Spread each slice with dressing; top with corned beef and sauerkraut. Cut cheese into pieces the size of the bread slices; place on top of sauerkraut. Bake 8 to 10 minutes or broil until cheese is melted. Sprinkle lightly with caraway seeds.

18 (2-piece) servings.
Preparation time: 15 minutes
Ready to serve: 25 minutes

Per serving: 135 calories, 6 g total fat (2 g monounsaturated fat, 3 g saturated fat), 8 g protein, 10 g carbohydrate, 25 mg cholesterol, 445 mg sodium, 1 g fiber.

Gazpacho

To make a crunchy low-fat tortilla to serve with this recipe, spray flour tortillas with nonstick cooking spray, sprinkle them with chili powder and reduced-fat cheddar cheese, then bake at 200°F for 15 minutes. Gazpacho supplies the antioxidants beta-carotene and lycopene.

4	large ripe tomatoes, peeled, seeded and chopped
4	green onions, chopped
1	red bell pepper, chopped
1	avocado, peeled, chopped (optional)
1	cup peeled, chopped cucumber
2	teaspoons chopped jalapeño pepper or 2 tablespoons canned diced green chiles
1	tablespoon sugar or equivalent sugar substitute
½	teaspoon garlic powder
¼	teaspoon salt (optional)
1	cup no-added-salt tomato juice
2	tablespoons lemon juice

1. In large bowl, combine tomatoes, green onions, bell pepper, avocado, cucumber, jalapeño pepper, sugar, garlic powder, salt, tomato juice and lemon juice; marinate in refrigerator 30 minutes.

2. Serve as a cold soup or salad with crunchy baked tortillas, or use as a dip with tortilla chips. Gazpacho keeps well for up to 3 days in refrigerator.

8 (¾-cup) servings.
Preparation time: 15 minutes
Ready to serve: 45 minutes

Per serving: 70 calories, 4 g total fat (2 g monounsaturated fat, 1 g saturated fat), 2 g protein, 9 g carbohydrate, 0 mg cholesterol, 85 mg sodium, 2 g fiber.
Star nutrients: Vitamin A (31%), Vitamin C (84%). **Antioxidants:** 1 mg Alpha-Tocopherol (vitamin E), 738 mcg Beta-Carotene, 1,185 mcg Lutein (+ Zeaxanthin), 4,702 mcg Lycopene

Parmesan, Crab & Artichoke Appetizer

Use the artichoke's tender heart in this delicious appetizer.

- 1 **cup 50% reduced-fat mayonnaise**
- 8 **oz. 50% reduced-fat cream cheese**
- ¾ **cup freshly shredded Parmesan cheese**
- 8 **oz. mock crab, finely shredded**
- 1 **(14-oz.) can artichoke hearts, drained, chopped**
- 2 **green onions, finely chopped (optional)**

1. Heat oven to 375°F.

2. In bowl, blend mayonnaise and cream cheese until smooth. Stir in Parmesan cheese, mock crab, artichoke hearts and green onions. Transfer to glass pie plate or shallow baking dish. Bake 15 to 18 minutes or until heated through. Serve with French bread wedges or rye crackers.

12 (¼-cup) servings.
Preparation time: 5 minutes
Ready to serve: 15 to 18 minutes

Per serving: 165 calories, 11 g total fat (5 g monounsaturated fat, 4 g saturated fat), 7 g protein, 7 g carbohydrate, 20 mg cholesterol, 515 mg sodium, 0 g fiber
Antioxidants: 10 mcg Beta-Carotene, 53 mcg Lutein (+ Zeaxanthin).

Sweet & Sour Meatballs

A must for any celebration or gathering!

1½	lb. lean ground beef
1	(8-oz.) can water chestnuts, drained, chopped
⅓	cup dry bread crumbs
1	egg or ¼ cup liquid egg substitute
1	tablespoon Worcestershire sauce
½	cup packed brown sugar
2	tablespoons cornstarch
1	cup beer
¼	cup vinegar
¼	cup ketchup

1. Heat broiler. In large bowl, combine ground beef, water chestnuts, bread crumbs, egg and Worcestershire sauce. Shape into 48 meatballs. Place on broiling rack; broil 8 to 10 minutes or until done.

2. In skillet, combine brown sugar, cornstarch, beer, vinegar and ketchup. Use wire whisk to stir, uncovered, over medium heat until thickened.

3. Transfer sauce to slow cooker or chafing dish. Place meatballs in sauce; keep warm. Serve with toothpicks.

24 (2-meatball) servings.
Preparation time: 15 minutes
Ready to serve: 25 minutes

Per serving (with egg): 101 calories, 5 g total fat (2 g monounsaturated fat, 2 g saturated fat), 6 g protein, 7 g carbohydrate, 28 mg cholesterol, 74 mg sodium, 1 g fiber.
Antioxidants: 18 mcg Beta-Carotene, 1 mcg Lutein (+ Zeaxanthin), 425 mcg Lycopene.

Fruit Pizza

This is a light and wonderful dessert, especially when these delicious fruits are in season.

Crust

- ½ cup low-fat margarine
- ¼ cup packed brown sugar
- 1 cup all-purpose flour
- ¼ cup quick cooking oats

Topping

- 1 (8-oz.) pkg. nonfat cream cheese
- ⅓ cup sugar
- ½ teaspoon vanilla
- 2 kiwi fruit, peeled, sliced
- 1 banana, chopped
- 1 pint fresh blueberries
- 1 pint fresh strawberries, sliced
- 1 (8-oz.) can crushed pineapple, drained
- ⅓ cup raspberry fruit spread
- 2 tablespoons water

1. Heat oven to 375°F. Spray 12-inch pizza pan with nonstick cooking spray.

2. In small mixing bowl, beat margarine, brown sugar, flour and oats until light and fluffy. Press dough into pan. Prick dough with fork. Bake 10 to 12 minutes or until golden brown. Cool.

3. In clean mixing bowl, combine cream cheese, sugar and vanilla; blend well. Spread over crust. Arrange kiwi fruit, banana, blueberries, strawberries and pineapple attractively on cream cheese mixture.

4. In small bowl, combine fruit spread and water. Brush or drizzle mixture over fruit to form a glaze. Chill pizza. Cut into wedges with pizza cutter.

12 servings.
Preparation time: 30 minutes
Ready to serve: 1 hour, 45 minutes

Per serving: 200 calories, 5 g total fat (1 g monounsaturated fat, 1 g saturated fat), 5 g protein, 36 g carbohydrate, 0 mg cholesterol, 295 mg sodium, 2 g fiber.
Star nutrients: Vitamin C (53%). **Noteworthy nutrients:** Phosphorus (17%). **Antioxidants:** 13 mcg Beta-Carotene, 16 mcg Lutein (+ Zeaxanthin).

Homemade Low-Fat Granola

Always a favorite, this low-fat granola also makes an excellent gift. Granola provides some of the nutrients we need daily, including 5 percent of our iron needs.

5	cups old-fashioned rolled oats
½	cup raw wheat germ
½	cup sunflower seeds
½	cup honey
¼	cup reduced-fat margarine
1	teaspoon ground cinnamon
½	cup cold water
1	teaspoon vanilla
1	cup golden raisins
1	cup banana chips

1. Heat oven to 300°F.

2. In large mixing bowl, combine oats, wheat germ and sunflower seeds. In another bowl, combine honey, margarine and cinnamon; add to dry ingredients, stirring until well mixed. In measuring glass, combine cold water and vanilla; slowly add to oat mixture, mixing until crumbly.

3. Pour mixture onto 15x10-inch baking sheet. Bake 40 minutes, stirring every 10 minutes. Turn off oven, leaving oven door ajar. Allow granola to cool ½ hour in oven.

4. When granola is room temperature, transfer to container with lid; stir in raisins and banana chips. Store in airtight container for up to 3 weeks.

32 (½-cup) servings.
Preparation time: 10 minutes
Ready to serve: 2 hours, 50 minutes

Per serving: 130 calories, 3.5 g total fat (0.5 g monounsaturated fat, 1 g saturated fat), 2 g protein, 23 g carbohydrate, 0 mg cholesterol, 10 mg sodium, 1 g fiber.

PART 6
Beverages & Smoothies;
Cookies & Desserts

Beverages & Smoothies
Cardamom Chocolate-Orange Shake
Papaya & Kiwi Froth
Strawberry Tofu Smoothies

Cookies
Allspice Apricot Crunchies
Megan's Cinnamon Chocolate Chip Oatmeal Cookies

Desserts
Zesty Anise Apple Crunch
Rock Star Brownies
Blueberry Nutmeg Soufflé
Strawberry Pie
Zucchini Brownies

Cardamom Chocolate-Orange Shake

Tea, an excellent source of flavonoids, teams with nonfat milk here to meet your low-fat calcium needs.

5 tablespoons sugar-free mandarin orange–flavored iced tea mix
2 cups nonfat milk
1 pint nonfat chocolate frozen yogurt
½ teaspoon ground cinnamon
½ teaspoon ground cardamom
½ cup cracked ice cubes

1. Place iced tea mix, milk, frozen yogurt, cinnamon, cardamom and ice cubes in blender; cover. Mix at medium-high speed 1 to 2 minutes or until smooth and creamy. Serve immediately.

8 (½-cup) servings.
Preparation time: 10 minutes
Ready to serve: 10 minutes

Per serving: 90 calories, 0 g total fat (0 g monounsaturated fat, 0 g saturated fat), 5 g protein, 16 g carbohydrate, 2 mg cholesterol, 80 mg sodium, 0 g fiber.
Noteworthy nutrients: Calcium (18%).

Papaya & Kiwi Froth

This frothy drink gives you vitamin A, lots of vitamin C and plenty of interesting flavor!

- ¼ cup decaffeinated diet lemon-flavored iced tea mix
- 1 packet sugar substitute
- ½ teaspoon fresh chervil
- ½ cup water
- ½ cup diet lemon-lime soft drink
- 1 papaya, peeled, quartered, or 1 cup raspberries (if in season)
- 1 kiwi fruit, peeled
- 1½ cups cracked ice cubes (about 10 cubes)
  Chervil blossoms, for garnish (optional)

1. Place iced tea mix, sugar substitute, chervil, water, soft drink, papaya, kiwi fruit, and ice cubes in blender; cover. Blend at medium-high speed 1 to 2 minutes or until smooth. Garnish with chervil blossoms, if using. Serve immediately.

4 (¾-cup) servings.
Preparation time: 10 minutes
Ready to serve: 10 minutes

Per serving: 65 calories, 0 g total fat (0 g monounsaturated fat, 0 g saturated fat), 1 g protein, 15 g carbohydrate, 0 mg cholesterol, 160 mg sodium, 2 g fiber.
Star nutrients: Vitamin C (117%).

Strawberry Tofu Smoothies

Tofu is a great source of isoflavones, which help reduce your risk of heart disease. Isoflavones may help men avoid prostate cancer, too. In addition, each serving here provides 13% of your daily fiber needs.

- 2 cups fresh or frozen strawberries (if fresh, reserve 4 with stems for garnish)
- ½ cup unsweetened pineapple juice
- 6 cracked ice cubes
- 2 kiwi fruit, peeled, sliced, 4 slices reserved for garnish
- 1 cup tofu, drained
- 1 packet sugar substitute

1. Combine strawberries, pineapple juice, ice cubes, kiwi fruit, tofu and sugar substitute in blender; cover. Puree until smooth. Pour smoothies into Champagne glasses or other stemmed glasses. Serve garnished with fresh strawberry and kiwi slice.

4 (1-cup) servings.
Preparation time: 15 minutes
Ready to serve: 15 minutes

Per serving: 135 calories, 3 g total fat (0 g monounsaturated fat, 0 g saturated fat), 7 g protein, 22 g carbohydrate, 0 mg cholesterol, 35 mg sodium, 3 g fiber.
Star nutrients: Vitamin C (143%). **Noteworthy nutrients:** Copper (15%).

Allspice Apricot Crunchies

Not only are cookies such as these sources of beta-carotene, but they taste good, too! Make these cookies ahead and freeze for up to 2 months.

½	**cup low-fat margarine**
½	**cup packed brown sugar**
¼	**cup honey**
1	**egg or ¼ cup liquid egg substitute**
1½	**cups quick cooking oats**
1	**cup whole wheat flour**
¼	**cup wheat germ**
1	**teaspoon baking soda**
½	**teaspoon salt**
¾	**teaspoon ground ginger**
¼	**teaspoon ground allspice**
¾	**cup chopped dried apricots**
1	**teaspoon vanilla**

1. Heat oven to 350°F. In mixing bowl, beat margarine, brown sugar, honey and egg until light and creamy. Stir in oats, flour, wheat germ, baking soda, salt, ginger and allspice; beat well. Stir in apricots and vanilla.

2. Drop by heaping teaspoonfuls 2 inches apart on ungreased baking sheets. Bake 8 to 10 minutes; cool 10 minutes. Cover with kitchen towel to cool completely before storing.*

20 servings.
Preparation time: 25 minutes
Ready to serve: 40 minutes

Per cookie (with egg): 110 calories, 3 g total fat (1 g monounsaturated fat, 1 g saturated fat), 2 g protein, 20 g carbohydrate, 10 mg cholesterol, 180 mg sodium, 2 g fiber.
Antioxidants: 867 mcg Beta-Carotene, 1 mcg Lutein (+ Zeaxanthin), 43 mcg Lycopene.

TIP * Covering baked good with a towel or loosely laid piece of aluminum foil "boxes in" the flavor and intensifies it. Old flour sack towels and modern light-weight cotton kitchen towels work well.

Megan's Cinnamon Chocolate Chip Oatmeal Cookies

Megan spent many hours making cookies at the Parson's Inn with her Gramma Mary. Mary learned her love of cookie baking from her mother, Megan's great-grandmother, Lottie Ackerman Mergen. These are their "coffee dunking" cookies. Plus, the oats provide a source of soluble fiber, and they help lower cholesterol too.

½	cup granulated sugar
½	cup packed brown sugar
¾	cup low-fat margarine, softened
2	eggs or ½ cup liquid egg substitute
1	cup all-purpose flour
1	cup whole wheat flour
1	teaspoon baking soda
½	teaspoon salt
½	teaspoon ground cinnamon
1	teaspoon vanilla
2	cups old-fashioned rolled oats
6	oz. reduced-fat chocolate-flavored baking chips or carob chips
36	pecan halves, for tops of cookies

1. Heat oven to 350°F. Coat baking sheets with nonstick cooking spray; set aside.

2. In large bowl, combine granulated sugar and brown sugar, margarine and eggs; mix well. In small bowl, combine all-purpose flour and whole wheat flour, baking soda, salt and cinnamon. Add to sugar mixture; mix well. Add vanilla. Stir in oats and baking chips.

3. Drop by rounded teaspoonfuls onto baking sheets. Lightly press pecan half into top of each cookie. Bake 10 to 12 minutes or until lightly browned.

48 cookies.
Preparation time: 15 minutes
Ready to serve: 30 minutes

Per cookie (with eggs): 90 calories, 4 g total fat (2 g monounsaturated fat, 1 g saturated fat), 2 g protein, 12 g carbohydrate, 10 mg cholesterol, 90 mg sodium, 1 g fiber.
Antioxidants: 1 mcg Lutein (+ Zeaxanthin).

Zesty Anise Apple Crunch

Although this dessert is a little higher in fat than others, nearly half of the fat is mono-unsaturated; the taste is most definitely worth it!

Nutmeg Ginger Crumb Topping

- 1 cup all-purpose flour
- ½ cup packed brown sugar
- ½ cup broken pecan pieces, coarsely chopped
- ½ teaspoon ground ginger
- ½ teaspoon ground nutmeg
- ¼ easpoon salt
- ½ cup low-fat margarine, cut into pieces

Apple Cranberry Filling

- 1 cup fresh cranberries
- ¼ cup packed brown sugar
- 1 tablespoon all-purpose flour
- 1 tablespoon grated orange peel
- 1 teaspoon anise seeds
- 1 (11-oz.) can light mandarin oranges, drained
- 5 medium baking apples, cored, sliced (Macintosh are great)

1. Heat oven to 350°F. Coat 2-quart baking dish with nonstick cooking spray; set aside.

2. In large mixing bowl, combine 1 cup flour, ½ cup brown sugar, pecans, ginger, nutmeg, salt and margarine.

3. In another bowl, stir together cranberries, ¼ cup brown sugar, 1 tablespoon flour, orange peel, anise seeds, mandarin oranges and apples; place in baking dish. Sprinkle topping over filling. Bake uncovered 45 minutes or until golden brown.

10 (⅔-cup) servings.
Preparation time: 15 minutes
Ready to serve: 60 minutes

Per serving: 195 calories, 9 g total fat (4 g monounsaturated fat, 1 g saturated fat), 2 g protein, 29 g carbohydrate, 0 mg cholesterol, 345 mg sodium, 4 g fiber.
Star nutrients: Vitamin C (28%). **Noteworthy nutrients:** Vitamin A (16%), Vitamin D (16%).
Antioxidants: 1 mg Alpha-Tocopherol (vitamin E), 18 mcg Beta-Carotene, 31 mcg Lutein (+ Zeaxanthin).

Rock Star Brownies

These low-calorie brownies provide omega-3 fatty acids, and the light cocoa flavor satisfies chocolate cravings.

- ¾ **cup sugar**
- 1 **teaspoon ground cinnamon**
- ⅔ **cup unsweetened applesauce**
- 1 **egg or ¼ cup liquid egg substitute**
- 1 **teaspoon vanilla**
- ¾ **cup all-purpose flour**
- ⅓ **cup unsweetened cocoa**
- ½ **teaspoon baking powder**
- ¼ **teaspoon salt**
- ¼ **cup walnuts**

1. Heat oven to 350°F. Spray 8-inch square pan with nonstick cooking spray; set aside.

2. In mixing bowl, combine sugar, cinnamon, applesauce, egg and vanilla. Stir in flour, cocoa, baking powder and salt; fold in walnuts. Pour into pan. Bake 20 to 25 minutes. Allow to cool. Cut into 16 pieces.

16 servings.
Preparation time: 15 minutes
Ready to serve: 60 minutes

Per brownie (with egg): 80 calories, 2 g total fat (0 g monounsaturated fat, 0 g saturated fat), 2 g protein, 16 g carbohydrate, 15 mg cholesterol, 130 mg sodium, 1 g fiber.
Antioxidants: 2 mcg Lutein (+ Zeaxanthin).

Per brownie (with egg substitute): 80 calories, 2 g total fat (0 g monounsaturated fat, 0 g saturated fat), 2 g protein, 16 g carbohydrate, 0 mg cholesterol, 130 mg sodium, 1 g fiber.

Blueberry Nutmeg Soufflé

Three successful soufflé secrets: Careful manipulation, slow baking and prompt serving.

- 1½ cups blueberries, fresh or frozen, unsweetened
- 2 tablespoons sugar
- ½ teaspoon ground nutmeg
- 3 packets sugar substitute

Custard

- 3 egg yolks, well beaten or
     ½ cup liquid egg substitute
- 1 cup nonfat milk or reduced-fat milk
- 2 tablespoons cornstarch
- 1 teaspoon lemon extract
- 3 egg whites, at room temperature*
- ¼ teaspoon cream of tartar

1. Spray 1-quart casserole or soufflé dish with nonstick cooking spray; set aside. Drain blueberries at least 30 minutes before using.**

2. Heat oven to 325°F. In small mixing bowl, combine blueberries, sugar, nutmeg and sugar substitute. Set aside.

3. For Custard: In 1-quart saucepan,*** blend egg yolks, milk and cornstarch over medium heat 4 minutes or until mixture thickens to medium-thick consistency. Stir constantly. Remove from burner; add lemon extract. Stir well. Let cool, stirring occasionally, 5 to 10 minutes. Meanwhile, in separate bowl, beat egg whites and cream of tartar with electric mixer 2 to 3 minutes or until stiff peaks form.

4. Stir blueberry mixture; combine with custard. Fold into egg white mixture. Pour into casserole. Bake 40 minutes or until top is golden brown and center is almost firm to the touch. Serve immediately.

6 (½-cup) servings.
Preparation time: 20 minutes. Ready to serve: 1 hour

Per serving (with egg): 105 calories, 3 g total fat (1 g monounsaturated fat,1 g saturated fat), 5 g protein, 14 g carbohydrate, 105 mg cholesterol, 55 mg sodium, 1 g fiber.
Antioxidants: 13 mcg Beta-Carotene, 13 mcg Lutein (+ Zeaxanthin).

TIPS * Egg whites form stiffer peaks when at room temperature before beating. Do not leave eggs at room temperature more than 1 hour.

** To thaw and drain frozen blueberries overnight, place them in a colander in the refrigerator. Remove excess liquid from blueberries with paper towels as necessary.

*** If you still have a double boiler, use it for this recipe.

Strawberry Pie

What could be more refreshing than strawberry pie? Pretzels give this dessert a salty twist to contrast the otherwise sweet taste.

Crust
- ¼ **cup low-fat margarine, softened**
- ½ **cup nonfat sour cream**
- ¾ **cup all-purpose flour**
- ½ **cup chopped pretzels***

Filling
- 1 **(3-oz.) pkg. sugar-free strawberry gelatin****
- 1 **cup boiling water**
- 2 **cups sliced strawberries****
- 1 **(8-oz.) container low-calorie whipped topping**
  Strawberry halves, for garnish

1. Heat oven to 350°F.

2. In mixing bowl, beat margarine and sour cream until light and fluffy; add flour and chopped pretzels. With fingers, press mixture into pie plate; flute edge. Bake 20 to 25 minutes. Cool 30 minutes on wire rack.

3. Meanwhile, prepare gelatin with boiling water. When cool, add sliced strawberries. When gelatin starts to set, pour into cooled pie shell. Chill 3 hours. Frost with whipped topping. Garnish with strawberry halves.

6 servings.
Preparation time: 15 minutes
Ready to serve: 3 hours, 30 minutes

Per serving: 210 calories, 8 g total fat (2 g monounsaturated fat, 5 g saturated fat), 3 g protein, 27 g carbohydrate, 0 mg cholesterol, 360 mg sodium, 2 g fiber.
Star nutrients: Vitamin C (45%). **Antioxidants:** 4 mcg Beta-Carotene, 15 mcg Lutein (+ Zeaxanthin)

TIPS * Chop pretzels in blender.
** Any fruit with corresponding gelatin flavor can be used.

Zucchini Brownies

Zucchini is the surprise ingredient that makes these brownies so moist … and good for you.

3	**cups peeled, grated zucchini**
1½	**cups granulated sugar**
⅓	**cup canola oil**
⅓	**cup nonfat sour cream**
1	**tablespoon vanilla**
2½	**cups all-purpose flour**
⅓	**cup unsweetened cocoa**
2	**teaspoons baking soda**
½	**teaspoon salt**
½	**cup chopped almonds**
⅓	**cup coconut**
	Powdered sugar, for dusting

1. Heat oven to 350°F. Spray 15x8-inch pan with nonstick cooking spray.

2. In 2-quart mixing bowl, mix zucchini, sugar, canola oil, sour cream, vanilla, flour, cocoa, baking soda, salt, almonds and coconut; spread batter in pan. Bake 25 minutes or until toothpick inserted in center comes out clean. Cool 15 minutes. Dust with powdered sugar and cut into 2x3-inch squares.

30 servings.
Preparation time: 15 minutes
Ready to serve: 55 minutes

Per brownie: 130 calories, 4 g total fat (2 g monounsaturated fat, 1 g saturated fat), 2 g protein, 21 g carbohydrate, 0 mg cholesterol, 290 mg sodium, 1 g fiber.
Antioxidants: 1 mg Alpha-Tocopherol (vitamin E), 46 mcg Beta-Carotene, 240 mcg Lutein (+ Zeaxanthin).

Selected References

American Cancer Society's Guide to Complementary and Alternative Cancer Methods (2000).

The American Dietetic Association. *What's in a Label? The Dietitian's Handbook for Helping Consumers Demystify Food Labels*. Omaha, NE: ConAgra, Inc., 1990.

The American Dietetic Association. *Snacking Habits for Healthy Living*, 1997.

The American Dietetic Association. *ProjectLean Resource Kit. Tips, Tools, and Techniques for Promoting Low-Fat Lifestyles*, 1995.

The American Dietetic Association. *Manual of Clinical Dietetics, Fifth Edition*, 1996.

Aspen Reference Group. Lawrence, Kenneth E., Director and Di Lima, Sara Nell, Senior Editor. *Dietitian's Patient Education Manual. Volume 1*. Gaithersburg, MD: Aspen Publishers, Inc., 1993.

Avery-Grant, Anika, RD. *The Vegetarian Female: A Guide To A Healthier Diet For Women of All Ages*. New York: Avery Publishing Group, 1999.

Barnard, Neal, M.D. *Turn Off the Fat Genes*. New York: Three Rivers Press, 2001.

Barrett, Judith. *Pasta Verde: More than 140 Vegetarian Recipes for Pasta Sauces, Soups, Salads, and Baked Pastas*. New York: Macmillan, 1995.

Bednash, Geraldine, PhD., RN, FAAN. *Ask a Nurse: From Home Remedies to Hospital Care*. New York: Simon & Schuster, 2001.

Bell, Graham A. & Watson, Annesley J. *Tastes & Aromas: The Chemical Senses in Science and Industry*. Sydney, Australia: University of New South Wales Press, Ltd., 1999.

Brill, Peggy W. with Gerald Secor Couzens. *The Core Program: 15 Minutes a Day That Can Change Your Life*. New York: Bantam Books, 2001.

Bryan, Mark; Cameron, Julia; Allen, Catherine. *The Artist's Way at Work: Riding the Dragon—12 Weeks to Creative Freedom*. New York: William Morrow & Company, Inc., 1998.

Busch, Felicia, MPH, RD, FADA. *Smart Nutrition: The Essential Vitamin, Mineral & Supplement Reference Guide*. Minnetonka, MN: National Health & Wellness Club, 2002.

Carr, Tanya and Descheemaeker, Koen, Edited by. *Nutrition & Health*. London: Blackwell Science Ltd, 2002.

Casar, Penelope. *Tapas: The Little Dishes of Spain*. New York: Alfred A. Knopf, Inc., 1996.

Castelli, William P. M.D. and Griffin, Glen C. M.D. *The New Good Fat Bad Fat: Lower your cholesterol & reduce your odds of a heart attack*. Tucson, AZ: Fisher Books, 1997.

Chopra, Deepak, M.D., & David Simon, M.D. *Grow Younger, Live Longer: 10 Steps to Reverse Aging*. New York: Harmony Books, 2001.

Clemen, Jane, RD, LD, Diana Kirkwood, M.A., and Bobbi Schell, P.T., with Daniel Myerson. *The Town that Lost a Ton*. Naperville, IL: Sourcebooks, Inc., 2002.

Connor, James R. and Beard, John L. Dietary Iron Supplements in the Elderly: To Use or Not to Use? *Nutrition Today*: Volume 32: Number 3; May/June, 1997.

Cordain, Loren, Ph.D. *The Paleo Diet: Lose Weight and Get Healthy by Eating the Food You Were Designed to Eat*. New York: John Wiley & Sons, Inc., 2002.

Corio, Laura E., M.D. and Kahn, Linda G. *The Change Before The Change: Everything You Need To Know To Stay Healthy in the Decade Before Menopause*. New York: Bantam Books, 2000.

Cull, Julie Metcalf, R.D. *Magic Herbs: More Than 200 Delicious & Healthy Recipes that Are Naturally Low-Fat & Fat-Free*. Minneapolis, MN: Chronimed Publishing, 1996. Now available through John Wiley & Sons, New York.

Cull, Julie Metcalf, R.D. *The Quality Time Family Cookbook: Over 200 Delicious, Healthy and Fast Family Favorites for Making Mealtime Creative and Fun.* Minneapolis, MN: Chronimed Publishing, Inc. 1995.

Dillard, James M.D. D.C. C.Ac. & Terra Zipory, Ph.D. *Alternative Medicine for Dummies.* Foster City, CA: IDG Books Worldwide, Inc., 1998.

Duke, James A., Ph.D. *The Green Pharmacy.* Emmaus, Pennsylvania: Rodale Press, 1997.

Duyff, Roberta Larson, M.S., R.D., C.F.C.S. *The American Dietetic Association's Complete Food & Nutrition Guide.* Minneapolis, MN: Chronimed Publishing, 1996. Now available through John Wiley & Sons, New York.

Eisenberg, D. 2001. Complementary, Alternative and Integrative Medical Therapies: Current Status and Future Trends. Rosenthal Lecture, Institute of Medicine. November 5, 2001.

Ferri, Fred F. *Ferri's Clinical Advisor. Instant Diagnosis and Treatment.* St. Louis, MO: Mosby, 2001.

Foco, Zonya, RD. *The Power of Positive Eating.* Walled Lake, MI: ZHI Publishing, 2001. Call toll-free at 1-888-884-LEAN.

Gadia, Madhn, M.S., R.D. *Lite and Luscious Cuisine of India: Recipes and Tips for Health and Guide Meals.* Ames, IA: Piquant Publishing, 1997.

Geil, Patti Bazel, M.S., R.D., C.D.E. *Magic Beans: 150 Delicious Recipes Featuring Nature's Low-Fat, Nutrient-Rich, Disease-Fighting Powerhouse.* Minneapolis, MN: Chronimed Publishing, 1996.

Gibran, Kahlil. *The Prophet.* New York: Alfred A. Knopf, 1972. (First printing, September, 1923.)

Goldberg, Israel. Edited by. *Functional Foods: Designer Foods, Pharmafoods, Nutraceuticals.* New York: Chapman & Hall, Inc.,1994.

Goldberg, Burton, Presented by. *Alternative Medicine: The Definitive Guide.* Tiburon, CA: Future medicine Publishing, Inc., 1997.

Greene, Bob and Winfrey, Oprah. *Make the Connection: Ten Steps to a Better Body and a Better Life.* New York: Hyperion,1996.

Hamilton, Eva May Nunnelley, Whitney, Eleanor Noss, 7 Sizer, Frances Sinekiewicz. *Nutrition Concepts and Controversies.* St. Paul, MN: West Publishing Co., 1985.

Haninson, Susan E., R.N., SC.D.; Colditz, Graham A., M.D.; Manson, JoAnn E., M.D.; and Speizer, Frank E., M.D. *Healthy Women, Healthy Lives. A Guide to Preventing Disease, from the Landmark Nurse's Health Study.* New York: Simon & Schuster Source, 2001.

Hartnell, Agnes Peg, EdD, RD, and Tyler, G. Scott, MD. *Dietary Triggers for Migraine.* Phoenix, AZ: Hancock Resources, 1996.

Health Magazine. *Women's Health Wisdom 2002.* Birmingham, AL: Oxmoor House, Inc., 2002.

Herbst, Sharon Tyler. *The New Food Lover's Companion.* Hauppauge, New York: Barron's Educational Series, Inc., 1995.

Hobbs. Christopher. L.Ac., Elson Haas, M.D. *Vitamins for Dummies.* Foster City, CA: IDG Books Worldwide, Inc., 1999.

Klag, Michael J., M.D., M.P.H., Editor-in-chief. *Johns Hopkins Family Health Book.* New York: Harper Collins Publishers, Inc., 1999.

Kris-Etherton, Penny, PhD., RD, & Burns, Julie H. MS, RD, Editors. *Cardiovascular Nutrition: Strategies and Tools for Disease Management and Prevention.* The American Dietetic Association.1998.

Kwiterovich, Peter, M.D. *Beyond Cholesterol. The Johns Hopkins Complete Guide for Avoiding Heart Disease.* Baltimore, MD: The Johns Hopkins University Press, 1989.

Larson, David, M.D., Editor-in-chief. *Mayo Clinic Family Health Book, Second Edition.* New York: William Morrow and Company, Inc., 1996.

Lee, Robert D., DrPH, R.D.; Nieman, David C. DrPH., F.A.C.S.M. *Nutritional Assessment, Second Edition.* St. Louis, MO: Mosby, 1996.

Lichten, Joanne V., R.D., Ph.D. *Dining Lean: How to Eat Healthy in Your Favorite Restaurants (Without Feeling Deprived).* 2000.

Mauskop, Alexander, M.D. and Fox, Barry, Ph.D. *What Your Doctor May Not Tell You About Migraines—The Breakthrough Program That Can Help End Your Pain.* New York: Warner Books, 2001.

McCully, Kilmer, M.D. *The Heart Revolution: The B vitamin breakthrough that lowers homocysteine, cuts your risk of heart disease and protects your health.* New York: Harper Collins, 1999.

McGee, Harold. *On Food and Cooking: The Science and Lore of the Kitchen.* New York: Collier Books, Macmillan Publishing Co., 1984.

The Moosewood Collective. *Sundays at Moosewood Restaurant.* New York: Fireside/Simon & Schuster, 1990.

Murray, Michael T., N.D., Pizzorno, Joseph E., N.D. *Encyclopedia of Natural Medicine, Revised 2nd Edition.* Roseville, CA: Prima Health, A Division of Prima Publishing, 1998.

National Health & Wellness Club. *Food for Health and Healing.* Better Homes and Gardens Books. James D. Blume, Editor in Chief; Kristi M. Fuller, R.D., Food Editor. Minnetonka, MN. 1999 by Meredith Corporation.

Nelson, Jennifer K., M.S., R.D., C.N.S.D.; Moxness, Karen E., M.S., R.D.; Jensen, Michael D., M.D.; Gastineau, Clifford F., M.D., Ph.D. *Mayo Clinic Diet Manual.* St. Louis, MO: Mosby, 1994.

Nelson, Miriam E., Ph.D. with Wernick, Sarah, Ph.D. *Strong Women Stay Slim.* New York: Bantam Books, 1998.

New England Journal of Medicine, Agency for Healthcare Research and Quality's Research Activities, No. 236; Vol. 342, No. 20.

Northrup, Christiane, M.D. *Wisdom of Menopause in 2002.* New York: Bantam Books, Inc., 2001.

Orman, Suze. *The 9 Steps to Financial Freedom.* New York: Three Rivers Press, 2000.

Ornish, Dean, M.D. *Eat More, Weigh Less: Dr. Dean Ornish's Life Choice Program for Losing Weight Safely While Eating Abundantly.* New York: Harper Collins Publishers, 1987.

Pawlak, Laura, Ph.D., M.S., R.D. *Appetite: The Brain-Body Connection, A Twenty-First Century Weight Management Program.* Hermosa Beach, CA: Independently Published, 1995.

Peeke, Pamela, M.D., M.P.H. *Fight Fat After Forty.* New York: Penguin Books, 2000.

Peirce, Andrea. *The American Pharmaceutical Association Practical Guide to Natural Medicines.* New York: The Stonesong Press, William Morrow and Co., Inc., 1999.

Pronsky, Zaneta, M.S., R.D., FADA. *Food-Medication Interactions, 12th Edition.* Birchrunville, PA: Food-Medication Interactions, 2002.

Reichler, Gayle, M.S., R.D., C.D.N., with Nancy Burke. *Active Wellness: A Personalized 10 Step Program for a Healthy Body, Mind, & Spirit.* Time-Life Books, Time Life Inc., 1998.

Roe, Daphne A. *Geriatric Nutrition. 3rd edition.* Englewood Cliff, New Jersey: Simon & Schuster Company, 1992.

Roizen, Michael F., M.D. *Real Age: Are You As Young As You Can Be?* New York: Cliff Street Books, an imprint of HarperCollins Publishers, 2000.

Rombauer, Irma S. *Joy of Cooking.* New York: Penguin Putnam, 1997.

Russell, Percy J., Williams, Anita. *The Nutrition and Health Dictionary.* New York: Chapman & Hall, 1995.

Schlosser, Eric. *Fast Food Nation: The Dark Side of the All-American Meal.* New York: Houghton Mifflin, 2001.

Simopoulos, Artemis P., M.D. and Robinson, Jo. *The Omega Diet. The Lifesaving Nutritional Program Based on the Diet of the Island of Crete.* New York: HarperPerennial, 1999.

Smith, M.J., M.A., R.D., L.D. *The Miracle Foods Cookbook: Easy, Low-Cost Recipes and Menus wiwth Antioxidant-Rich Vegetables and Fruits That Help You Lose Weight, Fight Disease, and Slow the Aging Process.* Minneapolis, MN: Chronimed Publishing, Inc., 1995.

Smith, M.J., M.A., R.D., L.D. *All American Low-Fat Meals in Minutes: Recipes and Menus For Special Occasions or Every Day.* Minneapolis, MN: DCI Publishing, Inc., 1990.

Smith, M.J., M.A., R.D., L.D. *60 Days of Low-Fat, Low-Cost Meals in Minutes That Fit Your Budget.* Minneapolis, MN: Chronimed Publishing, Inc., 1992.

Snowdon, David, Ph.D. *Aging with Grace. What the Nun Study Teaches Us About Leading Longer, Healthier, and More Meaningful Lives.* New York: Bantam Books, 2001.

Somer, Elizabeth, M.A., R.D. *Food and Mood: The Complete Guide to Eating Well and Feeling Your Best.* New York: Henry Holt and Co., an Owl Book, 1995.

Somer, Elizabeth, M.A., R.D. *The Origin Diet: How Eating Like Our Stone Age Ancestors Will Maximize Your Health.* New York: Henry Holt and Co., an Owl Book, 2001.

Symons, Michael. *A History of Cooks and Cooking.* University of IL Press, 2000.

Sykes, Bryan. *The Seven Daughters of Eve.* New York: W. W. Norton & Company, 2001.

Thomson, Cynthhia, M.S., R.D., C.N.S.D.; Ritenbaugh, Cheryl, Ph.D., M.P.H.; Kerwin, James P. M.D.; DeBell, Robyn, M.S., R.D., C.D.E. *Preventive and Therapeutic Nutrition Handbook.* New York: Chapman & Hall, 1996.

Toussaint-Sanrat, Maguelonne, translated by Anthea Bell. *A History of Food.* Malden, MA: Blackwell Publishers, Inc., 1992.

Tuft's University. *Health & Nutrition Letter.* 2002.

Tyler, Varro E., Ph.D. *The Honest Herbal: A Sensible Guide to the Use of Herbs and Related Remedies, Third Edition.* Binghamton, NY: Pharmaceutical Products Press, The Howorth Press, Inc., 1993.

U.S. Preventive Services Task Force, Report of the *Guide to Clinical Preventive Services.* Baltimore, MD: Williams & Wilkins, 1996.

Vliet, Elizabeth Lee, M.D. *Screaming to be Heard: Hormone Connections Women Suspect and Doctors Still Ignore.* New York: M. Evans & Company, Inc., 1995.

Warshaw, Hope S., M.M.Sc., R.D., C.D.E., *The Restaurant Companion,* Second Edition. Chicago: Surreybooks, 1995.

Waterhouse, Debra, M.P.H., R.D. *Female Fatigue: Eight Energizing Strategies for Lifelong Vitality.* New York: Hyperion, 2001.

Weight Watchers. *Stop Stuffing Yourself: 7 Steps to Conquering Overeating.* New York: Macmillan, 1998.

Weihofen, Donna L., R.D., M.S. with Marino, Christina, M.D., M.P.H. *The Cancer Survival Cookbook.* New York: John Wiley & Sons, Inc., 1998.

Weil, Andrew, M.D. *Eating Well for Optimum Health: The Essential Guide to Food, Diet, and Nutrition.* New York: Alfred A. Knopf, 2000.

Willcox, Bradley J., M.D., Willcox, D. Craig, Ph.D., and Makoto Suzuki, M.D. *The Okinawa Program: How the World's Longest-Lived People Achieve Everlasting Health—And How You Can Too.* New York: Crown, 2001.

Willett, Walter C., M.D. *Eat, Drink, and Be Healthy.* New York: Simon & Schuster, 2001.

General Index

Recipe Index